Foreign-Born
American Patriots

ALSO BY RENEÉ CRITCHER LYONS

*The Revival of Banned Dances:
A Worldwide Study* (McFarland, 2012)

Foreign-Born American Patriots

Sixteen Volunteer Leaders in the Revolutionary War

Reneé Critcher Lyons

McFarland & Company, Inc., Publishers
Jefferson, North Carolina, and London

LIBRARY OF CONGRESS CATALOGUING-IN-PUBLICATION DATA

Lyons, Reneé Critcher, 1961–
Foreign-born American patriots : sixteen volunteer leaders in the Revolutionary War / Reneé Critcher Lyons.
p.   cm.

Includes bibliographical references and index.

ISBN 978-0-7864-7184-3
softcover : acid free paper ∞

1. United States—History—Revolution, 1775–1783—Biography.
2. United States—History—Revolution, 1775–1783—Participation, Foreign.
3. United States—Biography.   I. Title.
E206L96 2014   973.30922'2—dc23   [B]   2013036630

BRITISH LIBRARY CATALOGUING DATA ARE AVAILABLE

© 2014 Reneé Critcher Lyons. All rights reserved

No part of this book may be reproduced or transmitted in any form or by any means, electronic or mechanical, including photocopying or recording, or by any information storage and retrieval system, without permission in writing from the publisher.

On the cover: *Die Helden der Revolution*, Frederick Girsch, between 1850 and 1890. From left, General Washington, Johann De Kalb, Baron von Steuben, Kazimierz Pułaski, Tadeusz Kościuszko, Lafayette and John Muhlenberg during the Revolutionary War (Library of Congress)

Manufactured in the United States of America

McFarland & Company, Inc., Publishers
Box 611, Jefferson, North Carolina 28640
www.mcfarlandpub.com

In memory of Howard Charles Critcher,
my father, who gave me a rebel's heart!
Huzzah, Dad!

Table of Contents

Acknowledgments ... ix
Preface ... 1

1 — Global Citizen "Adopts" America: Zealous Philip Mazzei ... 5
2 — Farmer of Thoughts: Thomas Paine ... 18
3 — Haym Salomon: Financial Hero ... 33
4 — Frontier Savior: Patriot Francis Salvador ... 41
5 — "I serve the Country for nothing": The Indestructible John Barry, Father of the American Navy ... 47
6 — Dunkirk Pirate: The Exploits of Gustavus Conyngham ... 61
7 — Going in Harm's Way: The Adventures of John Paul Jones ... 71
8 — The Versatile, Yet Forgotten, George Farragut ... 91
9 — Charting His Own Course: The Life of Pierce Butler ... 96
10 — Thaddeus Kościuszko: Prince of Tolerance ... 106
11 — The Daring and Dastardly Charles Armand ... 125
12 — Hungarian Hussar Michael Kováts ... 133
13 — Sacrificial Warrior Baron Johann De Kalb ... 141
14 — Thunderbolt of War: Count Casimir Pulaski ... 157
15 — Washington's One-Man Army: Peter Francisco ... 176
16 — The Revolutionary Pedagogy of Drillmaster Baron Friedrich Wilhelm Von Steuben ... 188

Bibliography ... 207
Index ... 211

Acknowledgments

I first want to say thank you to each and every philosopher, politician, naval officer, infantryman, cavalryman, soldier, financier, and privateer who fought for my freedom. Thanks to Europe for sending so many of your excellent officers and countrymen this way. Thanks to Thomas Paine and Philip Mazzei for setting all those crazy ideas of the time to paper, so eloquently, yet so simply. Thanks to Benjamin Franklin for reaching out in our time of need.

Thanks associated with the writing of this particular book, however, again go to my gracious and extremely independent mother, Anna Critcher Dyer, and my determined, insightful and intuitive daughter, Faith Marie. Love you, Woo, and love you, Mom. Also, I want to thank my stepfather, Tommy Dyer, doubly, for helping with the yard, the chores, the fix-it lists. Dripping faucets are not fife and drum corps.

Always, I must thank those who provide scholarly resources: thanks to the Sherrod Library at East Tennessee State University, especially the interlibrary loan staff. Special thanks to the Department of Curriculum and Instruction at East Tennessee State for supporting my scholarly endeavors as well. Huzzah to Travis Bowman, 6th generation descendant of Peter Francisco and author of *Hercules of the American Revolution,* for the interview regarding his ancestor's life and times. Thanks also to the Library of Congress (Print and Photograph Collection), the National Archives and Records Administration, and the U.S. Naval Historical Foundation for preserving images related to the American Revolution.

Friends who kept me going this time around include fellow wordsmith Helen Kampion and my mentor, Dr. Linda Veltze. Finally, I want to thank Pastor Brian Cornell for the CD of Revolutionary War tunes.

Liberty's torch kept the lights on!

Preface

Benjamin Franklin noted in 1777: "It is a common observation here that our cause is the cause of all mankind, and that we are fighting for their liberty in defending our own" (Franklin, letter to Samuel Cooper, May 1, 1777). At first reading, most believe Franklin's words apply to a time far removed from the Revolutionary period, deducing the great visionary was simply foreseeing a day when people across the globe would benefit from the sacrifice of the men and women of the Revolutionary period who forsook all for the sake of liberty. Not the case in any respect, for serendipitously, Franklin, from 1774 to 1780, would befriend and embrace several men "charged" by the cause of liberty, writing letters of recommendation which granted freedom-loving foreigners the means to *voluntarily* join the fight for American independence: prominent men such as Germany's von Steuben, but also so-called "ordinary" men seeking to rise above European rules of stature, such as Poland's Kościuszko or Scotland's John Paul Jones.

This book honors sixteen such foreign-born volunteer heroes of the American Revolution, immigrants who sacrificed home, family, finances, and in some instances their very lives for a sense of justice, the call of freedom. While many foreign champions advanced the American cause as the result of commissions in the French or Spanish armies, such as Rochambeau or Galvez, the men discussed in this volume volunteered either to join the American forces, finance the war effort, or incite popular appeal, beginning with Italy's Philip Mazzei, whose ideas influenced both Thomas Jefferson and James Madison, and ending with Baron von Steuben, who sought the "honor of having my name enrolled among those of the defenders of your liberty." While Alexander Hamilton and Lafayette also fit this definition, I have chosen to exclude these two heroes from the volume, for the works dedicated to these men are prolific, whereas many of the volunteers covered herein are almost unheard of in the annals of Revolutionary War studies. More's the pity, for as I discovered the background and exploits of these sixteen men, sweat covered my brow, so exhilarating are their stories! How many Americans realize Thomas Paine was a demoted British taxman? How many have even heard of founding father Pierce Butler, let alone read of his escape from British capture via the swamplands of South Carolina? Are Americans taught that virtual pirates, such as Ireland's Gustavus Conyngham, destroyed burgeoning English trade and commerce? Have school students heard of the death-defying exploits of John Barry or George Farragut? Is the general public aware that the cousin of Louis XVI formed a legion of cavalry at his own expense, capturing prominent Loyalists in daring night raids? The list goes on, but I, for one, remain discouraged over the fact I never before marveled at the feats of Peter Francisco, Hercules of the American Revolution, in American history classes, nor wept at the tenderhearted love story of Poland's Thaddeus Kościuszko, denied

love due to social status. I bow my head in respect to the foreign lives lost so that I may enjoy the freedom to even write this book: Hungary's Michael Kováts, Poland's Casimir Pulaski, Germany's Baron de Kalb.

Indeed, each of the sixteen foreign champions heralded herein experienced

TOP: *Die Helden der Revolution*, Frederick Girsch, between 1850 and 1890. From left, General Washington, Johann de Kalb, Baron von Steuben, Kazimierz Pułaski, Tadeusz Kościuszko, Lafayette and John Muhlenberg (Library of Congress).

BOTTOM: Benjamin Franklin, born in Boston, January 17, 1706, painted by Madame Filleul. Engraved by Louis Jacques Cathelin (1738–1804). The Latin epigram under the engraving, written by A. R. J. Turgot, reads, "Eripuit coelo fulmen spectrum que tyrannus," which is translated as "He snatched the lightning from the heavens and the scepter from tyrants" (Library of Congress).

personal trials which mirrored the cause of American liberty. Each chose to sacrifice personal gain for the rights of mankind. Some triumphed, others fell in battle, several were forgotten in old age, yet all contributed widely to the American cause, to the degree that the War would not have swayed in America's favor without the benefit of their vigor, courage, determination, inventiveness, intelligence, and love for the cause of liberty. Their experiences must be told, and retold.

I hope readers will use these profiles as a starting point and refer to the bibliography for additional enlightenment, discerning in greater detail the means employed by these Europeans as they dedicated themselves to the cultivation of human rights and liberties in our garden named "America." Collective contemporary works recommended include Bobrick's *Angel in the Whirlwind* and Flood's *Rise and Fight Again*. Individual works of note are Sorozynski's examination of Kościuszko, *Peasant Prince*, Evan Thomas' *John Paul Jones* and McGrath's *John Barry*. As listed in the citations, in many instances, research dictated traveling back in time to scholarly works penned in the early nineteenth century. What fun to sift through the language of the Revolutionary period, quiet foreign to many modern Americans. In this book I have opted to spell and capitalize words exactly as written by these witnesses to the Revolution when I am quoting them.

I also hope readers will venture out into the field, visiting the memorials and monuments described at the end of each profile, advocating for the erection of appropriate monuments where none exist. Happily, these memorials serve to dissolve geographic limitations, helping countries appreciate each other and collectively pay tribute to these very special volunteers, such gatherings spreading cheer and the good news that liberty is alive and well in the world, a world in which we may still bravely declare, as did volunteer mentor for most of these brave men, Benjamin Franklin: "Where liberty dwells, there is my country."

1

GLOBAL CITIZEN "ADOPTS" AMERICA
Zealous Philip Mazzei

Until July 4th, 1776, all the peoples of the world ... lived under the yoke of tyranny. They could not call their minds, their bodies, or their possessions their own.—Joseph Lewis

Philip Mazzei yearned to witness first-hand the "new-age" assurances of Dr. Benjamin Franklin, who touted America as a land of no aristocracy and no thrones, with elections and the rule of the elected, and the existence of municipal laws which met local needs. As fate determined, Philip was met on the shores of what would become his "adopted" land by George Washington, Thomas Jefferson, and jurist George Wythe, who Mazzei described as "one of the greatest characters the world has ever produced, unexcelled in law." (Mazzei, 200). Life-long friendships developed, and the word used most frequently by these friends to describe Mazzei's devotion to the cause of the American Revolution became: zealous. Thomas Jefferson wrote: "He has been a zealous whig from the beginning ... his early and zealous cooperation in the establishment of our independence having acquired for him a great degree of favor ... of solid worth; honest, able, and zealous in sound principles" (qtd. in Marraro "Philip Mazzei Virginia's Agent," 8). John Adams continued this characterization in his correspondence to Jefferson and Patrick Henry, respectively, in his letters from Paris: "He is ... a zealous defender of our affairs. His variety of languages, and his knowledge of American affairs, gave him an advantage which he did not neglect." "Mr. Mazzei has uniformly discovered in Europe an attachment and zeal for the American Honor and Interest, which would have become any Native of our Country" (qtd. in Marchione, "Philip Mazzei: Jefferson's Zealous Whig," 22).

Hailing from Tuscany during the "Age of Enlightenment," Italian-born Philip Mazzei, on the surface, sailed to America in 1773 for the purpose of introducing and producing "Mediterranean commodities, particularly wine, olives, and silk, an enterprise that had long engaged the fancies of that colony's enterprising elite" (Greene, 309). Benjamin Franklin, whom Mazzei had met in London when the Grand Duke of Tuscany requested he search out and buy two Franklin stoves (an invention lauded worldwide), congratulated Mazzei for his "laudable and meritorious endeavors to introduce new products," such as spades, bill hooks, flax sickles, vine cuttings, seeds, Italian and Maltese asses for the purpose of producing heartier mules, maize (which became known as Mazzei's corn), and new methods of clearing and cultivating land. Indeed, Mazzei was proud that "my name is applied to all the products I was the first to introduce and to whatever I taught the people to do or brought to their knowledge" (qtd. in Greene, 312). Nonetheless, in the deep waters of Mazzei's soul, he traversed the cold Atlantic in search of a political enlightenment yet only dreamed of in his native Italy.

Perhaps Mazzei's fervency and determination to advance such enlightenment was a result of his early upbringing, during which he was allowed to "have his way." Born at dawn in Poggio-a-Caiano, a small town near Florence, Italy, on December 25, 1730, Philip became his grandfather's favorite, to the point that his father and mother could not discipline him properly, thus shaping an "impetuous personality." Philip's grandfather, at times, even threatened to disinherit family members who dared to disagree with the youngster, a significant threat, for Giuseppe "was one of five property owners with homes, cottages, a storehouse and large tracts of farm land. He also had a monopoly over a vast territory for making brandy, as well as two large shops: one a blacksmith's; the other, a cartwright's" (Marchione, 34). (The Mazzei surname interestingly derives from the blacksmithing trade, meaning one who wields his iron mace with extraordinary force.)

Thankfully, Philip's strong will was balanced by both academic and character education. By the age of six, Philip began school in Prato, under the tutelage of Signora Bartoli, along with his brothers, Giuseppe and Jacopo. Philip was also taught to show compassion (in his *Memoirs* remembering accompanying his father to Carmignano to help with the annual distribution of bread to the poor, a duty required of one of the twelve ruling families of which he was a member) and to balance temperance with strength, for his grandfather taught him to avoid fights "but if you have one, stand your ground and be sure to strike first" (Marchione, "Adventurous Life," 34).

At the age of seventeen, Philip entered the school of medicine at Santa Maria Nuova Hospital in Florence. Marchione notes: "In Florentine circles, especially among the Jewish community, Mazzei was acquiring a reputation for his knowledge of medicine and his courage. One day while walking in the Jewish ghetto, he noticed an old man who was pushed to the ground by a scoundrel. He immediately unsheathed his sword and gave the culprit some hard blows with the flat of it, threatening to have him punished even more severely. His interest in the sick and his human qualities united with his happy disposition toward them attracted everyone's attention" (Marchione, "Adventurous Life," 38).

Though a devoted student, Philip soon encountered the strong arm of organized and unabashed religion. While ill from a cold, he drank a glass of water with mint syrup to soothe his throat, breaking the Church's obligatory fast during Lent (specifically on the Maundy Thursday before Easter). He was expelled from school, being forced to continue classes as a public student rather than an enrollee.

Yet another injustice surfaced in Philip's early life when first his grandfather died, and, shortly thereafter, his father. A professor at the University of Pisa, the eldest brother, Jacopo, relying on primogeniture, appointed himself administrator of the estate, and, despite the father's wishes, did not even leave him "crumbs," to use Mazzei's own word. Jacopo justified

Bust of Philip Mazzei, from a miniature made in Paris, 1790.

The Italian countryside, perfect for agricultural endeavors (Faith Marie Lyons).

his action by accusing Philip of "being a spendthrift and of dishonoring the family with behavior that violated moral and religious sentiments" (Marchione, "Adventurous Life," 36). During one particularly heated argument with Jacopo, Philip "ran home to get a saber that a Spanish officer had given his father" (Marchione, ibid, 42), deciding to lie in wait and ambush his brother as he crossed the bridge over the Ombrone River to Prato. Thankfully, Jacopo took a different route home than usual, most likely having been forewarned of his brother's anger.

Due to this family rift, Philip quit the medical school (but not before obtaining a surgeon's license at the advice of professor Dr. Antonio Cocchi) and left Florence for Livorno (traditionally Leghorn), planning to sail to South America to seek his fortune. Cousins and devoted family friends embraced Philip. Even the Spanish consul, Marquis Silva, sent a servant to the Mazzei brothers' shop to invite him to dinner. The Marquis thereafter assumed the fatherly role and "advised him to remain in Leghorn. He considered him too outspoken and too little experienced in the ways of the world to go to Spain or Portugal and then sail for South America. He stated that only when Philip learned to control himself and to hold his tongue, would he help him to leave Italy" (Marchione, 46).

While in Livorno, Mazzei "acquired a reputation as a doctor and especially a surgeon, so much so that a wealthy Jewish physician, Doctor Salinas, sought him out" (Masini, 114). (Philip himself wrote in his autobiography, "I was sought as a surgeon even by people I did not know, and although I had not manifested any desire to practice surgery, I began to earn more than I spent" [Mazzei, 65].) Dr. Salinas asked Mazzei to join him in Turkey, offering an excellent salary. Traveling through Hungary, across the Danube, to Bulgaria, and held by weather and illness in Constantinople for four months, Mazzei eventually arrived in Smyrna. The Orient revealed a rich, exotic culture, but also the horrors of justice gone awry. The Mullah, who invited Mazzei and Dr. Salinas to dinner upon their arrival, told the story of a baker who short-weighed loaves to a trusted customer. As punishment, the baker was thrown into a hot oven. A day or two later, Mazzei, while walking past a butcher shop, saw the corpse of the baker hanging on a hook next to lamb and poultry! The rationale explained to Mazzei was: "In your countries there is no end to it, but I assure you that for at least ten years no baker will dare to short-weigh a loaf of bread in Constantinople" (Mazzei, 100).

After a year, Mazzei tired of work as a physician, though excelling at the profession. He met several merchantmen in Smyrna who convinced him to take up a business in London. As transportation, Mazzei served as a doctor on the ship to London and used all the money saved in Smyrna to purchase "exotic" goods: raisins, figs, opium, and scammony (herb used by pharmacists of that time to produce a laxative). Though he met many important medical scientists in London, he opted for the business world, finally returning to Florence four years later, in 1761. Remaining in Italy for a year, Mazzei developed alliances with wine and olive oil producers and, once back in London, began an import business and invented an improved system for storing wine. His business became so successful he "formed a second company, moved into a beautiful house, and hosted a salon for many London personalities" (Masini, 115). He returned to Italy via France in 1765 and found cheese, pastas, and candies to add to his import business.

Unfortunately, Mazzei, once again, became the subject of religious intimidation, accused by the Inquisition of having shipped "forbidden books" to Italy. He received a letter from his friend Raimondo Cocchi which read, "A charge against you has been received here in which it is stated that you put an immense quantity of forbidden books on board a ship bound for Genoa, Leghorn, Civita Vecchia, Naples, and Messina in order to infect all of Italy" (Mazzei, 148). (Apparently, a Roman priest had accused Mazzei of being the "author and printer of several works of Voltaire and Rousseau ... and of three titles of books I do not think ever existed, namely, *The Roman Phantom, Hell Quenched,* and *Paradise Booed*" (Mazzei, 164.) To avoid arrest, he took refuge in Lucca, a Tuscan enclave, and began writing friends appealing for his exoneration. His Tuscan friend, Bernardo Tanucci, minister for the King of Naples, pleaded his case, and Mazzei was allowed to return to Tuscany, fully vindicated and determined to "hasten the abolition of the Inquisition in Tuscany."

Upon his return to London in 1767, Mazzei had "enlarged his circle of political and social friends in both England and the Grand Duchy of Tuscany, and in the Neapolitan kingdom in Italy" (Masini, 116) to include the Grand Duke of Tuscany himself, who asked Mazzei to seek out and purchase, as mentioned above, several Franklin stoves from the illustrious Benjamin Franklin, residing in London at the time as agent for Pennsylvania. As a result, Franklin also introduced Mazzei to other prominent American colonists residing in London, to include Thomas Adams. A Virginian merchant, Adams suggested to Mazzei that Virginia was an ideal location to grow "vines, olive trees, mulberry trees for silkworms, which meant a silk industry, and more" (Masini, 117). Additionally, Franklin and Adams, as stated previously, raved about America's nonaristocratic mindset, and the idea of America began to intrigue Mazzei. He wrote, "What contributed most to make up my mind was my clear perception of the aims of the British government (which were to push the colonists into rebelling, to subjugate them, to increase the number of civil servants to find it easier to achieve a despotism capable of enduring on its own foundation without the necessity of buying votes for a parliamentary majority) and the greatest unlikelihood that the government could achieve its ends. This made me hope that the Colonies would attain total independence" (Mazzei, 185). And, when John Wilkes' election to the British parliament was declared invalid (about the same time as he met Franklin), Mazzei defined the declaration as "a death blow to the solid and sacrosanct fundamental law of a free country, which is perfect freedom in the election of the representatives of the people" (Chamberlain, 1).

He sold his London business, no small feat, for he was required, three months before his departure, to give "public notice through the press, inviting my creditors to present themselves" (Mazzei, 186). He returned to Italy to prepare for his move to the New World, to settle accounts in Leghorn, Lyons, Genoa, and Florence, and to obtain permission from the Grand Duke to take along ten men. Mazzei also told the Grand Duke of the "serious dispute between England and her colonies. I knew that Lord Hillsborough, a bitter enemy of the Colonies, very shrewd, and a vile flatterer of the learned, vain, and ambitious Lord Bute, had said in the King's Council that the Colonies were getting too powerful and the time to curb them had come" (Mazzei, 193). Further, he told the Duke, "The Colonists are convinced that the Cabinet of St. James will not go so far as to want to use force of arms against them; that if it wanted to, Parliament would not permit it, and that if it did permit it, the nation would be against it. The Cabinet, on the other hand, believes that the Colonists would lack the courage to face regular troops and hence that a few regiments would be enough to keep them in line. This common self-deception cannot but cause them to push things so far, each being confident that the other will back down, as to make war inevitable" (Mazzei, 194).

Mazzei set sail for America on September 2, 1773, along with the approved farmers and tailor and his mistress (Madame Martin) and her daughter. Two months later, he landed in Virginia. Thomas Adams initially greeted Philip in Williamsburg ("a village rather than a town even though the Governor's Palace, the Assembly hall, the College, and the Bar were there" [Mazzei, 200]), thereafter traversing with his new friend to Jefferson's Monticello to rest before journeying into the Shenandoah Valley, where Mazzei was to either purchase or be granted land from the Virginia Assembly (about 5,000 acres). Jefferson and Mazzei, both knowledgeable in exotic trees and plants, walked around Monticello during the visit. Upon their return from their wanderings at Jefferson's Monticello, Adams looked at the pair and said to Jefferson, "I see by your expression that you've taken him from me; why, I expected as much" (Mazzei, 204). Mazzei purchased property adjoining Jefferson's and named his estate *Colle* (Italian for "hill"). Jefferson took the Tuscan under his wings, giving Mazzei an additional 2,000 acres and allowing him to stay at Monticello while land was cleared and a home built.

Jefferson and Mazzei immediately bonded, for Jefferson was "especially fascinated by Filippo's love for human liberty, the untouchable rights which he passionately supported" (Masini, 120). As is discerned from the account of Mazzei's adventures prior to his arrival in America, this zealous defense of liberty mirrored Mazzei's early to mid-life experiences: he advocated for freedom of religion due to having been spurned and oppressed by the Italian religious hierarchy on two separate occasions; he believed in a universal pursuit of happiness, his own personal quest having been quelled by a firstborn brother (the traditional authority figure); he stood for the rights of man, having witnessed the horrors associated with abuse of power in both "cultured" and exotic locales; he embraced his duty to improve mankind's lot as a result of his father's and grandfather's lead roles in assisting the poor and standing firm as justice beckoned; he freely spoke his mind and stood for freedom of speech, having witnessed John Wilkes expelled from the British Parliament upon expressing a personal voice in opposition to King George III; and he never backed down from a cause, having grown up "getting his way." In fact, Mazzei arrived in America with a hatred for English xenophobia and "the insolent way in which they expressed themselves about other nations" (Greene, 312), for, having traveled to London believing England was the freest country in the world by reason of its parliament and constitution, he discovered "the many flaws of English government" instead.

Mazzei immediately began cultivating the Italian seed, vine, and trees imported to America by his entourage: orange, lemon, peach, and olive trees; grapes; and corn and peas. Mazzei's project of organizing an agricultural company was endorsed and financed by notable Virginia planters and politicians, including George Washington, Thomas Jefferson, George Mason, and even Lord Dunmore, Virginia's governor. As in Europe, Mazzei's list of acquaintances grew quickly, becoming a *Who's Who* of Revolutionary Virginia. It included not only Jefferson, but also Peyton Randolph, Richard Bland, George Wythe, Robert Carter Nicholas, George Mason, George Washington, Archibald Cary, James Madison, and James Monroe. Obviously, these connections sprouted before Mazzei's arrival in America, for, while in London, Mazzei discussed political ideologies and the brewing troubles in the colonies with American businessmen, who wrote letters praising "Filippo Mazzei" for his "professional qualities, his culture, and his ideas about freedom"(Masini, 119). Referring to Virginia and America as his adopted country and a second motherland "chosen not by chance," Mazzei evidently found "the physical climate congenial to him as a Tuscan, and the ideological climate even more congenial as a man of Enlightenment" (Marchione, 60), sympathizing with the "colonists who were insisting on their rights as Englishmen in refusing to honor the Stamp Act" (Chamberlain, 2).

Thus, Mazzei immediately began "cultivating his political ideology amongst the American colonists, publishing through the Gazettes a periodic paper aiming to show the people how things really stood and how necessary it was to be prepared in order not to be caught by surprise in case of an attack" (Mazzei, 207). Interestingly, Virginia's English Governor, Lord Dunmore, invited Mazzei to discuss the Virginia Assembly (Lord Dunmore having been heavily reprimanded for failing to dissolve the Assembly) when Mazzei was commissioned a citizen of Virginia. Mazzei noted: "Thinking perhaps that he could make a proselyte of me, he unbosomed himself in such a way that I was able to see clearly the weakness of his mind and the meanness of his heart" (Mazzei, 207).

Eight months after his arrival, Mazzei was elected to the Committee of Twelve in Albemarle County, "to see that good order was maintained" (Mazzei, 206). (The Committee ensured that all colonies received correspondence regarding the English policy of *Divide et Impera,* an economic policy attack on the colonies, one-by-one.) The Committee's duties were to "correspond with the other Colonies at all times, provided the latter did likewise, as they all did, so that whatever happened in any one of them would immediately be known by all the others" (Mazzei, 206). Only five men received more votes than Mazzei, who was "greatly pleased to have been elected to the office because of the elation it caused among the poor people I had brought with me" (Mazzei, 208). And, "in private concerts, in public speeches given at various associations, and especially in his *Virginia Gazette* writings, he continuously warned his fellow Americans against jeopardizing and betraying freedom" (Masini, 120).

Though contributing to the revolutionary cause by way of these varying forums, Mazzei eventually began writing addresses in the *Virginia Gazette*, the ideas contained therein borrowed for such documents as the Declaration of Independence. (Jefferson mailed a draft of the Declaration to Mazzei upon its completion, July 3, 1776.) Jefferson translated these addresses from Italian to English and was therefore privy to the ponderings of his friend, a world citizen who understood the workings of governments across the globe. Mazzei, per Jefferson's suggestion, used the pseudonym *Furioso,* or Furious. One year before Thomas Paine's *Common Sense* and two years before the Declaration of Independence Mazzei wrote an article, eventually published in the *Gazette*, circa 1774–5, which read:

> In order to achieve our end, my dear fellow citizens, we must discuss man's natural right and the grounds of a free government. Such a discussion will clearly show us that the British Government has never been free at the peak of its perfection and that our own was nothing more than a bad copy of it.... But the time has come to change ways.... *All men are by nature equally free and independent. Their equality is necessary in order to set up a free government. Every man must be equal of any others in natural rights.* Class distinction has always been and will always be an effective obstacle and the reason for it is very clear. When in a nation you have several classes of men, each class must have its share in the government, otherwise one class will tyrannize the others [qtd. in Masini, 126].

Using his newspaper essays and speeches, as well as his social connections, in an attempt to sway public opinion in favor of independence, Mazzei showed "how fallacious the bases of public liberty were in England." As an example, at a dinner in Williamsburg (with George Mason and thirty other patriots), as the discussion led to independence vs. British governance, Carter Nicholas, Treasurer of the Virginia Colony, said, "'Mr. Mazzei, what I am afraid of is to lose the constitution.' Looking also at him, Mazzei replied: 'Mr. Treasurer, had I such a constitution, I would think myself consumptive.' Everyone liked his answer and laughed over it, but more than anyone else Mr. Richard Bland" (Mazzei, 211). (Bland was a delegate to the First and Second Continental Congress.)

Mazzei also wrote proudly in his *Memoirs* that "people came to consult with me from all parts of the country, which covered an area of about 150 square miles, seeking light on the true state of our affairs, explaining that since I was educated and they were not (and since I had lived in England and they had not), it was only right that I should inform them, just as they were in duty bound to tell their neighbors, what they learned from me" (qtd. in Greene, 313). In fact Mazzei wrote the *Instructions to the Freeholders of Albemarle County to Their Delegates in Convention*, in which he attempted to influence provisions of the Virginia Constitution, imploring citizens to "restructure the relationship between the ruled and the ruler. His plan called for political representatives to serve only as spokesmen and for their actions to be controlled by their constituents" (Billias, 101).

Addressing the citizens of Virginia as to oppressive British laws and policies (taxes, navigation, and trade acts), Mazzei noted, "If we do not wish to risk becoming its victim, we have to arm ourselves.... The result will necessarily be either complete freedom or the harshest slavery" (Mazzei, 210). As noted by Billias in *American Constitutionalism Heard Around the World*, "Having identified the moral corruption in the British government and believing in a tyrannical plot to enslave the American people, Mazzei argued that the colonists were justified in refusing further obedience to King George" (Billias, 100). Realizing the global nature of America's revolution, Mazzei also expounded the American cause abroad, publishing an article in defense of the Colonist's cause in the February 12, 1774, edition of Florence's *Notizie del Mondo*, a similar article appearing on June 10, 1775, in Tuscany's

Gazzetta Universale. (Both newspapers also published his translation of the Declaration of Independence in September 1776.)

In addition to his role as political informant, Mazzei volunteered not only his intellect but also his very life to the Revolution, joining the Albemarle "Independent Company," the local militia, as a private, along with Carlo Bellini (a fellow Tuscan and professor of languages at the College of William and Mary) and Thomas Jefferson. The militia met for recruitment purposes in April 1775, after Lord Dunmore, Virginia's royal Governor, seized ammunition from Williamsburg's magazine. As Patrick Henry marched the militia, to include Mazzei, Bellini, and Jefferson, to Williamsburg, picking up the Madison brothers along the way, Dunmore informed the citizens of Williamsburg that if the militia continued their march, he would emancipate the slaves, in turn, of course, precipitating an uprising. Peyton Randolph convinced the militia to disperse as a result of this threat (in the deal, the militia itself was paid for the confiscated ammunition). However, on January 11, 1777, preparing to "march to the Continental camp with as many volunteers as I shall be able to persuade" (Marchione, *Philip Mazzei: Jefferson's Zealous Whig*, 20), Mazzei, though intent upon fighting in the Army, was refused by Patrick Henry, who believed Mazzei should fight with the pen, rather than the sword.

From 1777 to October 1778, while Jefferson was away from Monticello, Mazzei supported the citizens of Albemarle, continuing to enlighten them as to the tyrannical nature of the British government, "unequivocally manifested by the Boston blockade, the passage of arms in the vicinity of that city, the conduct of our Governor, the landing of English troops at Hampton, etc.," also attending church every Sunday to "make a speech aiming to show the justice of religious freedom and the benefits that would derive therefrom, especially the removal of jealousies" (Mazzei, 222). As Jefferson and other Virginian assemblymen worked to create and revise the Virginia Code, they asked for Mazzei's opinion, based upon his internationally based knowledge of governing bodies. He also advocated for emancipation, predicated upon a successful education and the demonstration of "how to make good use of their freedom" (Mazzei, 223), and helped Washington recruit troops by accompanying recruitment officers when the need arose to "undeceive those good, over-credulous folk" and "unmask England's policy" (Mazzei, 224).

For some time in 1778, the Virginia Assembly discussed sending an agent to Europe on a mission to solicit financing. Jefferson, Patrick Henry, George Mason, and John Page decided to ask Mazzei to serve as such an agent, and Mazzei agreed "wholeheartedly" to accept the post. Mazzei's instructions were to travel to Tuscany and ask the Grand Duke for a loan and supplies. As Jefferson wrote to John Hancock, "Mazzei received his appointment from Governor Patrick Henry and the Virginia Council, in January 1779. He was authorized to obtain a loan of gold and silver, not exceeding £900,000, and to purchase goods in Italy for the use of the state troops. Mazzei asked for no compensation, but only desired to have his expenses paid. He signed the oath of allegiance to the Commonwealth of Virginia on April 21, 1779, and on June 19 sailed from Hob's Hole, on the Rappahannock, accompanied by his wife, his step-daughter, and a friend, Francesco del Maglio" (qtd. in Marraro, 9). He was given one hundred barrels of tobacco as well, for the purpose of fundraising.

Unfortunately, upon reaching Norfolk, Mazzei discovered the British had burned the ship readied to transport himself, his family, and the goods for sale. Patrick Henry recommended Mazzei sail on the *Johnston*, a brigantine commanded by Captain Andrew Patton, a Scotsman who pretended to be pro-American, but who was, instead, a spy for the English.

Patton charged Mazzei thirty guineas and three hundred liras in exchange for two small cabin places (around $250.00). Not thirty miles offshore, Mazzei noted "an English privateer coming towards us, which seemed to have been lying in wait for us" (Mazzei, 229). Having wisely placed all his instructions and credentials in a bag weighted with lead, Mazzei "went down to my cabin with my little bag in hand and as soon as the privateers came alongside, I threw it overboard without anyone's noticing" (Mazzei, 229).

Mazzei was captured, considered a maritime prisoner. He was taken to New York for interrogation. As his credentials were at the bottom of the ocean, and as Mazzei did not reveal the nature of his assignment, he was held in house arrest for three months both in New York and on Long Island, all the while insisting his business was a personal trip to Tuscany. Mazzei noted in a letter to Jefferson: "During our long delay in Rappahanock and York-River, the Captain's behavior to me and my family was intolerable; his insults were constant and certainly unprovoked, as I affected not to understand his insolence to avoid coming to extremities" (Marraro, *Philip Mazzei, Virginia's Agent*, 65).

At the English martial court while still in New York, before Sir George Collier, Mazzei and Jefferson were defined as "the biggest rebels in the colonies, deserving to be thrown into the sea with an anchor tied to their necks and feet" (Masini, 130). Mazzei insisted that he was bound to Tuscany for personal reasons and had boarded a vessel to Nantes, France, as it was the nearest port to Leghorn. Mazzei entreated to the commodore's examining lieutenant, "I was going to Tuscany, where my domestick affairs demanded my presence; as it appeared by Gen. Riedesel's testimony and other papers before us; that I never had any business with or from Congress; that he had seen by some of the papers that I had left enemies in Virginia, who on the great probability of my being taken might have formed a scheme to hurt me abroad, having been disappointed in the country" (Marraro, *Philip Mazzei, Virginia's Agent*, 68). The lieutenant advised Mazzei to write the commodore. Mazzei heeded and wrote a letter; "The purport of it was a description of my uncomfortable situation with a family in that hole, especially as the heat was very intense, and a desire of being suffered to go a shore on parole, and sent to England as soon as possible, under a guard if it was thought proper" (Marraro, *Philip Mazzei, Virginia's Agent*, 68). Fortunately, one General Patterson, an English troop commander on Long Island, knew of Mazzei's reputation as a businessman while in London and thus lightened his discomfort and spoke a good word for him. Mazzei was placed on a cargo ship bound for Cork, Ireland. While on the boat, he contracted "tertian fever, which did not leave me till about three weeks after I landed in Ireland" (Mazzei, 235). In Cork, Mazzei was befriended by one Mr. Cotter, who found Mazzei private lodgings and, upon the return of his health, money for passageway to Paris on a Portuguese boat, boarded "at night to avoid the risk of my being recognized, for the mere suspicion of my having some public mission might cause me to be arrested and held in the London Tower till peace was made, as happened to Mr. Laurens of South Carolina, who had been President of Congress" (Mazzei, 237). In the port of Nantes, France, Mazzei was befriended by a second Irishman, Mark Lynch, who gave Mazzei additional monies for his trip, as well as a fine dinner. Mazzei writes in his memoir, "You will marvel at the behavior of the two Irishmen towards me if you consider that neither one could have imagined that I even existed before we actually met. But you will marvel even more if I tell you that anyone not familiar with the facts would have to conclude from their letters to me that they were beholden to me instead of the other way around" (Mazzei, 241).

Once in Paris, Mazzei visited Benjamin Franklin in an attempt to receive a copy of credentials supposedly mailed to Franklin. Franklin knew nothing of Mazzei's directive, and indeed had never received any papers. Be it known, however, that Franklin was unaware his secretary was a British agent and spy who had confiscated the papers in an attempt to hinder Mazzei's mission (later delivered to the office of the representative of the Tuscan Grand Duchy in France). Plus, Franklin informed Mazzei that he "disapproved of the conduct of the State of Virginia, saying that foreign affairs should be left to the care of the Congress" (Mazzei, 246). Mazzei then wrote Governor Thomas Jefferson a total of twenty-three letters in an attempt to (1) relay the factual details of his capture; (2) plead for a copy of his papers; and (3) explain the destitute nature of his finances as a result of his imprisonment. Mazzei, without papers which authorized his ability to transact loans or financial arrangement for the State of Virginia, was rendered sterile. As Marchione notes, "Mazzei's mission was an utter failure. This was rendered all the more poignant by his failure to receive financial assistance throughout its duration" (76).

Returning to Italy, Mazzei addressed eleven letters to the Grand Duke of Tuscany asking for loans for the American cause, but his pleas fell on deaf ears due to lack of credentials and the Grand Duke's insistence that Great Britain would never allow her colonies to remain independent. Mazzei also wrote pamphlets and newspaper articles to support the American cause, including *The Justice of the American Cause, The Likelihood of a Happy Issue of the American Revolution, The Importance of Securing Trade with Virginia,* and *Why the American States Cannot Be Accused of Having Rebelled.*

When Great Britain ceded the land from Canada to Florida, and from the Atlantic to west of Mississippi, to the now independent United States of America, the new Governor of Virginia, Benjamin Harrison, recalled Mazzei to America (August 31, 1782) for the purpose of reporting to the General Assembly his unfortunate ventures since leaving the country and to pay Philip his due. Upon arrival in November 1783, he visited friends in Williamsburg, Petersburg, and New York and bought an estate in Richmond. Mazzei returned to a country in which "private interests, ancestry, and the social and cultural class divisions of the thirteen states' citizens who participated in the war were a remarkable obstacle to the creation of a united nation with a central government whose jurisdiction would extend over the entire territory. Each state jealously guarded its autonomy, and found it difficult to give up its sovereignty for the common good" (Masini, 133). Again, Mazzei's foresight spurred him into action, and, together with several eminent Virginians, he formed a Constitutional Society, whose aim was to discuss these important issues before the legislature and to "do something for the instruction of the mass of the people and promulgate and defend the principles of freedom and democracy" (Masini, 136–7) . Meetings of the prominent members of the Society (James Madison, James Monroe, Patrick Henry, John Marshall) took place at Anderson's Tavern in Richmond, Virginia. (Mazzei, upon his return to Europe in 1785, also suggested international members join the Society, to include Jurist Caesare Beccaria, Florentine philosopher Felice Fontana, biologist Lazzaro Spallanzani, and French liberal de la Rochefoucauld, personalities of the European "Age of Enlightenment," for Mazzei wished to "connect representatives from diverse backgrounds, but who shared, whether scientists or humanitarians, the will to defend religious freedom, the right to one's own opinions, and a belief in political democracy" (Masini, 137).

Mazzei described the nature of the Society in a letter to its duly appointed president, John Blair (Philip turned down the office when asked to do so): "It seems to me that in a truly free country, where national prosperity and happiness stand on the same foundation for everyone, the uneducated portion of the inhabitants has a right to be enlightened and advised by the educated citizens, just as a child is by his father" (Marraro, "Philip Mazzei on American Political," 377). The purpose of the Society is also defined in a letter to John Adams dated September 27, 1785:

> I have always been of the opinion that Freedom cannot subsist for long in any country unless the generality of the people are aware of its blessing, and tolerably well acquainted with the principles on which alone it can be supported.... A great deal is yet wanting to bring our Government to that degree of perfection, necessary to protect effectually the interest and honour of our country, and to transmit freedom to our distant posterity [qtd. in Masini, 134–5].

Remarkably, "three years before the Constitution was framed, Philip Mazzei served as chief organizer of its forerunner, 'The Constitutional Society,' whose historic function must have been as preface to the basic law of the land" (Furman, 1004), a "true embryo of the Constitution itself" (qtd. in Marchione, *Constitutional Society of 1784*, 12). The Society served as another example "of Mazzei's belief in the importance of ideas and power of the written word. It united his activities as propagandist — disseminator of ideas — and as a thinker.... It embodied for him, the important truth of the American experiment: that ideas are important, and that if freely and intelligently discussed by all voting citizens, they will exert real political influence" (Marchione, *Constitutional Society of 1784*, 11).

For several reasons, including the potentiality of receiving a diplomatic assignment in Europe, the fact that his friend Jefferson now lived in Paris as Minister to France, and irreconcilable domestic problems associated with the mistress he was forced to marry upon his arrival in America, Mazzei returned to Europe. Once in Paris, Jefferson explained to Mazzei his decision, similar to Franklin's, to discourage foreign agents from each state, instead supporting the appointment of federal agents and ambassadors. Alternately, Mazzei found another calling on behalf of His Country, "a far-reaching project to illustrate the new American reality, a voice for America, as almost daily he felt obliged to refute published canards, inaccuracies, and fabrications about his adopted country" (Marchione, 82). Part of this misinformation stemmed from a book *(Observations on the Government and Laws of the United States)* written by one Abbé Raynal, a French historian, who commented on the dangerous nature of commercial trade with the new United States of America. Mazzei noted, in his introduction to the book written between 1786 and 1788 entitled *Recherches Historiques et Politiques sur les États-Unis de l'Amerique Septentrional* (Political and Historic Research on the United States of America), "The Abbé Raynal does not seem to have shown with respect to us the accuracy of what he boasts" (qtd. in Masini, 140). He continued in the introduction to the English version of the four-volume *Recherches*: "We have seized the occasion to discuss, to clarify, to give details which will render the subject matter more interesting and the refutations less dull" (qtd. in Masini, 141).

The contents of Mazzei's volumes demonstrated the relationship between the colonies and Great Britain before the War and the causes of the War and "provided a complete picture of each state's conduct during the most critical phase between the end of the rule of the British monarchy and the creation of a republican government" (Masini, 141). Also, as Greene notes, Mazzei presented in great detail "what was most striking to most contemporary European visitors: the absence of legal social divisions and the vigorous commitment to personal liberty and political egalitarianism among the free population" (316). He also contended that Americans expected little from their government and supported economy and simplicity in governmental affairs, for "not to attend to one's business, and to increase the public expenditures unnecessarily, were condemnable" (qtd. in Greene, 317). To downplay de Mably's suggestion of a disorderly American society, Mazzei emphasized the docility of American citizens, pointing out that Shays' Rebellion (1786–7) was the only uprising during the eleven years following Independence, and writing: "A country where equal rights prevail will uphold a government believed to be good. As there are no unjust social distinctions, national dissensions cannot have deep roots, and when happiness and safety depend on good order, everyone will be interested in preserving it" (qtd. in Greene, 319). Mazzei described America as a "light, growing brighter every day ... with a model government and with laws whose wisdom and equity put to shame even the most enlightened nations," a country "closer to the principles of liberty than any ancient or modern republic" (qtd. in Greene, 322–3).

The Parisian reviews of *Recherches*, and its subsequent publication into German and English, written under the pseudonym, "A Citizen of Virginia," helped to dispel European fears, and as the Parisian reviewer Condorcet noted, "It is easy to recognize, through the veil that shrouds the author, an illustrious philosopher, worthy for genius and loftiness of character, to enlighten men and defend their rights, and destined through the power of his thought to exert influence on the happiness of his century and posterity" (Marchione, "Adventurous Life," 82). As Emery Neff of Columbia University has written, "Philip Mazzei draws attention to the multiracial origins of the Colonial Americans and to the generous aid which the young Republic received from idealists among many peoples. The publication of Mazzei's *Recherches* in Paris, and its review by Condorcet and other French thinkers, must be counted among the forces initiating the Revolution in the following year" (qtd. in Masini, 143).

Indeed, Mazzei became involved in the political thought behind the French Revolution and joined the Société de 1789 with Lafayette and other liberals who supported freedom, yet opposed Jacobin extremism. The King of Poland, Stanisław Poniatowski, also asked Mazzei to serve as his representative within the French government and as a personal political counselor, a position he accepted with gratitude. Mazzei's letters to the King greatly influenced Poland's democratic constitution of 1791 (though Poland was later partitioned in a coup). After leaving Paris and Warsaw, Mazzei did not return to Virginia, feeling "old and tired," but rather returned to Tuscany and settled in Pisa, continuing to sign his letters: Philip Mazzei, an American Citizen. A renewed correspondence with Jefferson kept Mazzei up-to-date on his beloved country, one from Jefferson in particular, written in 1803, stating, "You cannot imagine the progress republican principles have made. All is done smoothly and unanimously in both Houses. The Tories are generally either converted or silenced by the evidence of reason or by prudence. All the superfluous expenditures which steered the helm toward monarchy are being rapidly done away with and the fundamental principles of 1775 again thrive vigorously. In brief, it seems we are enjoying the effects of good laws administered with equal justice, without exclusive privileges of proscriptions for vile conduct. Our country will be the shelter of the oppressed" (qtd. in Masini, 154).

Devoting his life to a new wife and child in his later years, Mazzei no doubt missed his adopted land, having instinctively known in 1785 that he would never return, writing to James Madison: "I am leaving, but my heart remains.... America is my Jupiter, Virginia my Venus. When I think over what I felt when I crossed the Potomac, I am ashamed of my weakness. I do not know what will happen when I lose sight of Sandy-Hook. I know well that wherever I shall be and under whatever circumstances I will never relent my efforts towards the welfare of my adopted country" (qtd. in Marchione, *Philip Mazzei: Jefferson's Zealous Whig*, 23). Mazzei's sacrifices for America were indeed unrelenting: the sale of a successful London business, forced inattention to beloved agricultural pursuits, capture by the British army and ensuing imprisonment, poverty while in Ireland and Paris, twice sailing from his beloved adopted country in pursuit of the common good. Truly, Mazzei's contributions to American political thought and legislation reach beyond borders and time: the Declaration of Independence and United States Constitution mirror his writings and philosophies, time-bound documents that preserve the political and religious freedom and equality he worked tirelessly to propound, not only in America, but across the globe. His work, as described in a letter to John Adams, will benefit mankind across the ages, as unrelenting and zealous as the life which spurned a global political model: "The honest part of the inhabitants of this Globe are my brethren, Posterity my children; and was I to go and spend the remainder of my days in China, I would with pleasure, and in compliance with what I think my duty, contribute all my exertions to the forming of an asylum for Mankind from oppression" (qtd. in Marchione, "Adventurous Life," 88).

Memorials

John F. Kennedy, in A Nation of Immigrants, wrote: "The great doctrine 'All men are created equal' incorporated into the Declaration of Independence by Thomas Jefferson, was paraphrased from the writing of Philip Mazzei, an Italian-born patriot and pamphleteer, who was a close friend of Jefferson. A few alleged scholars try to discredit Mazzei as the creator of this statement and idea, saying that 'there is no mention of it anywhere until after the Declaration was published.' This phrase appears in Italian in Mazzei's own hand, written in Italian, several years prior to the writing of the Declaration of Independence. Mazzei and Jefferson often exchanged ideas about true liberty and freedom. No one man can take complete credit for the ideals of American democracy.

The 103rd Congress Joint Resolution 175, which designated October 1993 and October 1994 as "Italian-American Heritage and Culture Month" reads: "The phrase in the Declaration of Independence 'All men are created equal,' was suggested by the Italian patriot and immigrant Philip Mazzei" (U.S. Congress).

Governor Thomas H. Kean of New Jersey proclaimed October 27, 1984, as "The Constitutional Society Day" in "recognition of the 200th Anniversary of The Constitutional Society and in honor of its founder, Philip Mazzei." The Proclamation reads: "The Constitutional Society, which was founded in 1784, is considered the forerunner of the Constitutional Convention; and Philip Mazzei, one of the fathers of the American Nation and of American democracy, was the chief organizer of the Constitutional Society and was joined by 34 other leaders on the achievement of America's political independence; and the Constitutional Society encouraged discussion of important political issues before legislative decisions were made to preserve the 'pure and sacred principles of liberty' and emphasized that the Society's main purpose was 'to keep a watchful eye over the great fundamental rights of the people.'"

In 1980, a park at Mace and Pauldings Avenue on Williamsburg Road in the Bronx was renamed Mazzei Playground in honor of Philip Mazzei. In 1981, a 48-inch diameter steel and granite flagstaff was dedicated to Mazzei. In addition to new playground equipment, lighting, and benches, the park also fittingly planted lush vegetation, such as London plane trees, honey locusts, bayberry, witch hazel, reed grass, and lily turf.

Due to contributions from the American Society of Italian Legions of Merit, spearheaded by New York State Supreme Court Justice Dominic R. Massaro, a plaque and bust of Philip Mazzei now stands in the city town hall of Poggio-a-Caiano, Italy, Mazzei's place of birth.

2

FARMER OF THOUGHTS
Thomas Paine

Thomas Paine! A statue of gold should be erected to you in every city of the world!— Napoleon Bonaparte

Referred to in at least one account as "America's Godfather," Thomas Paine's writings "brought all diverse revolutionary activists together and gave them a common aim, which was the establishment of American independence" (Woodward, 14). They also "emboldened Americans to turn their colonial rebellion into a revolutionary war, defined the new nation in a democratically expansive and progressive fashion, and articulated an American identity charged with exceptional purpose and promise" (Kaye, 4). During the grueling and despairing days of the Revolutionary War, the inspirational musings contained in Paine's pamphlet *Common Sense* "kept the American Revolution from breaking down under the weight of defeat, hunger, and discord" (Woodward, 15). Honorably, his first essay for the series known as the *American Crisis,* written by the light of a campfire as he served in Washington's Continental Army in New Jersey, December 1776, was read to soldiers braving frostbite and blizzards as they made ready to cross the Delaware: "These are the times that try men's souls. The summer soldier and the sunshine patriot will, in this crisis, shrink from the service of their country; but he that stands it now, deserves the love and thanks of man and woman. Tyranny, like hell, is not easily conquered; yet we have this consolation with us, that the harder the conflict, the more glorious the triumph" (qtd. in Young, Nash, and Raphael, 89). Making him regarded as a hero during the Revolutionary period, Paine's motives, "to rescue man from tyranny and false systems and false principles of government, and enable him to be free" (qtd. in Fruchtman, 1), led even discerning, cautious John Adams to remark, "History is to ascribe the Revolution to Thomas Paine" (qtd. in Woodward, 14).

The first to pen the name "United States of America" and suggest a federal union of states, and one of the first, after Philip Mazzei, to propose independence from Great Britain (ironically, himself a British immigrant), Thomas Paine was born (1737) the son of Joseph Paine of Thetford, England, "a commonplace person ... placid and pious, industrious and poor," a staymaker (corset artisan) on the "same social level as the tailors, the shoemakers, and the blacksmiths" (Woodward, 18). His mother, Frances Cocke, eleven years Joseph's senior, was the daughter of a middle-class attorney (a social level above that of her husband) who traced his lineage back to legal scholar Richard Cocke, who wrote *English Law, or a Summary Survey of the Household of God Upon Earth in 1651.* Joseph was of the Quaker faith (in society of that period, considered second-class citizens without the right to vote or hold public office), and, Frances, an Anglican. Hence, Paine was born into a family of social and religious opposites, and "the resulting tension between Anglicanism and Quakerism — two very different, contrasting religions — had to have been a source of serious confusion to the boy" (Fruchtman, 21). Not only was Thomas subjected to religious contradiction, to the "Sunday piety of an established church which preached deference to a congregation that dare not be otherwise," but also to political polarities, the "measured tones of a constitution which called men free, to enslave them; of the majesty of a law that elevated itself, to mock justice" (Powell, 11). Early on, "young Thomas Paine would become sensitive to inequality and the possibility of reversals" (Kaye, 18).

Located seventy-five miles northeast of London, Thetford, at the time of Thomas' birth, was a market town of two thousand people (only thirty-one could vote, for "people without property or with an income of less than forty shillings a year were, simply put, disenfranchised: they neither voted nor held office" (Fruchtman, 17), dominated by the wealthy and

Golden statue of Thomas Paine in his hometown, Thetford (Norfolk), England (Ziko-C).

corrupt Duke of Grafton (the origin of the term "bunch of grafters"), primarily agricultural, with a definitive social order: aristocracy, gentry, artisans, laboring poor, paupers. In fact, the story in Thetford was "his Grace's three footmen earned less between them in a year than their master spent on his chocolates" (Powell, 9). In England as a whole, wealth was flaunted and poverty stigmatized, a stigma the landowners "sought to banish with a display of conspicuous consumption made the more conspicuous by the condition of the four million men, women and children lumped together as 'the poor' who lived out their lives at subsistence level, or below" (Powell, 7). Walpole, the first prime minister — and his kind — intent on consolidating "the authority of his class and its godhead, property ... pursued affluence based on landed interest, on capital speculation, on holding office under the crown; or a combination of all three" (Powell, 6). One visitor from Portugal noted, "The legislature here provides an abundance of excellent laws for the maintenance of the poor, and manufactures sufficient for all of them, and yet by indolent management few nations are so burdened with them, there not being many countries where the poor are in worse condition" (qtd. in Powell, 8).

Women fared worse than men, and many were forced down "the Norwich road to prostitution." The plight of pauper children proved worst of all, as many were apprenticed at the age of five or six, worked twelve to fourteen hours daily, and were subjected to diseased conditions. "With government imposing no controls whatsoever either on their hours of work or their work conditions, many simply starved or were beaten to death" (Powell, 9).

Writer Oliver Goldsmith noted, "Each wanton judge new penal statutes draws. Laws grind the poor, and rich men rule the law" (qtd. in Powell, 11). The majority of the laws passed were crimes against poverty. "By 1740 the theft of a shilling handkerchief was enough to send a child to the gallows" (Powell, 11). Men in need of relief were required to wear a large *P* on their right shirt sleeve; men and women caught begging could be stripped and whipped until bloody, the ears cut from a person who attempted to counterfeit the pass required for traveling from parish to parish, a feat necessary to find work, and an absconding child ringed by the neck or manacled.

Criminal court sessions were held in Thetford, at which time "the town's population ballooned and routine life gave way to a bizarre carnival of theatricals, amusements, trials, verdicts, and executions" (Kaye, 21). "Every spring, scores of hooded peasant convicts arrived to face the branding iron, life imprisonment, transport to the outlying colonies, or a session on the ducking stool at the river Thet. Those refused such mercies of the court would be led to the chalk ridge overlooking the Paine cottage, their bodies left to swing for an hour as the townspeople watched and laid wager as to the time of their passing" (Nelson, 15). Executions were held at Gallows Hill, in sight of young Thomas' home (the town stocks and pillory were near his schoolhouse). Thus, at a young age, Thomas would have been witness to such horrors as the execution of Amy Hutchinson, age seventeen: "Her face and hands were smeared with tar, and having a garment daubed with pitch, after a short prayer the executioner strangled her, and twenty minutes after the fire was kindled and burnt half an hour" (Conway, 9). As Conway notes, "Against the prevailing savagery a human protest was rarely heard outside the Quaker meeting" (9). Certainly, Thomas' later works were influenced by his childhood witness to "the corrupting influence of the aristocracy, the pomp of law, the evils of the unreformed corporations; the ruins of great ecclesiastical establishments" (Conway, 9). And, perhaps, his earliest writing as well, for as Conway continues: "Testimonies of the 'Spirit' against inhumanity, delivered beside instruments of legal torture, bred pity in the child, who had a poetic temperament. The earliest glimpses we have of his childhood are in lines written about a fly caught in a spider's web, and an epitaph for a crow which he buried in the garden:

> Here lies the body of John Crow,
> Who once was high, but now is low
> Ye brother Crows take warning all,
> For as you rise, so must you fall [qtd. in Conway, 10–11].

Though considered a woman of "sour" disposition, Frances Paine insisted that Thomas be enrolled in grammar school, perhaps to circumvent a pauper's fate for her son. With the financial assistance of a maternal aunt, Thomas began under the tutelage of the Reverend William Knowler, yet was forbidden by his father from reading books written in Latin, for the Quakers believed "Latin, the official language of states and churches, functioned to obscure the exercise of authority from the people" (Kaye, 22). Nevertheless, as Thomas wrote, "This did not prevent me from being acquainted with the subjects of all the Latin books used in the school" (qtd. in Conway, 12). Additionally, "what the boy missed proved to be no loss, for, freed of the classical affectations of the age, it did much to account for the vividness of his later prose style" (Powell, 13). Particularly, Thomas ingested the works of Shakespeare, John Milton, and John Bunyan. And, "there was an old book in Mr. Knowler's small library, *A Natural History of Virginia*, and from the first reading it enthralled Paine: 'My inclination from that day for seeing the western side of the Atlantic never left me'" (Powell, 13).

Thomas held an affinity for science, mathematics and poetry; the last he "rather repressed than encouraged, as leading too much into the field of imagination" (qtd. in Conway, 12). Perhaps the repression of imagination was the result of his religious rearing: "Though I reverence their philanthropy, I cannot help smiling at the conceit, that if the taste of a Quaker had been consulted at the creation, what a silent and drab-coloured creation it would have been! Not a flower would have blossomed its gaieties, nor a bird been permitted to sing" (qtd. in Conway, 11). Or, perhaps, as alluded to previously, imaginative thought in Thetford's pre-ordained world was severely punished. Whatever the reasoning, fortunately, Thomas' exceeding good moral education, tolerable stock of useful learning, excellent command of only one language, witness to intolerable injustices, and repressed poetic temperament and power would later break out into "glowing visions of ideal society and fiery denunciations of the unlovely world" (Conway, 13) which could be understood by all, for as Thomas later wrote: "As it is my design to make those that can scarcely read understand, I shall therefore avoid every literary ornament and put it in language as plain as the alphabet" (qtd. in Young, 89).

From the age of six to twelve, Thomas attended grammar school, yet was forced at age thirteen, due to his father's dwindling income, to become a staymaker apprentice, as most children adhered to the "general principles of a static society where each one followed the occupation of his family" (Woodward, 25). Bored with this arduous life, and remembering the stories of his schoolmaster who "told him about his escapades as a naval chaplain on a man-o'-war roaming from India, the Indies, and Africa to North America" (Fruchtman, 22), at sixteen, Thomas heeded a young man's call of adventure and attempted to escape from his father's staymaking shop to sail on a London privateer, *The Terrible,* with a captain whose last name was Death! He was quickly rescued by his father, whose Quaker sensibilities led him to discourage Thomas from such a violent life, Joseph having heard of Thomas' plans from a fellow master craftsman. Thomas remembered, "From this adventure I was happily prevented by the affectionate and moral remonstrance of a good father who, from his own habits of life, being of the Quaker profession, must begin to look upon me as lost" (Van der Weyde, 6). Joseph convinced the captain to free Thomas, literally saving his life, for "immediately after entering the Channel, the *Terrible* fell under assault from a French privateer, the *Vengeance;* only 17 English crewmen survived while more than 150 died, including Captain Death himself" (Nelson, 20). Staying in London to work under another staymaker, Paine did not return to Thetford, and three years later signed on to *The King of Prussia*, the experience forever quelching his desire to serve on another privateer and feeding his already established distrust of kings.

After his privateering experience, Paine returned to London for two years, eagerly seeking out London's café society, which "revolved around his profound interest in natural philosophy, the key Enlightenment enthusiasm that would sweep through every social class ... the most ardent students of nature were in fact artisans ... they called themselves 'mechanics,' and their great hero was the world's most celebrated self-made mechanic, Benjamin Franklin, who in *Poor Richard's Almanack* delineated their shared ideology: hard work, fortitude, thrift, patience, prudence, economy, moderation, sobriety, and self-improvement" (Nelson, 33). Paine writes, "As soon as I was able, I purchased a pair of globes, and attended the philosophical lectures of Martin and Ferguson, and became afterwards acquainted with Dr. Bevis, of the society called the Royal Society, then living in the Temple, and an excellent astronomer" (Conway, 15). He joined intellectual thinkers known as the Newtonians "with gusto, arguing with them in coffeehouses, reading the newest scientific publications; regularly attending evening lectures on the properties of air, the behavior of comets, the ingredients of light, and the engineering of pendulums; and watching eidophysicons (magic-lantern slide shows), globes and orreries, as well as demonstration of the powers of electricity, gas, chemicals, and magnets" (Nelson, 36). He noted, "Every person of learning is finally his own teacher. I seldom passed five minutes of my life however circumstanced in which I did not acquire some knowledge" (qtd. in Nelson, 36). These "moderns," nevertheless, did not limit their studies, for "the Enlightenment inspired them to question, debate, and ponder all received ideas, to reconsider all axiomatic opinion; the revolution of Newton had upended both cosmology and received wisdom" (Nelson, 38).

Heeding the economics of life, nevertheless, at twenty-two Paine opened a staymaking business in Sandwich (Kent) and married Mary Lambert. (Only one year later, she died, some sources believe in early labor. Paine wrote, "There is neither manhood nor policy in grief" [Nelson, 38]). Due to serious financial troubles, Paine's father-in-law convinced him to apply for a position as an excise officer, whose duty was to collect customs on alcohol, salt, soap, tobacco, and other goods. Passing an exam, which could only be taken pursuant to the recommendation of a local aristocrat, in Paine's case Lord Falkland, was a requirement. Paine studied for a year, passed the exam, and began work as an exciseman, "loathed by common folk and menaced by the kingdom's twenty thousand owlers (smugglers)" (Nelson, 38). Severely underpaid, the position spawned corruption and the acceptance of a shopkeeper's word, rather than an assessment, a custom also practiced by Paine. Initially fired, he returned, upon petition, to the town of Lewes, where he worked for six years, a harsh assignment, for "the southeast seaboard was popular with tobacco, tea, silk, and brandy smugglers working the Kent and Sussex beaches with Dutch gin and French imports" (Nelson, 39). He also married one Elizabeth Olive during this period, inheriting a tobacco and grocery store, and joined a workingman's club which met at the White Hart Inn. The members of this club encouraged political and literary debates and even awarded prizes (the Headstrong Award) to the best debater, Paine becoming known as "the General of the Headstrong War."

Paine also became somewhat of the local laureate, writing song lyrics for birthdays and other celebrations.

Freedom of movement in the corporate-owned town was almost extinct, parish officers removing those who did not belong to, or who were unwanted within, the parish. Paine noted, "This species of feudality is kept up to aggrandize the corporations at the ruin of the towns; and the effect is visible" (Williamson, 42). Being an exciseman who became, with "exceeding candor, and even tenderness, with which that part of the duty that fell to my share was executed" (qtd. in Conway, 35) a sort of trumpeter for his fellow excisemen, he wrote a pamphlet entitled *The Case of the Officers of Excise*, in which he revealed, "The salary of the inferior officers of the revenue has stood at the petty pittance of less than fifty pounds a year for upwards of one hundred years" (qtd. in Williamson, 50). He noted this salary was reduced to 35 pounds if the cost of maintaining a horse were considered.

Thomas Paine. Engraving of a 1792 painting by George Romney (1734–1802) (Library of Congress).

In the pamphlet, Paine noted, ahead of his time, that better pay would increase revenue, as workers would not carry out their duties poorly; that poverty bred dishonesty, even crime; and that social/economic reform was required. He wrote, "Poverty, in defiance of principle, begets a degree of meanness that will stoop to almost anything.... He who never was a'hungered may argue finely on the subjection of his appetite; and he who never was distressed may harangue as beautifully on the power of principle. But poverty, like grief, has an incurable deafness, which never hears; the oration loses all its edge; and '*To be, or not to be*' becomes the only question" (qtd. in Nelson, 44). Fellow excisemen raised money to publish the pamphlet and send Paine to London (Parliament) to argue their cause. In London, he was befriended by George Lewis Scott, a member of Parliament and Commissioner of the Excise Board, who introduced him to historian Edward Gibbon, author Samuel Johnson, and the Colonies' premier agent, Benjamin Franklin. Paine is said to have caught Franklin's fancy by quoting the Latin proverb "*Quisque suae fortunae faber*" (Every man is the artisan of his own fortune), ironic since Paine was not allowed to learn Latin in elementary school.

Because the public despised excise men and the government wished to pay its employees as little as possible, Paine's work was in vain and his petition to Parliament a debacle. On April 8, 1774, he was relieved from duty as an exciseman and became subject to immediate arrest for debt. A notice for the sale of all his worldly goods was placed in the *Sussex Weekly Advertiser*. He and his wife, Elizabeth, immediately separated, and he was paid 35 pounds for agreeing to hold harmless his wife from the sale of the business and home. All seemingly lost, Paine traveled back to London and visited George Scott and Benjamin Franklin, shortly thereafter sailing for the New World, for, as William Cobbett wrote: "A little thing sometimes produces a great effect; an insult offered to a man of great talent and unconquerable perseverance has in many instances produced, in the long run, most tremendous effects; and it appears to me very clear that some beastly insults, offered to Mr. Paine while he was in the Excise in England, was the real cause of the Revolution in America; for, though the nature of the cause of America was such as I have before described it; though the principles were firm in the minds of the people of that country, still, it was Mr. Paine, and Mr. Paine alone, who brought those principles into action" (qtd. in Nelson, 47).

On the boat across the Atlantic, Paine contracted typhus, arriving in Philadelphia in December 1774, so weak he had to be carried off the ship. His life was saved, primarily, by a letter found in his pocket from Benjamin Franklin, "better than a bag of gold" (Young, 88). It read: "The bearer Mr. Thomas Pain is very well recommended to me as an ingenious worthy young man" (qtd. in Young, 88). Dr. John Kearsley received word of the letter and cared for the "young" Paine extensively while he stayed in bed for six weeks before meeting Franklin's son-in-law, Richard Bache. Note: It should be noted that Paine and Franklin remained lifelong friends, and "after the great American hero lost both of his own sons — Francis, who died of smallpox as a child, and William, who abandoned his father to join the British during the Revolution — the bereaved father will turn again and again to Paine, calling him his adopted political son. In turn, Paine will discuss with Franklin all that he writes and all that he invents. Over the years, they will become more and more alike, coming to agree on nearly all matters large and small ... falling in synch politically on almost every issue ... of exactly the same mind when it came to religion" (Nelson, 47). In matters small, "Paine would regularly forego royalties to more widely distribute his writings, just as Franklin would never patent his lightning rod or stove (and would never make a penny from either) so that their designs could be shared beneficially by all" (Nelson, 50). In matters large, Franklin once stated, "Where Liberty is, there is my country," to which Paine responded, "Where liberty is not, there is my country," basically reflecting the same meaning.

Franklin's honored recommendation bode Paine well, and he obtained "many friends and much reputation." After a few temporary jobs as a teacher, he was hired by the *Pennsylvania Magazine* as the editor and stayed there eighteen months, attracting, by his writings, more than fifteen hundred paid subscribers and rendering the periodical the most widely read in the New World. This opportunity became "a seed-bag from which this sower scattered the seeds of great reforms ripening with the progress of civilization" (Conway, 47), allowing Paine to publish profound passages, such as:

- I am thus far a Quaker, that I would gladly agree with all the world to lay aside the use of arms, and settle matters by negotiation.
- The reasonable freeman sees through the magic of a title, and examines the man before he approves him.
- Who does not feel for the tender sex? ... Man with regard to them, in all climates and in all ages, has been either an insensible husband or an oppressor; but they have sometimes experienced the cold and deliberate oppression of pride, and sometimes the violent and terrible tyranny of jealously. When they are not

beloved, they are nothing; and when they are they are tormented. They have almost equal cause to be afraid of indifference and love. Over three quarters of the globe, Nature has placed them between contempt and misery.
- And when the Almighty shall have blest us, then may our first gratitude be shown by an act of continental legislation, which shall put a stop to the importation of Negroes for sale, soften the hard fate of those already here, and in time procure their freedom [qtd. in Conway, 44–60].

As Conway notes, amazingly, "The whole circle of human ideas and principles was recognized by this lone, wayfaring man. The first to urge extension of the principles of independence to the enslaved negro; the first to arraign monarchy, and to point out the danger of its survival in presidency; the first to propose articles of a more thorough nationality to the new-born States; the first to advocate international arbitration; the first to expose the absurdity and criminality of dueling; the first to suggest more rational ideas of marriage and divorce; the first to advocate national and international copyright; the first to plead for the animals; the first to demand justice for woman" (Conway, 47).

The *Pennsylvania Magazine* was indeed a hotbed of anti–British oratory, and Paine met many influential revolutionaries, notably Benjamin Rush, who, when introduced to Paine at the magazine's bookshop one day, "felt a kinship with the immigrant. Rush was pleased to learn that Paine had realized the independence of the colonies upon Great Britain, and that he considered the measure as necessary to bring the war to a speedy and successful issue" (Fruchtman, 61). When Rush suggested that Paine write a pamphlet to present, in writing, America's argument for separation, Paine agreed and began writing *Common Sense* (the title recommended by Rush himself upon Paine's soliciting title suggestions) in November 1775. As he wrote, Paine consulted Rush, who offered a few suggestions. Upon completion, Franklin, Rittenhouse, and Samuel Adams previewed the manuscript (though very few changes were made).

Printed by Robert Bell, Third Street, Philadelphia, on January 10, 1776, for the price of two shillings, the infamous pamphlet *Common Sense,* according to Dr. Rush, "burst from the press with an effect which has rarely been produced by types and paper in any age or country" (qtd. in Conway, 61), selling over 150,000 copies in 1776 in America alone (not to mention England and Ireland). (The title page initially read "Written by an Englishman." The total sales during the Revolution may have exceeded 300,000. Paine sent the first copy off the press to Benjamin Franklin, his mentor.) Ironically, on the same day, a speech by George III was made public, in which the King "reminded the Colonies of their dependence and the right of the British Crown to 'bind them in all cases whatsoever,' and warned them of the dire consequences of their disobedience to the Government's orders and demands" (Lewis, 42).

Paine never received a penny from the sale of the pamphlet, as he signed all his earnings over to the American cause, specifically to buy "mittens for the troops that were going to Quebec." Paine later wrote, "If there is any one circumstance in my character which distinguishes itself from all the rest, it is personal disinterestedness, and an anxiety to serve a public cause in preference to myself" (qtd. in Wood, 216). He aptly stated, "I am a farmer of thoughts, and all the crops I raise, I give away" (qtd. in Nelson, 63). That first year, more than one-fifth of the colonists read the pamphlet, or had it read to them. Scholars have noted that Paine's "stylistic qualities more than anything else made *Common Sense* one of the truly great bestsellers of the century" (Fruchtman, 63), such qualities including simple, straightforward, and understandable prose, rich in metaphor and imagery. For example, "The sun never shined on a cause of greater worth"; "Now is the seed-time of continental union, faith and honor"; "The present winter is worth an age if rightly employed"; "We have it in our power to begin the world again"; "A situation similar to the present hath not happened since the days of Noah until now"; "The birthday of a new world is at hand" (qtd. in Fruchtman, 63–4).

Scholars have also pondered the intellectual reception of *Common Sense*, which completed Washington's conversion to the cause of independence ("The sound doctrine and unanswerable reasoning contained in the pamphlet 'Common Sense' will not leave numbers at a loss to decide upon the propriety of separation"); influenced, or, as many believe, even constituted the Declaration of Independence (William Cobbett said, "Whoever wrote the Declaration of Independence, Thomas Paine was its author"); served as, according to the Rev. Theodore Parker "the arsenal to which colonists went for their mental weapons"; and, as later stated by John Quincy Adams, "crystallized public opinion and was the first factor in bringing about the Revolution" (qtd. in Van der Weyde, 31–2). Perhaps, in the end, the intellectual draw of *Common Sense* was its plea to a higher calling: "Paine raised the conflict between the colonists and the parent country above the level of an insurrection against taxation to a great human struggle for an ideal" (Van der Weyde, 33). As Paine himself wrote in the pamphlet, "'Tis not the concern of a day, a year, or an age; posterity are virtually involved in the contest, and will be more or less affected even to the end of time, by the proceedings now" (qtd. in Woodward, 77).

This far-reaching pamphlet, more than any other event or publication, turned the minds of the colonists to the cause of independence, persuading Americans to form a republic, separate, and broken from, the chains of Great Britain. Sir George Trevelyan, in the *History of the American Revolution*, in fact claims, "*Common Sense* turned thousands to independence who before could not endure the thought. It worked nothing short of miracles and turned Tories into Whigs" (qtd. in Woodward, 80) by reason of the following quotes:

- But examine the passions and feelings of mankind; bring the reconciliation to the touchstone of nature, and then tell me whether you can hereafter love, honor, and faithfully serve the power that hath carried fire and sword into your land?
- But Britain is the parent country, say some, then the more shame upon her conduct. Even brutes do not devour their young, nor savages make war upon their families; wherefore, the assertion, if true, turns to her reproach.
- A government of our own is our natural right; and when a man seriously reflects on the precariousness of human affairs, he will become convinced that it is infinitely wiser and safer to form a constitution of our own in a cool deliberate manner, while we have it in our power, than to trust such an interesting event to time and chance [qtd. in Woodward, 75–78].
- The monarchy has laid (not this or that kingdom only) but the world in blood and ashes.... Of more worth is one honest man to society, and in the sight of God, than all the crowned ruffians that ever lived" [qtd. in Kaye, 45].

Indeed, "Paine couched his argument in a language designed to inflame, to convince his readers that there were no alternatives to separation from England, and, in effect, to get them to go to war against the English government" (Fruchtman, 69). As Paine noted, "The cause of America made me an author" (qtd. in Kaye, 39). And, as Vermont minister Samuel Williams noted, "Paine, and other writers upon American politics met with amazing success:

Not because they taught the people principles, which they did not before understand, but because they placed the principles which they had learned of them, in a very clear and striking light, on a most critical and important occasion" (qtd. in Kaye, 41).

Based upon these principles, Paine sketched a federalist (a single nation state united for a common cause), republican (for the public good), and liberal-democratic (representative) plan of government in which the Continental Congress and provincial assemblies were to be one (no differentiation between federal and state assemblies), meet annually, and elect presidents, not governors. The assemblies were to determine domestic policy, only, and be subject to the Continental Congress, a three-fifths majority required to pass any law. Each colony was to have, at the very least, 30 delegates, with a president elected by the 13 delegations, subject to rotation among the colonies. As Paine noted, "By ingrafting representation upon democracy, we arrive at a system of government capable of embracing and confederating all the various interests and every extent of territory and population" (qtd. in Kaye, 47). Similarly, he advocated the convening of a conference to frame a Continental Charter, empowered by the people and containing a sort of Bill of Rights guaranteeing "freedom and property ... and above all things, the free exercise of religion, according to the dictates of conscience" (qtd. in Kaye, 48). He insisted, "we have every opportunity, and every encouragement before us, to form the noblest, purest constitution on the face of the earth" (qtd. in Fruchtman, 72) and warned, "If we omit it now, some Masaniello may hereafter arise, who, laying hold of popular disquietudes, may collect together the desperate and discontented, and by assuming to themselves the powers of government, may sweep away the liberties of the continent like a deluge" (qtd. in Williamson, 74). Finally, he encouraged an "American Independence Day," as follows:

> Let a day be solemnly set apart for proclaiming the charter; let it be brought forth placed on the divine law, the Word of god; let a crown be placed thereon, by which the world may know, that so far as we approve of monarchy, that in America the law is king. But least any ill should afterwards arise, let the crown at the conclusion of the ceremony be demolished, and scattered among the people whose right it is [qtd. in Kay, 48].

In response to the few critics of *Common Sense*, most notably William Smith, provost of the College of Philadelphia, his letters of attack simply signed "Cato," Paine wrote *Four Letters on Interesting Subjects*, a pamphlet published in the spring of 1776. In these letters, he advocated for a unicameral legislature ("The more houses the more parties; and perhaps the ill consequence to this country would be that the landed interest would get into one house and the commercial interest in the other"), habeas corpus, trial by jury, annual elections, a limitation on the terms of the President (finally addressed by the Twenty-second Amendment in 1951), a periodic examination of the Constitution "at certain periods according to its first principles to correct abuses," and a military membership in the throes of government, "for otherwise they would 'form a distinct party of their own'" (qtd. in Fruchtman, 87–8).

As noted by these discussions, Paine's writings crystallized in the minds of the colonists, and "the timid became courageous, the leaders became bold ... the demands swelled for Independence — that for government that represented the people.... They were ready and willing to lay down their lives, if need be, for this new Doctrine of Freedom" (Lewis, 49). Even Paine's libelous biographer, James Cheetham, admitted *Common Sense* was "terrible in its consequences to the parent country" (qtd. in Lewis, 52). Certainly our forefathers, whether consciously or subconsciously, heeded the below-given admonishment of *Common Sense* when organizing a committee to draft the Declaration of Independence:

> Were a manifesto to be published, and dispatched to foreign Courts, setting forth the miseries we may have endured, and the peaceful methods, which we have ineffectually used for redress; declaring at the same time, that not being able any longer to live happily or safely under the cruel disposition of the British Court, we had been driven to the necessity of breaking off all connections with her; at the same time, assuring all such Courts of our peaceable disposition towards them, and of our desire of entering into trade with them; such a memorial would produce more good effects to this Continent, than if a ship were freighted with petitions to Britain [qtd. in Lewis, 84–5].

And, in fact, some scholars believe Jefferson pulled many of the ideas and terms used in the Declaration from *Common Sense,* Joseph Lewis determining, "The one reflects the other as perfectly as the architect's plans mirror the building to be erected" (97). (Lewis theorized Jefferson simply copied a manuscript prepared by Thomas Paine, writing an entire book to justify his theory, entitled *Thomas Paine, Author of the Declaration of Independence.*)

Needless to say, after the dissemination of the Declaration of Independence, rhetoric met the reality of an escalating war. Through a telescope, on August 27, 1776, Washington watched the British storm Long Island, capturing, wounding, or killing over fifteen hundred Americans. On September 15, the British assaulted New York City. Those who held their hands up in surrender were shot in the face by hired Hessians. Within twelve hours, the British were marching down Broadway. Hearing such news from the front, Paine joined the Pennsylvanian Associators, a "Flying Camp" which "flew" into action whenever needed. Once in Fort Lee, he joined General Nathanael Greene's troops (a fellow Quaker), who appointed Paine as aide-de-camp and brigadier. On November 16 Washington, Greene, and Paine watched Cornwallis capture 2,858 men; on December 3, Newport, Rhode Island, and five days later Trenton, New Jersey. It was, Paine wrote, "the very blackest of times ... when our affairs were at their lowest ebb and things in the most gloomy state" (qtd. in Nelson, 107).

Paine immediately began writing a piece in honor of each colony, a series of thirteen letters, to become known as *The American Crisis*. The first was published one week before Christmas. The printers rushed eighteen thousand copies into the streets, again, at a minimal cost since Paine relinquished any share of the profits. One such copy reached the banks of the Delaware River and Washington's encampment. At dusk on December 23, 1776, in the wake of loss after loss, and with the realization that fifteen hundred Army contracts would soon expire, General Washington ordered his officers to gather the men in small groups and read aloud this first letter, which began:

> These are the times that try men's souls. The summer soldier and the sunshine patriot will, in this crisis, shrink from the service of their country; but he that stands it now, deserves the love and thanks of man and woman. Tyranny, like hell, is not easily conquered; yet we have this consolation with us, that the harder the conflict, the more glorious the triumph. What we obtain too cheap, we esteem too lightly: it is dearness only that gives everything its value. Heaven knows how to put a proper price upon its goods; and it would be strange indeed if so celestial an article as Freedom should not be highly rated. I thank God that I fear not. I see no real cause for fear. I know our situation well, and can see the way out of it [qtd. in Nelson, 109].

On Christmas Night, with these words now in the heart of every soldier, Washington crossed the ice-laden Delaware, surprising the Hessians and winning the Battle of Trenton. Scholar Van der Weyde notes, "There is no doubt whatever that 'Crisis I' won the Battle of Trenton" (41). Thereafter escaping Cornwallis' grip, Washington went on to win another battle at Princeton, fourteen hundred farmer-citizens agreed to extend their contract, and "These are the times that try men's souls" was "in the mouths of everyone going to join the army" according to one recruit. Prussia's Frederick the Great stated, "The achievements of Washington and his little band of compatriots (at Trenton and Princeton) is the most brilliant of any recorded in the history of military achievements" (qtd. in Nelson, 111). Paine himself did not just write letters (by the light of the Army's camp-fire on a drum-head nonetheless) but also participated in both campaigns alongside Greene and Washington.

Paine's accomplishments, accolades, and appointments multiplied accordingly, and he entered a triumphant period. He was appointed to the Council of Safety in Philadelphia to negotiate a treaty with the Natives, and Congress elected him as secretary of the Committee of Foreign Affairs. In Crisis II, he wrote: "The United States of America will sound as pompously in the world or in history as the Kingdom of Great Britain"; in Crisis III, "To know whether it be the interest of the continent to be independent, we need only ask this easy, simple question: Is it the interest of a man to be a boy all his life?" and in Crisis IV, "We are not moved by the gloomy smile of a worthless king, but by the ardent glow of generous patriotism. We fight not to enslave, but to set a country free, and to make room upon the earth for honest men to live in" (qtd. in Nelson, 113–4). In 1779, he was elected clerk to the Pennsylvania Assembly and wrote the preamble to the Act of Pennsylvania Abolishing Slavery, the first of all legislative measures for emancipation:

> It is not for us to enquire why, in the creation of mankind, the inhabitants of the several parts of the earth were distinguished by a difference in feature or complexion. It is sufficient to know that all are the work of the Almighty Hand. We find in the distribution of the human species that the most fertile, as well as the most barren parts of the earth, are inhabited by men of complexions different from ours and from each other; from whence we may reasonably as well as religiously infer, that He, who placed them in their various situations, has extended equally his care and protection to all, and that it becomes not us to counteract his mercies. We esteem it a peculiar blessing granted to us that we are enabled this day to add one more step to universal civilization by removing, as much as possible, the sorrows of those who have lived in undeserved bondage [qtd. in Van der Weyde, 104].

The University of Pennsylvania also conferred a Master of Arts upon Paine, the Quaker lad who had never learned Latin.

In early 1780, Paine again sought to lift the "souls" of Washington's troops. On May 28, Washington informed the Pennsylvania Assembly by letter, such correspondence read to Assembly members by Paine himself, who served as clerk: "I assure you every idea you can form of our distresses will fall short of the reality. There is such a combination of circumstances to exhaust the patience of the soldiery that it begins at length to be worn out, and we see in every line of the army the most serious features of mutiny and sedition" (qtd. in Van der Weyde, 107). Assembly members knew little money remained in the treasury, yet enough to pay Paine his salary. Paine, first to his feet, subscribed the whole amount, $500, to the relief of the patriot Army. That same night, Paine's sacrifice was noted at a coffeehouse in Philadelphia. Two financiers started a subscription, donating $200 apiece. In a short time, 300,000 pounds had been subscribed and a bank (the Bank of North America) established for the cause, incorporated by Congress! As further encouragement, Paine wrote Crisis IX, speaking to the patriots: "The man that does not now feel for the honor of the best and noblest cause that ever a country engaged in, and exert himself accordingly, is no longer worthy of a peaceable residence among a people determined to be free" (qtd. in Van der Weyde, 108).

Knowing that further aid from France was necessary, Paine also traveled to France with Colonel John Laurens, at his request, to request additional aid. Making an impression on the King, Paine was entrusted by Louis XVI with 2,500,000 livres in silver and a ship laden with military supplies and clothing, this gift financing the final campaign against Cornwallis. Again, Paine received no compensation for his services. As a final contribution to the Revolution and the establishment of the American States, Paine wrote letters for Rhode Island's *Providence Gazette* and *Newport Mercury* to convince the state of Rhode Island to enter the Union (the state objecting, jealous of its "sovereignty"). Paine wrote, "What would the sovereignty of any individual State be, if left to itself to contend with a foreign power?" (qtd. in Van der Weyde, 141). He wrote six letters in these newspapers, and, of course, Rhode Island became part of the Union. He also spoke to the whole of the Revolution in *The Last Crisis*, published on April 19, 1783, in celebration of the eight-year anniversary of the shot heard around the world at Lexington-Concord:

> The times that tried men's souls are over, and the greatest and completest revolution the world ever knew, gloriously and happily accomplished.... Never, I say, had a country so many openings to happiness as this. Her setting out in life, like the rising of a fair morning, was unclouded and promising. Her cause was good. Her principles just and liberal. Her temper serene and firm. Her conduct regulated by the nicest steps, and everything about her wore the mark of honor. It is not every country (perhaps there is not another in the world) that can boast so fair an origin. Even the first settlement of America corresponds with the character of the revolution.... As the scenes of war are closed, and every man preparing for home and happier times, I therefore take my leave of the subject. I have most sincerely followed it from beginning to end, and through all its turns and windings: and whatever country I may hereafter be in, I shall always feel an honest pride at the part I have taken and acted, and a gratitude to nature and providence for putting it in my power to be of some use to mankind [qtd. in Nelson, 164].

In October 1785, Congress paid an honorarium of $3,000 to Paine, and Pennsylvania offered 500 pounds. The state of New York honored him with 277 acres and a farmhouse outside New Rochelle. Amazingly, Paine, also a sort of engineer, began work on the invention of a steel bridge (at that point aspiring to once again cross the Atlantic and visit his mother and father). On April 26, 1787, he sailed for Europe, not to return to America for another fifteen years.

Of course, while in Europe, Paine wrote *The Rights of Man*, "the most forceful and most lucid exposition of basic human rights ever written" (Van der Weyde, 231). The volume was dedicated to George Washington, written in response to Edmund Burke's defense of the monarchy and aristocracy, and determined: "Every age and generation must be free to act for itself, in all cases, as the ages and generations which preceded it.... There is existing in man, a mass of sense lying in a dormant state, and which, unless something excites it to action, will descend with him ... to the grave. As it is to the advantage of society that the whole of its faculties should be employed, the construction of government ought to be such as to bring forward, by quiet and regular operation, all that extent of capacity which never fails to appear in revolutions" (qtd. in Kaye, 72). Therein, he continued to praise and admonish America:

> If there is a country in the world where concord, according to common calculation, would be least expected, it is America. Made up, as it is, of people from different nations, accustomed to different forms and habits of government, speaking different languages, and more different in their modes of worship, it would appear that the union of such a people was impracticable; but by the simple operation of constructing government on the principles of society and the

rights of man, every difficulty retires, and all the parts are brought into cordial unison [qtd. in Kaye, 75].

During the French Revolution, while supportive of the initial rebellion (in fact, Paine served twice on the National Convention, prior to The Terror, and served on the Committee of Nine which adopted a new Constitution, suspended, unfortunately, due to war) and the debunking of Louis XVI's reign, he voted against Louis' execution and was thus branded an enemy of France. Worried about the mob's intentions and anxious about his own morality, he wrote *The Age of Reason*, whose purpose was "to bring man to a right reason that God has given him; to impress on him the great principles of divine morality, justice, mercy, and a benevolent disposition to all men and to all creatures and to excite in him a spirit of trust, confidence and consolation in his Creator, unshackled by the fable and fiction of books, by whatever invented name they may be called" (qtd. in Kaye, 82). Dedicating the book to the citizens of America, he reminded humanity that "all national institutions of churches, whether Jewish, Christian, or Turkish, appear to me no other than human inventions, set up to terrify and enslave mankind, and monopolize power and profit.... The WORD OF GOD IS THE CREATION WE BEHOLD, and it is in this word, which no human invention can counterfeit or alter, that God speaketh universally to man" (qtd. in Kaye, 83).

As expected, Paine was arrested on Christmas Eve 1793, and remained in the Luxembourg Tower until July of the following year, released at the urging of James Monroe. Recovering from illness associated with his imprisonment (partial paralysis), Paine never failed in his defense of the afflicted or suppressed. In *Agrarian Justice*, he stated: "It is wrong to say God made both rich and poor. He made only male and female; and He gave them the earth for their inheritance" (qtd. in Kaye, 87). Returning to America at the age of sixty-six, he experienced a type of "fall from grace" due to the Federalists/anti–Federalists debate that engulfed the United States following the War, the growth of a propertied class, and religious fervor. Kaye notes, "While radicals and working people had continued to celebrate Paine and draw inspiration from his words, many among the powerful and the propertied had grown to despise him all the more. But he had antagonized far more than those who expected or longed to constitute America's governing class. His radical pronouncements on Christianity and the Bible had outraged many others, including those whom Paine had once inspired and empowered with his vision of an independent America. The man whom they saw as the champion of republicanism increasingly became in their eyes the champion of infidelity" (89).

Still, Paine, unappreciated at the hour of his death (only six people attended his funeral, one of which, Madame Marguerite de Bonneville, stood at one end as witness for a grateful France, placing her son at the other end as witness for a grateful America), has achieved immortality. Reformers throughout U.S. history have embraced and rediscovered his works, including Paine's writings in their rhetoric, narrative, and political philosophy, most notably George Lippard, Charles Sumner, Walt Whitman (the poet of democracy), Melville, Susan B. Anthony and Elizabeth Cady Stanton, Andrew Carnegie, Thomas Edison, Mark Twain, Franklin Roosevelt (in the throes of World War II), Bob Dylan, and Ronald Reagan. Ironically, in the modern day, "not only the left but also the right claims him as one of their own" (Kaye, 259).

Perhaps Paine understood his legacy would wax and wane, for, in 1800, during the Federalist debates, he wrote, "There is too much common sense and independence in America to be long the dupe of any faction, foreign or domestic" (qtd. in Kaye, 262). Though major monuments to one of the most ardent and sacrificial founding fathers have yet to be erected in our nation's capital, as Andrew Jackson noted, "Thomas Paine needs no monument by hands; he has erected a monument in the hearts of all who love liberty" (qtd. in Nelson, 335). Indeed, the love of liberty carried in human hearts, both past and present, as a result of his writings, is the quintessence, the faithful history of Paine's services and rewards. If truth be told, it is correct to parody *Common Sense* and declare *the cause of **Paine** is in great measure the cause of all mankind,* for, as Paine noted, "My principles are universal. My attachment is to all the world, and not to any particular part, and if what I advance is right, it is right no matter where or who it comes from" (qtd. in Wood, 216). To quote Whitman, Paine, in perpetuity, remains "large ... containing multitudes."

Memorials

A 12-foot carved and inscribed memorial column stands in New Rochelle, New York, erected in 1839 by educator Gilbert Vale, the first and longest standing monument. New Rochelle is also the site of the Thomas Paine Cottage, now open to the public, and the Thomas Paine Memorial Museum. Thomas Edison turned the first shovel of dirt for the construction of the museum.

In Thetford, England, a *gold* statute of Paine now stands, in accordance with Napoleon's famous quote. Paine holds a quill pen and a copy of the *Rights of Man* in his hands. In Thetford, the sixth form (secondary school) is also named after him. In a 2002 nationwide poll conducted by the BBC, Thomas Paine was ranked as #34 in the *100 Greatest Britons*! The Lewes Town Council in the United Kingdom celebrates the life and work of Thomas Paine each July.

Bronx Community College includes Paine in its Hall of Fame of Great Americans. Both Morristown and Bordertown, New Jersey, honor Paine with public statutes.

In Paris, a statue to Paine stands in Parc Montsouris, a green space ordained by Napoleon. A plaque erected in the street where Paine lived from 1797 to 1802 reads: "Thomas PAINE / 1737–1809 / Englishman by birth / American by adoption / French by decree."

The U.S. Postal Service issued a forty-cent stamp honoring Thomas Paine in 1968, and an eight-cent stamp in 1973 saluting the printers and pamphleteers of the Revolution, whose "presses and pens spread the idea of independence."

In October 1992 legislation was signed into law (PL102–407 & PL102–459) by President George H. W. Bush authorizing the construction of a memorial to Thomas Paine on the grounds of the U.S. Capitol. The memorial was to be built by private funds, yet to be erected.

Paine's premiere biographer, Dr. Moncure Conway, began the Thomas Paine National Historical Society in 1884. Thomas Edison was vice-president of the organization. The Society oversees the Thomas Paine Museum and Archives and held the first ever International Conference of Thomas Paine Studies in 2012.

3

HAYM SALOMON
Financial Hero

The kindness of our little friend in Front Street, near the coffee-house, is a fund which will preserve me from extremities.—James Madison

Lissa, Poland, 1740. Yiddish lines the tongues of residents, and synagogues line the streets. To a "highly respectable and learned" Jewish family is born Haym Salomon, one who never masters Yiddish, yet lives to speak seven other tongues: English, Spanish, French, Italian, Russian, German, and Polish. Salomon's family is strong and intact, "the central spiritual and social organ for the nation's Jews" (Schwartz, 6) after having moved to Poland from Portugal in the late 15th century at a time when the Catholic Church demanded that all Jews convert to Christianity. Having built their first synagogue in Lissa in 1626, Salomon's Jewish community enjoys religious freedoms. In 1764, however, Salomon's Poland comes under the rule of Stanisław August Poniatowski, a puppet of Catherine the Great of Russia. Poniatowski imposes strict and encumbering taxes on Jewish families. Salomon is forced to leave and begins traveling throughout Europe, learning language after language, striving to find "a country that encouraged education and religious freedom and that allowed its people a voice in the ways in which the government formed its policies. Salomon was unable to find such a country in Europe" (Amler, 10). Instead, he finds America and the Sons of Liberty, for "with his own unhappy country's history and with his hatred of despotic Russia, Salomon imbibed a love of liberty which extensive travel in Europe intensified, and, as might have been expected, the outbreak of the Revolution found him an ardent supporter of the Colonial cause" (Peters, 11).

Poniatowski proved a powerless and indecisive king. In fact he was the pawn and lover of Catherine the Great, and Russia, Prussia, and Austria longed for power over Poland. "And Poland, weakened by internal discord, by the spy systems of the three countries, could not resist" (Fast, 18). In 1768, the Polish people formed the Confederation of Bar in an attempt to save their homeland from foreign influence and control. Casimir Pulaski, discussed in Chapter 14, became leader of a group of patriots who, in 1771, conspired to force the King to defend his own country or withdraw from power. Unfortunately, the plan did not work, as the King's soldiers dominated the patriot forces. It cannot be definitively ascertained, but it is believed Salomon was "deeply involved in the futile but noble effort. The timing of his departure and his later demonstrations of both bravery and patriotism make him a prime candidate for involvement in the unsuccessful abduction attempt" (Knight, 16). Thus, due to religious persecution, unjustified taxation, and ruthless political forces,

Salomon left during the economic and social decline of 1764–68, for "the sake of easing the burden on the family" (Schwartz, 7). While in Europe, "he did acquire an unusual knowledge of finance and made friends among the bankers of the most important European commercial centers" (Lewis, 14). Fleeing to England after the unsuccessful kidnapping attempt long enough to prepare for a trip across the ocean, Salomon sailed in August of 1772 to America, landing in New York City, never again to return to the country of his birth, having "hitherto sustained the character of being warmly attached to America" (Schwartz, 9).

Salomon landed in the colonies, another land "verging on total collapse of its political and commercial structure," for "it was obvious that England was draining the colonies through continued taxation aimed at shoring up Britain's credit after the Seven Years' War; further, Britain looked upon the colonies as a British marketplace" (Schwartz, 8–9). Starting a personal business, no doubt taxed heavily by the British, he "became a fast friend of that fiery Scotsman, Alexander McDougall, and many evenings he spent in hot discussion with young Alexander Hamilton. He began to realize, as they did, that sooner or later war with England must come, that the Colonies must be free" (Fast, 19). Thus began the first of two periods in Salomon's service to the American Revolution, for, from 1776–1778, he apparently served as "an agent or even a spy for the Americans and helped in the escape of prisoners. Supposedly also he tried to subvert the Hessians ... and was even suspected of a part in a plot to burn the docks and British ships in port.... Salomon's activity during this period was political as well as economic and somewhat mysterious in character" (Rezneck, 82–3).

Salomon's first duty appears to have been that of a "sutler" for General Schuyler at Fort Ticonderoga in New York, or one who sold merchandise and supplies to the troops at military campgrounds from a tent or wagon. When New York City was occupied by British troops later that year, Salomon did not leave. A fire broke out and burned a quarter of the city on September 20, and shortly thereafter, presumed to have aided the Sons of Liberty in beginning the fire, Salomon was arrested by the British and imprisoned in the Provost, the worst prison on the island. (For four days before entering the Provost, he was placed in a jail called "Old Sugar House," "totally unlighted except for occasional slivers of light coming through holes in the roof" (Knight, 30). In the Provost, as many prisoners as could be were placed in a cell, sleeping shoulder to shoulder, and taken out from time to time for purposes of torture! Peters notes, "So closely were the prisoners packed there that when they laid down at night to rest, when their bones ached, on the hard oak plains, and they wished to turn, it was altogether by command, 'right — left,' being so wedged as to form almost a solid mass of solid bodies" (13). Salomon survived, as he later wrote to Congress, because of his appointment as a purveyor for a Hessian commander, a Lieutenant General Heister, who needed someone with a command of several European languages. In this position, Salomon knew "he could keep his finger on the pulse of the British campaign, sow discord among the Hessians, and smuggle information to the American army in the field" (Fast, 19). His "secret" activities for the Revolution included rendering aid to the French and American prisoners, in fact helping many to escape (with the help of a fellow prisoner, Samuel Demezes), and creating dissension among the Hessians, many of whom he convinced to resign their commission (Pennsylvania was giving 100 acres of land to any Hessian who agreed to desert the British and not take up arms against the colonists). It is believed "that he was personally responsible for several hundred desertions in just a few months' time" (Knight, 33).

During his forced service for the British, during which he was a secret service agent to the Americans, Salomon was released on parole. Picking up the pieces of his life, he married Rachel Franks, "sister of Colonel Isaac Franks, a Revolutionary officer of distinction, and of Mayer Isaac Franks, a judge of the Supreme Court of Pennsylvania" (Peters, 12). They soon had a son named Ezekiel, and Salomon moved his business to a larger office near the center of commerce, where he was "called upon to sell to the occupying British troops, and this may well have resulted in circumstances which would then permit him to serve as a spy for the Americans" (Knight, 36). In fact, it is believed that his growing contacts with international seafarers allowed Salomon and the Sons of Liberty to "smuggle both men and military intelligence across British lines to Washington's nearby outposts" (Knight, 36).

Salomon's secret activities soon "rendered him so obnoxious to the British headquarters that he was closely pursued by the guards" (Rezneck, 83). Intelligence worked against him, for in August 1778, he was again imprisoned by the British, escorted back to the Provost by "a drummer beating a slow cadence so that all who heard and observed the procession could comprehend the full power of the Crown" (Knight, 41). He was placed on "Congress Hall," housing many distinguished Patriots, many of whom were sent to the gallows, never to return to family and friends. Charged with treason, espionage, perfidy, arson, and the promotion of desertion and sedition, Salomon was sentenced to be hanged by the neck until dead. Note: As Schwartz reports, "Tradition has it that Salomon was responsible for both the 1776 and the 1778 fires. The dates fit neatly with his initial arrest and eventual flight" (29). Again, Salomon's wits paid off, for having concealed gold coins in his clothing prior to his arrest, he bribed a Hessian guard the night before his execution and escaped. On foot, over the next two nights, Salomon dodged Redcoats, despite a hacking cough (tuberculosis) acquired while in prison, barking dogs, and raiding parties on either side, finally reaching, fifteen to twenty miles later, Alexander McDougall's Continental Army regiment. Escaping safely to Philadelphia, and attended to by the Jewish Congregation Mikveh Israel (at the home of Joseph Cauffman), he reported to the Continental Congress on August 25: "Your Memorialist has upon this Event most irrevocably lost all his Effects and Credits to the amount of Five or six thousand Pounds Sterling and left his distressed Wife and a Child of a Month old at New York waiting that they may soon have an Opportunity to come from thence with empty hands" (qtd.

Bust of Haym Salomon created by the George Washington Bicentennial Committee (National Archives and Records Administration).

in Schwartz, 28). According to Rezneck, "the document indicates either a brazen boldness or a merited right to the attention of Congress" (83).

Denied employment by the Congress due to financial concerns, a deaf-ear which "worked for the ultimate good both of Salomon and the young country" (Peters, 14), Salomon entered the second part of his revolutionary career, "in which he conducted himself more openly and certainly with great skill and patriotism" (Rezneck, 83), becoming a commission merchant and broker, "buying and selling for a commission, both foreign and American currencies. He provided his talents as an agent for the trading of merchandise, but acted on his own as a dealer in various commodities and goods. On occasions, he financially backed the captains and owners of privateers and blockade runners. Salomon shared in their spoils when their raids against the British were successful" (Knight, 52). Again, overnight, Salomon's enterprise, a brokerage run from the corner of a coffeehouse, worked for the good of the nation, as his "eminent respectability, remarkable intelligence, irreproachable integrity, his delicate sense of mercantile honor, his unbounded benevolence for all mankind, and, above all, his undying hatred of English tyranny, soon led to his recognition by the leading men of his time" (Peters, 15). Newspaper ads placed by his firm advertised his ability to deal with bills of exchange on France and Holland. The ads in the *Pennsylvania Packet* read,

> Haym Solomons, Broker, sells Bills on Holland, France, Spain, England, St. Croix, &c. He likewise sells, on commission, Loan-office certificates, and all other Kinds of Merchandise. He gives constant attendance at his Office in Front-street, between Market and Arch-streets, from 9 to 12 in the forenoon; likewise attends at the Coffee-house from 12 to 2.
>
> Haym Salomon, Broker, at his office in Front-street, between Market and Arch-streets, TRANSACTS all kinds of business on Commission. Buys and sells Bills of Exchange on any part of Europe. As also, Pennsylvania and other State money, and which he receives in payment for Bills of Exchange, at the highest price given. He gives constant attendance at his Office, from nine to one in the forenoon and from three to seven in the afternoon.

Peters records, "For the most part the money advanced by Louis XVI and the proceeds of the loans negotiated in Holland passed through his hands. He was entrusted with the negotiation of all the war subsidies of France and Holland on his own personal integrity, which were sold to the resident merchants in America without any loss, at a credit of two and three months, for which he received the small commission of one-fourth of one per cent. Several European finance houses did business with him" (15–6). By November, he had saved £1,200, and "Salomon's newfound prosperity also brought him back his family, which suggests that he had to pay for their safe passage" (Schwartz, 35). His financial service and fluency in the French language soon came to the attention of Chevalier de la Luzerne, the French minister, who appointed Salomon Paymaster General of the French Army and Navy in America. As such, he provided loans to General Lafayette until supplies arrived from France.

From his own purse, Salomon subsidized Spanish and French ambassadors, as well as Dutch officials. Don Francisco Rendon, ambassador from Spain, wrote to the Spanish governor of Cuba, "Mr Salomon has obtained money for his most Catholic Majesty, and I am indebted to his friendship in this particular for the support of my character, as his Most Catholic Majesty's agent here, with any degree of credit and reputation, and without it I would not have been able to give that protection and assistance to His Majesty's subject which His majesty enjoins and my duty requires" (qtd. in Peters, 22). Peters even believes, "The secret support of Charles III of Spain is said to have been due to Salomon's efforts" (22).

Salomon loaned money not only to foreign ambassadors who furthered the American cause, but also to major players of the Revolution. James Madison, Father of the Constitution, called Salomon his "private benefactor," and wrote,

> I am almost ashamed to reiterate my wants so incessantly to you, but they begin to be so urgent that it is impossible to suppress them. The kindness of our little friend in Front Street, near the coffee-house, is a fund which will preserve me from extremities, but I never resort to it without great mortification, as he obstinately rejects all recompense. The price of money is so usurious, that he thinks it ought to be extorted from none but those who aim at profitable speculations. To a necessitous Delegate he gratuitously spares a supply out of his private stock [qtd. in Knight, 59].

It is also known that Salomon offered support to Thomas Jefferson and James Monroe, and, possibly, sundry Revolutionary founders, directly financing the armies of Lafayette and Baron von Steuben. John Paul Jones received aid for his buccaneering efforts, as did Pennsylvania's Governor Thomas Mifflin; James Wilson; first signer of the Declaration of Independence and an early federal judge; General Arthur Saint Clair (original governor of the Northwest Territory); Edmund Randolph; and Robert Morris, congressional treasurer. And, undoubtedly, Arthur Lee, Joseph Jones, John Mercer, Joseph Reed,

Statue of Haym Salomon, George Washington, and Robert Morris in Chicago (Teresa Smith).

and William McPherson also received Salomon's financial assistance. No matter the names and numbers, "Unquestionably, Haym Salomon served the fiscal needs of the Revolutionary government ably and even unselfishly and deserved well of the country, and his contributions do not need to be exaggerated by later fictions" (Rezneck, 94). All in all, Salomon contributed between $600,000 and $800,000 toward the revolutionary cause, whether by supporting troops, military and governmental leaders, or patriots. According to Lewis, "taking the $800,000 figure and adding interest over 217 years, one arrives at a debt amounting to over $2.5 trillion owed to the heirs of Salomon" (15).

On June 8, 1781, Superintendent of Finance for the American colonies, Robert Morris, entered an agreement with Salomon to "assist me in the sale of the Bills ... his Brokerage to be settled hereafter, but not to exceed half a per cent" (Rezneck, 85). Thus began Morris and General Washington's "habit" of "sending" for "Mr. Salomon desiring him to press the sale of Bills" (Rezneck, 85). So insistent were Morris' demands, legend states that Morris actually "sent" for Salomon on *Yom Kippur*, the holiest day on the Jewish calendar. When Salomon was not found at the coffeehouse, "Morris, over his courier's vehement protest, sent him to the synagogue to get Haym Salomon out of the meeting to appeal for his help. On *Yom Kippur,* no Jew is even supposed to think about money. It would be blasphemous to touch money, write a check, or enter into any kind of financial transaction" (Lewis, 25). Supposedly shocked by this interruption, the congregation nonetheless listened to Morris' pleas. As the story goes, Salomon personally donated $3,000, and, within minutes, $20,000 was raised, to be donated only after sunset and the end of the Holy Day. Legends aside, all-in-all, Morris' diary, as kept during the Revolution, contains over seventy references to pleas for Salomon's aid. And, history records that Washington asked Morris to "send for" Haym to raise $20,000 during the summer of 1781, in order to "pay the expenses of leading his army to Yorktown and a possible end of the war.... It was necessary that Washington convince the French that he was now able to meet the financial obligations, even though this had not always been the case in the past.... With Salomon's cash in hand, Washington joined Rochambeau and crossed the Hudson River on August 20 and ... on October 21, 1781 Great Britain suffered the greatest military defeat in its history" (Knight, 64).

Salomon also became a stockholder in the newly established Bank of North America, keeping "a substantial account in it, out of which were made payments to the government" (Rezneck, 86). Chartered not as a federal bank, incorporated within the state of Pennsylvania, it was "the first commercial bank in the United States" (Lewis, 33). He believed the bank would "facilitate the management of the finances of the United States. The several states may ... derive occasional advantages" such as "discounting notes of individuals, and thereby anticipating the receipt of public money: besides which, the persons who had contracted for furnishing rations to the army were also aided with discounts, upon the public credit" (qtd. in Rezneck, 54). The bank insured the guarantee of foreign loans and the upkeep of Washington's Army (food and clothing).

Due to his expertise in brokering monies necessary for the war effort, Morris allowed Salomon to advertise as "Broker to the Office of Finance," within the *Packet*, the *Independent Gazeteer*, and the *Chronicle of Freedom*. On one occasion, after the war, when soldiers were rebelling and demanding back-payments for their service, Morris, unable to meet the financial demands ($140,000 owing, Morris lacking $101,000), ordered "Solomon the Broker to sell more Bills to provide for the balance" (Rezneck, 89). Salomon again performed a miracle, rendering the United States government solvent in an after-war crisis. Scholar Charles Russell wrote, "The romance of business remains unwritten in America. It has nothing more remarkable than this triumph of a Polish immigrant, nine years in the country, and the price he paid for it. The whole American Revolution seems now to the sober inquiring sense a thing incredible, but even that wild story has no chapter more startling" (276).

One of Salomon's last duties to our country was to take a stand for religious freedoms and rights, addressing the Pennsylvania Council of Censors, who had placed a "Christian test oath" for officeholders in the state constitution. He and five other Jewish leaders wrote: "Your memorialists ... with great submission apprehend that a clause in the Constitution which disables them to be elected by their fellow citizens to represent them in the assembly is a stigma upon their nation and their religion, and it is inconsonant with the second paragraph of the said Bill of Rights" (qtd. in Rezneck, 96). They continued, "The Jews of Pennsylvania, in proportion to the number of their members, can count with any religious society whatsoever the Whigs among them. They have served some of them in the continental Army; some went out in the Militia to fight the common enemy; all of them have cheerfully contributed to the support of the Militia and the government of this state" (qtd. in Rezneck, 96). By 1790, following the example of the United States Constitution, Pennsylvania repealed the clause, becoming "one of the first states to establish religious equality in the political realm" (Rezneck, 96).

Salomon finally succumbed, at the premature age of forty-five, to the tuberculosis ravaging his lungs (since the British imprisonment). The *Pennsylvania Packet* wrote: "An eminent broker of this city, he was a native of Poland and of the Hebrew nation. He was remarkable for his skill and integrity in his profession and for his generous and humane deportment" (qtd. in Rezneck, 96). Harvard historian Albert Bushneff, believes "all Americans may acclaim Haym Salomon as a patriot, a benefactor to his Country, an inciter of patriotism to members of his race, to his countrymen, and to later generations. It looks as though his credit was better than that of the whole 13 United States of America" (qtd. in Lewis, 29).

Would such a benefactor assist the United States of America so generously and with such devotion in the 21st century if push came to shove? The answer lies to fate. Whether yea or nay, despite this century's financial failings, should not "the people of this peerless, unrivalled, unapproached and unapproachable Republic, now in the days of their prosperity, erect to this early benefactor a monument at Washington, a memorial to this ardent lover of human freedom, who did in his little office in Front Street, Philadelphia, for the Nation's credit, what Washington did on the field of battle for the people's freedom?" (Peters, 35).

Memorials

A congressional enactment of August 6, 1956, provided: "The Mikveh Israel Cemetery, located in Philadelphia, Pennsylvania, and containing the graves of Haym Salomon and other outstanding patriots of the Revolutionary War who played important parts in the early history of the United States, shall be declared to be a unit of the Independence National Historical Park."

A report from the 29th Congress determined, "Abundant proof is presented that Haym Salomon rendered very essential aid to the cause of the Revolution, and that he did so, judging by so many of his acts, disinterestedly and from a sincere and ardent love for human freedom."

In A Senate Committee on Revolutionary Claims, dated July 2, 1865, the attestation read: "All the former reports from the committees of both houses show that Haym Salomon supported from his private means many of the principal men of the Revolution, who otherwise, as stated by themselves, could not have attended to their public duties, among whom are mentioned Jefferson, Madison, Lee, Steuben, Mifflin, St. Clair, Blond, Jones, Monroe, Wilson and others."

President Franklin Roosevelt referred to Washington, Morris, and Salomon as "this great triumvirate of patriots," and the evening before December 7, 1941, noted, "Their genius in finance and fiscal affairs and unselfish devotion to the cause of liberty made their support of the utmost importance when the struggling colonies were fighting against such heavy odds."

On March 25, 1975, the Postal Service issued a stamp bearing the legend: "Haym Salomon: Financial Hero." On the reverse an inscription read: "Businessman and broker Haym Salomon was responsible for raising most of the money needed to finance the American Revolution and later to save the new nation from collapse."

On the 150th anniversary of the approval of the Bill of Rights, a statue was unveiled in Heald Square on Wacker Drive in Chicago, Illinois, depicting General George Washington, Robert Morris, and Haym Salomon.

In Los Angeles, California's MacArthur Park, a larger-than-life statue honors Haym Salomon's legacy.

4

FRONTIER SAVIOR
Patriot Francis Salvador

He asked whether I had beaten the enemy. I told him yes.—Major Andrew Williamson, on the South Carolina frontier, 1776

Patriot Francis Salvador, whose last name meaning "Savior" was constructed in England to preserve his family's lineage and very existence, in fact saved many lives on the South Carolina frontier during the early years of the American Revolution, yet lost his own for America's noble cause. Salvador hoped to redeem a slight upon his uncle Joseph and his entire family by the British Parliament and monarchy while forging a nation which embraced religious freedom and abolished, once and for all, anti–Semitism. His family was no stranger to oppression, having run from European persecution for centuries.

The Salvadors were Sephardic Jews (Spanish-Portuguese residents, expelled from Iberia during the Inquisition, who worshipped in Hebrew, Spanish, and Portuguese), shortly based in London, having also run from oppression in Holland (Francis was only the fourth generation Londoner). Due to these experiences, Francis' paternal role models certainly instilled a sense of justice and duty within his character. Francis' grandfather, also named Francis, remembering the persecution of his own childhood, worked to send members of his synagogue to a safer locale. The stock company which sought to develop the colony of Georgia commissioned three prominent London Jews, Anthony da Costa, Francis Salvador, and Alvaro Lopez, to help raise investment capital. In turn, forty-two Spanish–Portuguese Jews, living in London, were granted leave to make passage across the Atlantic in 1733, settling in Savannah without religious recourse.

In the streets of London, Francis' uncle, Joseph, exhibited true humanitarianism to his nephew, as "notwithstanding the extensive financial and mercantile transactions in which he was engaged, he devoted a portion of his time to the improvement of the condition of the needy. He not only gave largely to all existing institutions, but was ever seeking new places for conquering the hydra-headed evil of pauperism ... always a liberal donor to the necessitous" (Elzas, 109). Francis most likely chose the colonies himself due to the growing anti–Semitism resulting from the Naturalization Act of 1753, which made displaced Jews English citizens. Due to public outcry, the act was repealed the following year, receiving no support from Parliament or the monarchy, even though Francis' paternal line had become prominent businessmen who loaned money to the English government, and even though a seven-man Jewish delegation organized by Francis' Uncle Joseph had visited and congratulated King George III upon his coronation. (When Joseph later pressed for the return of a law making Portuguese Jews citizens of England, he was booed out of a theater.) No doubt, Francis and his drifting family "shared in the strong anti–British sentiment characteristic of the frontier" (Rezneck, 23).

Born in 1747 in London, Francis' name in the London synagogue in which he was reared became "Daniel Jezurun Rodrigues," as Francis' forefathers in Portugal had been known as Jessurun Rodrigues (such name retained as late as 1764). Though his father, Jacob, died when Francis was two, he was raised in luxury in London due to his grandfather's business acumen, trained by private tutors, and became an extensive European traveler. At age twenty Francis married his cousin, Sarah, and took his place in the family shipping business. Events soon devastated the family fortune. As Pencak notes, Joseph "lost much of his fortune in the failure of the Dutch East India Company and the Lisbon earthquake, the latter a sign that despite the Inquisition, Jews remained silent and significant partners in the Portuguese economy" (124). An American fortune remained, however, for, in 1755, Joseph had bought over one hundred thousand acres in the district known as Ninety-Six (present day Abbeville, South Carolina), referred to as "Jews Land." Thus, Joseph convinced Francis to travel to America, promising to sell him a large tract. Francis agreed, hoping to restore the family's economic gains by growing indigo.

South Carolina proved a friendly environment for Francis as John Locke had ensured a religious tolerance in the early colony of South Carolina, making it favorable for the establishment of a Jewish community. Locke was friends with the Earl of Shaftesbury, Lord Ashley, who wrote the charter for the colony and asked Locke for assistance. "It gave Locke the opportunity to include some of his favorite ideas on religious toleration in the 'Fundamental Constitution of Carolina.' For Carolina the advantages were soon discernible since it attracted talented dissidents such as Jews and Huguenots to that population-starved colony" (Feingold, 29). Scholar Walter Edgar acknowledged this early Jewish presence, centered primarily around Charleston: "Because of its policy of religious tolerance, South Carolina attracted a sizable percentage of the Jewish residents of British North America. They were primarily Sephardic Jews who had been expelled from Spain and Portugal, and they came to South Carolina via the Netherlands, England, or the West Indies" (qtd. in Hirschman and Yates, 147). Experiencing only good will from the host city of Charleston, nearly five hundred Jews settled in the area, making Charleston the fourth oldest Jewish community in the Americas, behind New York, Philadelphia, and Savannah. (Charleston's Beth Elohim was established in 1749.) Hirschman and Yates note this population was "the largest, wealthiest and most cultured Jewish community in the Colonies" (158). Jewish reformer Issac Harby wrote, "Carolina Jews joined other religious groups to form one great political family, not a despised sect, but a portion of the people."

Arriving in the colony in 1773, Salvador was virtually destitute, having left behind a wife and four children, whom he hoped to bring across the ocean at some point. Salvador dedicated every moment to the task of cultivating the rich land of his estate, which he named Coronoca, or "Corn-acre." Within a year he became a wealthy, distinguished member of the Charleston and District Ninety-Six community, and the first Jew elected to a high office in the English colonies (Salvador served at this post until his death). Hirschfeld notes, "His English birth notwithstanding, he was impelled in part toward the Whig side because the gentry, the upper classes with which he was associated, were anti–British" (93). In 1774, as the largest land owner in District 96, having purchased 7,000 acres from his uncle, he was the logical choice to serve on South Carolina's first provincial Congress along with his planter friend, Richard Rapley, for "most low country planters became increasingly agitated during the 1760s as Parliament sought to tighten its economic grip on the American Colonies. Like most colonial legislatures, the South Carolina Commons was concerned that its legislative power was being usurped by Parliament" (qtd. in Hirschman and Yates, 93). Francis Salvador represented the colony of South Carolina at both the First and Second Provincial Congress (1773–1776), at a time when Jews could not vote in Britain because they would not swear an oath to be a "good" Christian. "His personality, level of education, and enthusiasm for the cause of independence were sufficiently strong credentials to overcome his youth (twenty-eight in 1774) and the fact he was a Jew" (Hirschman and Yates, 93).

In his term for the Provincial Congress, Salvador actively assisted in the drafting of South Carolina's first constitution, "drawing up the declaration explaining the purpose of the provincial congress to the people, obtaining ammunition, assessing the state of the interior parts of the country, and making sure the state constitution was accurately engrossed" (Pencak, 125). He served on the Committee attempting to preserve peace in South Carolina's interior, where the British were negotiating an alliance with the Cherokees, and on the ways and means committee, "a select committee authorized to issue bills of credit to pay the militia" (Feldberg, 35). He also assisted South Carolina's Provincial Congress in framing a bill of rights and preparing an address to the royal governor of South Carolina, presenting grievances to the British crown. In the Second Provincial Congress, he urged the body to "instruct the South Carolina delegation in Philadelphia to vote for independence" (Feldberg, 35). He next served in the state's General Assembly, and, as a state representative, served on the committee responsible for the enforcement of the Continental Association, becoming friends with significant revolutionary leaders from South Carolina, including Andrew Pickens and fellow congressman Andrew Williamson, commander of the district militia, whose duty was to defend the settlements from raiding Cherokees.

When militia were needed by either side in the South Carolina backcountry, meetings were held to win converts, at which volunteers signed an oath of loyalty to the cause of independence and the decisions of the Continental Congress (considered by the British an act of treason, punishable by death). As noted above, the South Carolina Provincial Congress had appointed Salvador to "a commission to negotiate with Tories living in Northern and Western parts of the colony to secure their promise not to actively aid the royal government" (Feldberg, 35). History details that on a late afternoon in August 1775, Salvador attended such a meeting at Fort Boone, also asking local farmers at the meeting to discontinue trade with England. In fact, Salvador apparently was responsible for the quill, inkwell, and paper for the meeting, saving the signatures for congressional purposes and safekeeping the list so that it did not fall into British hands. As Loyalist backcountry men suspiciously looked on, calling Congressman William Tennent a traitor after his two-hour sermon that supported a motion to sign the oath, Salvador bravely seconded the motion and compiled the signatures.

Returning from his duties in the General Assembly to Ninety-Six and Coronaca on July 1, 1776, Salvador's ardor for the cause of the Revolution impelled him to volunteer for the local militia under Major Andrew Williamson, who was asked to "engage a band of Cherokee Indians incited by local Tories" (Rezneck, 24). For, beginning in May 1776, the Cherokees, at the bidding of the British, plundered the South Carolina backcountry, murdering all within their wake. As the Cherokees approached Ninety-Six on the same day as Salvador's return, July 1, a neighboring planter, Aaron Smith, rode to Coronaca. Two of his fingers were shot away, and he informed Salvador that the Cherokee had murdered his father, mother, five brothers and sisters, and five slaves. Salvador ordered his best horse saddled, and, "in an act reminiscent of Paul Revere, mounted his horse and galloped nearly 30 miles to give the alarm" (Feldberg, 35). He rode to the home of fellow planter and friend, Major Williamson, warning all along the path of the advancing war party. Williamson and Salvador began rallying ammunition and troops, and by July 15 gathered over 1,150 muskets and rifles, along with 450 men. Attacked on the 15th by 88 Cherokee and 100 Loyalists, they won a victory that "gave heart to the embattled frontier. When news of British defeat at Charleston (June 28) reached the backcountry, many doubters were persuaded and began to arrive in numbers to join Andrew Williamson and Andrew Pickens' in a punitive expedition against the Cherokee" (Lumpkin, 29).

Though warned by veteran Indian fighter Andrew Pickens not to advance any deeper into Cherokee territory, Williamson proceeded at the prompting of Chief Justice William H. Drayton, who had written Salvador, bluntly insisting that Williamson and his men were to "punish the Indians mercilessly. Their cornfields were to be cut up, captive Indians were to be enslaved, their towns burnt, their land confiscated, and the nation extirpated" (Marcus, 125).

On July 31, as two white Loyalist guides captured by Williamson led his 330 men into an ambush near the Keowee River, British commander Alexander Cameron and 1,200 Cherokee and Seneca Indians awaited the arrival of the district militia, even though Williamson had informed the two prisoners that "if I found they deceived me, I would

The Cherokee as depicted near the time of the American Revolution.

order them instantly put to death" (Marcus, 128). Williamson describes the awaiting ambush in a letter to the governor of South Carolina, John Rutledge:

> "The River Keowee lying in our route, and only passable at a ford at Seneca, obliged me (though much against my inclination) to take that road; the enemy either having discovered my march, or laid themselves in ambush with a design to cut off any spies or party I had sent out, had taken possession of the first houses in Seneca and posted themselves behind a long fence, on an eminence close to the road where we were to march. And, to prevent being discovered, had filled up the openings betwixt the rails with twigs of trees and corn-blades. They suffered the guides and advanced guard to pass when a gun from the house was discharged meant, as I suppose, for a signal for those placed behind the fence, who, a few seconds after, purged in a heavy fire upon my men, which, being unexpected, staggered my advanced party" [qtd. in Marcus, 128].

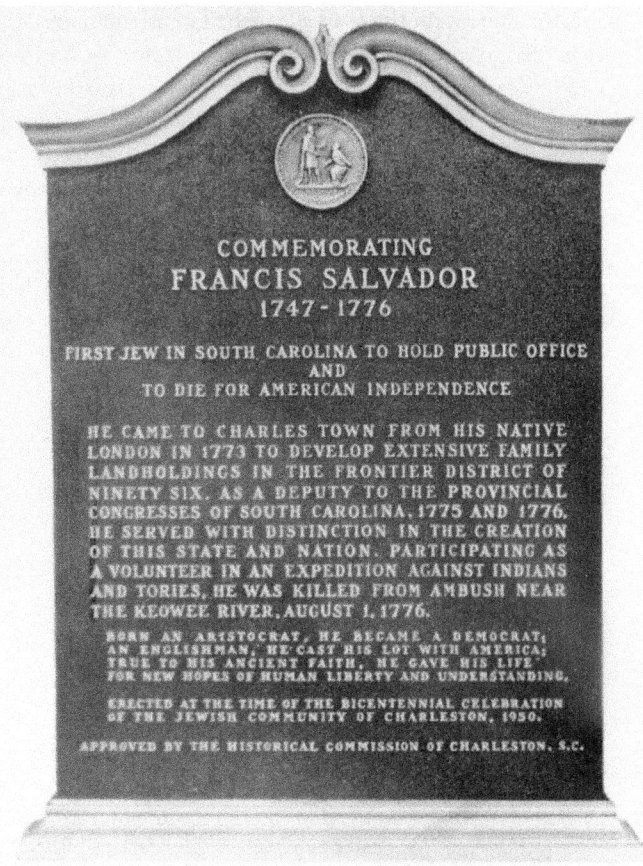

Marker to Francis Salvador, Washington Park, Charleston, South Carolina.

Caught in the ambush (which occurred August 1, 1776, at 2:00 A.M.), Salvador was shot from his horse, receiving three bullets, and subjected to the mutilation of a scalping. Major Williamson witnessed Salvador's death and was at his side upon his death. "He died, about half after two o'clock in the morning, forty-five minutes after he received his wounds, sensible to the last. When I came up to him, after dislodging the enemy, and speaking to him, he asked whether I had beaten the enemy. I told him yes. He said he was very glad of it and shook me by the hand, and bade me farewell, and said he would die in a few minutes" (qtd. in Pencak, 24). Thus, as the first Jewish casualty of the American Revolution, Salvador's body unfortunately "lies in an unknown grave on South Carolina's frontier" (Rezneck, 24). Nevertheless, South Carolina's Jews have commemorated his memory in Charleston City Park.

A Charleston publication, the *Remembrancer*, reported, "The whole army regretted his loss, as he was universally loved and esteemed by them" (qtd. in Elzas, 76). Chief Justice and historian of South Carolina, John Drayton, Salvador's friend and colleague in the first legislature, spoke highly of Salvador: "The fate of this gentleman excited universal regret.

His manners were those of a polished gentleman and as such he was intimately known and esteemed by the first revolutionary characters of South Carolina" (qtd. in Rezneck, 24).

Salvador died in service to the two dreams he brought across the Atlantic: economic independence from Britain and religious freedom, two dreams posthumously realized. True to his bidding before the South Carolina Provincial Congress, yet unfortunately unknown to Salvador before his death, the Declaration of Independence was adopted on July 4. True to Salvador's service toward the legislative advancement of his adopted Colony, in 1790, South Carolina, in its second constitution, gave Jews the legal right to hold elective office. And, without a doubt true to posterity, as quoted by fellow Patriot and friend, Henry Laurens, Salvador's untimely death remains "universally regretted."

Memorials

To celebrate the two hundredth anniversary of Charleston's Jewish congregation, in 1950, a monument was erected in Charleston's City Park in memory of Francis Salvador, reading:

Commemorating
Francis Salvador
1747–1776
First Jew in South Carolina to hold public office
And
To die for American independence

He came to Charlestown from his native
London in 1773 to develop extensive family
landholdings in the Frontier District of
Ninety-Six. As a deputy to the Provincial
Congresses of South Carolina, 1775 and 1776,
he served with distinction in the creation
of this state and nation. Participating as
a volunteer in an expedition against Indians
and Tories, he was killed from ambush near
the Keowee River, August 1, 1776.

Born an aristocrat, he became a democrat;
An Englishman, he cast his lot with America;
True to his ancient faith, he gave his life
For new hopes of human liberty and understanding.

5

"I SERVE THE COUNTRY FOR NOTHING"
The Indestructible John Barry; Father of the American Navy

When Britain held the bold tyrannic rod, and cry'd 'Ye slaves obey our sov'reign nod,' The patriot sons of virtue took the flame, and fill'd the lists with hardy deeds of fame; Amongst the first, the boldest, and the best, Brave Barry stands intrepidly confest.—Revolutionary Philadelphia verse sung to "Sons of Neptune"

John Barry was born near the sea in the year 1745, in County Wexford, Ireland, "a prostrate land beneath English monopolists and a penal code that permitted a Roman Catholic barely the means to eke out a miserable existence" (Clark, 4). Though the son of a farmer, Barry's soul left the land and became one with the sea, perhaps because, for an Irish Catholic of that age, "mere survival was success enough" (McGrath, 4). The Irish of that time were forbidden, by England's penal laws, to worship, receive religious education, own weapons or land, hold office, speak the Gaelic language, or inherit property. As a farmer, John's father, James, could earn only one-third of his annual harvest; he was required to move from one estate to another, similar to America's post–Civil War sharecroppers, never allowed freedom of his own person. James and his wife, Ellen, lived in a one-room thatched-roof home, in which John was born. Yet, just ten miles away, the busy port of Wexford was sending ships to the Americas stocked full of linen, wool, ale, and beer, offering John an out to ports beyond, one of which, Philadelphia, became "home" during his adult years. Arriving in Philadelphia at the young age of fifteen, John immediately determined to make America the country of his adoption.

Three options were available to Barry as an adult: "remain home, and confront hardscrabble poverty; join one of the Irish Brigades far flung across Europe, and face death by battle or disease; or go to sea, and live a life fraught with hardships, risking mortality on the world's oceans in service to the British Empire" (McGrath, 7). Of course the third choice, ironically, was the "best" choice, one made by John's uncle, Nicholas, who proved to be a sort of saint by providing a berth to "his nine-year-old nephew as cabin boy on a Wexford merchant ship, probably his own" (McGrath, 9), as Nicholas, by that time, had remained safe and earned enough on his journeys to build his own ship, one of the few things not banned by the penal laws.

Though educated from the age of six to nine in a government-run charter school (the price for which was the child's conversion to the Church of Ireland), John, once on board, had to "learn the ropes," literally, running rigging, scrubbing the deck, serving the captain, steering, and splicing. Traveling to and from European ports for six years, "before the mast," as a teenager John became big-boned, cleared six feet in height, and sported thick dark hair and eyebrows and gray-brown eyes, an assuming figure later described as "graceful and commanding. His whole deportment was marked by dignity unmixed with ostentation; and his strongly marked countenance was expressive at once of the qualities of his mind and the virtues of his heart" (Kessler, 166). No doubt, he carried with him "hatred of the oppressors and recollections of the misery and want of his childhood years, which stayed with him through his life" (Clark, 13). Two lifelong acquaintances John met in his early years in Philadelphia described not his impressive physique, however, but his "strong and active mind," and "indefatigable industry ... not long without employment," the path to his "ascendancy" (Kessler, 156). For, upon arrival in Philadelphia, most likely a trip to visit an aunt, Jane Barry Wilcox, who had married an Irish-born merchant and moved to America, Barry found work on ships bound to the West Indies, and, over the next six years, demonstrated his "nautical skill, the steadiness of his habits, and the integrity of his character" (Kessler, 157), becoming a ship's mate trusted by prominent Philadelphian merchants, one of which, Edward Denny, decided to make Barry captain of the first ship purchased from personal funds, the *Barbados*.

Ironically, on his first several voyages, Barry faced life-and-death situations, sailing through hurricanes of "monstrous proportions," the *Philadelphia Gazette* reporting, "Captain Barry's Vessel was thrown on her Beam Ends for 24 hours, shifted her Cargoe, and he lost his Mainsail and Topsail" (qtd. in McGrath, 22); "thrown on her Beam Ends meant that the *Barbadoes* was sailing almost sideways, her sails reefed or in tatters, and perilously close to capsizing" (McGrath, 22). No doubt, these trips were training for the life-and-death battles Barry would endure in years to come. Returning home safely, Barry gladly spoke nuptials with his Irish sweetheart, Mary Cleary. His popularity as a captain of the sea increased, and within two years, Barry himself had purchased two ships, aptly named *Industry* and *Frugality*.

During the next six years, Captain John Barry was home in Philadelphia for only six months, Mary dying in her 29th year from an unknown illness. McGrath quotes, "In the midst of his mourning came a new career opportunity, one that would move the young captain to the pinnacle of Philadelphia's merchant trade. In March 1774, Barry received a message from Robert Morris" (37), treasurer of the American Revolution itself. (No doubt Morris "caught wind" of Barry's participation in Philadelphia's own "Boston Tea Party," when one British Captain Ayers was taken off the British ship *Polly*, paraded down the streets at Gloucester Point by an angry mob, and subjected to the threats of the "Committee on Tar and Feathering." Promising to return to England if so allowed, Ayres set sail the next day, Barry sailing behind him in the *Peggy* to insure compliance. Morris discovered Barry's political leanings due to his attendance at the *Polly* affair, discerning "there was not one tug of conscience regarding the rights of the British Empire in the heart and mind of this Irishman, exiled because repression and religious intolerance reigned over his native land. If the time came to fight, John Barry would fight" (McGrath, 40). Barry in fact had been involved with the Cause from day one, subscribing to and signing the Non–Importation Resolves in 1770, entered into by "gentlemen of the house of burgesses and the body of merchants assembled in Williamsburg, Fairfax County, Colony of Virginia, in opposition to taxes imposed by England to raise revenue upon the people of the colony" (Meany, 3). Note: Frost wrote in his *Naval Biography:* "We may be sure he was earnest and active in any measures to restrict the operations of those inimitable to Liberty or engaged in efforts detrimental to the Patriots' endeavors" (qtd. in Griffin, 11), speaking of Barry's November 25, 1776, participation in the gathering at the Indian Queen Hotel in Philadelphia to consider accusations against those suspected as Tories and unfriendly to the cause of America. Certainly, "the spirit of the colonies had entered his soul and childhood experiences had fitted him admirably to be a Rebel against Parliamentary oppression" (Clark, 13). Clark further notes: "John Barry could never subscribe to adulation of anything British. His early life had created an antipathy in that direction, which time could not heal" (359).

Morris commissioned Barry to sail his new ship, *Black Prince*, a "ship beautiful to behold: 91 feet 5 inches long, 26 feet 1 inch at the beam, with the blunt bow and raised quarterdeck easily recognized on both sides of the Atlantic as that of a Philadelphia merchantman.... Her figurehead was a handsomely carved knight, sword and shield at the ready" (McGrath, 42–3), to England with a load of wheat and flour, asking for ballast in lieu of trade goods in return. Barry accepted the commission even as "his business affairs then were at the height of their prosperity, but his sympathies were so strongly and fervently with the cause of the Colonies that he sacrificed his fortune and private interests and at once enlisted in the Continental Navy" (Meany, 4). While Barry was in port at Bristol, the Boston ports were closed by the British, and he was deliberately held in port while in Great Britain, as "stevedores worked at a snail's pace.... Sometimes only three hundred barrels a day were removed." Four months later, in London, shortly after the Battle of Lexington and Concord, the unloading of the *Black Prince*'s cargo was again delayed, and Captain Barry slept on board ship for his own safety. Finally allowed to leave London on August 5, Barry urgently pushed the *Black Prince* homeward, recording, on September 12, 1775, "Dist. Logged-237." As Clark notes in the *Naval Documents of the American Revolution,* "there is no faster known twenty-four hours of sailing in the eighteenth century" (qtd. in McGrath, 51).

As if waiting on Captain Barry, on October 12, 1775, Congress passed legislation, largely due to the advocacy of John Adams, creating an American Navy, the first ship purchased by Congress being the *Black Prince.* Sadly, Barry gave up command of his ship. He was not offered a commission, but instead served as a type of naval inspector. Though hard for a sea captain, Barry graciously assisted in the preparation of several frigates for the purpose of war, also overseeing construction of four new ships, "literally dry-docked, preparing other captains' vessels for war and watching them sail away" (McGrath, 61). Due to his gracious, volunteer spirit, John Hancock and Robert Morris eventually offered Barry a commission aboard a ship, aptly named *Lexington*, Barry of course accepting the command. Hancock, at the Marine Commission meeting informed Barry, "We understand a commission in the Continental Navy will not be displeasing to you and your reputation as an excellent seaman and a man of resolute courage is not unknown to us. If 'tis to your liking, a commission is already drawn up appointing you captain of the Lexington effective this day." Barry replied, "I accept the command with a determined resolution of distressing the enemy as much as is in my power" (qtd. in Clark, 73).

On April 7, 1776, outwitting a British frigate loaded with gunpowder, near Cape Charles, Virginia, Barry and his crew witnessed "the first time British colors were lowered by a British ship of war in combat with the Continental Navy" (McGrath, 75). An admirer of Barry, himself a lieutenant in the Navy, author James Fenimore Cooper later described this first Continental battle in *The History of the United States Navy*: "On the morning of April 7, 1776, the Lexington, Captain Barry, a small brig of 14 guns, fell in with the *Edward*

Barry's first ship, the *Lexington*, named for the Revolution's first battle, from a painting by F. Muller (National Archives and Records Administration).

an armed tender of the Liverpool, off the Capes of Virginia, and, after a close and spirited action of nearly an hour, captured her" (qtd. in Meany, 5). Richard Henry Lee narrated in a letter, "The enemy did not submit until he was near sinking" (qtd. in Meany, 11). Barry modestly wrote to the Continental Marine Committee:

> Gentlemen, I have the pleasure to acquaint you that at one PM this Day I fell in with the sloop *Edward*, belonging to the Liverpool frigate. She enjoined us near two glasses. They killed two of our men, and wounded two more. We shattered her in a terrible manner, as you will see. We killed and wounded several of her crew. I shall give you a particular account of the powder and arms taken out of her, as well as my proceedings in general. I have the pleasure to acquaint you that all our people behaved with much courage. I am gentlemen, John Barry [qtd. in McGrath, 76].

As Reilly notes, "Philadelphia acclaimed the Irish seadog when he brought his prize up the bay four days later. John Adams wrote of the battle: 'We begin to make some figure here in the navy way'" (1). Biographer Clark notes "that Barry had captured a well-armed tender, given safe convoy off the capes to a number and merchantman, and eluded an enemy fleet,

John Barry, from a painting by Alonzo Chappel (1828–1877) (National Archives and Records Administration).

were matters discussed freely in Congress and coffee house. How completely he had outwitted one of England's best sea captains, however, was not then, nor later, understood or appreciated" (87).

Barry's next feat was to save "265 heavy Barrels of Powder, 50 Muskets, 2 three Pounders, swords, and about 1,000 pounds worth of dry goods" from a beleaguered ship known as the

Nancy, beached and surrounded at Turtle Gut Inlet, New Jersey, by the British warships *Orpheus* and *Kingfisher*. Arriving on barges from the *Lexington*, Barry's crew boarded the *Nancy*, priming the 3-pounders. Once the British longboats closed in and were within range, Barry ordered "Open fire!" While the Americans hurriedly unloaded the powder from the cargo hold of the *Nancy*, Barry continued his assault on the *Kingfisher*. Eventually, however, the *Orpheus* closed in, early in the morning of June 29, 1776, and the *Nancy* "was shot full of holes, the main mast shot in two, and her deck was littered with spars, canvas, rope, and tackle" (McGrath, 92). Barry ordered all Americans to shore, with orders for one longboat to return for the captains and gun crew. He asked the crew to take 40 of the remaining 121 half-barrels of powder to the captain's cabin. He personally placed a running fuse from the deck down into the hold and cabin and poured 50 pounds of powder on to the mainsail, dropping two hot coals on the edges. Thirty minutes later, British soldiers stormed the *Nancy* with cheers, right before a mighty explosion heard "40 miles above Philadelphia." The supposed "victors" and the soldiers accompanying within the rowboats went flying "30 or 40 yards high" and "eleven bodies, two laced hats, and a leg with a white spatter dash" splashed into the water. Those that survived the explosion "in a shattered condition and weakly manned" rowed back to the *Kingfisher*. Note: Barry was so busy making decisions during the affront, he forgot to take the *Nancy's* Grand Union flag. Another "daring but fool hardy seaman," ironically named John Hancock, jumped back onto the ship, took down the flag, dove back into the water, and boarded Barry's barge! Five days hence, July 4, 1776, Barry and his crew no longer fought for the United Colonies, but for the "United States of America," having saved much needed gunpowder for the War effort! (*Connecticut Currant*, July 15, 1776.)

Aboard the *Lexington*, Barry found two more prizes, the *Lady Susan*, owned by Virginia's Royal Governor, Lord Dunmore, and therefore a particular prize for Barry and the Continental Navy, and the *Betsy*, taken as a result of Barry's cunning in running a British flag up the *Lexington's* post and fooling the *Betsy's* crew, who gave three cheers for their presumed comrades. In turn "the sardonic Barry ordered the three cheers returned by his men. Taking speaking trumpet in hand, he informed Kerr (the captain) of his true identity, and of Kerr's new standing in the war: as a prisoner of the Continental Navy" (McGrath, 100).

As new ships were built for the Continental Navy, Barry was assigned to the *Effingham*, the *Lexington* assigned to an alternate naval captain. Again without a ship until the *Effingham* was finished, Barry became a land captain for a few short months, on shore long enough to meet, fall in love with and marry Sarah Austin (who stitched the first American flag to be saluted in Europe high atop John Paul Jones' *Ranger*). Some accounts state he assisted in the crossing of the Delaware during this period. For instance, Reilly writes: "Though a sailor and a commissioned captain, he organized a company of volunteers and aided in the transport of the troops across the icy waters, and was in the thick of the strife at Trenton and Princeton. Thus ably did he sustain the Father of His Country in his and its greatest trial" (1). And, Griffin believes, "Captain John Barry, with a company of volunteers, in December 1776, took part in the Trenton Campaign. In co-operation with the Marines under Captain William Brown, he lent efficient service in transporting Washington's army across the Delaware, when they took part in the battles of Trenton and Princeton" (48). Griffin also states Barry, during this service, was an aide to Washington in the safe conduct to Philadelphia of the baggage of captured Hessians, also escorting surgeons and physicians necessary to the war effort to Princeton. The Ancient Order of Hibernians, the oldest, largest Irish-American fraternal organization in the United States, resolved: "John Barry briefly enlisted in the Continental Army and participated in the battles of Trenton and Princeton and was principally responsible for organizing the crossing of the Delaware River by General Washington and his Army in December 1776 (qtd. in "Resolution"). Alternatively, McGrath notes, as Barry served under a Lt. Cadwalader at the time, "The legend that Barry fought at Trenton is a false one. Cadwalader's forces were to cross at Bristol and attack the Hessians from the rear, but Cadwalader found 'It is impossible to pass above Bristol with the ice' and saw no way to get the cannon Barry had delivered across the river" (107–8). Clark agrees with McGrath: "Much as we regret to admit it, John Barry was not at Trenton. His experiences that day were with Cadwaleder's brigade at Bristol. They, too, had expected to cross and come upon the enemy from the rear. Floating ice above Bristol had frustrated an attempt at that point ... then the tide turned and a vast field of ice shifted in and cut off the Jersey shore. It prevented the landing of any cannon and without cannon Cadwaleder felt the effort would be futile" (109).

Upon the first sail of the *Effingham*, when finished, up the Delaware to face Britain's Admiral Howe, Barry faced a test of integrity. Just a few miles up from Philadelphia, a rowboat pulled aside the *Effingham*, with a lone messenger, asking to visit with the captain. Once aboard, the messenger conveyed a treasonous offer: "15,000 Guineas if Barry would come in with the ship ... and, if he wished, Barry could retain command of the *Effingham* under British colors with the Commission of her in the King's Service" (qtd. in McGrath, 122). In a rage, Barry "spurned the eydee of being a Traitor to my Country" (Clark, 124) and assured the messenger that "he had devoted himself to the cause of his country, and not the value and command of the whole British fleet could seduce him from it" (qtd. in Gilmore, 35). James Fenimore Cooper wrote of this incident, "Commodore Barry as an officer and a man ranked very high. His affection to his adopted country was never doubted and was put to proof, as the British government bid high to detach him from its service during the Revolution" (qtd. in Meany, 68). Alas, the *Effingham*, in September 1777, upon the British occupation of Philadelphia, was ordered sunk by General Washington, in order to keep the ship out of the hands of the British. Meany states, "Barry, with violent emphasis, opposed her destruction, and left no doubt in the minds of the Committee of his serious earnestness — and, again, time proved the correctness of Barry's judgement" (16).

Never backing down from his duties, in order to obtain cattle for the Continental troops, Barry rowed with his men on barges down the icy Delaware River in February 1778, heading south and burning haystacks (over 400 tons) as a decoy for those on land moving cattle. The British changed plans, and instead of heading north to Burlington, and therefore in the path of General Anthony Wayne, busy "purchasing or requisitioning cattle from the farms dotting the river's shoreline" (McGrath, 151), headed south to confront Barry. Wayne thus successfully passed the Cooper's Ferry crossing at Philadelphia, journeying north to Burlington, Bristol, and eventually, on to Valley Forge and Washington's starving troops.

By March, the British, despite Barry's midnight torch party, had occupied the Delaware River for four months. Keeping a lookout on Reedy Island for an opportune moment, Barry summoned his men (only 27 in number) on March 7, 1778, hoping to surprise three approaching British transports. Leading seven barges and a few small cannon, Barry and his crew closed in undetected by the *Mermaid*, which carried much needed forage, and the *Kitty*, sporting two 4-pound cannons. Barry's men, in an act of daring, scrambled over the gunwales of both ships. Barry himself, "cutlass in hand, led his men as they clambered over the bulwark to find they, too, had captured a British ship loaded with forage" (McGrath, 157). Turning the barges and the *Kitty* toward a third British ship, the *Alert*, Barry "suggested that the British captain surrender the schooner as well" (Gilmore, 35). The *Alert* became quite the prize, carrying "eight Double fortified four-pounders and twelve four Pound howitzers," and "a hold full of engineering tools and a huge compilation of correspondence, mostly belonging to British Chief Engineer Montresor and Hessian General Knyphausen. While ransacking the galley, other sailors came across a well-stocked pantry, including a huge cheese oval together with a jar of pickled oysters" (McGrath, 159). The cheese and oysters, along with the cannons and howitzers, were sent to General Washington. Barry also burned the transports and schooner, and after a determined but unrealistic fight with the British to keep the *Alert,* instead sank it. "The embarrassment the British felt at losing three fine ships along with one major, two captains, three lieutenants, and a quantity of armed sailors to a force of only 27 men in rowboats must have been extreme" (Gilmore, 35). Barry became the "hero of the Delaware," the *Pennsylvania Gazette* writing, "Captain Barry has distinguished himself exceedingly on the river" (qtd. in McGrath, 165), George Washington himself writing to John:

> Sir—I have received your favor of the 9th inst. I congratulate you on the Success which has crowned your Gallantry and Address in the late Attack upon the Enemie's Ships—although circumstances have prevented you from reaping the full benefit of your Conquest, yet there is ample consolation in the degree of Glory, which you have acquired—You will be pleased to accept my thanks for the good things which you were so polite as to send me, with my wishes that your suitable recompense may always attend your Bravery [qtd. in McGrath, 166].

Frost later wrote, in his *Naval Biography*, "For boldness of design and dexterity of execution, it was not surpassed during the war" (qtd. in Meany, 18). Despite a chilly relationship between Barry and the oldest founding father, Franklin wrote: "Nothing will give us greater weight and importance in the eyes of the commercial world than a conviction that we can annoy on occasion their trade and carry our prizes into safe harbors" (qtd. in Meany, 19). Alexander Hamilton, writing from Valley Forge, wrote to Governor Clinton of New York, "We have nothing new in camp save that Captain Barry has destroyed with a few gunboats two large ships belonging to the enemy, laden with forage from Rhode Island. He also took an armed schooner which he has since been obliged to run ashore after a gallant defense. 'Tis said he has saved her cannon and stores among the ordinance four brass howitzers" (qtd. in Griffin, 19).

Due to Barry's bravery, in early 1781, he was awarded command of the finest ship built by the Continental Navy, the *Alliance,* "178 feet long, with a 36-foot beam and 12 feet 6 inches depth of hold. Her draft was 16 feet 6 inches; she displaced 910 tons. She mounted thirty-six guns. So beautiful was she to the nautical eye that one French official declared that 'there is not in the King's Service, nor in the English Navy a frigate more perfect and more complete in materials or workmanship'" (qtd. in McGrath, 219). Revolutionary poet Philip Freneau wrote:

> When she unfurls her flowing sails, undaunted by the fiercest gales,
> In dreadful pomp she plows the main, while adverse tempests rage in vain.
> When she displays her gloomy tier, the boldest Britons freeze with fear,
> And, owning her superior might, seek their best safety in their flight.
> But, when she pours the dreadful blaze and thunder from her cannon plays,
> The bursting flash that wings the ball, compels those forces to strike a fall
> [qtd. in Griffin, 30].

Washington's troops, at that time, were, according to Lafayette, "naked, shabbily naked," and Washington wished for John Laurens to return to France to seek additional financial backing, to be transported by Barry on the *Alliance,* "to seek an immediate ample and efficacious succor in money, large enough to be a foundation for substantial arrangement of finance, to revive public credit and give vigor to future operations" (qtd. in Griffin, 30). Barry wrote, "I know how essential it is to my Country that Col. Laurens should be landed in France with the greatest expedition, ... but how poorly the ship *Alliance* is mann'd and the great risque we run'd in coming to Sea with such a Paltry Crew" (qtd. in McGrath, 223). Near Newfoundland, Barry had to sail through twenty miles of glaciers, and a "barrage of frozen shards," which Thomas Paine, also on board, described as a "thundering ... succession of Icy Rocks" (qtd. in McGrath, 227). However, once in France, Laurens indeed received six million livres (gold) from the King, "buying money, food, clothing, and munitions of war, enabling Washington to compel the surrender at Yorktown" (Meany, 24).

During the journey, Barry also overtook a British ship, the *Alert,* which was, against international law of the time, holding a Venetian ship, *La Buonia Compagnia,* hostage. Barry immediately released the hostage ship, allowing it to sail back home to Venice, thus improving international opinion of the newborn "United States of America." The Venetian Senate wrote to Benjamin Franklin of their "grateful sense of the friendly behavior of Captain Barry, commander of the *Alliance* in rescuing one of the ships of their State from an English privateer and setting her at liberty" (qtd. in Griffin, 31).

On the way back to America, Barry weathered a mutiny of the British soldiers (war prisoners) who manned the ship and planned to "take the ship on her passage, and all the officers, in the middle of the watch of the night, except Lieutenant Patrick Fletcher, who was to navigate her to some port in Ireland, or, on failure, to be destroyed. A quarter master, one of the mutineers, was to have command" (Kessler qtd. in Griffin, 34). Subsequent to Barry's successful squelching of the mutiny, the *Alliance,* named for the alliance between France and the United States, came under attack by the British sloops of war *Atalanta* and *Trepassey.* Clark describes the attack: "The hot afternoon rolled along, a living hell on the face of the placid ocean. The roar of cannon fire was almost incessant, punctuated by the crack of muskets, the screams of the wounded and dying, the shouts of the sweaty, powder-grimed combatants. Over all hung the battle smoke, a gray pall whose pungent odor sent men coughing and choking about their duty. Through it John Barry moved a charmed figure on that bloody quarter deck. His voice rose encouragingly to stimulate the exhausted crew to fresh efforts. His command rang out, clear and distinct above the tumult. Here was a fighting man to be obeyed" (224). During the battle, Barry received a grape ball in his left shoulder. He tried to stay on deck and in command, but due to profuse bleeding, was carried below and to surgery. McGrath describes the ordeal: "The wound thus opened, and with Barry flat on his back in quiet suffering, Kendall took his bullet forceps — a scissor like instrument with cupped ends — to reach the projectile, and cut into the wound. Widening around the grapeshot (and adding more suffering to Barry's condition), Kendall grasped the forceps around the projectile. Slowly, he removed it from Barry's shoulder. The original 1 ½-inch hole was considerably wider now. With the grisly piece of iron removed, Kendall let the wound bleed awhile. Then he cleaned the area out, using straight turpentine or a mixture of turpentine and egg yolk. Either would send the most stoic of souls into further agony" (256).

All seemed lost as Lieutenant Hacker went below to inform Barry of the "shattered state of the sails and rigging, the number of killed and wounded, and the disadvantages under which they labored, for the want of wind" (qtd. in McGrath, 257–8). Barry, when asked if colors should be struck, thundered "No! If the ship can't be fought without me, I will be carried on deck" (qtd. in McGrath, 258). To his credit, the lieutenant informed the crew of Barry's determination, and "informed of their captain's decision to keep fighting, the crew 'one and all resolved to stick by him'" (qtd. in McGrath, 258). Providence smiled, and the breeze shifted. The *Alliance*, back under Barry's command, turned and fired fourteen 12-pounders into the *Trepassey*, taking the ship and turning 180 degrees to wreck the *Atalanta* as well. Graciously welcoming the British captain to his cabin that night, Barry directed the *Trepassey*, with all prisoners aboard, to Halifax, and the *Atalanta* and the *Alliance* to Boston for repairs. This particular voyage, "during which he captured seven prizes, was the most successful one made under the direction of the Board of Admirality" (Paullin, 206). Once in port, Barry convalesced, healing from his wounds while receiving national praise and commendation from Congress. As Dennie, Barry's contemporary and a journalist and graduate of Harvard who edited the *Pennsylvania Gazette*, wrote, this prize was "considered at the time of its achievement a most brilliant exploit, and as an unequivocal evidence of the unconquerable firmness and intrepidity of the victor" (qtd. in Meany, 64). Williams Collins' poem, written to honor the battle, reads:

> In the brave old ship Alliance, We sailed from sea to sea,
> Our proud flag in defiance, still floating fair and free.
> We met the foe and beat him, as we often did before,
> And ne'er afraid to meet him, was our brave old Commodore [qtd. in Reilly, 6].

After Cornwallis' surrender at Yorktown, Robert Morris asked Barry to deliver Lafayette and his entourage of fifteen to France and "to avoid all Vessels and keep in mind, as your sole object, to make a quiet and safe passage to some port in France" (qtd. in McGrath, 280). Despite encountering a British ship, Barry followed orders and "put the good of his country ahead of his personal wishes — he ordered his crew to avoid the ship, despite their loud grumblings about wishing 'Lafayette was in France' and missing out on a possible prize" (Gilmore, 35). Barry noted, "I serve the Country for nothing" (qtd. in Griffin, 40).

As one last service for the cause of the Revolution, Barry overcame the charge of Britain's *Sybil* on March 10, 1783, off Cape Canaveral, Florida, after the historical "end" of the Revolutionary War, but before the Treaty of Paris, cutting the sailing and rigging of this particular ship "all to pieces." The commander of the *Sybil* may have known the *Alliance*, on this particular voyage, was carrying a large sum of money ($72,000) en route to Congress (Philadelphia) from Havana. Due to the treaty, just a month thereafter, Congress declared a "cessation of arms," rendering Barry's battle with the *Sybil* the last naval battle of the American Revolution (remember, Barry had also fought the very *first* naval battle of the Revolution), having "in the space of nine years ... brought Congress its first armed prize, its last war money, and, in between, captured more than 20 British vessels and given our country loyal and versatile naval service" (Gilmore, 35).

George Washington organized and created the United States Navy in March 1794, authorizing the construction of six ships. Then Secretary of War Henry Knox wrote Barry, "The President has appointed you to be a Captain of one of the ships provided.... It is understood that the relative rank of the Captains is to be in the following order: John Barry, Samuel Nicholson..." (qtd. in Gilmore, 35). Barry replied simply: "The honor done me in appointing me Commander in the Navy of the United States is gratefully acknowledged and accepted by your most obedient and humble servant John Barry" (qtd. in Griffin, 40). Three years later, after the building of the ship the *United States*, Barry's official commission (February 22, 1797), marked "Reg. No. 1," was issued by President Washington, who placed "special trust and confidence in Barry's "patriotism, valor, fidelity, and abilities." Regarding his ship, the *United States*, Griffin notes, "In the long list of splendid vessels which in a hundred combats have maintained the honor of our national flag, the *United States* stands at the head. She served our country well in the war with France under Barry; also in the war with England in 1812–15 and in subsequent duties, peaceful or warlike" (Griffin, 53). Her figurehead was described by a spectator at the commissioning: "She is crest with a Constellation, her hair and drapery flowering. Suspended to the ringlets of hair, which fall or wane over her Breast; reclining in her bosom, is the portrait of her favorite son, GEORGE WASHINGTON, PRESIDENT of the UNITED STATES; her waist bound with a Civic band. In her right Hand, which is advanced, she holds a spear, suspended to which is a Belt of Wampum, containing the emblems of Peace and War. On her left side is a Tablet, which supports three large volumes which relates to the three branches of government; the Scale, emblematic of Justice, blended with them. The left hand suspends the Constitution over the Books, etc; on the tablet the EAGLE with his wings half extended, with the Escutcherns, etc. of the ARMS of the United States on the Right, designates the attributes COMMERCE and AGRICULTURE, and a modest position of the ARTS and SCIENCES" (qtd. in Clark, 383).

Barry, at this point known as Commodore Barry, now served as Commander of the U.S. Navy. In an 1813 portfolio, Dennie wrote: "His [Barry's] opinion was very influential in the adoption by the government of that excellent model for ships of war, the superiority of which over every other has been so strikingly proved, as to have extorted the acknowledgment even of our enemies" (qtd. in Meany, 41). In this service, he also commanded all vessels in the "quasi-war" with France (during the chaos of the French Revolution) and commanded a naval station in the West Indies, training many of the naval officers involved in the War of 1812. Barry also wrote a signal book, suggested and began the organization of naval yards for ships and supplies, and established the earliest traditions of the Navy: faithful devotion to duty, honoring the flag, and vigilant protection of the rights of the sovereign United States. It is ironic that "it has been beautifully said of Washington that under the Divine plan he was to be childless that a nation might call him Father. May not in a lesser degree the same sentiment hold good for the Father of the American Navy?" (Reilly, 7).

When Jefferson became President in 1801, all naval ships were "called in" and Barry, though retained in service of the government, was paid half-time. Alas, Barry's health was also failing (occupation-related asthma), and by December 1802, "ill health was enfeebling him, destroying his wonted activity" (Griffin, 63). Commodore Barry eventually succumbed to acute asthma on September 13, 1803. The *American Daily Advertiser* in Philadelphia, September 15, 1803, read: "It may be needless to observe that Captain Barry espoused with ardor the cause of liberty early in the year 1775, or to say with what constancy of attachment and boldness of enterprise he supported her interest during the war; all who have read the details of that glorious struggle must be familiar with the name of Captain Barry, and view in him a patriot of true integrity and of undoubted bravery" (qtd. in Meany, 69). An ode appeared in the same publication on September 24, 1803, *Lines on the Death of Commodore Barry*:

> Beneath His Guidance, Lo! A Navy Springs
> An infant Navy, spreads its canvas wings;
> A rising Nation's Weal, to shield, to save,
> And guard her commerce on dang'rous wave.

The epitaph on his gravestone was written by Dr. Benjamin Rush, first surgeon-general and signer of the Declaration of Independence: "Let the patriot, the soldier, and Christian who visits these mansions of the dead, view this monument with respect. Beneath it are interred the remains of John Barry. He was born in the County of Wexford, in Ireland. But America was the object of his patriotism and the theater of his usefulness" (qtd. in Meany, 72). In 1813, Barry's contemporaries, Rush and Kessler, wrote for Philadelphia's *Portfolio:* "So many of the distinguished naval men of the present day commenced their career under Commodore Barry that he may justly be considered the father of our Navy" (qtd. in Clark, 497).

In 1895, General St. Clair Mulholland of Ireland, as a copy of Gilbert Stuart's portrait of Barry was placed in Independence Hall, described John Barry as "one of the most illustrious of Ireland's sons, a brilliant child of the wind and waves, a heroic warrior of the sea who never knew defeat, the Father and Founder of the Navy of the United States, the Navy that from the beginning has been the admiration and model of all the nations of the Earth" (qtd. in Griffin, 66). Truly, a study of John Barry's life provides a lesson for all present and future Americans: "Barry loved the United States. He was at the service of his country at any time; at the service of a faction, never. That was his creed, as he lived it through the Revolution, and would live it to his death" (Clark, 359).

Memorials

In the research and scholarship associated with the American Revolution, as well as the history taught to America's citizenry, Barry's name is, according to Reilly, ignored: "The friend of Washington and Lafayette, who was twice thanked by Congress, who was in command of the Continental sea forces when Cornwallis surrendered, who suggested the creation of the Navy Department and held its first commission, seems to have been strangely ignored" (8). Nevertheless, one statute honoring John Barry is in one of the most revered historical sites in our country, at the formal entrance to Independence Hall. This statue depicts Barry pointing to the sea. The inscription reads: "Father of the Navy of the United States. Born in Wexford, Ireland, 1745. Died in Philadelphia, 1803. Presented to the City of Philadelphia by the Friendly Sons of St. Patrick, 1907."

A statue of Barry stands in Franklin Park, Washington, D.C., dedicated in 1914 by Woodrow Wilson. A wayside marker explaining Barry's contributions was placed beside the statue in 2012.

The Commodore Barry Bridge crosses the Delaware River from Chester, Pennsylvania, to Bridgeport, New Jersey.

A statue of Barry overlooks the Crescent Quay in Wexford, Ireland, a gift to the town by the United States. To celebrate "Barry Day," each year a parade and wreath-laying ceremony takes place at the statue, sponsored by the Irish Naval Service and the Minister for Defense.

September 13 is "John Barry Day" in New Jersey Public Schools.

In Brooklyn, New York, the oldest park in the borough is named Commodore Barry Park, renamed for the Commodore in 1951 due to its location next to the Brooklyn Naval Yard founded by Barry.

Barry and the crew of the *Alliance* are commemorated for the final naval battle of the American Revolution in a plaque located at Jetty Park in Cape Canaveral, Florida.

Barry's grave site is located at Old St. Mary's Church in Philadelphia, Pennsylvania.

Four U.S. Navy ships have been commissioned in John Barry's name:

5—"I serve the Country for nothing" 59

Statute of Commodore John Barry pointing out to sea, Independence Hall, Philadelphia (author's photograph).

USS *Barry* (DD-2) (1902–1920)
USS *Barry* (DD-248) (1921–1945)
USS *Barry* (DD-933) (1956–1983)
USS *Barry* (DDG-52) (1992–)

On May 21, 2011, the Ancient Order of Hibernians (AOH), the largest Irish American Catholic organization in the United States, announced approval by U.S. Naval Academy officials of their proposal to erect a memorial on Academy grounds in Annapolis, Maryland, to honor Commodore John Barry. The "Barry Memorial Project" will be completed in two phases, the first being an arching sign over the Academy's new pedestrian gate, naming it the "Commodore John Barry Gate." The second phase will be the construction of an 8-foot tall granite memorial honoring Commodore Barry, inside the Barry Gate and within the Barry Plaza.

6

DUNKIRK PIRATE
The Exploits of Gustavus Conyngham

In a word, Cunningham, by his first and second bold expeditions, is become the terror of all the eastern coast of England and Scotland.—Robert Morris, 1777

Britain, at the time before, near, and during the American Revolution, gained its great wealth from naval commerce. Accordingly, "being a great commercial nation, anything that would interfere with her commerce would be most disastrous in its effects, and would be most keenly felt by her people in their homes" (Jones, 6). As the conflict between the colonies and Britain escalated, commerce between the two powers ceased; however, Britain concentrated her trade with the rest of the world in the English and Irish Channels and adjacent seas, such routes "carefully guarded by large, vigilant, and fully equipped English fleets" (Jones, 7). Any brig or frigate from the colonies brave enough to trespass these waters, in an attempt to capture British commerce vessels and claim prize merchandise, assisted the efforts of the American Revolution by "eating away" at the core of Britain's economic, and, consequently, military, might. Such bravery was exhibited over and over again by Irish-born Captain Gustavus Conyngham, who volunteered his services to Benjamin Franklin, received a temporary commission, and "took thirty-one prizes while in command of *Surprize* and *Revenge*, more than any other American naval officer did in the Revolutionary War. His legacy to the United States Navy is one of determination, imagination, and success" (Bowen–Hassell, 41).

Born in Ireland, specifically the County of Donegal in 1747, in the town of Largyreagh, close to where, 30 years on, he would capture the British frigate *Venus*, Gustavus immigrated to America in his early youth (1763) with his father, also named Gustavus. He was sponsored by his uncle, the Reverend William Conyngham of Letterkenny, entrusted into the care of Redmond Conyngham, nephew to the elder and first cousin to Gustavus, as an apprentice. He entered the port of Philadelphia, which became his adulthood home while on land, where he lived with his wife, Anne Hockley (Philadelphia is also the site of his burial in St. Peter's churchyard).

Redmond Conyngham had immigrated to America (Philadelphia) in 1740 and established a shipping mercantile, which became "eminently successful." He eventually owned and sailed merchant ships in coordination with his partner, also from Ireland, John Nesbitt, the firm becoming known as Conyngham and Nesbitt. Redmond, in 1765, protesting the Stamp Act, signed the Non–Importation Agreement (also signed by John Barry from Chapter 5). Redmond Conyngham "thought that nature, or rather his natural genius, pointed out the sea as the element on which Gustavus was to live, and therefore placed him in a vessel of his own under the command of Captain Henderson.... With this ship Gustavus remained, learning the business of navigation, until Henderson's death, when he was promoted to the command of the ship 'Molly'" (Conyngham, David, 20). (Captain Henderson regularly carried goods to and from Antigua, and Gustavus "gained leadership as well as seamanship skills under Henderson's fatherly guidance" [Hayes, 16].) Young Gustavus found himself surrounded by the independent and hard-working merchantmen of Philadelphia, who no doubt instilled a hatred of Britain's oppressive tax laws into the equally hard-working ship's apprentice. And, Gustavus watched as his second cousin and son to Redmond, David Conyngham, sailed, in 1772, to France, Poland, and Great Britain, as a secret agent of the colonies, returning in 1774 "having added in his humble capacity to the character of America" (Conyngham, David, 18). Within a year, "finding then that separation from the mother country was imminent, he decided to take the part of America.... The foreign business of the firm of Conyagham, Nesbitt, & Co. required his presence once more in Europe" (Conyngham, David, 18). On this particular trip, David sailed on the brig *Charming Peggy* owned by the firm, by this time, pursuant to David's promotion, commanded by Captain Gustavus Conyngham, "laden with flaxseed ... to return with powder and other needful things for the Colony" (Conyngham, David, 18), for "the merchant company of Conyngham and Nesbitt decided to take a financial risk by sending its vessels through waters dominated by the Royal Navy in order to bring back the necessary war supplies" (Hayes, 17).

Entering the English Channel, trying to use fog to hide his passage into Holland, Conyngham finally arrived at Dexel Island, and "the cargo was brought out to her by two Dutch vessels employed for the purpose" (Jones, 7). Unfortunately, winds prevented a return for several days, and, in the meantime, in the words of Conyngham, "I am sorry to say an Irish sailor on board the name of Brackenridge ... deserted and informed the British Consul of every particular" (qtd. in Neeser, 10). Arrested, with a guard on board, Conyngham and his crew overthrew the captors, "breaking an arrest under that despotic Government" (qtd. in Neeser, 10). Winds prevented a return for several days, however, and British authorities by that time had complained to Dutch authorities as to the nature of the return cargo. The *Charming Peggy* was prevented from sailing home to

Captain Gustavus Conyngham. Painting by V. Zveg, based on a miniature by Louis Marie Sicardi (U.S. Naval Historical Center).

The Dunkirk Pirate, an engraving found in English coffee-houses during the Revolution (U.S. Naval Historical Center).

America, and the ship was sold. Conyngham and all his crew were forced to find other means of passage home, and "like many a Yankee shipmate, found himself stranded in Europe, on the lookout for anything to fill up his spare moments and burning to do something" (Neeser, xxx).

Conyngham found himself in Dunkirk, France, whereby, through friend and merchantman John Ross, he became acquainted with William Hodge, a Philadelphia merchant purchasing vessels for the Continental Navy, as well as Benjamin Franklin. Recommended by Hodge, and pursuant to Conyngham's wish to serve America, Franklin issued Conyngham a commission signed by John Hancock on March 1, 1777. Hodge placed Conyngham in command of a lugger of English construction which he had purchased in Dunkirk, renamed the *Surprize*. That self-same night, after Conyngham slipped on board with carriage and swivel guns, the "*Surprize* sailed from Dunkirk under the guise of a bona-fide smuggler. But, once clear of the roads, she threw off the mask, hoisted the Continental colors, and began to cruise off the mouth of the Meuse" (Neeser, xxx). Eluding British watches, Conyngham sailed up the coast of Holland, and, by May 3, the *Prince of Orange*, loading wine, lemons, and oranges, was "brought to" by Conyngham, after he had engaged the captain in conversation while studying the ship's ability to defend itself. Once satisfied as to the superiority of the *Surprize*, running his colors up the pole, Conyngham asked the captain to "surrender his vessel to the Congress of the United States ... and an eleven man crew climbed over the bulwarks and took control" (Hayes, 20). The next day, Conyngham intercepted another British merchant vessel headed to Germany with a load of fruit and wine, the *Joseph*. Conyngham ordered both prizes and the *Surprize* back to Dunkirk, an imprudent move in international terms and one taken at great personal risk.

Unfortunately, Conyngham was unaware a treaty between Britain and France (the Treaty of Utrecht which followed the Nine Years War and the War of Spanish Succession) allowed official British observers to prevent privateering. Thus, once in port, the minister for foreign affairs, Comte de Vergennes, confiscated Conyngham's prizes and jailed the American crew (released a month later), to simulate the image of neutrality. While the prizes were confiscated and the crew remained unreimbursed, as a result of Conyngham's brave feats in British waters, "the British admirality ordered at least five warships to cruise the English channel" (Hayes, 28). Insurance rates rose anywhere from 10 to 40 percent, averaging 28 percent, "higher than anytime during the global conflict of the Seven Years War" (Hayes, 27). Conyngham himself became the hero of the hour, the "Pirate of Dunkirk," and "his deeds were discussed in the coffee-houses, and prints representing him with his rattle-snake flag and his captures were displayed in the shop windows" (Jones, 11). As for the American commissioners, they saw "an opportunity to intercept British commerce in the unprotected northern approaches to Great Britain and launch raids on the west coast of England.... Franklin and Deane sent a request to Congress asking that the Marine Committee send two or three frigates to cruise in British waters. In the meantime, the commissioners worked to get Conyngham back out to sea and add to the pressure on enemy trade" (Hayes, 28).

Of course, outfitting Conyngham with another ship now required deception and cunning. Hodge clandestinely bought a ship named the *Greyhound*, a cutter of about 130 tons, supposedly selling it to an Englishman, Richard Allen. He also bought fourteen 4-pounder cannons. A passport for the *Greyhound* was approved for Bergen, Holland, as a vessel of commerce. Conyngham even found a place on shore to test the cannons, and, upon his satisfaction, he "placed them in the ship's hold rather than on deck in order to maintain the appearance of a merchant ship fitting out for a voyage across the Atlantic" (Hayes, 28).

Slyly, the crew was hired one by one from the local, unemployed seamen, most of whom were smugglers, constituting "a gang of desperadoes." Since Richard Allen was supposedly an Englishman, the French did not examine the sale closely and allowed Mr. Allen to leave Dunkirk's port without a security escort. Of course, Richard Allen was "none other than Gustavus Conyngham himself, and the sale was a fraud" (Hayes, 30). A second commission was given to Conyngham by W. Carmichael, secretary to the American commissioners at Paris, attested to by Charles Thompson. Changing the cutter's name to the *Revenge*, he set sail on July 17, 1777, during the absence of two British warships which had been watching the port. His papers identified him as Richard Allen, Englishman and captain of the North Carolina privateer *Pegasus*. And, "when she went to sea she had on board fourteen carriage- and twenty-two swivel-guns, and a crew of one hundred and six men, sixty-six of whom were Frenchmen. In his written sailing orders, Conyngham was instructed to proceed directly to America as bearer of dispatches, and was not to molest British shipping unless he was attacked; but the verbal instructions he received from Mr. Carmichael, the Secretary of the Commissioners, were exactly to the contrary. And these verbal orders he at once proceeded to faithfully carry out. One of them was to intercept, if possible, and capture the transports carrying Hessian troops to England for service in America" (Jones, 15). Leaving a day too late for this last directive, Conyngham believed the Continental Navy had "lost a glorious opportunity" (qtd. in Neeser, 3). His written directives also provided the leeway of obtaining prizes in the event he found himself short of provisions or attacked by the enemy.

Immediately, the *Revenge* began capturing prizes, aptly earning its name and vindicating Conyngham for the ordeal endured on Dexel Island and in Dunkirk. Conyngham, with a renegade crew eager to earn prize money, seized on the exceptions in his orders, since a British frigate fired several guns toward his ship the day following his launch (18th), which the *Revenge* outsailed. On the 19th, "the scenario was repeated with another British frigate, only this time the American vessel passed into the open waters of the North Sea.... Thus Gustavus decided to begin a cruise against British shipping" (Hayes, 30), an act considered "so unexpected, so bold, so audacious that British ships were no longer considered safe, even in the English Channel" (Neeser, xxxvi). The British merchant ships captured by Conyngham from July 17, 1777, to May 20, 1778, all within European waters, included:

Eighteenth-century French engraving, reproduced in "Letters and Papers relating to the Cruises of Gustavus Conyngham," edited by Robert Wilden Neeser, 1915 (U.S. Naval Historical Center).

Ship and Locale	Date	Cargo Seized	Disposition
Scottish smuggler—East Coast of Britain	July 20, 1777	Illegal gin	Set on fire, crew taken prisoner
Northhampton—East Coast of Britain	July 21, 1777	Merchandise	Prize crew placed on board under command of Benjamin Bailey with orders to sail to Bilbao, Spain
Maria—East Coast of Britain	July 21, 1777	None	Burned
Patty—East Coast of Britain	July 21, 1777	?	Ransomed for 600 guineas (with prisoners from all three captures of the day on board)—payment to be sent directly to American commissioners in Paris
Venus—West Scottish Coast	August 4, 1777	Whaler	Prize crew ordered to take vessel to Martinique in the French West Indies for sale
Black Prince—Northern coast of Spain	August 23, 1777	Wine, fruit, oil	Escorted into the Spanish port of El Ferrol, sent to Bilbao, Spain
4 vessels—Northern coast of Spain	Fall, 1777	Assorted	Bilbao, Spain, or West Indies
Gracieux (only French ship captured)—French coast	December 21, 1777	Woolen goods	Bilbao, Spain
Peace and Harmony—French coast	March 10, 1778	Oranges	Ordered to Massachusetts
Betsy—French Atlantic	March 11, 1778	?	Ordered to Massachusetts
Fanny—coast of Portugal	March 12, 1778	?	Ordered to Massachusetts
Enterprize—French coast	March 20, 1778	?	Set ablaze
Hope—Straits of Gibraltar	March 24, 1778	Letter of Marque	Prize crew placed on board
Maria off Cape Finisterre, two brigs in the Bay of Biscay, one brig off the mouth of the Straits	April, 1778	Varying	Sold in Spain, most likely by Le Couteulx and Co.
Honoria Sophia (Swedish)—coast of Spain and Portugal	May 20, 1778	Dry goods	Ordered carried into an American port

All of these captures achieved, pursuant to Conyngham' journal, in "those seas covered by British Cruzers of every description and with orders from their Government to follow the *Revenge* into any harbor she might be in and destroy her" (qtd. in Neeser, 7), were not without consequence, both positive and negative. At first, Conyngham developed a warm relationship with the Spanish governor of El Ferrol, who even helped him to sell prizes and/or reclaim deserted sailors. Note: One such deserter, John Jordan, ran to the British consul at Corunna, who placed him on board an English merchant vessel ready to leave port. Conyngham ordered five men from the *Revenge* and two of the Governor's Spanish soldiers to board the merchant vessel the night of November 20, 1777, and forcibly remove Jordan, returning him to the *Revenge*. Conyngham also was successful in selling his prizes, with the assistance of Spanish firms Lagoanere & Company (El Ferrol and Corunna) and Joseph Gardoqui & Sons (Bilbao), both having "long done business with the American colonists, and they were eager to support the new nation in a cause with which they sympathized ... some of the money used to purchase weapons and goods for the Continental Army.... American Commissioner John Adams was able to draw $3,000 from the account for traveling expenses when visiting Corunna in February 1780" (Hayes, 36).

News of Conyngham's success "within sight of the very shores of England caused great excitement in London" (Neeser, xxxvi), for "Conyngham could not be caught; even in the sight of British men-of-war he continued his depredations, and on one occasion, off Cape St. Vincent, he actually brought to and burned the tender to H.B.M.S. Enterprize under the very guns of that frigate" (Neeser, 152). Silas Deane, the American commissioner in Paris, wrote to Robert Morris, treasurer of the Revolution, "In a word, Cunningham, by his first and second bold expeditions, is become the terror of all the eastern coast of England and Scotland, and is more dreaded than Thurot was in the late war" (qtd. in Neeser, 98). Jones indicates that "the King of England is reported to have said to his Minister that it would give him pleasure to be present at the hanging of Conyngham, if he could only catch him. There was no occurrence in that part of the world at this time that attracted more attention than these valiant cruises of Conyngham" (19).

Yet, due to the nature of the clandestine crew members on board the *Revenge*, as mentioned above, Conyngham, to avoid a mutiny, captured a French vessel, *Gracieux*, and a Swedish vessel, *Honoria Sophia*, in an attempt to placate and provide provision and payment for his crew, "not always amenable to discipline or willing to abide by the laws of civilized warfare" (Neeser, xliii). Jones notes, "There were a 100 or more of these fellows, speaking different languages and presenting every form of racial temperament and disposition. They were not easily governed, even by this resourceful man. Discipline became next to impossible, and frequently his crew became rebellious, up to the point of mutiny" (19).

The capture of these non–British vessels enraged the Spanish, as it "was a flagrant violation of the customs of naval warfare" (Neeser, xl) and "no sooner had the brig dropped anchor in port than the prize crew were thrown into prison, and it was only with the greatest difficulty and by his submitting to the arbitrary terms of the Spanish governor that Conyngham was able to obtain their release" (Neeser, xl). Conyngham was reprimanded by the American commissioners, but "angrily responded that 'damned policy' would not satisfy sailors, and that he was being criticized for doing exactly what British captains had done on many occasions" (Hayes, 36). Upon Conyngham's capture of the *Honoria Sophia*, Franklin himself denounced the "act of piracy" and indicated Conyngham "will certainly be punished when duly prosecuted, for not only a regard to justice in general, but a strong disposition to cultivate the friendship of Spain" (qtd. in Neeser, 147). Indeed, upon the capture of the *Honoria Sophia*, Spain closed its ports entirely to Conyngham, and "fortunately, an anchorage in a small neighboring inlet was allowed by some of his friends, and here, under the bold headlands of the Galician coast, he repaired his vessel and refitted her for another cruise" (Neeser, 7). Necessarily, Conyngham set sail, on September 1, 1778, for a Caribbean cruise of the Continental Navy cutter *Revenge!*

Arriving in St. Pierre, Martinique, on October 9, 1778, Conyngham's ship was refitted and replacements for crew members recruited. Sailing toward the British-controlled islands later that fall, Conyngham captured the following prizes while in the Caribbean (November 13, 1778, being his busiest day of the War):

Ship and Locale	Date	Cargo Seized	Disposition
Two Friends— near St. Lucia	November 13, 1778	Casks of water	Sent back to Martinique
Two small schooners	November 13, 1778	?	Sent into St. Eustatius and sold
Admiral Barrington	November 13, 1778	Privateer with six 2-pounders and fourteen swivels	Prize crew sailed back to Martinique
Loyalist	November 16, 1778	Privateer with 50 men and ten 3-pounders and fourteen swivels	Escorted back to Martinique
Lukey	December 9, 1778	?	Sold at Martinique

No international incidents haunted Conyngham during this particular cruise, and, as Conyngham put it, "the *Revenge* kept the British privateers in Good order in those seas" (qtd. in Neeser, 9). In early 1779, the *Revenge* was needed to deliver a shipment of arms to Philadelphia; "thus nineteen months after being commissioned into the service of the United States, *Revenge* arrived at a home port" (Hayes, 39), making "an uneventful passage. Not a sail was sighted during the voyage, and Philadelphia was reached without mishap on February 21, 1779. Here Conyngham delivered a precious cargo of arms and munitions of war to the Continental military authorities, and not long after the *Revenge* herself was turned over by him to the Marine Committee to be sold by them at public auction" (qtd. in Neeser, 154–5).

The career of the Continental cutter *Revenge* was at an end, leaving as her legacy the fact that "English ships were afraid to leave their harbors. English merchants refused to load their wares except in French and Dutch bottoms.... The sales of her prizes in Spain realized sums which were of great moment to the American commissioners in Europe" (Neeser, xvi). As for her captain, "Conyngham became the most dreaded man in Europe.... The eyes of Europe were centered upon him. His name became a catchword in the taverns of the Continent. His achievements aroused the enthusiasm of the people of the Bourbon countries. His captures embroiled the Courts of St. James and Versailles. From that moment the intervention of France in the American Revolution became an assured fact" (Neeser, xviii). Jones even asserts that during this nineteen months, Conyngham's fame was exceeded by no other officer in the Continental Navy, not even John Paul Jones, and that Conyngham "had swept these seas with such intrepid energy that the attention of all Europe was called to his movements and they gave rise to protracted discussion and diplomatic conversation between the statesman of England, France, and Spain" (24). Of course France and Spain, clandestinely, had provided friendly merchants, the means for refitting and unemployed crew members, arms and supplies, and open harbors.

Sadly, after the state of Pennsylvania bought the *Revenge* and hired Conyngham, under his naval commission, to sail the Delaware in defense of the coast and for the protection of ships conducting business in Philadelphia's harbors, Conyngham's luck changed (apparently depleted with the capture of *Lukey* in the Caribbean), and he was captured by the British frigate *Galatea*. (Two enemy privateers led Conyngham into the Delaware capes, near New York, into the very jaws of the frigate.) Though Conyngham tried to escape, the British bound him and placed him in irons beneath the British prison in New York, threatening to execute him for piracy. He lived on stale bread and bad water for fourteen days, thereafter being put on a vessel crossing the Atlantic, "to receive that punishment from his injured country, which his crimes shall be found to deserve" (Neeser, 183). At Pendennis Castle,

Falmouth, and Mill Prison, Plymouth, in England, Conyngham lived on three ounces of beef a day, placed into the dungeon for forty-two days at a time. There, he and fellow prisoners, according to his journal, ate "dogs, cats, rats, even the grass.... This is hard to be credited, but is a fact" (qtd. in Jones, 27). Congress informed Conyngham's captors that a British naval prisoner would be executed in retaliation if Conyngham were condemned, yet, at Plymouth he was confined "to stand a tryale with his most Gracious Sovering George the 3rd" (qtd. in Neeser, 171).

Not one to accept such a fate, Conyngham attempted an escape on three occasions, the first time walking out the front gate dressed as a visiting doctor, succeeding on the third attempt, along with fifty-three additional American prisoners, by tunneling under the prison wall (November 3, 1779), committing "treason through his majesties earth" (qtd. in Neeser, 194). Finding his way to London and a friend who was an American sympathizer, he placed himself under the auspices of John Paul Jones while awaiting instructions from Benjamin Franklin. ("While in London, in disguise, he was entertained by the prints he saw of himself, in the shape of a monster, in the shop windows" [Jones, 28].) Conyngham even joined John Paul Jones on another short cruise against enemy trade in the English Channel, eventually departing from Jones in Corunna, Spain, and boarding a merchant vessel to America. Alas, a British vessel captured the merchant ship on March 17, 1780, and Conyngham, once more, found himself back at Mill Prison, his second stay lasting over a year. A prisoner exchange was not feasible at this point, and Conyngham again found a means of escape in June 1781, taking a few prisoners with him and safely ensuring transport for himself and these prisoners aboard the *Hannibal* to America. As Jones dictates, "These periods of adversity and cruel suffering are to be remembered by this later generation of his countrymen, in connection with the years of his brilliant and uninterrupted success, for together they measure the debt of gratitude that is due to his memory. His imprisonment was the penalty imposed upon him for the injury he inflicted during those years of fruitful service upon this implacable enemy of his country" (28).

Upon his return to America, petitioning Congress for remuneration for his years of service, an unfortunate decision of Congress quashed Conyngham's expected reward for services rendered (as well as future recognition). Apparently, the commission delivered to him by Franklin in March 1777, had been confiscated by the French at Dunkirk (upon the taking of *Gratieux*). The congressional commission reported that the lost document "did not give him rank in the Navy" and had been "intended for temporary expeditions only" (qtd. in Neeser, 209). Accordingly, "his suit for the restitution of funds owing him and back payments was held not proven" (qtd. in Neeser, 158). James Fenimore Cooper, in his *Naval History of the United States*, denounced such decision, writing, "That there was some irregularity in giving Captain Conyngham two commissions for the same rank, and bearing different dates, is true, but this arose from necessity; and want of regularity and system was a fault of the times, rather than of those who conducted the affairs of the American Marine during the Revolution. There can be no reasonable doubt that both the Surprise and the Revenge were public vessels of war, and that Gustavus Conyngham was a captain in the Navy of the United States of America, in virtue of two commissions granted by a competent authority; and that, too, subsequently to the declaration of independence, or after the country claimed all the political rights of sovereign power" (qtd. in Neeser, liii).

Despite this rebuke, Conyngham served his country in the subsequent quasi-war with France (1798–1801) aboard the vessel *Maria*, even attempting to serve once more during the War of 1812, his health forbidding such efforts. Up until his death on November 27, 1819, however, Conyngham continued to petition Congress for recognition associated with his services aboard the Continental Navy cutter *Revenge*.

Conyngham's lost rank affected his long-term legacy immensely, as well as the honor to which he is still due, for no statues, bridges, or other honors exist for Captain Conyngham. Thankfully, the words of his most prominent biographer, Charles Henry Jones, provide the most profound tribute, one which will most likely, as time progresses, cure this oversight and produce a grateful American citizenry:

> There is something nearly approaching splendor in the valor and self-reliance of this remarkable young man. He found no discouragement in treacherous, narrow seas with which he was unfamiliar and over which his enemies boasted of their supremacy, hemmed in by bitterly hostile shores on one side and by harbors that were only friendly in secret on the other; he was not discouraged by rebellious crews or dishonesty in those to whom he was obliged to entrust his prizes; by exhausted supplies and the uncertainty as to how or where they were to be replenished, or how his weather beaten little cruiser was to be refitted. For nearly two years he sailed defiantly upon these venturesome reprisals, and always with success, and always from devotion to the cause of his country. *It was this same spirit which pervaded Conyngham that made American independence possible* [30].

Memorials

The U.S. Navy named three ships for Conyngham:
USS *Conyngham*—a destroyer (1915–22)
USS *Conyngham*—a destroyer (1936–46)
USS *Conyngham*—a guided missile destroyer (1963–90)
Conyngham Borough in Luzerne County, Pennsylvania, is named in Conyngham's honor.

7

GOING IN HARM'S WAY
The Adventures of John Paul Jones

When the enemies' land force is once conquered and expelled from the continent, our Marine will rise as if by enchantment and become, with the memory of persons now living, the wonder and envy of the world.—*John Paul Jones, 1778*

Off the coast of England in 1779, during the battle for the British man-o-war *Seraphis,* John Paul Jones stubbornly refused to surrender or give up the flag for the Continental Navy ship under his command, the *Bonhomme Richard* (named after Franklin's *Poor Richard's Almanac*). Though his ship was burning, leaking, and sinking, when a petty officer attempted to haul down the flag and save what was left of ship and crew, Jones threw a pistol at his head. For, this Scottish-born officer meant "to go in harm's way," not simply for hire, but "in defense of the violated rights of mankind," becoming the first commissioned lieutenant in the Continental Navy, six months before the Declaration of Independence. Known for his determined statement, "I have not yet begun to fight," and for being the first naval officer to hoist the American flag over a warship, Jones was, according to Herman Melville, "an audacious Viking ... intrepid, unprincipled, reckless, predatory, with boundless ambition, civilized in externals but a savage at heart" (qtd. in Thomas, 6). John Adams described Jones as "the most ambitious and intriguing officer in the American Navy.... His eye has keenness and Wildness and softness in it" (qtd. in Thomas, 7). No matter his flawed genius and personality inconsistencies, Jones loved the ideals of his adopted country and "imagined America as a mighty sea power long before the country had the capacity or the will to become one," prophesying, "Without a respectable Navy — alas America!" (qtd. in Thomas, 9).

The man who believed "boldness, not caution, wins," and who exclaimed, "The flag and I are twins, born the same hour and from the same womb of destiny" (GPO, 37), was the son of John Paul, Sr., an unlettered Scottish gardener. John Paul, Jr., was born July 6, 1747, in Arbigland, Scotland, near the Solway Firth, and christened, simply, John. John Paul, Sr. would today be considered a landscape architect, for he was recruited all the way from the east coast of Scotland, specifically Leith, by one local gentry, a Mr. Craik, for the purpose of creating "romantic vistas, ponds, glades, groves, hillocks, and glens and dales" (Thomas, 13). To this area of Scotland, one historian attributed pride and intractability, "steeped in the traditions of centuries of independence" (qtd. in Lorenz, 5). No doubt, John Paul, Jr., was destined to adopt the love of freedom, the same as "warriors like Wallace and Bruce, literary geniuses like Scott, Carlyle, and Burns, leaders in religion like Knox and the Covenanters" (Lorenz, 6). John Paul, Jr.'s niece stated in her memoirs, "If ever localities might be inferred to have determined the intellectual bias of an individual, the birthplace of John Paul, and the scenery and associations of its vicinity, may be cited as admirably calculated to lay the groundwork for the restless spirit of adventure, an inclination for poetry, and an occasional imaginary longing for solitude" (Taylor, 12).

Mr. Craik was domineering, and, according to his daughter, Helen, "ardent to make himself completely master of whatever he took in hand" (qtd. in Thomas, 14). John Paul, Sr., was to do as he was told; thus, the proud father and the lordly English sympathizer butted heads on occasion. One story passed through time relates that when Mr. Craik insisted, for the sake of symmetry, that John Paul, Sr., build two summer houses in the garden, the frugal Scotsman thought two homes extravagant. To prove his point, John Paul, Sr., upon catching another employee stealing fruit, locked him in one summer home and John Paul, Jr., in the other. When Mr. Craik asked the elder John Paul why the boy was locked up in one of the summer homes, John Paul, Sr., replied, "for the sake of symmetry." John Paul, Jr., as a sensitive child, "could not have missed the tension between his proud father and the lordly Mr. Craik, especially when he was sitting locked in the summer house, wondering why he had been put there. John Paul, Jr. observed his father's seethings and vowed not to cringe himself. John Paul Jones's sense of resentment and wounded pride were never far from the surface in later life. He came by them naturally" (Thomas, 15).

His mother, Jean McDuff, daughter to a farmer from a village known as "Sweetheart Abbey," was housekeeper to Mr. Craik, who built a "neat stone cottage of three or four rooms" for the couple. Jean has been described as "a Celtic daughter of Caledonia whose blood in the veins of her offspring pulsated with the characteristic fervor of the adventurous Highland clans. She also transmitted her inheritance of a time-honored tradition of the sea bred at the Solway's shores and inborn from Norse migrants to Galloway with the bold instincts of their Viking ancestors" (Lorenz, 4). John became the fourth of seven children to live in the small cottage of the Scot gardener who "was independent in his views and took no back wind from anyone" (Morison, *Jones*, 6). Seemingly destined to a life of obscurity and poverty, John "doubtless went barefoot most of the year like other boys of his class, and wore tough, warm, woolen clothes either handed down by his elder brothers or cast off by the boys in the Great House" (Morison, *Jones*, 7). He attended the Kirkbean Presbyterian Church each Sunday with his parents and attended its parochial school until the age of thirteen, the schoolmaster being the Reverend James Hogg, an alumnus of King's College, Aberdeen, and no doubt an excellent instructor, for John always expertly expressed himself in writing. (In a small museum near Kirkbean is preserved John Paul's original geometry book with his "bold, round, thirteen-year-old signature," the name of the book being *Euclide's Elements: The Whole Fifteen Books, Compendiously Demonstrated: with Archimedes's Theorems of the Sphere and the Cylinder*. Scottish schools of that era and locale promoted excellence, as Brady notes: "No claims of labor were allowed to interfere with the claims of education. On Sundays he was regularly and religiously marched to the kirk to be duly inducted into the mysteries of the catechism, and thoroughly indoctrinated with the theory of predestination and its rigorous concomitants" (5). He spoke in the "braid Scots" dialect of poet Robert Burns and never traveled more than twenty miles from his place of birth until the age of thirteen, when he "packed a sea chest" and became the apprentice of a Mr. Younger on a brig known as the *Friendship*, departing from Whitehaven, a port he later raided.

No doubt, the sea was his destiny, as recalled by Mr. Craik's son after John Paul became famous. This childhood friend remembered John Paul "would run to Carse-thorn whenever his father would let him off, talk to the sailors and clamber over the ship…. He taught his playmates to maneuver their little rowboats to mimic a naval battle, while he, taking his stand on the tiny cliff overlooking the roadstead, shouted shrill commands at his imaginary fleet" (qtd. in Morison, *Jones*, 9). Jones explained to Benjamin Franklin, "I had made the art of war at sea in some degree my study, and had been fond of the navy, from boyish days up" (qtd. in Thomas, 16). Jones' niece even postulated: "At this time, the town of Dumfries carried on a considerable trade in tobacco with America, the cargoes of which were unshipped at the Carse-thorn.... His daily intercourse with seamen here tended of course to strengthen and confirm his nascent passion. It is also observed that his passion for America, and his willingness to descend with fire and sword, in her cause, upon the shores of his native land, which were thought unnatural, may have had their origin in the conversations of mariners from the discontented colonies" (Taylor, 15).

John Paul Jones. Engraving by J.B. Fosseyeux, 1781, from drawing by J.M. Moreau, Jr., 1780. In French: "Rarely are such men made, but when they fall from the sky, the faint enjoy" (National Archives and Records Administration).

The *Friendship* first sailed to Barbados for rum and sugar, proceeding to Hampton, and thereafter Fredricksburg, Virginia, where John Paul met his eldest brother William, who had immigrated to that area and established himself as a tailor. For several years, John Paul made one round trip per year between Scotland and Fredricksburg, able to spend time with family on both sides of the Atlantic. Thus, John Paul familiarized himself with, and no doubt learned from, the lively culture of Barbados' seaports and the refined character of Fredricksburg, meeting gentlemen in his brother's tailor store, listening to their conversations, and imitating their manners, for John Paul, throughout his life, "grasped every occasion to improve himself, socially and otherwise" (Morison, *Jones*, 12), developing the habit of "midnight study." In Fredricksburg, John Paul's "prepossessions in favor of America, and sympathy with colonial feelings, were here naturally fostered under circumstances calculated to make them keen and enduring" (Taylor 16). On board the *Friendship* he learned to navigate ships celestially (the octant he acquired at a young age may be found in the Naval Academy Museum in Annapolis), and developed a respect for the power of the oceans, writing "the awful majesty of the tempest ... surpassed the reach even of poetic fancy and the pencil" (qtd. in Thomas, 21).

Four years later, the brig was sold and John Paul released from his apprenticeship. For a term "neither long nor happy," he served upon a British man-o-war, finding the British Navy as "autocratic as the French, which required as a feudal tradition that an officer should inherit the blood of four generations of the nobility" (Lorenz, 14). Thus, upon perceiving that "family interest had more influence than personal merit," John Paul abandoned "that insolent and faithless nation" (qtd. in Lorenz, 14). He became a third mate on a "blackbirder" named *King George* out of Whitehaven for two years, and thereafter the chief mate of the slaver *Two Friends* out of Kingston, Jamaica. After one round trip from Jamaica to Africa and back again, John Paul obtained his discharge, for he would have no more of what he described as an "abominable trade." As Morison relates, "The slave traffic not only outrages his sentiments of humanity; it was a nasty business" (Morison, *Jones*, 13). Jones' niece believed, "It is fair to infer that the exhibition of these horrors, at which his feelings revolted, strengthened his love for that liberty in whose cause he afterwards fought, and for that land which knew how to vindicate the cause of liberty" (Taylor, 17). Lorenz noted that a man who stood against slavery in 1768, and who opposed it not only in principle but also in practice, stood apart from his contemporaries. Jones' turn from the abhorrent institution "gave proof of an independent, just spirit. Poor, he turned away from the lure of large profits; rugged himself, he was keenly sensitive to suffering of others; restricted by his own birth, he was the more alive regardless of color to the violated liberty of human beings" (Lorenz, 15). Note: Later in life, Jones befriended the African American Revolutionary era poet, Phyllis Wheatley, sending amateur verse to her upon occasion. His favorite poet was James Thomson (whose verse denounced the horror of slavery), and he referred to Shakespeare in many letters during his adulthood, even acting for a short period in a troupe touring the West Indies before heading back out to sea.

In port, an unemployed John Paul met Samuel McAdam from Cork, who offered him a free passage home. During the voyage to Kirkcudbright, both the master and mate died of a fever. As John Paul was the only passenger aboard who could navigate, he assumed command and brought the vessel and her crew of seven safely to Scotland. Ironically, the name of the vessel was *John*, and the owners were so pleased about the safe arrival of the ship, they appointed John Paul master of the next voyage to America. Thus, "John Paul, Jr., at the age of twenty-one, was master of a merchant vessel in the West Indies trade" (Morison, *Jones*, 14), and had "crossed the line from servant to master" (Thomas, 22). For the next two years, he served as master and selling agent; "his opportunities were not provided to him; he made his own way and at a young age had achieved much" (Conrad, 50).

On his second voyage aboard the *John*, John Paul encountered the discretionary and abusive powers of the gentry. Using disciplinary procedure standard to the merchant vessels of the era, John Paul ordered a crew member, Mungo Maxwell, flogged for "mouthing off at him, shirking duty, and doing his work sloppily" (Thomas, 23). Upon reaching Tobago, Maxwell visited the British court, charging John Paul with unjust abuse. The admiralty judge examined Maxwell's wounds "and found them to be neither 'mortal nor dangerous.' The judge ruled that the carpenter had earned the stripes across his back by his incompetence and disobedience" (Thomas, 24). Angrily, Maxwell returned to Scotland, yet died on the return voyage. His distraught, powerful, and influential family (a clan of southern Scotland, earls of Nithsdale, living in a castle thirty-five miles from Kirkcudbright) convinced the vice admiral of Scotland to place John Paul under arrest when he next entered the Scottish port, charged with the murder of Mungo, the father stating Mungo had been "most unmercifully, by the said John Paul, with a great cudgel or batton, bled, bruised, and wounded upon his back and other parts of his body, and of which wounds and bruises he soon afterwards died" (qtd. in Thomas, 25). John Paul, upon arrival, was "escorted on a walk of shame. He was marched up High Street, past Grayfriars Church and MacLellan's Castle, to the Tolbooth, the local jail. There he was clapped into irons and left, either in the 'laich sellar,' the low cellar where a local witch had been imprisoned before she was executed (strangled by the neck) some years earlier, or possibly in the new debtor's prison on the third floor" (Thomas, 25).

Posting bond, John Paul set out on a course of defense. He returned to the Caribbean to obtain evidence that he had been exonerated by the Admiralty Court in Tobago. He obtained a statement that Maxwell had seemed "in perfect health" at the time he boarded the ship which was to transport him back to Scotland, that he had caught a fever thereafter and died at sea. Though the charge was dismissed, Mr. Craik, who had known John Paul since a boy, siding with Scotland's upper class, scorned John Paul to the point he was required to produce character testimonials from local acquaintances. John Paul wrote to his mother, "Mr. Craik's nice feelings will not perhaps be otherwise satisfied. His ungracious conduct to me before I left Scotland I have not yet been able to get the better of. It is true that I bore it with seeming unconcern, but Heaven can witness for me, that I suffered the more on the very account" (qtd. in Thomas, 26). Jones was bitter and resentful toward the upper class for the remainder of his life; this incident deepened his resolve to advance his situation by merit, not birth. Accordingly, shortly after his release, he became a Freemason, "an essential social elevator in the eighteenth century" (Thomas, 26), which "later helped him to establish himself at *Fredricksburg*, Boston, Portsmouth and Paris" (Morison, *Jones*, 18).

John Paul also became part-owner and commander of the *Betsy*, a large, square-rigged ship which traded between England, Ireland, Madeira, and Tobago. By the age of twenty-five, he was earning enough money to consider retirement, settling down, marrying, and becoming a Virginia gentleman farmer. But, fate determined otherwise, and, again, on a second voyage, John Paul encountered "the greatest misfortune of my life," one that dashed his hopes for retirement. Failing to advance money to his crew in Tobago, hoping to invest in a return cargo, he planned on paying his crew in Great Britain. The crew would have none of this plan, and the ringleader of a mutinous attempt to row to shore, whom John Paul described as "a prodigious brute of thrice his strength who neglected and even refused his duty with much insolence" (qtd. in Thomas, 31) rushed John Paul with a bludgeon, even though John Paul had presented a good-will offering of "frocks and trousers." As he swore "the grossest abuse that vulgarism could dictate" and swung at his commander to inflict a lethal blow, John Paul, "thunderstruck with surprise," retreated until he felt his heel strike the edge of a hatchway. Trapped, John Paul defended himself, and his sword thrust into the ringleader, a local and one of about 300 white men who lived on the island. Fearing the locals would side with the ringleader and come for his head, or at least condemn him for murder, John Paul "hastened to his friends in Tobago."

He offered himself freely as a prisoner to a justice of the peace. As the case came within the jurisdiction of the admiralty courts and no admiralty commission was then at the island, the justice stated that he need not surrender himself until one was convened. His previous supporters, James Simpson the former Judge Surrogate who had given him in Tobago his affidavit concerning Maxwell, and William Young the Lieutenant Governor before whom it had been sworn, concurred in the opinion that he should absent himself, pending the next session of a commission. All his friends, in fact, urged that for the present he should leave the country. They saddled his horse and insisted that he ride" (Lorenz, 26–7). Jones himself later wrote, "It was the advice of my friends ... that I should retire incognito to the Continent of America, and remain there until an admiralty commission should arrive in the island, and then return" (qtd. in Lorenz, 28). Morison notes, "One can only assume that the death of the Ringleader, a Tobago man, had so stirred up local sentiment that John Paul's friends could not be responsible for his safety and prevailed upon him to escape at once" (*Jones*, 23). Thus, a mysterious period in Jones' life began. Disguised in appearance, in a manner unrecognizable to the locals, and with a new name in tow, "at the close of 1773 John Paul of Arbigland and possibly Paul Jones of the Masonic of Kirkcudbright became John Paul Jones of history" (Lorenz, 28), sailing to safety, and to a greater destiny, in America.

With the blood of independent, freedom-loving, and sea-faring peoples in his veins, having experienced the injustices associated with class structure, the horrors of enslavement, and the sometimes frightening consequences of mob rule, John Paul Jones proved ripe for a stand against British oppression, ever ready to fight for the cause of liberty. Having been steeped in the standards of educational excellence, gaining habits of life-long study, while also being exposed to the manners and standards of a true gentleman and the arts of landscaping, poetry, and theatre, he also knew well how to conduct himself in professional society. And, finally, spurned by a marriage prospect to one Dorothea Dandridge, cousin to Martha Washington, while residing at the "Grove" (no doubt licking his wounds) with fellow Scot Dr. John K. Read, Master Mason of Fredericksburg, for the simple reason he was not from a "socially acceptable" family, Jones, in his own words, relinquished his "prospects for domestic happiness to restore peace and goodwill among mankind." (Dorothea would choose Patrick Henry as a husband, twice her senior, at the insistence of her father.) Indeed, as John Adams aptly discerned, Jones now carried the "wild, keen, and soft eye" which would carry him into the midst of Revolutionary War command.

Indeed, as Thomas notes, "Jones had plenty to offer the American rebels: seamanship, navigation skills, experience commanding a ship. He knew something about gunnery" (42). And, as English biographer Sherburne noted, "It is singular that during the first years of the American Navy, with the exception of Paul Jones, no man of any talent is to be found directing its operations, and had it not been for the exertions of this individual, who was unsupported by fortune or connexions, it is very probable that the American naval power would have gradually disappeared" (qtd. in Taylor, 27–8). Thus, Jones was certainly recommended to the Continental Congress' Naval Committee by the "angel of my happiness," Joseph Hewes, a North Carolina merchant, Freemason, delegate to the Second Continental Congress, and member of the Marine Committee. Upon traveling to Philadelphia and offering his services to an as yet nonexistent Navy, in order "to teach the enemy humanity by some exemplary stroke of retaliation" (qtd. in Lorenz, 50), Jones was commissioned a first lieutenant ("John Paul Jones, Esq., reads the parchment, and that 'Esq.,' a gentleman's title, meant the world to Jones" [Thomas, 45]), placed in command of the *Alfred*, named after the founder of the British navy.

On December 3, 1775, John Paul Jones is credited with raising the first American flag aboard a ship, a hybrid with thirteen red-and-white-striped bars to represent the colonies, and the crosses of St. George and St. Andrew in the canton to symbolize the British union. (The Stars and Stripes were two years away.) And, when he accepted his commission on December 7, 1775, the earliest naval lieutenant's commission granted by Congress, at "a date when only a few radicals wanted a complete separation from England — he well and truly believed that he was fighting not for American independence but for the principle of liberty—the right of a free people to determine their destiny without coercion by a misguided king and a corrupt ministry. And the flag he raised with his own hands on the jackstaff of his first temporary command ... was not the Stars and Stripes of an independent republic, but the 'Grand Union Flag,' the Union Jack and Stripes, which symbolized a united resistance to tyranny, but loyalty to the English King" (Morison, *Jones*, 30).

Jones' luck had most decidedly changed, for "on January 3, a raw, wind-whipped day, a large crowd came to the harbor side to watch the hope of the navy sail down the Delaware, toward the sea and the enemy beyond. A fife and drum corps gaily played; the crowd cheered. There was the *Alfred*, rated thirty guns; the *Columbus*, twenty-eight guns; the *Cabot*, fourteen guns; the *Andrew Doria*, sixteen guns; and the *Providence*, twelve guns" (Thomas, 46). Or, was luck simply on Jones' side? For, in later reflections, Jones wrote, "Was it proof of madness in the first corps of sea officers to have at so critical a period launched out on the ocean with only two armed merchant ships, two armed brigantines, and one armed sloop, to make war against such a power as Great Britain?" (qtd. in Thomas, 46). (Jones also later recalled, "The first beginning of our Navy was, as navies now rank, so singularly small that I am of opinion it has no precedent in history" [qtd. in Lorenz, 54].)

Under Commodore Hopkins and aboard the *Alfred*, Lieutenant Jones was in charge of the lower gun deck, training the crew and directing fire when needed. The most famous battle gauged by the *Alfred* was against the British H.M.S. *Glasgow*, which sustained "ten shots through her mainmast, 110 holes in her mainsail, 88 in her foresail, 52 in her mizzen staysail, some spars carried away, and her rigging cut to pieces" (Morison, *Jones*, 49). Commodore Hopkins, by May 1776, placed Jones in command of the *Providence*, a sloop whose first order was to deliver one hundred soldiers for Washington's Army from New London to New York. In port, he wrote a letter to Joseph Hewes, now famous for its profession as to the appropriate qualifications of a Naval officer: "In my opinion a Captain of the Navy ought to be a man of Strong and well-connected Sense with a tolerable Education, a Gentleman as well as a Seaman, both in theory and practice—for, want of learning and rude Ungentle Manners are by no means the Characteristick of an Officer, nor is any man fit to command a Ship of War, who is not also capable of communicating his Ideas on Paper in Language that becomes his Rank" (qtd. in Morison, *Jones*, 54). His next orders included escorting the vessel *Fly*, carrying cannon for Washington's army to Long Island Sound, and escorting a convoy of colliers to Philadelphia, doing so despite the presence of British cruisers and Admiral Lord Howe's fleet.

In Philadelphia, Joseph Hewes, sitting in Congress at the time, introduced Jones to congressional chairman John Hancock and financier Robert Morris, resulting in a captain's commission dated August 8, 1776, directed to "Seize, take, Sink, Burn or destroy" British vessels, obtain intelligence if possible, protect and aid American vessels, and treat prisoners humanely. This cruise, according to Morison, proved "the happiest and most rewarding of Paul Jones's naval career. He had a crew of over seventy men, the best (he declared in later years) that he ever commanded. He was on his own with nobody to give him orders once he had dropped down the Delaware. He had plenty of sport, made numerous prizes, and at last was ahead of the game financially" (*Jones*, 59). Sailing on August 21, 1776, independence having been declared, *Providence*, within a week, captured the *Britannia*, a whaling brigantine, the known listing of prizes captured on this cruise being:

Ship and Locale	Date	Cargo Seized	Disposition
Britannia—one week outside of Philadelphia toward Bermuda	August 28, 1776	Whaling	Sent to Philadelphia with a prize crew
Sea Nymph—West Indies	September 3, 1776	Rum, sugar, ginger, oil, London market Madeira wine	Sent to Philadelphia with a prize crew
Favourite—West Indies	September 6, 1776	Sugar	Recaptured by H.M.S. *Galatea*
Alexander, Sea Flower, Ebenezer, Alexander, Kingston Packet, Defiance, and *Success*-Nova Scotia	September 20, 1776	British fishing fleet	Back to New London with the *Alexander, Kingston Packet,* and *Success. Sea Flower* burned, *Ebenezer* dragged onto a reef and broken up; *Defiance* put to sea
Portland—Nova Scotia	September 26, 1776	Whaling sloop	Escorted to New London

All-in-all, Jones "during the last six months of 1776 ... captured or destroyed five transports, two ships, six schooners, seven brigantines, one sloop, and a sixteen-gun privateer" (Bobrick, 385). Before departing on his next cruise, Jones informed Congress that crew members would be hard to come by on naval ships unless prize percentages were increased, writing unless "the private Emoluments of individuals in our Navy is made superior to that in Privateers it never can become respectable — it never will become formidable.... If our Enemies, with the best established and most formidable Navy in the Universe, have found it expedient to assign all Prizes to the Captors — how much more is such policy essential to our infant Fleet" (qtd. in Morison, *Jones*, 65). Heeding this wise advice, Congress upped the prize contention to fifty percent, rather than thirty-three percent, and granted the entire value of a prize if the ship captured were a privateer or man-of-war.

Jones believed his next course was to capture British merchant vessels off the coast of New York during the winter months, but Commodore Hopkins presented Jones with a higher calling, rescuing one hundred American prisoners then subjected to slave labor in the coal mines of Nova Scotia. Jones responded in the affirmative, later writing, "All my humanity was awakened" (qtd. in Thomas, 67), reflecting to Joseph Hewes, "Since liberty hath chosen America as her last asylum every effort to protect and cherish her is noble and will be rewarded with the thanks of future ages" (qtd. in Thomas, 70). (In this same letter he reflected that the Navy should institute "unlimited enlistment periods, an impartial Board of Admiralty to run the navy [rather than a highly politicized congressional committee], and wages and prize shares competitive with those of the Royal Navy and American privateers" [Thomas, 70].) In mid–November, racing to the prisoners in the cold, blustery waters off Nova Scotia, Jones' next prize helped to clothe the soldiers who crossed the Delaware on Christmas Day to defeat the Hessians, for the British transport, *Mellish*, was carrying "chests of medicine, fine silks, some important British citizens bound for Halifax, and, most critically, *thousands* of winter uniforms" (Thomas, 71). The uniforms had been destined for General Burgoyne's winter army, who had planned to "split the South" with a march down through Lakes George and Champlain. Jones wrote Robert Smith, a fellow Mason in North Carolina, "This will make Burgoyne 'shake a cloth in the wind' and check his progress on the Lakes" (qtd. in Thomas, 71). Near Thanksgiving, Jones captured a collier carrying the coal from the Cape Breton coal mines to the British army in New York. He also sent armed boats, in the fishing port of Canso, to destroy an oil warehouse, thus further affecting Britain's winter war efforts. Discouragingly, he learned from the collier's crews that the American prisoners, in order to survive the cruel winter, had already joined the British navy.

Due to political meanderings and strife, i.e., a listing of naval command developed by the Marine Committee which placed Jones eighteenth on the list (as he had no local political backing and Joseph Hewes was absent at that time), and a rift with Commodore Hopkins over Robert Morris' insistence that Jones be "pushed out" to the Caribbean, Captain Jones did not return to action until nearly a year later, November 1, 1777. He was provided command of the sloop-of-war *Ranger*. Humorously, Morison notes, "No more appropriate name for a ship commanded by John Paul Jones could have been devised" (*Jones*, 103). Note: The date the command was issued, June 14, 1777, was the same day Congress

> *Resolved* That the Flag of the thirteen United States be thirteen stripes, alternate red and white; that the union be thirteen stars, white in a blue field, representing a new constellation [qtd. in Morison, *Jones*, 101].

Jones informed the Marine Committee of his plan to surprise and attack with advantage, writing, "It is true I must run great risk, but no gallant action was ever performed without danger. Therefore, though I cannot insure success, I will endeavor to deserve it" (qtd. in Thomas, 109). Note: Before sailing Jones ordered his own personal coat-of-arms, using the arms of a Jones family in Wales with those of a Paul family in Gloucestershire. "He surrounded this with swords, cannon, an anchor, a Masonic emblem, dolphins, and the flag he had sailed under: the Grand Union, but with red, white, and blue stripes, the blue command pennant, a red, white, and blue striped flag, and a variation of the New England pine tree" (Balderston, 82).

The launching of *Ranger* was quite a show, as "topsail yards were braced sharp, precisely at nine o'clock a gun was fired, and the Marines' drums and fifes beat a merry tune while the men heaved on the capstan bars to break out the anchor, and as *Ranger* whipped around under the fresh breeze from the White Mountains, with a strong ebb current under her keel, Captain Jones on the quarterdeck in his best blue uniform and Major Frazer in continentals waved their cocked hats to the ladies ashore" (Morison, *Jones*, 113). After the show, however, Jones was all business, landing in Nantes, France, to begin his campaign, writing Congress, "As America must become the first Marine Power in the world, the care and increase of our seaman is a consideration of the first magnitude, and claims the full attention of Congress" (qtd. in Morison, *Jones*, 117). Once settled in France, Jones received his orders from Franklin and Deane: "After equipping the *Ranger* in the best manner for the cruise you propose ... proceed with her in the manner you shall judge best for distressing the Enemies of the United States, by sea or otherwise, consistent with the laws of war, and the terms of the commission" (qtd. in Morison, *Jones*, 125). When Jones and his crew and an American convoy sailed from Quiberon Bay early on the morning of February 13, a squadron of French battleships and three frigates escorted Jones safely from the coast. Jones, with the new American colors, saluted the French naval command with thirteen guns, the French returning the salute with nine guns (their traditional salute to international allies, such as "an Admiral of Holland or of any other Republic"). This salute became the first for the United States from a foreign power under the first official American flag and "symbolized the secret alliance which had been signed between the two countries a week earlier" (Morison, *Jones*, 129).

Jones' immediate objective was to "raid an English seaport, destroy shipping and capture some important person as hostage, in order to force the British government to exchange American sailors taken prisoner" (Morison, *Jones*, 133). (Jones always considered American prisoners of war, no doubt due to his early life experiences in which he was unjustly imprisoned.) Ironically, Jones turned to the land of his youth. His first capture (again, ironically, April 19, the anniversary of Lexington and Concord three years earlier) was of a Scottish schooner loaded with oats and barley, which he sank, taking the crew prisoner, also sinking a Dublin-based sloop, the *Lord Chatham,* "to prevent intelligence." And, in order to seal the "propaganda value of raiding an English seaport" (Morison, *Jones*, 139), and to avenge the fact that French intelligence had informed him Britain's plan was to burn American seaports, Jones and his Lieutenants, Meijer and Wallingford, along with midshipman Ben Hill, left the *Ranger* at midnight in row boats, with a total of forty men. Their purpose was to raid and burn the ships within the harbor of Whitehaven, the very port from which Jones sailed from Scotland to America at the age of 13. After three hours of rowing, they reached shore, throwing "candles" (canvas dipped in brimstone, ignited with fleet and steel) into the ships at port, Jones himself scaling the walls by standing on the shoulders of his men and securing the guards. Around five A.M. they returned to their boats, Jones the last, for "the sun was a full hour above the horizon, and as sleep no longer ruled the world, it was time to retire," said Jones (qtd. in Morison, *Jones*, 140). That same morning, rounding to St. Mary's Isle, a peninsula in Kirkcudbright Bay, Jones and his men again rowed to shore, hoping to imprison one Lord Selkirk with hopes for a prisoner exchange. As the lord was not then home, and as his crew insisted on looting the mansion, Jones allowed the officer and mate to enter the mansion and take only the silver, returned to the countess after the War with a personal apology. These raids on two tiny seaports shocked the whole of England, for letters from the area asking for protection were immediately delivered to the British Admiralty.

Next, in the North Channel of the Irish Sea, from a captured fishing boat crew, Jones learned that the H.M.S. *Drake* was upon him, anchored at Carrickfergus Harbor, Northern Ireland (near Belfast). On April 24, as a decoy, Jones slid a British flag up his ship's pole and sailed into Belfast Lough. The captain of the *Drake* sent members of the crew to investigate the supposed merchant vessel. The six men soon were on board the *Ranger,* instantly informed as to their status as prisoners of Captain Paul Jones of the United States Navy. Throughout these captures and raids, Jones also endured the threat of mutiny from his crew (for they were receiving no prizes), placing a gun to the head of one ringleader to stop a mutiny and having his first lieutenant stand at the boat at Whitehaven to ensure his passage back to the ship. But, when British prisoners were taken, "it tickled their caprice and soothed them again into good humor" (qtd. in Lorenz, 170), explained Jones, for "the crew had watched the capture with enchantment, hailed it as an omen of victory, and was electrified with the will to fight" (Lorenz, 170).

Captain Jones led the *Drake* into the middle of the Channel, in open water off the coast of Donaghadee, near the Copeland Islands. (The battle became known in Ireland as the Battle of the Copelands. Irishmen rowed their fishing boats to sea to witness the battle firsthand.) As the night engulfed the islands and ships, and as the *Drake* came within pistol shot of the *Ranger,* the battle ensued, described by Jones thusly:

> The battle was warm, close, and obstinate. It lasted an hour and four minutes, when the enemy called for quarters; her fore and main-topsail yards being both cut away, and down on the cap; the top-gallant yard and mizzen-gaff both hanging up and down along the mast; the second ensign which they had hoisted shot away, and hanging on the quarter gallery in the

water; the jib shot away; her sails and rigging entirely cut to pieces; her masts and yards all wounded, and her hull also very much galled. I lost only Lieutenant Wallingsford and one seaman, John Dougall, killed, and six wounded.... The loss of the enemy ... was in killed and wounded forty-two men. The Captain and lieutenant were among the wounded; the form, having received a musket ball in the head the minute before they called for quarters, lived and was sensible some time after my people boarded the prize. The lieutenant survived two days. They were buried with the honors due to their rank and with the respect due to their memory" [qtd. in Lorenz, 172].

Jones usurped all of the rules of British warfare, opening the battle at close quarters, concentrating his gunfire upon the sails rather than the hull of the enemy ship, making use of muskets and grenades to sweep the decks, and in position to board the *Drake* if need be, a type of guerrilla warfare at sea (George Washington used the same strategies on land). Certainly, growing in his capacity as a naval warrior, and finally earning the well-deserved respect of both his nation and his crew, Jones, in Lorenz's words, "at this point was practically invincible. The wide margin of his victory demonstrated in itself his powers in reserve. The marred initial plans to attack the *Drake* by day or night, the two unsatisfactory undertakings at Whitehaven, the humiliating as well as unsuccessful enterprise at St. Mary's Isle, and the increasingly obstructive and vicious behavior of the *Ranger's* men from the first episode with the *Drake* at the beginning of the cruise almost to the very moment of the ultimate conflict with her — all had moved the heart and mind of the Captain to a cumulative fixity of will as set as the coils of a tense spring for the final dramatic moment of action. Even the gallant behavior of the sailors at the crisis had been the sheer result of his magnetic personality. Jones alone was the imponderable human factor that had won the battle" (Lorenz, 174). Again, John Paul Jones wrote history, winning the first victory of a Continental Navy vessel over an English man-o-war.

Back in port in France, Jones dealt with his prisoners of war (and an exchange with Admiral Howe in America) and the court-martial of one of his lieutenants, who absconded with the *Drake*, after Jones placed him in charge of the prize, recaptured by Jones himself. As the demeanor of his crew convinced Franklin that Jones needed another ship, Jones wrote the philosopher, who quickly became Jones' proponent, "Nothing would give me more pleasure than to render essential services to America, in any measure that you may find expedient" (qtd. in Taylor, 107).

In Britain Jones' escapades were causing a stir, indeed a type of hysteria, described by Jones' early biographer, Mrs. Reginald De Koven:

Chap books depicted Paul Jones as a buccaneer, armed to the teeth, in highly colorful pictures, bloody and terrifying. Mothers frightened their children with the bare mention of his name. From this time on he was celebrated in popular song, and took his place with Captain Kidd in the histories of the Pirate Kings [qtd. in Thomas, 136].

Jones became part of the folklore of the British Isles. In pubs and taverns, ballads were written of his exploits, one of which sang:

> You have heard o' Paul Jones?
> Have you not? Have you not?
> And you've heard o' Paul Jones?
> Have you not?
> A rogue and a vagabond;
> Is he not? Is he not?
> He came to Selkirk-ha,

Paul Jones, the Pirate. Engraving (full-length caricature) published by A. Park, London (National Archives and Records Administration).

> Did he not? Did he not?
> And stole the rings and the jewels a,'
> Did he not? Did he not?
> Robeed the plate and jewels-a,'
> Which did his conscience gall,
> Did it not?

Back in America, privateer captain Thomas Bell wrote John Paul that Joseph Hewes and Robert Morris were "in raptures" over the *Ranger*'s success, and that "the public to the Southward thinks you the finest fellow belonging to America" (qtd. in Thomas, 156). In a return reply, Jones dreamt of a bright future for America's Navy, believing "When the enemies' land force is once conquered and expelled from the continent, our Marine will rise as if by enchantment and become, with the memory of persons now living, the wonder and envy of the world" (qtd. in Thomas, 156–7).

The ship eventually assigned to John Paul was the *Bonhomme Richard*, named for Franklin's almanac, as mentioned earlier, which took sail on August 14, 1779. First, Captain Jones fooled the captain of a fifty-gun ship, the *Romney*. Sailing up to the ship dressed in British naval uniforms and carrying the British colors, Jones listened as the British captain asked for gunpowder. Jones obliged, and, when the captain was aboard, asked, "What news? The pilot said that the pirate Jones was off the coast and deserved to be hanged. Jones smiled. 'I am Paul Jones'.... The poor pilot dropped to his knees and begged for his life. 'Get up!' Jones commanded. 'I won't hurt a hair on your head, but you are my prisoner'" (Thomas, 175).

On September 21, 1779, the *London Evening Post* reported: "Expresses also arrived on Saturday from Sunderland, stating that Paul Jones had taken sixteen sail of colliers. In consequence of the capture of so many colliers, and the interception of the trade, the price of coals will be enormous. Instead of having the dominion of the sea, it is now evident that we are not able to defend our own coast from depredations" (Seitz, 45). Shoring along the

Memorable battle between the *Seraphis*, commanded by Captain Pearson, and the *Bonhomme Richard*, commanded by John Paul Jones. Engraving from painting by Richard Paton, 1779–80 (National Archives and Records Administration).

coast of Scotland, working up the Forth, Jones' presence also placed the locals in a state of panic, as families fled, banks closed, weapons were found (stored after the 1746 disarmament) and "an aging Presbyterian minister went to the shore, settled his chair in the surf, and prayed for a strong wind to blow the Americans away" (Thomas, 175). Indeed, a gale ensued which thwarted Jones' plans to raid the coast at Leith and led him on a course northward and into the path of the infamous *Seraphis*.

Acclaimed as the greatest naval battle of the Revolutionary War, the *Richard* and *Seraphis* met each other off the cliffs of Flamborough Head, on the Yorkshire coastline "just as the moon was rising," on September 23, according to midshipman Nathaniel Fanning. Amidst a calm and clear sea, Captain Pearson of the *Seraphis* hailed, "This is his majesty's ship *Seraphis*. What ship is that?" (No easy foe, Pearson was a 30-year veteran at sea, six of which were served in the Royal Navy, seeing three fleet actions and commanding two ships of war, *Seraphis*, with forty-four guns on two decks, the third. Jones, through his spyglass, noticed Pearson nailing his flag, an enormous, blood-red Royal Navy ensign, to the staff.) Jones replied, "Come a little nearer and I will tell you." Pearson replied, "What are you laden with?" to which Jones exclaimed, "Round, grape, and double-headed shot!" The American flag immediately rose, instigating firepower from both sides. As Thomas notes, "The sound was appalling: the tremendous concussion of forty-two cannon and scores of small arms fired at nearly the same instant, the cracking of splintered wood, the jarring clang of a cannonball striking an iron muzzle or an anchor fluke, and, very soon thereafter, the shrieks and cries of the wounded. At the range of twenty-five yards, every gun hit home" (183). Jones noted, "The battle thus begun was continued with unremitting fury. Every method was practiced on both sides to gain an advantage, and rake each other; and I must confess that the enemy's ship, being much more manageable than the *Richard*, gained thereby several times an advantageous situation in spite of my best endeavors to prevent it" (qtd. in Bobrick 389).

Going into battle, the *Richard* was outgunned forty-four to forty, and Jones' convoy, the *Pallas, Alliance,* and *Vengeance*, abandoned him to the British man-o-war. Initially, Pearson outfoxed Jones, steering the wheel at just the right moment to rake and cross the stern, sending grapeshot down the length of the ship. Guns were overturned; twenty-two out of twenty-five men on the poop deck were dead or severely wounded. Rounding leeward, the *Seraphis* continued its assault, pouring shot from a broadside every two minutes or so. Ocean water poured into the *Richard's* splintered hull, and pumps did not keep up.

The wind and breeze saved the day for Jones, for "feeling a puff from the dying southerly, he ordered the sailing master, Samuel Stacey, to 'lay the enemy's ship on board.' ... Jones was able to blanket his opponent and steal her wind, catching what little zephyrs still rippled the water in the settling darkness" (Thomas, 187). Upon collision, "the bowsprit of the British ship drove into the *Bonhomme Richard's* mizzen rigging" (Thomas, 188). The two ships were hopelessly intertwined. Jones himself climbed the ladder on the poop deck and tied the line between the mizzenmast. He ordered a heavier rope tied between the *Seraphis'* jib boom and the *Richard's* mizzenmast, himself tying the rope with the help of his sailing master Stacey, commenting to the cursing sailor, "Mr. Stacey, it's no time to be swearing now. You may by the next moment be in eternity, but let us do our duty" (qtd. in Thomas, 188).

The battle was now an hour old, and "a few miles away, atop the cliffs of Flamborough Head, large crowds were gathering. About a thousand people had walked or ridden from the surrounding villages, lured by the news that a British man-o-war had trapped the Pirate Jones. Under the silvery moon, across the glistening water, they witnessed a fantastic sight. The two warships were locked inside a yellowish cloud that pulsated with flashes of orange and white light. In the dead calm, the smoke from the cannon and numerous small blazes created a thick blanket of sulfurish smoke, eerie and ghostly to the onlookers on the cliff, choking and toxic to the men trapped within" (Thomas, 189).

Jones' men began shooting across the decks of the *Seraphis*, forcing Captain Pearson to go below deck. The cannon of the *Seraphis* continued pounding its opponent. Both ships caught fire. The carpenter, John Gunnison, believing the ship sinking and the captain dead, asked the gunner's mate, Henry Gardner, to call quarters. Hollering "Quarters! Quarters!" the two men headed to the mainmast to strike the American flag. Jones, leaning over a 9-pounder to fire another shot, wheeled immediately, asking, "Who are those rascals? Shoot them! Kill them!" Lunging at the men, he pulled his pistol and fired (the chamber was empty). He hurled the pistol at Gardner's head as he was scrambling down the ladder, knocking him cold. Pearson, having heard the cry, yelled, "Have you struck?" As a result of this question, America has one of its primary, immortal quotes, a legacy born, for Jones replied (according to Lieutenant Richard Dale), "I have not yet begun to fight." (In a memoir written to Louis XVI, Jones stated he said: "Je ne songe point a me render, mais je suis determine a vous faire demander quartier," or "I haven't as yet thought of surrendering, but I am determined to make you ask for quarter," most likely a mouthful at a time of crisis. One contemporary account suggests he said, "I may sink, but I'll be damned if I strike" (qtd. in Thomas, 192).

The British, at that point, even tried to come on board *Richard*, but with Jones at the head, "wielding a boarding pike," the crew forced the British sailors back to their ship. Thomas notes, "The end came with surprising suddenness." And, it came at the hand of brave sailors who climbed to the maintop, forty feet above the deck, shooting at their enemy below. Sailor William Hamilton, a fellow Scotsman, at the fourth hour, or around 10:15 P.M., edged along the footropes of the main yard with a leather bucket of grenades (about the size of baseballs) and a lighted slow-match. Hamilton threw the grenades, which detonated twenty seconds after being lit, below, finding holes in the ship in an attempt to find *Seraphis'* gun deck. The ball met its target, powder cartridges left out in the throes of battle by the gun crews. A chain reaction caused a flash fire in the gun deck, sailors on fire diving into the sea. Jones also continued to pound the *Seraphis'* mast with the 9-pounder.

Captain Pearson could stand no more, as the *Seraphis* was "in deplorable shape. Her spars, sails, and rigging were destroyed, and the dead and dying scattered about her deck. At length, when her mainmast began to topple, Captain Pearson 'lost his nerve,' and struck" (Bobrick, 389). Jones replied, "If you have struck, haul down your ensign." As no member of the crew would "expose themselves to American marksmen, he had to ascend the quarterdeck himself and haul his standard down" (Bobrick, 389). "Jones ordered, 'Cease fire,' and Captain Pearson walked onto the *Richard* to hand Captain Jones his sword. Pearson said, 'It is with the greatest reluctance that I am now obliged to resign you this, for it is painful to me, more particularly at this time, when compelled to deliver up my sword to a man who may be said to fight with a halter around his neck.' Jones replied, 'Sir you have fought like a hero, and I make no doubt but your sovereign will reward you in a most ample manner for it.' Pearson then asked the nationality of his crew. 'Americans,' said Jones. 'Very well,' said Pearson, 'it has been "diamond cut diamond" with us'— in disparagement of the French" (qtd. in Bobrick, 390).

Midshipman Flanning wrote of the battle: "The tangle of mangled corpses was enough to appall the stoutest heart.... Upon the whole, I think this battle and every circumstance attending it minutely considered, may be ranked with propriety the most bloody, the hardest fought, and the greatest scene of carnage on both sides, ever fought between two ships of war of any nation under heaven" (qtd. in Bobrick, 390). The state of the *Richard* was "frightful. Her rudder was hanging by one pintle, her stern frames and transoms were almost entirely shot away, the quarterdeck was about to fall into the gunroom, at least five feet of water were in the hold, and it was gaining from holes below the waterline ... and her topsides were open to the moonlight. The timbers of her lower deck from the mainmast aft, 'being greatly decayed with age, were mangled beyond my power of description,' observed Jones in his narrative of the battle, 'and a person must have been an Eye Witness to form a Just idea of this tremendous scene of Carneg, Wreck and ruin that Every Where appeared. Humanity cannot but recoil from the prospect of such finished horror, and Lament that War should be capable of producing such fatal Consequences'" (qtd. in Morison, *Jones*, 239–40). British and American sailors now worked side by side to ensure the ships did not explode, dropping cartridges into the ocean. By the evening of September 24, the *Richard* sank, Jones transferring his crew aboard the *Seraphis* and sailing onward. Of course, the British were already after him again, searching for Captain Jones "to the northeast, toward Scandinavia, to the southeast, toward Holland and France, and all around the British Isles. They never found him.... Jones's legend was made. 'Paul Jones resembles a Jack o' Lantern, to mislead our mariners and terrify our coasts,' wrote the *London Morning Post*. 'He is no sooner seen than lost'" (qtd. in Thomas, 199). (Jones zigzagged in the North Sea for ten days and thereafter headed into Dexel Island in Holland, three days later rowing to Amsterdam in order to negotiate a prisoner exchange. The Dutch treated him as a hero, escorting him to the theater and down the streets with "Huzzahs," even writing a folksong which children continue to sing in the Netherlands: "Here comes Paul Jones; such a nice fellow! His ship went down at England's End. Had we him here, had they him there, He'd know what to do; fortune may turn. Here comes Paul Jones; such a nice fellow! A born American; no Englishman at all. Here comes Paul Jones; such a nice fellow! He does many bold deeds for the good of his friends" [qtd. in Morison, *Jones*, 257].) American Agent Dumas noted the Dutch were "overjoyed and mad to see the vanquisher of the English. They applaud him and bowed down to his feets, ready to kiss them" (qtd. in Thomas, 202). Note: While in Holland, Captain Jones met Gustavus Conyngham, recently escaped from a British prison (see Chapter 6), befriending Conyngham and welcoming him aboard his new ship, the *Alliance*, until Conyngham could receive a new command.

The *Alliance* sailed to Spain and thereafter Paris to reach a safer port on December 27, again outfoxing the British, who were of course after Jones' head, by taking the direct route, over the holiday, straight down the English Channel "while British seamen were still recovering from their Yuletide carousing" (Thomas, 209). Thick weather also helped Jones slip by another British man-o-war fleet off the Isle of Wight.

In Britain Jones became known as "a daring pirate who has for some time past done so much mischief on the coast of Great Britain," and another verse was added to the folksong referenced above:

> He took the *Seraphis*
> Did he not? Did he not?
> He took the *Seraphis*, tho' the battle it was hot;
> But a rogue and vagabond,
> Is he not?

On the other hand, France was "electrified." Franklin wrote to Jones, "Scarce anything has been talked of at Paris and Versailles but your cool Conduct & persevering Bravery" (qtd. in Bobrick, 390). John Adams remarked, "The cry of Versailles and the Clamour of Paris became as loud in the favour of Monsieur Jones as of Monsieur Franklin, and the inclination of the Ladies to embrace him almost as fashionable and as strong" (qtd. in Bobrick, 390). King Louis XVI himself formally honored Jones, presenting him with a gold-hilted sword, the words engraved thereon being: *Vindicati Maris Ludovicus XVI remunerator Stenua Vindici* (reward from Louis XVI to the valiant avenger of the rights of the sea). The sword was also adorned with medallions of Mars, Hercules, Neptune, and Minerva. The King also made Jones a member of the Ordre du Mérite Militaire, the equivalent of a French knighthood. (Subsequently, Jones preferred the title of "Chevalier," sometimes signing his name "Chevalier Paul Jones".)

Jones sailed home to Philadelphia in February 1781, aboard the *Ariel*, delivering 437 barrels of gunpowder and 146 chests of arms to the Continental Army (which helped Washington in his Southern campaign). Jones' prize for all his valiant efforts and commands was the promise of a seventy-four-gun ship being constructed in Portsmouth, the *America*. Nevertheless, the war ended before Jones could take command and reenter battle (he hoped to return to the British Isles). In 1787, Congress voted him a gold medal, designed by Augustin Dupré, with a bust of Jones on one side and the *Richard* and *Seraphis* on the other. The medal reads on the bust side: "To John Paul Jones, Commander of the Fleet. The American Congress." The ship side reads: "The Enemy's Ships Captured or Put to Flight. At Scotland's Shore 23 Sept. 1779."

Returning to Paris in hopes of obtaining a French commission, which never materialized, Jones spent his last days in ill health, "worn by care and the exposure of too many years, staying awake for days at a time, standing alert on the quarterdeck of troubled ships in troubled seas" (Thomas, 305). He died on July 18, 1792. Ironically, Jefferson, then secretary of state, had appointed Jones to lead an American delegation to free thirteen American prisoners, "sailors seized from merchantmen and thrown in the grim cells of Algiers" (Thomas, 305), which for years had troubled John Paul to the point he had corresponded with Jefferson on numerous occasions about the fate of "our poor countrymen." (Brady notes: "Practically his first military effort was an attempt to set free American prisoners, and his last Commission from the United States was the appointment to effect the release of the unfortunate Americans held by the Barbary States. Thus he fought not only for the establishment of civil liberty and national independence, but with an eye single to the individual prisoner" (341). The orders, "the kind of recognition that Jones so craved during his life" (Thomas, 305), unfortunately arrived at the end of July, subsequent to John Paul's demise. The French government rescued Jones from a pauper's grave, placing his body "pickled in alcohol, in a lead-lined coffin, should more enlightened American governments seek to reclaim and properly honor their hero's remains" (Thomas, 306). Note: Many have tried to prove that Jones received his last name from a friend in North Carolina, Willie Jones, a contention never proved and highly unlikely. However, the state of North Carolina figured heavily in both the beginning and end of John Paul Jones' life, i.e., "at the beginning of his career in the Navy, when Joseph Hewes got him his commission and became his confident, but also at the very end of his life. Colonel Samuel Blackden, formerly of a North Carolina regiment of dragoons, was one of two friends who stood by John Paul Jones in his final illness, the last gentleman who saw him alive, and the man who interceded with M. Simonneau, Commissaire of the Paris section where Jones died, to have his body placed in a lead coffin which could eventually be transported overseas and given a dignified public funeral. Thus, we owe it to one North Carolinian that Jones entered the service to which he was such a glory; and, to another

North Carolinian that it was possible, in 1905, to have his body disinterred and transferred to Annapolis" (Morison, "Willie Jones," 206).

The site of Jones' grave was quickly forgotten. His fame as a naval hero continued throughout the nineteenth century, but it was not until the twentieth century that biographers began to understand his abilities as a naval *officer*. For, his strategic vision, which placed the nation's interest over his own personal gain, "his rise to the top levels of the new American navy through dint of hard work and application, his skill as a naval architect, his continued study to better himself as an officer and commander, and his attempts to reform the Navy and to substitute merit and ability in place of nepotism and influence, all marked him as one who sought to professionalize the early Navy" (Conrad, 69).

Jones' legacy also speaks to his love for freedom, his love for America, where he spent "fifteen years among an enlightened people, where the press is free, and where the conduct of every man is open to discussion, and subjected to the judgment of his fellow citizens," fighting for a "world in which men might advance by their merits and drive, and not be pegged by their birth or place" (Thomas, 308). America's great tribute to Jones occurred over a century after the Revolution. In 1899, American Ambassador to France, General Horace Porter, used his own funds to find Jones' grave, now below Parisian sheds and buildings of a decrepit nature. Excavation began in 1905, and the body was remarkably preserved (by the alcohol no doubt). Physicians were even able to perform an autopsy, revealing the cause of death as liver disease, pneumonia, and jaundice. President Theodore Roosevelt sent four cruisers to retrieve Jones' body. An elaborate service was held in France, and once on the shores of America, eleven ships fired a 15-gun salute as Jones' body sailed up the Chesapeake. The body was taken to Annapolis for a proper burial at the United States Naval Academy, a commemoration held on April 24, 1906 (the anniversary of Jones' capture of the Drake in 1778 off Carrickfergus). General Porter remembered Jones' massive courage in a commemoration address, stating:

> Paul Jones never sailed in a man-of-war whose quarter-deck was worthy of being trodden by his feet. His battles were won not by his ships, but by his genius. Employing the feeble vessels given him or which he himself procured, he sailed forth boldly to strike the enemies of his country's liberty wherever he could find them and paused not till he dipped the fringes of his banners in the home waters of the mistress of the seas. He captured some sixty vessels from the foremost of naval powers, made four bold descents upon the land, seized large quantities of arms and military stores, destroyed more than a million dollars' worth of property on the sea, and took hundreds of prisoners whose capture was used to force an exchange and release our men, who were being slowly tortured to death in the loathsome, pestilential prison hulks in Brooklyn.... He was the very personification of valor. He ranked courage of the manliest of human attributes. He loved brave men; he loathed cowards. He believed that there was scarcely a sin for which courage could not atone. He showed this trait in all the aphorisms he uttered, such as: "Boldness, not caution, wins"; "Men mean more than guns in the rating of ships"; "I am not calculating risks, but estimating the chances of success"; "The sources of success are quick resolve and swift stroke"; "Bravery is that cheerful kind of spirit that makes a man unable to believe that there is any such word as danger in the dictionary, or, if so, not able to see why it should be there." As long as manly courage is talked of or heroic deeds are honored there will remain green in the hearts of brave men the talismanic name of Paul Jones [Porter, 29].

Assuredly, John Paul Jones' spirit could not be locked inside a garden gate, extinguished by imprisonment, blasted away by grapeshot, or severed at the hand of bodily demise. It continues to sail atop the waves, creating foam which lands, sometimes firmly, sometimes ever so softly, on shore, known as: universal human rights.

John Paul Jones Monument, Washington, D.C. (D. E. Baird).

Memorials

The John Paul Jones Memorial is located in West Potomac Park in Washington, D.C., dedicated on April 17, 1912. On each side of the monument, water flows from the mouth of a fish into a small pool. On the reverse side of the monument, Jones is seen hoisting the flag on the *Bonhomme Richard*. The statue is listed on the National Register of Historic Places as part of the American Revolution statuary group.

A bronze statue stands in the Garden of the Heroes in the west side of the Philadelphia, Pennsylvania, art museum.

The state of Maine instituted the John Paul Jones Memorial Park in Kittery, Maine, on May 31, 1926, a site now listed on the National Register of Historic Places. The site of the park commemorates the nearby site where in 1777 the *Ranger* was built and launched.

John Paul Jones is now buried inside the Chapel of the United States Naval Academy. A magnificent crypt, reminiscent to that of Napoleon's, distinguishes his grave site. The crypt is shaped in the form of a ship with seaweed entwined thereon, dolphins guiding the ship on each side. The crypt is surrounded by plaques, famous sculptor Houdon's bust, and John Paul Jones memorabilia. A plaque with comments from President Theodore Roosevelt reads:

> **John Paul Jones**
> 1747–1792
>
> Fearless in battle, and successful in keeping a large portion of the Royal Navy from our shores during our revolution, Jones also urged the establishment of navy officer schooling ashore. He gave our Navy its earliest traditions of Heroism and Victory.
>
> * * * * *
>
> "Every officer in our Navy should know by heart the deeds of John Paul Jones. Every officer in our Navy should feel in each fiber of his being the eager desire to emulate the energy, the professional capacity, the indominitable determination and dauntless scorn of death which marked John Paul Jones above all his fellows."
>
> President Theodore Roosevelt

A memorial plaque is on the last residence of John Paul Jones in Paris, France, and reads:

> "I have not yet begun to fight."
>
> John Paul Jones
>
> Capitain de Vaisseau
> de la Marine des Etats Unis.
>
> Chevalier de L'ordre
> du Mérite Militaire
> L'un des heros de la Guerre
> de L'independance Americaine
>
> Est mort dans cette maison
> le 18 Juillet 1792

The two-roomed cottage where John Paul Jones was born in Arbigland, Scotland, is now a tourist attraction. The John Paul Jones museum is also located on the property. A rose garden is near the museum, in honor of Jones' father.

The JOHN PAUL JONES HOUSE (private), at the corner of Lafayette Blvd. and Caroline St. in Fredricksburg, Virginia, a small half-brick, half-frame structure, is the only house in America the naval hero called home. It was owned by his older brother, William Paul, who conducted a tailoring business after migrating from Scotland in 1758.

8

THE VERSATILE, YET FORGOTTEN, GEORGE FARRAGUT

I recollect well that the cavalry was twice, during the action, between our army and the enemy.—Major Thomas Young, Battle of Cowpens, 1781

Specialization in a certain area of warfare was the gift of many of the heroes of the American Revolution, but the genius of Spanish-American George Farragut no doubt rested in his versatility. A seaman, guerrilla, artilleryman, and cavalry officer, he may be considered "the most versatile hero of the Revolution" (Munro, 12). Described by George Servier, son to John, as "a short, chunky man; very brave and a funny genius," Farragut sailed for the Carolinas in March 1776, loaded with cannons, muskets, powder, shot and ball for the rebelling colonies. He commanded a gun battery during the siege of Charleston, burning "as much powder and with as much annoyance to the enemy as any one officer in the American Army" (qtd. in Munro, 12). He helped to annihilate "Bloody Tarleton's" unit and even engaged in hand-to-hand combat with the ruthless British commander during the Southern campaign. His cavalry unit snarled, nipped, and bit at the heels of Cornwallis' rear flanks as he moved through the Carolinas, instituting a type of guerrilla (Spanish for "little war") warfare. No doubt George, or Jorge in his native land, fighting throughout the South during the American Revolution, lived up to the name of his thirteenth-century Spanish ancestor, Don Pedro Farragut (or Ferragut), styled *El Conquistador*, or "The Conqueror," "a renowned warrior in the service of King James I of Aragon when that Monarch expelled the Moors from Majorca and Valencia" (Haywood, 91). And, due to his service, offered to that victorious cause which advocated the advancement of human liberty and justice, he also lived up to the enunciation of his surname, pronounced "Farragood."

Born Don Jorge Ferragut Mesqueda (his baptismal, Anglicized name being George Anthony Magin) on September 29, 1755, to Antonio Ferragut and Juana Mesqueda on the Spanish island of Minorca in the township of Ciutadella, George, upon his birth, though a full-blooded Spaniard, was a French citizen, for the French seized the island in the self-same year. Most likely educated in Barcelona, it may be that he "gained some knowledge of English while there; for, after coming to America, he showed himself quite proficient in the language of his adopted country" (Haywood, 91). However, as mentioned, in all likelihood, he was trained in the way of a warrior as well. One visitor to the island at that time noted: "To make their sons good marksmen, it was a custom of parents to hang the breakfast upon boughs of lofty trees, to remain there until brought down by the boys with a sling. The strong arms of manhood, thus trained, would hurl with tremendous power the 'smooth stones.' When the warriors went into battle, a sling was suspended from the neck, another from the waist, and a third carried in the hand for immediate use" (Headley, 17–8).

George most likely also learned other lessons about the perils of inequity and injustice, witnessing some of the extreme poverty belaying the isolated island. One account from an American midshipman in the early 1800s reads: "One of the most striking contrasts Minorca presents is its extreme poverty. Proofs of this meet you on all hands, and in every shape. You see them in the number of mendicants that crowd the street, in the modes to which many of the inhabitants resort to obtain sustenance, in the fare to which they are obliged to submit, and in the low prices affixed to manual labor and domestic services" (Headley, 14–5). By his own account, George began sea travel at the age of ten, doubtless working from time to time aboard a merchant ship. As a young adult, he joined the merchant marines and came to command a vessel which traded goods between Veracruz, Mexico, New Orleans, Havana, and other Caribbean ports. Apparently, for a time he also "served aboard a fireship in the Russian Navy, fighting against the Turks at the battle of Chesna in July 1770" (Babits 64).

George Farragut, from the portrait attributed to William Swain (1803–1857).

Following the end of the Seven Years' War in 1763 (known in the United States as the French-Indian War), Farragut's birth island reverted to British rule. As Munro notes, "Farragut's antipathy toward the British for their long occupation of Minorca probably made him receptive to the new political ideas to which he was exposed in North America" (12). Mahan believes: "Having grown to manhood a subject to Great Britain, but alien in race and feeling, he naturally espoused the cause of the colonists, and served gallantly in the war" (1). Farragut immigrated to America in 1776, probably at the urging of his friend, Fernando Leigh of Norfolk, Virginia, whose father, Colonel William Leigh, had served in the Spanish cavalry at an early age and later settled in Sussex County, Virginia, as a planter. While a sea captain, Farragut most likely brought Spanish wines and other sundries to his Virginia friends, who in turn gave him an "entrée into social circles in the southern colonies" (Munro, 12). Thus, upon sailing into the then–Spanish-owned port of New Orleans in 1775, the news of Concord and Lexington upon every tongue, Farragut changed his course in life, forfeiting the money he was no doubt earning as captain of a merchant ship. He set sail for Port-au-Prince, Saint-Domingue (now Haiti) with a cargo of merchandise he planned to exchange for weaponry and ammunition. The exchange occurred, and Farragut set sail for the Carolinas, landing in Charleston in March 1776, "laden with arms for the rebelling colonists" (Munro, 12).

Upon arrival, Farragut volunteered to serve as an officer on a rebel privateering vessel with twelve guns, then as a lieutenant in the South Carolina Navy where he supervised shipbuilding for the colony and helped in the defense of Savannah. When the British occupied Savannah in December 1778, Farragut escaped to Charleston and continued to fight at sea under Commodore Abraham Whipple. On January 27, 1780, the commissioners of the South Carolina Navy appointed Farragut to command the *Revenge,* a prize claimed by Thomas Pickering and converted to a galley with two carriage guns (probably 6-pounders), and eight or ten swivels. Farragut was to ready the *Revenge* for sea and "enlist the usual complement of officers, plus forty seamen, including blacks. He was allowed to offer a one hundred dollar bounty to new recruits" (Sayen 233). The *Revenge* was then ordered to Georgetown.

As Sayen notes, "Whipple proved an unfortunate choice as naval commander" (234). Though it took the British sixteen days to get their ships across Charleston Bar, for they had to unload guns and stores before crossing, Whipple did not play the part of the aggressor, but instead sequestered all of South Carolina Navy's ships (*Carolina, South Edisto, Marquis de Bretagne, Lee, Revenge*) between Charleston's Neck and Shute's Folly to form a type of boom to block passage. Nevertheless, the British were still able to move gunboats overland, across Stono, through Wappoo Creek and across the Ashley to "invest the City and compel its surrender along with nearly 7,000 soldiers and sailors, all the remaining ships and all the galleys. It was a tragedy that the galleys and the other vessels of the South Carolina Navy, which could have done so much for the defense of their state, ended up by doing so little" (Sayen, 235).

The British also seized Georgetown, and most likely the remaining ships, yet Farragut "managed to take his galley so far up the Sampit River and to conceal her so well, that she was never discovered by the British or Loyalists and survived to be recommissioned in South Carolina service under Captain Jacob Milligan on May 27, 1782. She operated out of Georgetown until March 15, 1783, when she was decommissioned with the end of the war" (Sayen, 235).

Having escaped the British, this time, and forced once more back onto shore, Farragut commanded a gun battery, hence his comment about burning enormous amounts of powder. During this service, on May 20, 1780, Major Benjamin Lincoln, leading Farragut's unit, was forced to surrender to Lord Cornwallis, Lieutenant General Charles, and Lieutenant General Henry Clinton, these British officers having earlier led "a 90 ship invasion force carrying 8,500 soldiers and 5,000 soldiers and marines" (Munro, 12) toward Charleston Harbor. The forces surrendered, the city came under seize, and Farragut became a prisoner of war. Thanks to his friendship with wealthy Spanish merchant Juan de Miralles, a prisoner exchange occurred and Farragut regained his freedom. Sailing from Philadelphia, Farragut again commanded a privateer vessel, and, meeting a much heavier armed British man-o'-war, during the engagement received a musket ball to his right arm. Thankfully, the ship's surgeon saved the limb.

After healing from his wound, Farragut turned again to land, revealing another talent, skill with horses. He joined the North Carolina Cavalry (State Legion of Mounted Rangers) as a Trooper of 100 men under General Nathanael Greene and Captain Daniel Morgan. Haywood notes: "This organization of light horsemen was largely entrusted with guarding the western settlements, and much of its warfare was waged against the Indians and their Tory instigators in that section of North Carolina which is now the State of Tennessee" (92). At the Battle of Cowpens, January 17, 1781, he saved the life of his immediate commander, Lieutenant William Washington. During this particular battle, Lieutenant Colonel Banastre "Bloody" Tarleton pursued Morgan's column, including Farragut's cavalry unit. Greene placed his militia at the lead to fire two volleys, saving the more highly trained Continental Army to deliver a deadly volley upon Tarleton's advancing troops. The cavalry, at the same time, skirted the edges of Tarleton's back right troops, while the militia returned to rake the left back. Major Thomas Young's memoir relates: "After the first fire, the militia retreated, and the cavalry covered their retreat. They were again formed and renewed the attack, and we retired to the rear. They fought some time, and retreated again and then formed a second time. In this I can hardly be mistaken, for I recollect well that the cavalry was twice, during the action, between our army and the enemy" (qtd. in Southern, 183). During the ensuing scrimmages, Farragut "saved Washington's life during a desperate hand-to-hand encounter with Tarleton. Tarleton, himself wounded, escaped with a mere 10 percent of his men. The once-elite Tarleton's Legion had been effectively annihilated" (Munro, 14).

North Carolina Governor Abner Nash subsequently appointed Farragut to command an artillery detachment, yet another mode of military service. Fighting in a fray at Beaufort Bridge, the artillery proved cumbersome and vulnerable in the Carolina backwoods; thus Nash allowed Farragut to recruit, organize, and command a group of cavalry men, and when "Cornwallis moved through the Carolinas in 1781, he found both Farragut and Colonel Francis Marion's mounted guerrillas harrying his rear and flanks" (Munro, 14). Note: As a result of the Spanish support of the American Revolution, a Franco-Spanish expeditionary force landed on Minorca on February 5, 1782, and returned the island to Spanish rule.

Farragut was promoted to captain in May 1782, the state of North Carolina resolving "that Captain George Farragut, of the State Legion, be allowed three hundred dollars in full for six months' pay and subsistence money, which shall be received in the sales of confiscated property as gold and silver, and any Commissioner may be allowed the same in the settlement of accounts" (Haywood, 92). Three years after the war the North Carolina Senate styled him "Mr. George Farragut, late a Captain in the State Calvary of the State of North Carolina," resolving "that this General Assembly are led to adopt this measure from conviction of the faithful, voluntary, and public-spirited services of the said Mr. Farragut, he being a native and subject of the Kingdom of France" (Haywood, 93).

Unfortunately, at the close of the war, Farragut, who had given up the life of a privateer, was left "poor and penniless." He did, however, recover financially, to an extent, first serving as major of a militia cavalry unit fighting off Indian raids in Eastern Tennessee, marrying Elizabeth Shine from North Carolina, "a cool headed, hard-working, and courageous Irish American woman of 30" (Munro, 15), and eventually moving his family to Mississippi, where he served as sailing master on the Mississippi River for the United States Navy. He also fathered Admiral David Farragut, who became the Navy's first admiral, serving the Union during the Civil War. As Munro writes: "The Spanish have a saying, '*De tal palo tal astilla*,'— from a tree such as George Farragut, one could expect a splendid splinter.... George Farragut ... never abandoned the flag of his adopted country — and neither did David Glasgow

Farragut when Tennessee and Louisiana seceded from the Union in 1861, despite his mother's and his wife's Southern connections" (15).

Despite all these sacrifices and military accomplishments, little has been written about George's life, though much about the life of his son, David. Truthfully, the obscurity surrounding George's name is inconceivable based upon his willingness to serve America's revolutionary cause in multitudinous life-threatening capacities. For a conqueror whose warrior spirit backed America's conquest of tyranny, our country's abandonment of tribute needs now to be remedied!

9

CHARTING HIS OWN COURSE
The Life of Pierce Butler

In private, as in Publick life, the freedom and prosperity of the United States will always be near and dear to me. — Founding Father Pierce Butler

Considered a founding father, Pierce Butler, a major in the South Carolina militia, delegate to the Continental Congress, delegate to the Constitutional Convention, and U.S. Senator, was, ironically, "the youngest captain in his Majesty's 29th Regiment" (qtd. in Bell, 1) at the age of twenty-one. Initially serving in Halifax, Nova Scotia, defending Britain in the French-Indian War, he was sent to Philadelphia to determine how best to fortify that city in association with the unrest created by the Stamp Act. A trip to Charlestown (Charleston), South Carolina, changed his mind, for that city carried the same degree of unrest, opportunities for status and success which would never befall a third-born child in British society (based upon primogeniture), and an opportunity "for the first time to chart his own course, independent of his family's expectations" (Lipscomb, xvi). Making a three hundred and sixty-degree turn, Pierce wrote, "No Man on Earth has the *Cause* more at heart, or wishes more ardently to Serve it than I do" (qtd. in Lipscomb, xvii). No doubt his decision rested in the heart, for joining the Patriot cause placed Butler's very life, as well as his newly found economic success, in jeopardy. Resigning in 1773 from the British army, selling his commission, Butler became a hunted man, the British especially wishing to make an example of this "prominent rebel." He "escaped being taken prisoner by a British column by only the narrowest of margins" (Lipscomb, xiv) and endured British looting of his properties. As Lipscomb notes, "As a former British officer and high-profile patriot, he was a special object of British resentment, and it is reasonable to assume that General Provost's troops wreaked havoc on the Butler properties in May 1779 during their feint against Charleston. The financial impact plagued Butler for years afterward, and it was the ultimate cause of the money worries that fill much of his correspondence during the 1790s" (xix).

Pierce was born in County Carlow (Garryhunden), Ireland, on July 11, 1744, to a prominent family, his father, Sir Richard Butler being a baronet and a member of the Irish Parliament, his mother, Lady Henrietta Percy. His family claimed descent from the Butler family which produced the Ormondes, and his mother's father was mayor of Dublin; thus Pierce carried pride in name. His aptitude in forming a new government came naturally, as his "family tree was well stocked with legislators and politicians. Between 1692 and 1800, five baronets in succession — his great-grandfather, his great-uncle, his father, his brother, and his nephew — represented county Carlow in the Irish Parliament, and his Percy great-grandfather had been the lord mayor of Dublin" (Lipscomb, xv). No doubt he understood the need for a change in political systems within the Colonies, for "during the eighteenth century the government of Ireland was characterized by political corruption, religious intolerance, economic oppression of the tenant class, and the presence of a standing army that was characterized in 1798 by its own commander in chief as 'formidable to everyone but the enemy'" (Lipscomb, xv). And "his mature judgment of his native country's shortcomings — perhaps formed after years of life abroad — affected his vision of the government he wanted for his adopted country" (Lipscomb, xv).

Though he had the aptitude in his blood, the family did not direct Pierce toward a career in government, as he was the third son. Titles, Estates, and Seats were reserved for the eldest son. Many times sons other than the eldest were directed toward a career in the military, and commissions were not directly associated with education, but were instead purchased by prominent families. Pierce's commission was arranged at the age of eleven, and by the age of fourteen he was serving as a lieutenant for his Majesty's army in Nova Scotia, Canada, engaged in combat against the French, and wounded in action.

Due to his aristocratic birth, Butler would have enjoyed an excellent basic education, but was apparently a self-learner as well, as evidenced by references to ancient and modern authors and scholars within his letters and speeches. Winters in Canada during his service as a teen also lent free reading time, and "perhaps his political thought began to take a progressive turn during the long stretches of his youth spent at Canadian army posts, where except for hunting and fishing he would have had little to occupy his free time other than reading books, pamphlets, and newspapers. The printed page could have become a ready source of the ideas that later turned the soldier into a nation builder and senator. It could also explain a predisposition toward radical politics that his family in Ireland did not share" (Lipscomb, xvi).

In 1767 at the age of twenty-three, Butler traveled to Charlestown (Charleston), South Carolina, with a detachment of his regiment, the town he would embrace as his new home, and in which he would garner a new family. He found Charleston a "sophisticated low country outpost in marked contrast to the cold Nova Scotia he had left" (Bell, 2). Charleston in turn appreciated Butler's Irish wit, elegance, and determination, as he made quite an impression and wooed many feminine hearts. When he returned to his regiment, which had moved to Boston, the streets were steeped in revolution. Butler actually witnessed the Boston Massacre, the soldiers involved in the skirmish being members of the 29th Regiment, but was not one of the British officers who fired on the Boston crowd. To ease ill will, the 29th was sent to New Jersey.

Butler, again, took leave to Charleston where he met his soon-to-be wife, Mary Bull Middleton (the Bull family having produced two royal governors), an heiress to three plantations (Toogoodoo, Bull's Island, and Hilton Head), whose father and brother had just died, leaving the estate in a state of disarray. Butler and Mary's remaining brothers were asked to manage the affairs of the diverse lands, and Bell writes, "His forthright manner and his ability and readiness to take command were qualities sorely needed to bring order to the chaos of the estates of Mary Butler's father and brother. Pierce embraced this administration (purchasing 9,000 acres in South Carolina between 1772 and 1786), and quickly began the management of the diverse properties inherited from Mary Bull" (18). Pierce must have been incensed when he heard that, due to his already having received a commission, an eleven-year-old brother would inherit the seat in Irish Parliament after his father and two elder brothers passed away in 1772, for "the Butlers were conspicuous for high and independent feelings, united with a chivalric contempt for danger" (Bell, 2). However, in marrying Mary Middleton, he had found the life and inheritance denied to him in Ireland as a result of his birth order: land, money, and even romance. He became quite a successful land speculator, and was also surrounded by other "prominent rebels," as Mary's cousins were married to Charles Pinckney and Edward Rutledge (who signed the Declaration of Independence).

Accordingly, he resigned his commission in 1773, sold it, purchased seventeen hundred acres on St. Simons Island in Georgia to add to the marital holdings, and "became caught up in the American Revolution on the patriot side" (Lipscomb, xvi). He abandoned the "grace and favor" of the Crown and denied "King and Country" to join his newfound family in the cause of liberty and freedom. Pierce apparently also forfeited a merchant schooner, offering it to the colony, as early as 1775. In a letter of March 21, 1776, to another of Mary's cousins, Arthur Middleton, a patriot from the low country who would sign the Declaration in a few months, Butler strategized the necessary enforcement: "Unless we have an *immediate* reinforcement from the Nor'd, and a proper military establishment here, these Colonies are lost" (Bell, 26). Further, in the letter, Pierce "called for a standing Army of no less than five thousand men to protect the Carolinas and Georgia from the British and asked Arthur Middleton to prevail upon the Congress to have General Charles Lee come down and take charge" (Bell, 26).

Butler cared for his plantations, served as justice of the peace, and was a member of the South Carolina House of Representatives (1776–77) prior to Britain's decision to turn the War southward. Note: Historical records of South Carolina's General Assembly during this period (journals or rollcalls) have not been found, and the newspapers reported few legislative debates prior to 1780. However, in all likelihood, Pierce helped to create South Carolina's constitution, drafted not by a convention but by the Assembly. The constitution also addressed (and addresses) "matters that were dear to Butler's heart: separation of church and state through disestablishment of the Anglican Church (which his hatred of the Irish tithe system would have led him to support),

Founding Father and Constitutional Framer Pierce Butler.

prohibition of dual office holding and the political corruption it invited, and broadening the political base of government through measures such as the popular election of senators" (Lipscomb, xx).

Upon the War's return to the South, "several gentlemen" asked Butler to serve as South Carolina's first state adjutant general (the same as a brigadier general), and he was named to the post on February 17, 1779. Within a month, Butler and his cousin-in-law John Rutledge had inspected South Carolina's interior militia, conferring with Continental Army General Benjamin Lincoln on March 18 in Purrysburg. Butler's role as brigadier general was varying, and he performed "an exemplary job of mobilizing and inspiring the troops, collecting intelligence, handling refugees, and even on occasion commanding troops in the field. During Gen. Augustine Prevosts's raid in May 1779, Butler took 130 horses, reinforced Gen. William Moultrie's army, and defeated a foraging party of the Seventy-first Regiment sixteen miles south of Parker's Ferry. At some point in 1779, he paid a personal visit to George Washington's encampment in New Jersey, where he met Nathanael Greene, later commander of the Southern Army, and presumably conferred with the Continental high command" (Lipscomb, xviii). Note: Prevost was a British officer who conducted a cattle raid upon the Georgia Sea Islands and marched on Charleston. During the march, Butler organized "harrying attacks on the enemy's columns" (Coghlan, 108).

Of course, Butler was highly concerned about his family while away, writing General Benjamin Lincoln on May 3:

> Believe me dear Sir that new terms of expression are yet to be found to make known my Distress on account of my Family. I heard they had set out by Water some days ago for Charles Town. They must then have either fallen into the hands of the Enemy or in the Arms of the Deep — All my hopes and Happiness in life centered on them. If they are gone there is no happiness left in me in this world. Nothing to wish for so much as Death. I entreat you to ask Captain Morgan to go in an armed boat in Search of them [qtd. in Bell, 29].

In the self-same letter, Butler told General Lincoln of intelligence gathered from a British prisoner by means of a "pistol at his temple," who then revealed the size and forces of Prevost's British forces. He ended by adding, "I wish I was possessed of Powers Sufficient to enable me to be more serviceable to a Country that is Dearer to me than the one I first breathed in" (qtd. in Bell, 29).

As previously mentioned, the British specifically targeted Butler and his plantations (even his primary residence, Eutaw Plantation), looting and burning many of his properties, absconding with the rich household furnishings the Butlers had moved to a country storehouse, confiscating 200 of his slaves, and sinking his ships. The Butlers' financial empire was disrupted to the point that Pierce had to sell three hundred head of cattle for living expenses. Most alarmingly, "like other high-level government officials, Major Butler left Charleston before its surrender, but as the trap closed around the city in mid–April, he escaped being taken prisoner by a British column by only the narrowest of margins. He disappeared into the swamps on the eastern branch of Cooper River and made his way to North Carolina" (Lipscomb, xix). (Butler was in fact up-country in an attempt to recruit militia at the time of the surrender.) Butler's family remained trapped in Charleston until the fall of 1781, negotiations with the British for their safe delivery completed by General Nathanael Greene, at Butler's request. The family was not reunited until December 1781. During Butler's absence, his three-year-old son died in an accident associated with fire, the details of which remain lost to history. However, Butler himself blamed his son's death on the British, writing to his friend James Iredell in North Carolina, "But all of this and more

I could bear without a Sigh were it possible to have restored to me my Favourite Son, the Promising Prop of my latter days, that they wantonly robbed me of" (Bell, 30). For protection, while in North Carolina, Butler attached himself to General Gates' army, commanding a group of men guarding British prisoners at Salisbury for the remainder of 1780 and most of 1781.

When reunited with his family, he left for Philadelphia, where, at that point, according to Butler, "trade flourishes and plenty abounds, the war is not felt here, while the Carolinas groan under the weight and miseries of it" (qtd. in Bell, 38). From Philadelphia, as the war ended, Butler also wrote, "Thank God it is not in the powers of any one man to involve us in the horrors of war.... I have suffered so greatly by war that I shall for the rest of my days pray for Peace on Earth" (Bell, 41). He wrote of the Dutch desire to enter war with Austria in 1784, "I am sure if they had drunk as deep of the bitter cup as some Americans have, they would use every effort to avoid it. When they beheld their wives and children, that were used to live not only in affluence but luxury, turned out of their comfortable habitations! And without one provision as was the case of many of the first families in America, they will wish that they had been wise before it was too late" (qtd. in Coghlan, 110).

After the War, the Butlers returned to Charleston, and Pierce returned to work on his plantations, also traveling to England to (1) obtain an appropriate minister for St. Michael's, the church of which he was a member, and to recast the bell for the church, confiscated by the British; (2) find educational placements for his children; and (3) secure a loan on which to rebuild his plantation and build a new home. When he returned to America, the South Carolina General Assembly both appointed Butler to a commission which determined the border between South Carolina and Georgia (the Treaty of Beaufort) and as a delegate to the Constitutional Convention in Philadelphia, "this honor conferred upon him as a feeble testimony of the gratitude and high opinion of his countrymen for his Revolutionary services" (qtd. in Lipscomb, xxii), according to a Charleston newspaper. First, however, the Assembly offered him the South Carolina governor's office, a position he declined. Butler felt an obligation to accept the offer to attend the Convention, nevertheless, for he favored "forming a more Energetick federal Government," for the purpose of settling interstate disputes, developing a strong military, and fostering a staunch financial solidity, contributing to safe trade and respectful negotiating powers between nations. Apparently, by the time of the convention, Butler had healed many of the emotional and financial wounds incurred in the War and was described as "enthusiastic, enterprising, gallant & resolute. Of a tall and well proportioned frame, dignified carriage & deportment, accompanied with courtesy of manners, the result of much travel and military habits" (qtd. in Lipscomb, xxii). A source during the meetings at Philadelphia reported that Butler "wore a powdered wig, a handsome stock, gold lace on his coat" (qtd. in Lipscomb, xviii), a stock being a military officer's neck cloth of silk or velvet with a silver buckle. A fellow delegate from Georgia, William Pierce, noted, "Mr. Butler is a character much respected for the many excellent virtues which he possesses.... He is a gentleman of fortune, and takes rank among the first in South Carolina" (qtd. in Lipscomb, xviii).

It seems that Butler used the "high Irish style of parliamentary rhetoric ... a language of baroque metaphor and personification, punctuated by brutal rejoinders" (qtd. in Lipscomb, xxvii) during his speeches at the Convention, making his presence known frequently and being described by Clinton Rossiter, who classified the delegates at the Convention, as one of the "Very Usefuls." And, while fifty-five delegates attended and participated in the Convention, only thirty-nine actually signed the Constitution, Butler being one of the thirty-nine. Note: Humorously, Butler was the only framer who doodled in a notebook during the Convention, and actually drew cartoons of the other delegates as they spoke.

Butler's contributions to our Constitution were varied. First, he rebuked the opinion of James Madison and his followers regarding the issue of dual office-holding (Madison believing it would improve the talent pool). Butler argued, "We have no way of judging mankind but by experience. Look at the history of the government of Great Britain, where there is a very flimsy exclusion — Does it not ruin their government? A man takes a seat in parliament to get an office for himself or friends, or both; and this is the great source from which flows its great venality and corruption" (qtd. in Lipscomb, xxv). Of course, Butler was also pondering the corruption apparent in his country of birth, where Crown office-holders in the Parliament perpetuated Britain's control of Ireland.

Second, Pierce contributed to the delegates' decision associated with qualifications for U.S. Senators, to include residency requirements, using his own situation as an example. The collected Convention records include:

> Mr. Butler was decidedly opposed to the admission of foreigners without a long residence in the Country. They bring with them, not only attachments to other Countries; but ideas of Government so distinct from ours that in every point of view they are dangerous. He acknowledged that if he himself had been called into public life within a short time after his coming to America, his foreign habits, opinions, and attachments would have rendered him an improper agent in public affairs. He mentioned the great strictness observed in Great Britain on this subject [qtd. in Lipscomb, xxv].

To Butler's satisfaction, the residency and citizenship requirements for the House of Representatives became seven years, and for the Senate, nine years. The President of the United States, of course, had to be "a natural born citizen." The Convention delegates robustly debated the position of the executive in an attempt to prevent any sort of monarchy. According to Ulmer, "Butler's fear of executive abuse is almost pathological and is reflected in virtually all his comments on the chief magistrate" (Ulmer, 363), and he was "extremely 'power conscious' throughout the Convention" (Ulmer, 364). He did not want the Executive to have veto power or the power to make peace treaties, writing:

> The President of the United States is the Supreme Executive Officer. He has no separate legislative power whatever. He can't prevent a Bill from passing into a law. In making Treaties, two-thirds of the Senate must concur. In the appointment of Ambassadors, Judges of the Supreme Court, & ca., He must have the concurrence of the Senate. He is responsible to His Constituents for the use of his power. He is Impeachable.... Yet, after all, My Dear Sir, I am free to acknowledge that His powers are full great, and greater than I was disposed to make them. Nor, Entre Nous, do I believe they would have been so great had not many of the members cast their eyes toward General Washington as President; and shaped their Ideas of the Power to be given to a President, by their opinions of his Virtue. So that the Man, by his Patriotism and Virtue, Contributed largely to the Emancipation of his country, may be the Innocent means of its being, when He is lay'd low, oppressed [qtd. in Ulmer, 367].

Butler in fact argued for a "plural executive" of three or more, and he intimated: "I think by being in Publick life I have acquired a more intimate Knowledge of Man than I should otherwise have had. I wish I could say that my respect had increased with my Knowledge of him" (qtd. in Ulmer, 370). Despite Butler's contentions, one executive prevailed in convention.

Thus, the question of electing this one executive became the argument. Butler authored the Electoral College constitutional mandate (Article II, Section I) from decisions made in

Site of the Constitutional Convention as attended by Pierce Butler, the Pennsylvania State House, Independence Hall, Philadelphia (author's photograph).

a committee of eleven. In a letter to Weedon Butler of May 5, 1788, Pierce indicated "I had the honor of proposing in the Committee ... the mode" of the executive's "Election" (qtd. in Ulmer, 363). To understand how difficult a consensus in association with this "mode" proved to be, consider the fact that "election by electors chosen by and from the national legislature was favored at one time by Daniel Carroll of Maryland. At another point election by the people was supported by Carroll, Morris, Williamson, and Madison. Choice of a president by electors chosen by the people was preferred at one time by Carroll, Morris, King, and Madison. At other points, Dickinson, Williamson, Sherman, and Brearly spoke out for election by the national legislature. One member of the Committee, Nicholas Gilman of New Hampshire, expressed no view of any kind in the Convention" (Ulmer, 365). As originally worded, the electors were determined by the state legislators, Butler seeing this language as "an alternative to putting the election in the hands of either Congress or the people" (Lipscomb, xxv). He noted, "The two great evils to be avoided are cabal at home, & influence from abroad. It will be difficult to avoid either if the Election be made by the Natl Legislature. On the other hand, the Govt. should not be made so complex & unwieldy as to disgust the States. This would be the case, if the election should be referred to the people. He liked best an election by Electors chosen by the Legislatures of the States" (qtd. in Lipscomb, xxv). Notably, Butler's reason for fear of a congressional election was the fact that South Carolina's General Assembly was most frequently lobbied by British interests. Butler was determined the British Crown would have no say in the election of the President of the United States.

Late in these meetings, Butler's idea caught fire, described by Abraham Baldwin of Georgia as "perfectly novel, and therefore occasioned a pause; but when explained and fully considered was universally admired, and viewed as the most pleasing feature in the Constitution" (qtd. in Lipscomb, xxvi). As a senator from South Carolina in the First, Second, and Third Congress, Butler defended the electoral system as originally written, vehemently objecting the eventual amendment and countering with the draft of an amendment which would limit presidential terms (a modified version later ratified as the Twenty-second Amendment). His campaign against the Twelfth Amendment failed, but his final speech associated therewith still carries a degree of truth: "Pass this amendment, and no man can live in the small States but under disparaging circumstances; they will have about as many rights left in society as the Helots of Greece. And why is all this done? For the purpose of showing one of the least becoming of the weak passions of man, resentment, you pursue a line of conduct reprobated by yourselves in the time of your predecessors" (qtd. in Lipscomb, xxxv).

Other major legacies associated with Butler's terms in the Senate include introduction of the bill which moved the capital to Washington, D.C., introduction of the resolution which eventually required Senate sessions to be made public (instead of being held in secrecy, such as was the case until 1796), and a consistent and "flaming" opposition to the creation of a federal district court system (which he believed was a threat to state sovereignty). While he was in office, French diplomats considered Butler a reliable ally. And, finally, Butler condemned the Whiskey Rebellion of 1794, attributing the act to "a few bad men who wished to proceed to extremities at Once and to draw the Sword of Civil discord for a small aggression against a handful of men not sensible of doing wrong. May such unfeeling blood thirsty Scoundrels be banished from Society!" (qtd. in Coghlan, 118).

Though now haunted by his political positions regarding slavery and his use of the institution to advance the economic standing of his plantations, Butler, a victim of the economic realities of the time, would write in 1788: "If America should be the means of opening the eyes of the Enslaved, so as to make them cast off their Chains, I shall be better reconciled

The room in which Pierce Butler introduced and debated the U.S. electoral system, the Pennsylvania State House, Independence Hall, Philadelphia (author's photograph).

to my sufferings and losses. You may naturally ask me Why, with these sentiments, do you hold so many in Bondage? I answer You, that I would free every one of them tomorrow if I could. That is if the Legislature would permit it. I ardently wish that I never had anything to do with such property" (qtd. in Bell, 48). It does seem that Butler continued to gravitate more and more in his political beliefs to one who advocated for *all* who are oppressed, not only American patriots, but also Loyalists who were mistreated following the Revolution and backcountry South Carolinians, whose grievances were noted by Butler (in this regard he misaligned himself with the Charleston establishment). Lipscomb notes, "Probably, he had always sympathized with backcountry interest, but by the late 1780s his commitment to reform was becoming evident through his support for moving the state capital inland, debtor relief, and reapportionment" (xxi), considered a blow to the political power of the planters or merchants of the low country. As Ulmer notes, "Butler was more favorably inclined toward the South Carolina aristocracy prior to 1787 and less favorably inclined toward it subsequent to 1793 (373). In fact, in 1794, C. C. Pinckney penned, the "upper country had already their Senator, as Major Butler looks upon himself to be of that part of the State" (qtd. in Ulmer, 373). Coghlan continues, "Major Butler's aristocratic attitudes were firmly mixed with a genuine attachment to democratic ideals" (118).

Assuredly, in his younger years Pierce Butler joined the revolutionary cause as a result of a denial of his right to self-determination and unlimited achievement. His life first ruled by the laws of Britain, his country of birth overrun with corruption and intolerance, Butler offered his life to a higher calling. As Lipscomb notes, "Anyone seeking to understand Pierce Butler cannot ignore his origins" (xv). Nonetheless, as a mature adult who had survived what he termed a "civil war," as well as many political and personal battles, Butler obviously turned his life lessons inward, not only attempting to improve his own morals, and acting upon the virtues for which he fought ("In private, as in Publick life, the freedom and prosperity of the United States will always be near and dear to me"), but also exemplifying for future Americans the manner in which our collective inner lives will be the foundation sustaining these freedoms: "I am free to confess, that after all our Endeavors, Our System is little better than Experiment; and that much must depend on the Morals and manners of the People at large" (qtd. in Ulmer, 374).

Memorials

Unfortunately, Butler's death attracted little attention in South Carolina newspapers, or elsewhere. By today's standards, he would have been afforded a state funeral.

Butler's tombstone lies in the historical Christ Church graveyard in Philadelphia, Pennsylvania (his last years were spent in Philadelphia near his daughter, who had married a doctor living in that city). Coghlan writes: "Although Major Butler's tombstone in Christ Church, Philadelphia, bears no epitaph, he would have gloried in one word, 'republican,' with the small *r*."

10

THADDEUS KOŚCIUSZKO
Prince of Tolerance

Bless, O God, my country, my relatives, my friends, my benefactors, my countrymen, the whole human race.—Thaddeus Kościuszko

Thaddeus Kościuszko. Engraving by H. B. Hall after Joseph Grassi (1822) (National Archives and Records Administration).

Many pictures of Polish military engineer for the American Revolution, Thaddeus Kościuszko, show him wearing a red four-cornered hat adorned with a bright feather. In the Polish "Krakowian" tradition, such a hat represents duty, honor, liberty, and freedom. If any historical personality exemplifies these virtues, it is Thaddeus Kościuszko. Referred to by his friend Thomas Jefferson as the "true son of liberty," Kościuszko's life was immersed in the pursuit of liberty, not just for Boston or Philadelphian merchants, but for all, for "his deep sense of respect extended to all races, religions, classes, genders, and nationalities.... He also spoke for peasants, Jews, American Indians, women, and everyone else who was being discriminated against" (Storozynski, xiii). Indeed, when he left a liberated America for the last time, having served as a military engineer and cavalry man for the Continental Army, contributing to the victory at Saratoga, fortifying West Point, and contributing to victory in the South,

Kościuszko willed his fortune to assist in the eradication of slavery, for as Lech Wałęsa remarked: "Kościuszko understood freedom as complete, not only from the outside oppressor, but also from internal tyranny" (qtd. in Pula, 13).

Kościuszko was born in the ancient land of Poland, tolerant and liberal up through and until the Russians invaded and eliminated the *Pacta Conventa* of 1574, in which "all Polish citizens were given the legal right to withdraw their allegiance from the king if he broke any law passed by parliament or the specific conditions of his election" (Pula, 19). Though Poland enjoyed the centuries-old historical tradition of ethnic and religious diversity and monarchial limitation, Russia tore the political gains of the country in two and, by 1746, the country "languished in a state of political decay" (Pula, 21). Into this environment Thaddeus was born (February 12, 1746), youngest child of four born to Ludwig Tadeusz and Tekla Ratomska Kościuszko. Thaddeus' family status was "minor," his father being a sword bearer, an honorary title given to local officials. The family was well-off, but not wealthy, maintaining an estate which sustained 31 different families in the province of Polesie (a small town called Mereczówszczyźna). Overseer of these families, Ludwig taught his children "that treating the peasants fairly and providing them with a greater share of the fruits of their labor would make them more productive. Ludwig was a loving husband, father, and landlord who believed that all people were entitled to hope and happiness" (Storozynski, 3). Thaddeus took this lesson to heart, playing with the children of the peasants and taking them to his favorite spot, a boulder from which he would observe the world below.

The Kościuszkos (pronounced *Kost-iuszko* and meaning "small bone") were part of the top ten percent of Polish society; however, the top one percent, land magnates who hired small armies to protect their wealth, allied themselves with the Russians, creating chaos and abolishing established political advancements. The rest of the nation suffered, even the ten percent mentioned, to include Thaddeus' family. Pursuant to custom, Thaddeus was educated at home for the first nine years of his life. His mother, Tekla, "a woman of character, energy, and some education" taught her children to respect learning and the history and culture of Poland, while Thaddeus' uncle introduced him to drawing, mathematics, and French. At the age of nine, he was sent to the Catholic Piarist Fathers College at Lubieszow, under the tutelage of Father Stanisław Konarski, who revolutionized and enlightened his curriculum with the teachings of John Locke. Introduced to the democracy of the Greeks and Romans, Thaddeus became engrossed with the biography of Timoleon, the Corinthian (Greek) statesman and general who freed his fellow countrymen and the Sicilians from the tyranny of Carthage, a "scenario the young Pole could not help but equate with the plight of Poland during his formative years" (Pula, 23). Kościuszko later lauded his hero: "He overthrew tyrants, set up republics and never demanded any power for himself" (Storozynski, 3). Of course he compared "Timoleon's Greece to Poland's subjugation by czarist Russia, whose army was growing more assertive in controlling Polish affairs. He saw in Timoleon a lesson in freeing his own people from Russian domination. Kościuszko realized early on that Europe's unjust class structure and agrarian economy allowed the rich to get richer by exploiting the peasants. To him the notion of happiness meant self-determination" (Storozynski 3).

When his father died in 1758, Thaddeus returned home for five years, continuing under his mother's instruction, who also relied, again, upon the uncle, as well as a nearby priest. At this point, Thaddeus excelled in geometry and art. He also assisted his mother in the work of the estate, helping her glean the most out of the plantation's many pursuits: "fruit orchards, vegetable gardens, wheat fields, bakery, brewery, malthouse, grain silos, dairy, cheese-making cribs, chicken coops, pigsties, and barns stocked with horses and cows" (Storozynski, 10). When Kościuszko was eighteen, one of Poland's princes, Czartoryski, initiated a Royal Knight School, a military academy and "school of patriotism" which "offered a general liberal education ... to educate a new corps of officers and produce enlightened public leaders" (Pula, 25). Recommended by the Czartoryski family and local gentry Józef Sosnowski, Kościuszko was admitted to the inaugural class to study English, history, philosophy, ethics, and mathematics, along with, most importantly, military engineering and fortification (mapmaking, trigonometry, drawing). Czartoryski's own rendition of his intent for the cadets reads: "He, whom the chance of birth and fortune has chosen for active civic duties, should strive to perfect himself in such knowledge.... You, who now find your Homeland in the most lamentable state conceivable, should populate it with citizens ardent for its glory, for increasing its internal vigor and its international prestige, for improving its government, which is of the worst possible kind.... May you, the new generation, change the old form of your country" (qtd. in Pula, 26). So eager was Kościuszko as a student at the Academy, he would tie a string to his hand, leaving the other end in the hallway. When the night watchman began his rounds at 3:00 A.M., he would pull the string to awaken Kościuszko.

Kościuszko continued to excel academically, graduating at the top of his class. He also perfected his physical stature, aggressively practicing swordsmanship without bullying less accomplished cadets. He earned the nickname the "Swede" among his classmates, for he identified with the Swedish King Charles XII, whose success fighting Russian troops rendered him another of Kościuszko's role models. Kościuszko also practiced and perfected negotiating skills, representing the cadets in the presence of the Polish King when a slight from a provincial governor insulted a particular cadet at a reception in Warsaw. The King was so impressed with Kościuszko's explanation and plea, he ordered the governor to apologize to all of the Royal Academy cadets and periodically invited Kościuszko to visit the castle to provide progress reports. Upon graduation, Kościuszko was awarded one of four scholarships provided for the continuation of studies in France. For a year prior to his continued studies, Kościuszko was employed by the Royal Military School as an instructor, with the rank of artillery captain "because of his mathematical skills and ability to project accurately the range and line of fire for cannons" (Storozynski, 11).

In Paris, Kościuszko learned war strategies from Marshal Sébastien le Prestre de Vauban, Europe's premiere authority on fortification, and bridge building and architecture from Jean-Rodolphe Perronet, who had "built the most beautiful bridges, roads, and buildings in Paris" (Storozynski, 12). In the cafés Kościuszko became enthralled with physiocracy, a political philosophy which, if implemented in his country of birth would end feudalism, for the physiocrats believed "that land was the only true source of wealth, and agriculture the key to prosperity. They believed that only those who owned or leased land should be taxed. They opposed forced labor for serfs and argued that peasants should be able to migrate to find work. They advocated a natural law under which government took a hands-off, laissez-faire approach to economics. They opposed taxes on farmers and their harvest and argued that free markets would bring individual liberty and economic security" (Storozynski, 12). Next, Kościuszko visited Holland to learn how to build dikes and/or solve water management problems in Poland, also visiting England, Switzerland, Saxony, and the ancient ruins of Rome, his travels helping him discover "what was necessary to attain durable government and the due happiness of all" (Storozynski, 13).

The coalescence of his cultural background, education, philosophical ponderings, and the practice of Deism undeniably "reinforced in Kościuszko the egalitarian idea that the peasantry should be treated with the same respect accorded other human beings, a belief that would come to fruition later in his life" (qtd. in Pula, 29). Profoundly, Kościuszko wrote: "This immense universe—filled with an infinite number of stars and our hearts seeking refuge in unhappiness speak for the existence of the Supreme Being. We do not understand it, but we feel it everywhere and we all have to worship it.... God does not interfere with *homo sapiens*.... The will of God is identical with character, justice, and the humanistic conduct of man" (Pula, 29). The precepts of the Enlightenment ingested during his studies also led Kościuszko to reach the stance that "philosophers should actively fight 'against ignorance, injustice, and the inequality of societies and nations'" (qtd. in Pula, 29).

Upon Kościuszko's returning home, the conditions in Poland had worsened. The country had been attacked by neighbors and partitioned into three divisions. Commissions in Poland's now almost non-existent army required payment, and Thaddeus' elder brother had squandered the family inheritance. In a sense overqualified and unable to find employment, Thaddeus traveled to Warsaw to visit his military friends at the Academy. He was hired to tutor the daughters of Lord Joseph Sosnowski, "one of the richest noblemen in Kościuszko's region" (Storozynski, 14), Ludwika (who beamed with "a gleaming light of awareness" with "an intellect well beyond her years") and Catherine. Kościuszko grew enraptured with Ludwika, finding that she "had been the first to translate a book by Quesnay about physiocracy and agricultural reform from French into Polish. Ludwika and Kościuszko were kindred spirits. The passion beating in his chest for the rights of the peasants melded into romantic love for Lodwika as he discovered that the worldviews of the hetman's feisty daughter were similar to his own" (Storozynski, 14). Ludwika (Louise) certainly served as the one true love in Kościuszko's life.

What followed in Thaddeus' life is as tragic as a Shakespearean drama. First, upon conversing with Ludwika's mother, he inferred his financial situation did not allow him to ask for Louise's hand. Thus, Kościuszko traveled to Pulway to visit with his friend, Prince Czartoryski, also his Royal Academy benefactor. The prince informed Kościuszko he had considered asking for Ludwika's hand himself, and explained the impossible politics behind marriages among the nobility. Kościuszko's princely friend, nevertheless, suggested that Kościuszko take his case to King Stanisław, vowing "that whatever the outcome, he would support his infatuated protégé" (Storozynski, 14).

The King kindly provided Kościuszko an audience, displeased upon hearing his request. Having survived a disastrous relationship with the Czarina of Russia, who had appointed him as a puppet King, Stanisław advised Kościuszko to forget the "silly notion" of love, explaining he could not provide a captain protection against a wealthy and prominent lord. Forlorn and devastated, Kościuszko, together with Ludwika and his fellow military school cadet, Julian Ursyn Niemcewicz (who later became one of the nation's most prolific writers), planned an elaborate elopement, complete with "a comfortable carriage, war fast horses, a priest willing to marry them, and ways to cover their tracks and find safe houses in which to hide in the forests and mountains" (Storozynski, 15). As love is sometimes indiscreet, the two young men did not cover their tracks, and the King learned of their plans. Since the cadet he had supported did not listen to his advice, Stanisław informed Lord Sosnowski of the lovers' plans.

On an autumn night in 1775, the couple attempted to elope. As they raced over the dirt roads to find a priest, galloping horsemen rode up to the carriage and reined in the harnessed steeds. Kościuszko leapt from the carriage, leaving his love inside, and drew his sword. Due to his training, he could have fought off up to three guards, and in fact was ready to. Nonetheless, past his blade stood Louise's father himself, whom Kościuszko could not harm in front of his lover's eyes. As he placed the blade back in its sheath and asked for Louise's hand, the lord replied: "Pigeons are not meant for sparrows and the daughters of magnates are not meant for the sons of the common gentry" (Storozynski, 1). The guards attacked Kościuszko and knocked him unconscious. When he awoke, Kościuszko found Louise's white handkerchief, dropped in the scuffle. Placing the treasured possession in his pocket, Kościuszko began the long walk home in the dark. The truth of this rendition bears great weight, for "three men who knew Kościuszko, from three different countries, wrote similar accounts of his attempt to run off with Louise" (Storozynski, 2). The ending was sour; the lovers did not win out, and Kościuszko never married. As scholars have noted throughout the nineteenth and twentieth century, "Clearly Kościuszko's rejection by Lord Sosnowski was the pivotal moment of his life" (Storozynski).

Lord Sosnowski, as a matter of honor, sought revenge (remember, he had been one of the magnates who had recommended Kościuszko for the Royal Academy and had entrusted him with the education of his daughters). Confining Ludwika to a convent until she could marry a prince decided on as the result of a land deal, Lord Sosnowski wished Kościuszko dead, threatening violence and prosecution for ravishing his daughter. Thus, "the painful reality of class distinction grew even harsher once Kościuszko realized that he had not only lost the love of his life but also faced the loss of his life…. The outraged hetman was so influential and vengeful that Kościuszko, broke and broken hearted, was forced to flee his homeland" (Storozynski, 15).

Again coming to the rescue, lifetime friend Prince Czartoryski, gave Kościuszko five hundred ducats for traveling expenses. Not exactly understanding the course he might take, Kościuszko pondered whether to find work in the Saxon Court of Dresden, apply for a military position in France, or sail to America. He wished to find a purpose associated with his ideals, as "the affair with Ludwika Sosnowska had a clear effect on his psyche, and for the rest of his life he was drawn to the underprivileged, as well as those who were willing to help them" (Storozynski, 16), also hoping to be of service to Poland again someday and pay her back "with the obligations of citizenship."

Not finding his calling in Saxony, Kościuszko traveled to Paris, a city abuzz with news of the American Revolution. He ingested playwright Beaumarchais' (*The Barber of Seville* and *The Marriage of Figaro*) criticisms to Louis XVI (prior to the monarch's alliance with America): "How can you allow your vessels to take by force and bind suffering black men whom nature made free and who are only miserable because you are powerful? How can you suffer three rival powers to seize iniquitously upon and divide Poland under your very eyes?" (qtd. in Storozynski, 17). Becoming acquainted with Beaumarchais, who had received a letter from Virginian Arthur Lee requesting "arms, powder, and above all engineers," and upon Beaumarchais developing a clandestine trading firm (with French and Spanish support) named "Roderigue Hortalex & Cie," Kościuszko left on the first ship carrying ammunition and supply to Saint Dominique (Haiti), and from there to the colonies. (Traveling via Saint Dominique allowed secured safety in the face of British ships, for the French were still, in theory, neutral, and this French-controlled port was a short distance from the American coast.) An early historian, Neilson, relates: "This celebrated engineer came to this country utterly unprovided with letters of recommendation or introduction and nearly penniless and offered himself as a volunteer in the American cause and solicited an interview with Washington" (qtd. in Haiman, 6). Note: Other historians believe Thaddeus may have carried one recommendation, that being from Prince Czartoryski, addressed to General Charles Lee, second in rank only to Washington.

Kościuszko's crossing proved as dramatic as his lost love affair, for, sailing in June 1776, at the beginning of hurricane season, his ship was blown off course by a tropical storm, ground into the coral reefs off Martinique. Kościuszko and five of his compatriots, also crossing to volunteer for the American cause, rescued themselves by grabbing the ship's masts and kicking to shore. This fate allowed Kościuszko to discern firsthand the horrors associated with the slave trade, as he witnessed Africans in shackles and chains at the horrendous slave auctions. Gathering himself long enough to find a small fishing vessel headed to the Bahamas and along North America's coast, Kościuszko's very life was spared at the same moment when men of like mind were signing the Declaration of Independence. In fact, when Kościuszko disembarked in Philadelphia, "the capital was still pulsating with excitement over the Declaration of Independence and the idea that a new nation had been created" (Storozynski, 20). Fate indeed had a hand in Kościuszko's crossing and his subsequent contributions to the American Revolution, for, as best summarized by Pula:

> The vessel brought with it a man whose historical traditions, cultural values, education, and personal experience forged a personality rich in patriotism, support for national self-government, advocacy of political liberty and personal freedom, tolerance for divergent religious and cultural traditions, and a general humanitarianism spanning all classes and varieties of people. He had a strong sense of patriotism forged over centuries of historical tradition and reinforced by the unfortunate situation of Poland he witnessed as he grew to adulthood in a nation that had lost its own political liberty, fostering in him a strong appreciation for the American quest for independence. Further, the Poland of Kościuszko's youth was a multi-cultural state, a nation comprising great cultural, national, and religious diversity. It was in this society of various groups living together under allegiance to a single central government that Kościuszko grew to manhood. This familiarity with the concept of unity in diversity — "E Pluribus Unum" the Americans would call it — was yet another personal experience he could relate to the American determination to preserve a harmonious society tolerant of diversity. Possessing these traits, as well as valuable training as a military engineer, he was well-suited to his imminent role in support of American independence and democracy.

According to a description Kościuszko later provided to his personal aide, his first steps off the boat included walking through the door of Benjamin Franklin's shop, at which point "the old sage of Philadelphia peered through the top half of his bifocals at the unannounced visitor" (Storozynski, 20). Kościuszko introduced himself and offered his services to a new nation, offering to take the appropriate exam. Franklin asked for letters of recommendation, to which Kościuszko replied, "I do not have any. A talented person should be able to show his worth, and not letters of recommendation. I want to show my competence by taking your placement exam." Franklin, seeing Kościuszko did not understand the fact that a nation of farmers and merchants, heretofore under Britain's supposed protection, did not have a military exam, interrogated Kościuszko about news from Europe as well as his background and political ideals. When satisfied, Franklin rose to his feet and kissed Kościuszko's forehead, saying, "But you have to admit, young man, that it was pretty unwise to travel two thousand miles without any commitments or connections" (qtd. in Storozynski, 20–1). Nevertheless referring Kościuszko to David Rittenhouse, a surveyor and scientific instrument expert, for a geometry test, upon Kościuszko's passing the exam, Franklin introduced the young man to Congress. When he presented himself to the Congressional Board on War on August 30, in what was, at the time, known as a "Memorial," the Board's report resulted in the October 18, 1776, resolution "that Thaddeus Kościuszko be appointed an engineer in the service of the United States, with the pay of sixty dollars a month, and the rank of colonel" (Haiman, 9). John Hancock wrote Kościuszko on the same day: "We reposing especial Trust and Confidence in your Patriotism, Valour, Conduct and Fidelity, do by these Presents, constitute and appoint you to be an Engineer with the Rank of Colonel in the Army of the United States, raised for the Defence of American Liberty, and for repelling every hostile Invasion thereof ... and we do strictly charge and require all Officers and Soldiers under your Command to be obedient to your Orders as Engineer" (qtd. in Storozynski, 22).

Franklin first put Kościuszko to work fortifying Philadelphia against an expected British attack. Also working for the commander of the city's forces, General Israel Putnam, Kościuszko designed and supervised the construction of a redoubt on the shores of the Delaware at Billingsport, New Jersey. After his commission was signed, he was asked to build Fort Mercer high atop a forty-foot cliff at Red Bank, New Jersey. These defenses were "resilient enough to last well into the twentieth century," and as described by Christopher Ward, these fortifications were "a double line of *chevaux-de-frise* that extended from the Jersey shore across the channel to Billings Island. They were crate like structures made of heavy timbers, loaded with stones and sunk in the water. They were mounted with wooden beams, shod at the upper end with iron points, slanting upwards to within four feet of the surface of the river at low tides and pointing downstream. They were capable of ripping open the bottom of any ship that tried to pass them over" (qtd. in Pula, 41).

What followed was a scramble for a highly qualified engineer. Putnam still wanted Kościuszko to continue his work on the Delaware; thus at Fort Mifflin "Kościuszko ordered the orchards north of the fort cut down to clear a line of fire at any approaching enemy. His men also dug deep trenches outside the fort's walls and another row of breastworks along the river bluff. These were filled with another row of abates to deter an infantry attack" (Storozynski, 23). But, George Washington wrote John Hancock on December 20th, frustrated with his present engineers, stating, "There is one in Philadelphia whom I am told is clever, but him I have never seen" (qtd. in Storozynski, 23). And General Horatio Gates strove to develop a tight friendship with Kościuszko.

General Gates won the battle, and eventually appointed Kościuszko Engineer of the Northern Army. His first advent into the lines of battle occurred in April of 1777 at Fort Ticonderoga and Fort Edward, Kościuszko directed to "examine and report the condition of that fortress; the extension (if any) to be given to Fort Independence, and lastly, whether Sugar Loaf Hill could be made practicable to the ascent of guns of large caliber" (Pula, 51). Calling Sugar Loaf Hill not only an excellent place to resist the enemy, but also beat them, Kościuszko recommended fortification and cannon placement atop the slope of Mount Defiance. Gates and his emissary, Colonel Wilkinson, along with Major John Armstrong, agreed, Armstrong believing the hill "would permit the ascent of the heaviest cannon ... [and] furnish a good site for a battery, ... which so placed, from elevation and proximity, would completely cover the two forts, the bridge of communication and the adjoining boat harbor" (Storozynski, 26).

However, political intrigue interfered, as Gates' nemesis, General Schuyler, became Gates' superior. Inspecting Kościuszko's plans, he noted that no other engineer, French, British, or American, had recommended fortification of the Hill, and that he was "not disposed to embarrass himself or his means of defence, by making the experiment; and the less so, as he was fully convinced that between two and three thousand men could effectually maintain Fort Independence and secure the pass" (Pula, 58). Though maintaining his demeanor in front of his superior, Colonel Wilkinson "detected under Kościuszko's placid silence, more than a little anguish and mortification" (Pula, 59). Kościuszko continued to build defenses for the Fort, nonetheless, including breastworks, redoubts, and batteries, along with a large star-shaped redoubt. When the British eventually moved upon the 2,066 Continentals, 450 militia, 229 artillerists, and 183 rangers and engineers, they found "on the summit of the mount ... a star fort made of pickets, well supplied with artillery, and a large square of barracks within it; that side of the hill which projects into the lake is well intrenched, and has a strong abates close to the water, which is lined with heavy artillery pointing down the lake, flanking the water battery, and sustained by another about half way up the hill. Fortified as the enemy are, nothing but a regular siege can dispossess them" (qtd. in Pula, 60).

A determined British General Burgoyne, with the recommendation of his Swiss engineer, Lieutenant William Twiss, discovered that Sugar Loaf was in range of Fort Ticonderoga. Cutting a passageway for artillery, his General William Phillips commented, "Where a goat can go, a man can go, and where a man can go he can drag a gun" (Pula, 61). The artillery was placed atop Sugar Loaf, ironically, on July 4, 1777, and the next day, after the Americans had celebrated the first anniversary of the Declaration of Independence, they awoke to find "soldiers in crimson jackets perched atop Mount Defiance aiming a cannon down on them" (Storozynski, 28). The first shot was directed at a rebel boat on the lake, but the next cannonball landed inside the fort. Blockhouses were set on fire, and the Americans were forced to evacuate, sneaking out of the fort at ten o'clock at night, using the floating log bridge luckily constructed by Kościuszko to retreat south, toward Albany. As the evacuation ensued, however, a French general, passed out in an alcoholic stupor, failed to warn his man, torched his quarters, and the resulting fire lit up the night sky, allowing the British to observe the fleeing colonials. The Mohawk, Onondaga, Cayuga, and Seneca siding with the British were sent into the night to hunt down and scalp the fleeing Americans.

A regretful Schuyler placed Kościuszko in charge of preventing the British advance, also placing a fine horse and tons of axes in his care. As Storozynski describes, "With Adirondack blackflies biting the backs of their necks and timber rattlesnakes nipping at their feet, three hundred wool-clad, sweating Continental soldiers under Kościuszko's command toiled in the heat to chop down trees to block roads and destroy bridges over streams as soon as the rebel troops had crossed them" (30). A British soldier noted, "The felled trees were as plenty as lampposts upon a highway about London" (qtd. in Storozynski, 30). Fires were also set to fields of corn and grain and cattle were driven away, all in all slowing the British supply line to the degree it took the force twenty days to cover twenty-two miles. Finally, Kościuszko raced through the wilderness searching for a safe campsite for the retreating rebels who had not been scalped, placing batteries around the camp. Major John Armstrong wrote, "In the retreat of the American army, Kościuszko was distinguished for activity and courage and upon him devolved the choices of camps and posts and everything connected with fortifications" (Storozynski, 30). Schuyler was removed from his post.

The Northern Army regrouped at Saratoga, joined by Benedict Arnold's 1,200 troops and some Connecticut infantry. As Colonel Morgan Lewis set up camp, he was approached by Kościuszko, who had followed General Gates, and told of the indefensible locale of the encampment. Lewis reported Kościuszko's comment, "From Yonder Hill, on the left, your encampment may be cannoned by the enemy, or from that on our right they may take aim at your shoe-buckles" (qtd. in Storozynski, 33). Given leave to find an appropriate site, Kościuszko rode north, reaching an elevated pasture on the road to Albany along the Hudson. Lewis noted Kościuszko's enthusiasm as he galloped his horse in circles on the apex of the hill, for he remarked, "This is the spot!" Major Dearborn marked it a "very advantageous Post," described by one biographer as "a strategic bottleneck which could neither be forced nor avoided without difficulty" (Pula, 80). Below the Bemis Heights bluffs (named for a tavern run in the vicinity by Jotham Bemis) stood open fields and ravines. To the east was a narrow riverside passage, and to the west hills with thick forests. Immediately, Kościuszko inquired as to the "number of divisions in the Army and their names, took a piece of paper from his portfolio, and drew in pencil the plan of the camp, and assigned the location of several regiments and in conformity with that plan they were speedily marched to the ground and they proceeded to erect breastworks and fortifications" (Storozynski, 33). One thousand troops were placed at Kościuszko's command, carrying out his plans for redoubts, batteries, bivouacs, and roads. Entrenchments made of earth, logs and fence rails started near Bemis Tavern; redoubts guarded the lowlands; lines were constructed to prevent bayonet charges; four deep ravines formed a natural barrier near the woods; gun emplacements were placed on the heights; woods and hills were improved with fieldworks; the Neilson barn was turned into a strongpoint supported by a well-entrenched battery; bridges were destroyed to prevent an advance; and, finally, riflemen were used as a sort of screen at Freeman's Farm. George Otto Trevelyan wrote, "He had crowned Bemis Heights with a stronghold which resembled a citadel rather than a temporary field work" (Pula, 81).

In large part due to all these feats of engineering, the Battle of Saratoga was a smashing victory, as "two lieutenant generals, two major generals, three brigadiers, with their staffs and aides, 299 other officers ranging from colonels to ensigns, chaplains and surgeons, 389 noncommissioned officers, 197 musicians, and 4,836 privates passed out of the armed forces of Great Britain in America. The material captured was of vast importance, including 27 guns of various calibers, 5,000 stand of small arms, great quantities of ammunition, and military stores and equipment of all kinds" (Pula, 99). Turning the tide of the Revolution, victory at Saratoga convinced France and Spain to form an alliance with the American cause just days later, specifically February 6, 1778, bringing additional arms, ammunition, and, eventually, the force of the French army and navy to America! (The battle is considered one of the ten most important in history, and, as Pula strategizes, "Saratoga made Yorktown possible.") Due to site location and ravines, the rebels had a clear shot on the enemy's path. At the Hudson River passage, cannons were readied. Kościuszko's fortifications could not be challenged, channeling the British attack to the left away from riverside meadows. The British were forced to march around redoubts, ending in the forest, ambushed by Daniel Morgan's sharpshooters, who even climbed trees to get better shots, hitting every artillery officer save one and 36 of the 48 gunners. Kościuszko's field obstacles also provided quick egress to facilitate counterattacks.

The battle actually encompassed two phases. During the first phase, six hundred Redcoats were killed or wounded. The large wolf packs which ensued forced the British to enter the second phase of the battle two weeks hence (to avoid the onset of plague or disease), the Redcoats swinging even further in the forest to avoid Kościuszko's defenses. Again, Morgan's snipers killed hundreds, the British were surrounded, and, as General Gates informed his wife, "Burgoyne and his whole army have laid down their arms, and surrendered themselves to me and my Yankees.... If Old England is not by this lesson taught humility, then she is an obstinate old slut, bent upon her ruin" (qtd. in Storozynski, 39).

Gates told Benjamin Rush a year later, "Let us be honest. In war, as in medicine, natural causes not under our control, do much. In the present case, the great tacticians of the campaign were hills and forests, which a young Polish Engineer was skillful enough to select for my encampment" (qtd. in Storozynski, 39). Historian Channing, who has recognized no other foreign hero besides von Steuben (see Chapter 16), believed "whatever credit there may be would seem to belong to Gates and to his engineer, Kościuszko, the Polander" (qtd. in Mizwa, 131). And, finally, Woodrow Wilson in his *History of the American People* said, "It was the gallant Polish patriot, Tadeusz Kościuszko, who had shown General Gates how to intrench himself upon Bemis Heights" (qtd. in Mizwa, 131). Though a promotion was offered to Kościuszko by Gates, Kościuszko understood a promotion would promote jealousies, and, unlike his compatriot at Saratoga, Thaddeus suggested to Gates' traveling subordinate, "My dear Colonel if you see that my promotion will make a great many Jealous, tell the General that I will not accept of one because I prefer peace more than the greatest Rank in the World" (Haiman, 34). Biographer Haiman notes, "It was one strand of Kościuszko's greatness that he shunned even deserved recognition; he preferred to serve disinterestingly; the public cause, which he embraced, was always first in his mind" (34).

At this point in the War, prevention was the key. A post initiated at West Point by Brigadier General Samuel Parsons languished as "almost every obstacle within the circle of possibility has happened to retard their progress," and Parsons, "finding it impossible to complete the Fort and other defenses intended at this post, in such manner as to render them effectual early in the spring, and not choosing to hazard his reputation on works erected on a different scale, has desired leave" (qtd. in Pula, 119). To fill this spot, Gates nominated Kościuszko before the Board of War on March 5, 1778, to serve under the command of General Alexander McDougall, commander of the Hudson Highlands. General Washington emphasized to McDougall: "I need not observe to you that West Point is to be considered as the first and principal object of your attention. I am persuaded you will neglect nothing conducive to its security, and will have the works directed for its defense prosecuted with all the vigour and expedition in your power. You are fully sensible of their importance and how much their completion will ease and disembarrass our future general operations" (qtd. in Pula, 120). The objective at West Point was to create a headquarters for the Continental Army on the banks of the Hudson, 50 miles north of New York City, which would also allow the army to fire upon any passing British ships and prevent Redcoat soldiers from scurrying up the banks. Thus, Kościuszko became engineer of a parcel of land with thin rocky soil, solid rock underneath, set in a bitterly cold landscape, with a lack of manpower, equipment, and draft animals. First, he concentrated on the eventuality of a land attack, constructing obstructions to interdict river traffic, a water battery, permanent barracks, outworks, an abatis, magazines, and a *chevaux-de-frise* (a wooden frame with wooden spikes therein which form a type of X shape). By June 12, when Dr. James Thatcher climbed an adjacent mountain, he reported "a picturesque scenery of peculiar interest ... Fort Putnam, on its most elevated part, the several redoubts beneath, and the barracks on the plain below, with numerous armed soldiers in active motion, all defended by the most formidable machinery of war" (Pula, 125).

Much work remained, including "the chain and boom across the river had to be reinforced and the wood repaired and treated with tar as a preservative. The initial works constructed on land had to be woven into an intricate system by the creation of supporting blockhouses, redoubts, and *chevaux-de-frise*. To house troops and supplies, barracks, magazines, and bombproofs had to be constructed within the primary works" (Pula, 125). Washington, upon inspection, was pleased, and West Point became his headquarters. Continental Army historian Lynn Montross concluded, "Clinton could no more dream of attacking this stronghold than Washington could hope to storm the works of New York" (qtd. in Pula,

133). The winter season was waning, nonetheless, and fears regarding a British attack on West Point increased. While plans were set, construction wavered due to lack of manpower. Kościuszko was forced to complain to McDougall and write General Washington, informing, "These works want at less six hundred men, one hundred and sixty Carpenters, twenty Masons, and twelve Miners, ten teams for two months" (qtd. in Pula, 139). Washington responded, and 2,500 men were employed for the project, placed under Kościuszko's command. With this number also came human resource challenges, such as provision, pay, clothing, illness, health, and disputes. Among his workers, however, grew a deep sense of respect for their commander, described by one, Samuel Richards, as elevated "in mind which gave fair promise of those high achievements to which he attained. His manners were soft and conciliating and, at the same time, elevated. I used to take much pleasure in accompanying him with his theodolite, measuring the heights of the surrounding mountains. He was very ready in mathematics" (qtd. in Pula, 141). The British were also impressed with the engineer, respecting his engineering marvels and deeming the fortifications surrounding West Point insurmountable, for, over the next year, Kościuszko built "a bombproof shelter and cistern to catch rainwater; erecting a stone wall around the Webb redoubt and putting in a bombproof storage magazine; building a redoubt and bombproof shelter on Matters Rock Hill; finishing another battery along the river overlooking the chain; and building one redoubt and designing another on Constitution Island" (Storozynski, 75).

Kościuszko's intellect, however, struggled against this isolated, friendless, and somewhat static assignment, the continual construction amidst harsh conditions and diminished labor, the winter of 1779–80 being "one of unexampled severity at West Point.... So intense was the cold, that for a period of forty days, no water dripped from the roofs which sheltered them. The snow was four feet deep on a level, requiring a heavy force to be constantly engaged in keeping open the communication with the six or seven redoubts built and building. Twice during the winter the North Redoubt barely escaped total destruction by fire. The parapet, built of logs, covered with earth, and difficult of access, burned nearly three days before the fire could be extinguished. The South Barrack in Fort Arnold was entirely consumed, with a large quantity of stores" (qtd. in Pula, 142). Reconstruction was required, along with the building of additional outworks, barracks, and magazines.

As spring arrived during this solitary period, Kościuszko began a garden during his off-duty hours "among the rocks that jutted from the sides of the cliffs fronting the Hudson River" (Pula, 143). To this difficult-to-reach point, he lowered pails of dirt with ropes, planting flowers and shrubbery and constructing a marble fountain with spouting jets and cascades, a spot maintained to this day by West Point cadets, known as Kościuszko's Garden. Samuel L. Knapp in *Tales of the Garden of Kościuszko,* described:

> It was here, when in its rude state, that the Polish soldier and patriot sat in deep contemplation on the loves of his youth, and the ills his country had to suffer. It would be a grateful sight to him if he could visit it now, and find that a band of youthful soldiers had, as it were, consecrated the whole military grounds to his fame. His martial spirit would take fire in beholding such exact military maneuvers, as are exhibited by the scientific corps; and in the pride of his soul he would declare that a country who gave her sons such an education could never be conquered or enslaved [qtd. in Pula, 143].

Similar to the huge rock Kościuszko meditated upon as a child, the tiny garden constructed between the boulders of Fort Arnold offered a place of solace, a chance to ponder the ideals for which he worked and to consider "the predicament of the subjugated peasants in his own country, and the plight of America's citizen militia, and the African slaves in the United

States" (Storozynski, 71). Kościuszko even showed compassion to the British prisoners of war held at West Point, offering them food from his own rations. (Many years later a Polish traveler was nursed back to health from a bout of malaria by an Australian shopkeeper, who cared for the Pole because "his grandfather would have starved to death as a prisoner of the American Revolution, if not for a Polish soldier named Kościuszko who shared his bread" [Storozynski, 72].) Another story relates that on one occasion, Kościuszko's African servant, Grippy, was left to watch Kościuszko's log cabin quarters for three days. Grippy invited the slaves and free black men from the camp to a party while his supervisor was away, dressing up in Kościuszko's uniform (complete with the four-cornered cap adorned with ostrich feathers), shining his legs with black shoe polish to resemble boots. Kościuszko returned to the party unexpectedly. Expecting to be beaten, Grippy fell at Kościuszko's feet, "cowering and crying, 'Whip me, kill me, Massa; do anything with me Mr. General.' Kościuszko took Grippy by the hand and said, 'Rise, Prince. It is beneath the dignity of an African prince to prostrate himself at the feet of anyone'" (qtd. in Storozynski, 73). Introducing Grippy as an African prince to those officers who were to determine his punishment, Kościuszko used dignity and humor to diminish an expected harsh and severe whipping. The officers instead, due to Kościuszko's introduction, subjected Grippy to a forced intoxication, offering wine, brandy, and a cocktail named Hollands (Dutch gin distilled from rye, barley, and juniper berry flavorings). Grippy later noted the next morning's hangover was comparable to a crucifixion. After the war "Agrippa Hull" settled in Massachusetts, opened a catering business, bought land, and built a house, telling his story of the tolerant Kościuszko and his gift of a flintlock pistol made by an eminent Polish gun maker upon their parting of ways.

All in all, West Point became, due to Kościuszko's diligence, "a fortress far ahead of its time," according to Dave R. Palmer. The skill associated with this feat is described by American historian George Bancroft: "Until 1778 West Point was a solitude, nearly inaccessible; now it was covered by fortresses with numerous redoubts, constructed chiefly under the direction of Kościuszko as engineer, and so connected as to form one system of defense, which was believed to be impregnable" (qtd. in Pula, 144). The fort effectively circumvented the British from use of the Hudson River and protected the valley's valuable food stock of grain and corn which fed Washington's army, the general noting, "To his care and sedulous appreciation, the American people are indebted to Kościuszko for the defense of West Point" (qtd. in Pula, 145). The British forces were effectively bottlenecked in New York City, effecting their turn to the Southern campaign, for, as Hoffman Nickerson concluded, "From the moment when its works came into existence the army of Sir Henry Clinton on Manhattan Island was held in a vise" (qtd. in Pula, 145). As noted by General John Armstrong, "Kościuszko's merit lies in this, that he gave the fortifications such strength that they frightened the very enemy from all temptations of even trying to take the Highlands" (qtd. in Pula, 145).

At this point in the War, due to the strength of West Point and the Northern Army, Washington needed to strategize how he would defend the forthcoming Southern campaign by the British. Hence, aware of the need for engineers on the battlefield, Washington offered Kościuszko a position under General Nathanael Greene. Riding to Richmond, Virginia, with his free black servant, Grippy, where he stopped to deliver correspondence to then Governor Thomas Jefferson, Kościuszko was surprised to learn that the man who had written "all men are created equal" owned slaves. He would establish a lifelong relationship and correspondence with Jefferson, nonetheless, and would make Jefferson the executor of his will, in which he left $30,000 for the establishment of a school for African American children in Newark, New Jersey, Kościuszko's final legacy to America.

Unfortunately, Benedict Arnold took the reins at West Point, tactfully destroying its forces, weakening the river chain, reproducing Kościuszko's blueprints, betraying the nation in an attempt to deliver West Point into the hands of the British. What schoolchildren are not taught when they learn of Arnold's betrayal is that the prize Arnold was attempting to sell to the British for the sum of twenty thousand pounds was "Kościuszko's handiwork of two and a half years in the Hudson Highlands" (Storozynski, 92). Arnold's treachery, thankfully discovered, was unforgivable in light of the fact that the sacrificial Pole Kościuszko had given his lifework to creating "the palladium of American independence ... the grand link in the chain of our union," for, if Kościuszko's fortress had fallen, the newly formed United States, according to Major Samuel Shaw "would have been reduced to an extremity from which nothing, in the present spirit of the times, but a creating power could have extricated us" (qtd. in Storozynski, 93).

Kościuszko headed to Charlotte, North Carolina, to join General Greene and several other friends from the Northern Army, to include Daniel Morgan, Lewis Morris, and Major John Armstrong. First, Greene directed Kościuszko to explore the Catawba River and report "the depth of water, the rapidity of the stream, the rocks, shoals or falls you may meet with and every other information necessary to enable me to form an accurate opinion of the transportation which may be made on the river in the different seasons of the year" (qtd. in Pula, 159). During this expedition, Kościuszko and his companion, Captain William Thompson of South Carolina, were exposed to grave danger, for Loyalists were "as thick as the trees." These reports were the first surveys of their kind for the western North Carolina rivers and "were of inestimable value to Greene in his campaign" (Haiman, 105).

Next, Kościuszko was to find an appropriate camp for Greene's army. Finding the area around Charlotte, North Carolina, insufficient, he thus also traversed the Pee Dee River from the mouth of the Little River, accompanied by Major William Polk. Finding a strategic position near Cheraw, South Carolina, rich in food stock, supported by Francis Marion's guerrilla force, and situated at a point which would disrupt British couriers, Kościuszko fortified the camp. In order to ensure escape from Cornwallis' troops, numbering in the thousands, if the need should arise, Greene also ordered Kościuszko to construct a small fleet of boats. Kościuszko designed and supervised construction of the light watercraft, easily carried from one river to another within North and South Carolina. This fleet "became critical after Greene sent Daniel Morgan's unit into South Carolina, where the rebels routed the British calvary and infantry unit of Col. Banastre Tarleton at the Battle of Cowpens on January 17, 1781 (Storozynski, 97). Furious, Cornwallis determined to find Greene's army. Knowing he could not meet Cornwallis' army full-force, Greene entered into a game of cat-and-mouse in which he led Cornwallis deep into North Carolina, far from his line of supply, all the while biding time and awaiting French reinforcements. As Pula notes, "Greene's plan called for excellent timing, hard marching, and diligence. Moving too fast might discourage Cornwallis from following. Moving too slow, or being unable to cross a river, would mean destruction at the hands of Cornwallis's well-trained regulars. Probably the greatest post of responsibility on this hectic race against time and redcoats was that of Greene's director of transportation. On the shoulders of this man lay the responsibility for selecting routes of march, providing the appropriate transport at the correct time and place, and insuring that measures were taken so the various rivers along the route of march would be passable. A mistake on any one of these and disaster could overwhelm Greene's army. The man chosen for this manifestly important task was Tadeusz Kościuszko" (163).

Blazing the path, Kościuszko determined the best course throughout the march, a two hundred-mile course through the Carolinas to the Dan River. As Pula notes, "Kościuszko appeared to be everywhere handling the myriads of details necessary for success, planning lines of march, gathering and dispatching crucial boats, and seeking little known shortcuts" (164). Cornwallis, always just a couple of hours behind, believed his efforts would result in the annihilation of the remainder of the Southern army. Yet, Greene marched his troops 47 miles in 48 hours in a February rain, red clay roads first turning to mud, and, thereafter, when temperatures dropped and the weather turned to snow, into a frozen mire. Once reaching the Dan, the crossing was crucial; boats needed to be readied, earthworks formed, and occupants on the other side informed of the arrival of the troops, these tasks also coming under Kościuszko's purview. Again, Kościuszko's work was crucial: he "kept constantly busy seeing to the safety of the supplies, planning routes, and galloping ahead to see whether the marshy roadways needed bridging, rushing to the Dan himself to lay out defensive works to protect the crossing" (Pula, 165). Once across the Dan, a few of Greene's men heckled and thumbed their noses at the Redcoats as they arrived on the southern bank. Many of these same men were barefoot by that time, with bloody feet, and Greene described them to Jefferson as "almost fatigued to death, having had a retreat to conduct for upwards of two hundred miles" (qtd. in Storozynski, 98). Basically, the Continentals, in what became known as "The Race to the Dan," outmarched the Redcoats by a one-third ratio due to Kościuszko's

Washington saying goodbye to his officers. Engraving by Phillibrown from painting by Alonzo Chappel (1828–1877) (National Archives and Records Administration).

tireless efforts. British Colonel "Bloody" Tarleton concluded, "Every measure of the Americans during their march from the Catawba to Virginia was judiciously designed and vigorously executed" (qtd. in Pula, 165). However, as Pula notes, "the strongest appraisal of Kościuszko's work is the fact that Greene's entire force escaped across the Dan without loss, preserving the Southern Army from destruction" (165).

When Cornwallis did not pursue the Continentals into Halifax, Virginia, Kościuszko received a long sought-for post as field commander, given command of Ashley Ferry, nine miles north of Charleston, to keep an eye on the last British stronghold between New York and Savannah. Developing a rapport with the African American community near his post, Kościuszko used a network of slaves to channel information about British movements to his post, as well as a silversmith's son (Petrie) and three men known as W, P, and X, who delivered information about British troop movements. Traps were subsequently set, Kościuszko and his men stealing horses from the enemy (on one raid 60 horses were taken from the cavalry), also clandestinely obstructing supply lines, driving cattle behind the Continental line, and, on one occasion, capturing one of the largest food supplies, one thousand head of cattle. Kościuszko's unit also won two skirmishes with the British on the outskirts of Charleston. The third skirmish turned out to be the last of the Revolutionary War, and, ironically, "Kościuszko was carrying a spontoon, a half-pike blade with a pointed crossbar at its base, which shattered in his hand when it was hit by English gunfire. Four musket balls pierced his coat, yet he escaped unhurt. These are believed to be the last shots fired during the American Revolution" (Storozynski, 109). General Greene lauded Kościuszko's service in the Southern campaign, writing:

> Among the most useful and agreeable of my companions in arms was Colonel Kościuszko. Nothing could exceed his zeal for the public service, nor in the prosecution of various objects that presented themselves in our small but active warfare, could anything be more useful than his attention, vigilance and industry. In promoting my views to whatever department of the service directed, he was at all times, a ready and able assistant. One in a word whom no pleasure could seduce, no labor fatigue and no danger deter. What besides greatly distinguished him was an unparalleled modesty and entire unconsciousness of having done anything extraordinary. Never making a claim or pretension for himself and never omitting to distinguish and commend the merits of others. This able and gallant soldier has now left us for the North; intending to return directly to his own country, where he cannot fail to be soon and greatly distinguished [qtd. in Pula, 200].

Kościuszko's joy, associated with the American victory, knew no bounds, but in a letter to his friend Colonel Williams, he tried to explain his feelings: "O how happy we think our Self when Conscious of our deeds, that were started from principle of rectitude, from conviction of the goodness of the thing itself, from motive of the good that will Come to Human Kind" (qtd. in Haiman, 144).

Remaining in service until Congress completed back-payment negotiations, assisting Greene in procuring rice for the troops as they gathered and dispersed, and remaining on duty near Washington's headquarters, Kościuszko was presented a personal gift of a sword and set of pistols from General Washington. Washington also made a triumphal entry into New York City on November 25, 1783, Kościuszko part of the procession. On December 4, Washington took leave of his officers, asking each to "come and take me by the hand." Upon Kościuszko's turn to embrace his commanding officer and say his good-byes, Washington removed a cameo ring of the Society of the Cincinnati from his finger and placed it on Kościuszko's finger as a tribute to his service for the cause of American independence.

This poignant moment served as the end of Kościuszko's service to the cause of liberty and justice in America. His service was not only brave, commendable, and expertly wrought, but "during seven years of constant service from 1776 to 1783, Kościuszko took only one leave of absence, the brief time he spent at Traveler's Rest with Gen. Gates's dying son. He was always loyal to his commanding officers, speaking highly of St. Clair, Gates, and Greene both in private letters and, when occasion permitted, in public forums. Kościuszko was also a humane officer who readily gained the friendship of his colleagues, cared for the needs of his men, sought to relieve the suffering of British prisoners, and did what he could to better the plight of the slaves he encountered" (qtd. in Pula, 210). He became a member of the Society of the Cincinnati and the American Philosophical Society.

Kościuszko returned to Poland a national hero, settling on his father's estate and pondering how the lessons of the American Revolution could be applied to his own country. He brought from America the deep love of freedom, a republican spirit, and "the consciousness that even an undisciplined and ragged citizen army, if fired with zeal for a sacred cause, can win victories against a powerful nation" (Mizwa, 135). A new constitution for Poland was even ratified in 1791, "adopted in the midst of national rejoicing, many of the old abuses were swept away, the system of elective kings was abolished, constitutional and hereditary monarchy (to insure continuity and strengthen the central government) was established, burghers were granted equal rights with nobility, and the condition of the peasants was ameliorated" (Mizwa, 135). Unlike America, however, Poland was surrounded by autocracy. Russia and Prussia continued their assault upon the nation, and continued to partition the nation's land holdings. Kościuszko again rose to the call of the downtrodden, this time establishing Kraków as a seat of rebellion, calling upon the country's peasants to unite. On March 24, 1794, he proclaimed an insurrection in the market square of this city, took an oath as commander-in-chief, and called upon all able men to bear arms (again, unlike America, the working class was not accustomed to bearing arms). The nobles shared equally in the defense of their country. Poles were not accustomed to rifles and muskets as Americans were, and most had only scythes with which to defend their country. Nevertheless, the Poles, under Kościuszko's leadership, did win the first battle at Racławice, capturing Russian artillery and guns. And, the citizens of Warsaw managed to oust Russian troops. Unfortunately, Prussia and Austria joined forces with Russia, and Kościuszko and his people's uprising could not remain victorious against three nations (remember, Poland's peasantry were not literate, either, as had been America's militia).

At the battle of Maciejowice, Kościuszko was gravely wounded and imprisoned for over a year at the Peter-Paul fortress in St. Petersburg. Upon the death of Catherine I, her son Paul I, freed Kościuszko, but only upon meeting Kościuszko's conditions: 12,000 other Poles in Russian prisons were to be set free. Traveling to America to completely heal his wounds, both physical and emotional, he was lauded as "one of the greatest men of our century." America greeted him again with open arms, the citizens of Philadelphia unhitching the horses from his carriage and pulling it to his quarters on Fourth Street. Kościuszko told the welcoming delegation, "I look upon America as my second country, and I feel myself too happy when I return to her" (qtd. in Mizwa 140). Washington wrote Kościuszko from Mount Vernon, welcoming him "to the land whose liberties you have been so instrumental in establishing," noting "no one has a higher respect and veneration for your character than I have" (qtd. in Mizwa, 140). During this visit to America, his friendship with Jefferson was renewed and deepened, Jefferson writing, in 1798, as mentioned previously, "He is as pure a son of liberty as I have ever known, and of that liberty which is to go to all, and not to the few and rich alone" (Mizwa, 140). Leaving America when the French Revolution began, believing he might help Poland again, Thaddeus left a last will and testament in the hands of his friend, Jefferson, bequeathing his American property (including lands upon which the city of Columbus, Ohio, now stands) for the purpose of "purchasing Negroes from among Jefferson's own or any others and giving them liberty in my name, in giving them an education in trades or otherwise and in having them instructed for their new condition in the duties of morality which may make them good neighbors, good fathers or mothers ... and in whatsoever may make them happy and useful" (Mizwa, 140–1). As a final gift to America, in 1800, he wrote the military treatise *Maneuvers of Horse Artillery*, becoming the first effective system for the organization of the American artillery, one used in the War of 1812, for the Army, at that time, had no other system.

Working from Paris for the Polish cause, Kościuszko finally settled in his later years in Switzerland, living with his friend, Francis Zeltner, and dying in Soleure on October 15, 1817, from a stroke incurred when his horse stumbled on a mountain near Lake Geneva. The undertaker found a white handkerchief on Kościuszko's breast, the same one dropped by Louise as her father pulled her from the carriage during the botched elopement. His heart was removed and placed in a bronze urn, to remain in free Switzerland, and only returned to Poland when the country became free. His body was laid to rest on the Wawel Hill in Kraków, among Polish kings, Czar Alexander sending his personal carriage to Switzerland to recover the body. The whole world, and every religious faction, mourned the Polish hero, and "when news of his death in exile spread through Europe, funeral masses were held in Catholic, Lutheran, and Calvinist churches. Jewish synagogues and Muslim mosques also held services where worshippers prayed for Kościuszko's soul" (Storozynski, 278).

In his later years in Switzerland, Kościuszko's love of humanity continued to pour forth. Seeing a Polish regiment in the Czar's army attempting to confiscate the villager's stocked fishponds, he yelled in Polish, "Stop, soldiers, stop!" The peasants of the village took off their hats and formed a protective circle around Kościuszko. The annoyed soldiers asked Kościuszko who he was to order them so, to which he replied, "I am Kościuszko." The soldiers fell at his feet, throwing their arms to the side. When the Czar who freed him from the St. Petersburg prison returned to the throne upon Napoleon's defeat, Kościuszko was escorted into his presence, humbly asking the returning Czar to "grant amnesty to the peasants drafted into the armies of the countries that divided Poland promising to abolish serfdom within ten years; to declare himself king of Poland under a constitutional monarchy like that of England, and to establish schools using government funds to educate the peasants" (qtd. in Storozynski, 267). (Czar Alexander hugged and kissed Kościuszko as if they were life-long friends.) When Poland became no longer a sovereign nation, to Prince Czartoryski Kościuszko pleaded "for estate owners to establish a school for peasants in each estate. In every town the government should establish a school for burghers and peasants teaching them mechanical crafts" (qtd. in Storozynski, 271). Indeed, education, as at the beginning of his life at the Royal Academy, became a calling in Kościuszko's twilight years, as he tutored the four Zeltner children, always ready with sugar plums for his students and their friends after their history, math, and art lessons. He also rode through neighboring towns, searching for people suffering tragedies, such as fires, floods, or crop failures, asking local ministers to point out the needy. Note: African American educator and former slave Booker T. Washington visited Kościuszko's tomb in 1910, thereafter writing: "As I looked upon his tomb, I thought how small the world is after all, and how curiously interwoven are the interests that bind people together. Here I was in this strange land, farther from my home than I had ever expected to be in my life and yet, I was paying my respects to a man whom the members of my own race owed one of the first permanent schools for them in the United States. When I visited the tomb of Kościuszko I placed a rose on it in the name of my race" (qtd. in Storozynski, 283).

This profile of Kościuszko's life serves to educate and nourish the spirit of this writer, all Americans, and all citizens of this globe who hereafter read this story. Kościuszko's wisdom might enlighten the current status of our political system as well, for in his later years he forewarned: "Riding over the highest mountain tops and through the lowest valleys, has taught me to hold the middle of the road as much as possible. I want to follow this approach in my thoughts" (qtd. in Storozynski, 270). And, a final story from Kościuszko's life must "cure" our personal and collective spiritual malaise (fostered by materialism): An old beggar visited Kościuszko's residence at the Zeltner home instead of waiting for his trip to the village. Kościuszko let the suffering man inside and gave him a coin. The visitor thanked him, but, alas, on the way out the door stepped on Kościuszko's pet bird, crushing him to death. The look of dismay on the faces of both men was acute. The needy visitor turned pale and tried to speak, but could not. Kościuszko, seeing the old man's sorrow, returned to his desk, took out another gold coin, and gave it to the troubled man, saying, "Here, my poor friend, something more for your pain," turning away to hide his own sorrow.

In closing, Kościuszko's prayer, written for the "whole human race," speaks to every heart:

Kościuszko Mound, Bronisława Chapel at its foot.

Almighty God, who enlivens the world's millions with your Spirit,
  Who has ordered me to live in this valley of tears for designs hidden from me,
  Grant that I may wend my way through it over roads pleasing to You;
  Let me do good; keep me from evil; restrain the unruly impulses of my impetuosity;
  Let me come to know your genuine truth unmarred by any human error.
    Bless, O God, my country, my relatives, my friends, my benefactors, my countrymen — the whole human race.
    And when my last hour comes, when my soul takes leave of my body, grant that it may stand
    Before your countenance in the dwelling of the blessed and comprehend the mystery of the world which today is beyond my comprehension. Do not send me to eternal perdition; but permit me to Stand before your countenance in the abode of the blessed. I ask this through Jesus Christ our Savior. Amen.

Memorials

Poland's freedom was not restored until after World War I, at which time the citizens of Poland brought the bronze urn holding Kościuszko's heart back to his homeland.

The Thaddeus Kościuszko National Memorial stands at the corner of 3rd and Pine Streets in Philadelphia, Pennsylvania, honoring this hero of two continents. It maintains and celebrates the home Kościuszko stayed in during 1797–98 as he convalesced from wounds incurred in the Polish uprising, permanently exiled from his home country.

Historian Stanisław Herbst wrote in the *Polish Biographical Dictionary* that Kościuszko might be the most popular Pole ever, both in Poland and beyond.

A statue of Kościuszko stands in Lafayette Park, Washington, D.C., a contributing monument to the National Register of Historic Places' American Revolution Statuary listing.

Statues of Kościuszko stand in Philadelphia, Detroit, Chicago, Milwaukee, Cleveland, St. Petersburg, and Pennsauken, New Jersey.

A statute of Kościuszko overlooks the Hudson River at West Point in New York.

In Poland stands the Kościuszko Mound in Kraków, built in the years 1820–1823. Monuments are also found in this city (designed by Leandro Marconi) and in Łódź.

A monument to Kościuszko stands in Solothurn, Switzerland, as well as a museum at the site of his last residence.

Twin Bridges over the Mohawk River in the State of New York, leading to the Adirondacks, is named after Kościuszko.

The tallest mountain in Australia is named Mount Kościuszko.

An island in Alaska is named Kościuszko Island, as is Kościuszko County, Indiana, and Kościuszko, Mississippi.

The Polish-American Kościuszko Foundation was organized in Thaddeus' memory.

Kościuszko is the subject of a sonnet by Samuel Taylor Coleridge and a poem by John Keats. A panaroma stands in Racławice, Poland, depicting the battle of Racławice, created for the centenary anniversary by Jan Styka and Wojciech Kossak.

11

THE DARING AND DASTARDLY CHARLES ARMAND

Justice to that gentleman obliges me to express the Esteem I have of him, as an intelligent, active, and very deserving officer. — George Washington, Yorktown, Virginia, 1781, speaking of Charles Armand

The French court. A Buddhist monastery. Daring and dastardly Charles Armand Tuffin, Marquis de la Rouërie embraced both these forms of living. A brigadier general in the American Revolution. A staunch supporter of King Louis XVI in the French Revolution. Impetuous and adventure-seeking, Charles Armand lent his bravery and courage to both conflicts, earning glory as both a revolutionist and royalist. Careless and frivolous as a youth, Armand's inner core was not immediately apparent; however, when push came to shove, the young aristocrat evaded the wrath of the French monarchy, swam the angry Atlantic to evade the British, walked one hundred miles on foot to join the American cause, recruited a "Legion" of cavalry and infantry men, and became the first officer crossing over the parapet at Yorktown. An amalgamation of personality, Armand "pleased the Americans by the simplicity with which he adopted republican morals, he won the affection of the French by his bravery and modesty, he gained the admiration of both by his heroic courage and his unconquerable firmness" (Rosengarten, 236).

Bringing in the New Year in 1750 (January 1), Charles' birth home was Brittany, France. The son of an old aristocratic family, left at an even earlier age by the death of his father into the care of a pretty, pleasure-seeking mother, Charles entered the Royal House Guards (French military) at the age of ten under the command of Duke de Biron. The Tuffins were feudal lords of an area encompassing about ten miles, holding the courts of justice for the people and receiving all tithes. Privileged and spoiled, considered compulsive and headstrong by his guardian, the uncle who raised him, his fellow officers and the ballet dancers of the Paris opera no doubt found Armand "quick-witted, utterly fearless, a loyal friend, a gay companion, and an expert horseman. Above all, he was full of charm" (Whitridge, "Marquis," 49). Kite relates, "The boy, gentle and modest by nature, winning and affectionate, grew up in the company of his mother and his tutors, docile to their teaching, inured to all manly sports and exercises, and for recreation dashing at break-neck speed over the countryside, his pet monkey seated on the pummel of his saddle" (452). In Paris, he received a brilliant education, learned to speak English and German, and danced to his heart's content. An attempted elopement caused Armand great remorse, and he sought refuge at a Trappist monastery (Monastery of La Trappe), staying two years, with every idea of becoming a monk. Forgiven by his ever patient guardian (uncle), however, who convinced him to reject this lifestyle, he returned to Brittany. His youthful impetuous nature, however, did not abate, and, after severely wounding the nephew of Louis XVI during a duel over a mutual love interest, at one point he believed he had killed him; his guilt resulted in an attempted, self-imposed, poisoning (opium). Having experienced the dark depths of the soul, and no doubt exposed to the concept of collective well-being while an apprentice monk, Armand pondered the fresh paradigms of the American Revolution, the values associated therewith firing his imagination and adventurous spirit. As Whitridge notes, "Just as today a certain section of the younger generation feels stifled by standards and conventions that seemed natural enough to their parents, so many of the more generous-minded nobility in France felt stifled by the atmosphere of Versailles. Fortunately for them, there was a new Arcady across the sea where men could breathe more freely, a land of noble savages, romantic scenery, and social equality, where a struggle for liberty was going forward under the banner of a leader who might well have stepped out of the pages of Plutarch" (50).

No doubt news of the Declaration of Independence reached Brittany, for Armand sought out and obtained, at risk of personal harm, a letter of recommendation from Silas Deane in Paris. Leaving a natural son, born from one of his many love affairs, and his mother behind in France to sail for America, Armand boarded a ship owned by Robert Morris and filled with munitions and other valuable dry goods for the Continentals, which was chased by a fleet of three British men-o-war while in the Chesapeake Bay. John Adams described the incident in a letter to his wife in April 1777, describing how the captain blew up the ship rather than have it fall into British hands. The captain died in the course of this endeavor, Adams lamenting, "I regret the loss of so brave a man more than that of the ship and cargo. The people are fishing to save what they can, and I hope they will save the Cannon. The French Gentlemen, it is said, have brought dispatches from France to the Congress" (qtd. in Whitridge, 49). Prior to ignition, Armand and his valet, rather than surrendering to the British, jumped into the stormy Atlantic. Momentarily deprived of worldly

Charles Armand Tuffin, Marquis de la Rouërie (1750–1793).

belongings, but with French dispatches in hand, Armand and his valet walked 100 miles on foot to Philadelphia, there appearing before the Continental Congress, tendering their services to the American cause.

The Congress, upon receiving foreign volunteers, many times would "pass the buck" to General Washington, forcing the commander to determine the character of the volunteer and/or an appropriate vacancy within his command, a task he did not relish. On May 16, 1777, just three days prior to meeting Armand, Washington wrote: "I shall inform Monsieur Armand, and reconcile him to it the best way I can, that there is no vacancy for him at present. And I would beg leave to suggest that where promotions are made in future, from Political and Honorary Motives, that it will be well for Congress to explain the Gentleman, that it may be some time before they can be put in actual command. This might prevent their entertaining suspicions of neglect on my part, which the situation of the Army will not allow me to obviate" (qtd. in Whitridge, *Marquis*, 48).

Armand apparently impressing George Washington upon introduction, the commander had changed his mind by May 19, writing to Robert Morris: "Armand is a modest, genteel, sensible young gentleman, and I flatter myself his conduct will be such as to give us no reason to repent any civilities that may be shown him" (qtd. in Whitridge, *Marquis*, 48). Washington's letter continues to inform Morris that Armand had requested to command a partisan corps of Frenchmen. Washington granted Armand's request, informing him to engage up to 200 men and decide upon appropriate officers. The fact that Washington apparently changed his mind upon meeting Armand, offering him a carte blanche command, is significant to Armand's ability to convey an impression of strength. Yet, Armand also carried recommendations from Robert Morris' French friends, was a graduate of the Garde du Corps, spoke and wrote English fluently, and was willing to spend his own money to organize, equip, and pay those under his command.

A wild and undisciplined youth was transformed, once he reached the shores of America, to a responsible and reliable officer, his fearless nature having always run deep, but the lessons learned from two near brushes with death, the unbounded love of his guardian, the social conventions of his class, and the spiritual contemplation in which he participated while living in the monastery, molding the young man who sacrificed the remaining years of his youth for the cause of American independence. A fatherless child also may have subconsciously considered Washington the father he never knew, his first letter to the General reading, "My General, I am come into your Country to serve her, and perfect my feeble talent for war under the command of one of the greatest generals of the world" (qtd. in Whitridge, *Marquis*, 50). To Robert Morris he wrote, "We love and honor this good general as our father. These are the true sentiments of every Frenchmen in your Country" (qtd. in Whitridge, *Marquis*, 50).

Having given up the title of "Marquis" at the moment he reached America's shores, Armand still found trouble recruiting 200 of his fellow countrymen and was thus placed in charge of a rag-tag infantry corps of German-speaking Pennsylvanians serving as outposts and, at times, pretending to be Hessians in cattle raids across the countryside. This group was known as Ottendorff's Corps, assigned to Armand after the original commander, Baron de Ottendorff, a German, deserted to the British and received a captaincy in Benedict Arnold's American Legion. Armand's first battle occurred on June 26, 1777, as he led his German recruits against the British at Short Hills, New Jersey, losing nearly a third of his men, yet personally rescuing a cannon from capture. Washington praised Armand for recovering "a piece of artillery which, but for your spirited behavior, would have been taken by the enemy." After also entering a skirmish with the British at the Head of Elk on the Chesapeake Bay, Ward believes Armand next served at Red Bank (helping Lafayette hold back a Hessian artillery force of 350), Brandywine, and Germantown, and a letter written by Armand on October 11, 1778, from near Kingsbridge, New York, says, "The Legion again went into Winter Quarters on the upper Delaware, where, with Pulaski's Corps, it served as a protection to Pennsylvania" (Ward, 6).

Next assigned to Valley Forge, impatient with the inaction associated with that bitter winter, Armand began picking up recruits from Hessian prisoners of war. Congress authorized Armand, after months of debate, to gather a "legion" of 450 men to be known as the "free and independent chasseurs." Armand dressed these men, at his own expense, in splendid uniforms (olive-colored coatees and brown breeches) and paid for a coach to parade them before old comrades. Note: Armand's uniform was a "coat and waistcoat of very dark green and light brownish buff, with small brass buttons, epaulettes of gold braid, with a silver star on the right one; bright red stock tied over a white stock, ... shako of black fur, with an aigrette and a white ornament" (qtd. in Haarmann, 100). He trained the men in cavalry techniques, forming a unit of dragoons followed by a group of light infantrymen for coverage purposes. Washington finally gave Armand permission to raid between Manhattan and the main American line, resulting in his delight at Armand's success, as "his operations consisted mostly of hit-and-run tactics, and though his encounters with guerrilla bands and other cavalry patrols were on too small a scale to be decisive, they were important as raising the morale of the army during an otherwise dismal period of inaction in New York and New England and defeat in the South" (Whitridge, *Marquis*, 53).

Under Colonel Lee's command, Armand's cavalry took Simcoe's Corps (the Queen's Rangers), who had executed several successful undertakings against the Americans, as prisoners near the Raritan River, South Amboy, New Jersey, Simcoe at the time undertaking an expedition to destroy several American boats. In another famous raid on November 7, 1779,

The left bank of the Hudson River three miles above Still Water, the inhabitants thereof counting Charles Armand as their friend. Engraving by Barlow; published by William Lane, London, 1789 (National Archives and Records Administration).

Armand captured a high-ranking Loyalist in his personal home as he slept, Alderman Leggett. Ward writes, "Colonel Armand proceeded with his corps from near Tarrytown to the vicinity of Morrisania, to the house of Alderman Leggett, where he surprised and took Major Baremore and five other prisoners. The secrecy, precaution, gallantry, and discipline exhibited by the Colonel and his corps on this occasion did them much honor. In the capture of Major Baremore, the inhabitants of the adjacent country were relieved from the frequent excursions of a troublesome officer" (8). Armand accomplished this mission by first securing William's Bridge over the Bronx River, as German mercenaries patrolled the area. Next, he led twenty-two dragoons to Baremore's home, surrounding it, Armand also entering the home to seize the Major. Additionally, near Morrisania on December 2, Armand and some of his corps imprisoned Captain Cruser and two other prisoners.

Armand's daring raids became legendary in the Hudson Valley, such legends preserving the impressions he made upon the valley's citizens. One such citizen, George D. Wildes, relates:

> Armand was an officer of light horse, stationed in 1779 at Croton ... near the Hudson, and was distinguished for a dashing courage and admirable address, in successive forays and expeditions down the valley ... the scene of many a fierce encounter between the Hessian Yagers and De Lancey's Loyalist on the one side, and on the other, Col. Greene's, Col. Sheldon's, and Col. Armand's Horse. Armand especially seems to have distinguished himself repeatedly in bold night attacks upon the quarters of the Hessians at or near Kingsbridge. Bolton, the historian of Westchester County, and tradition, alike identify Armand as the hero of one remarkable encounter.... A small stream, still called Tippet's Brook, or the Mosholu, runs southward through this valley. Colonel Armand having ridden rapidly under cover of the night from his quarters on the Croton, certainly twenty or more miles, charged a full speed upon a body of the German Yagers, whose outposts were at Warner's Store.... Armand came cautiously upon a vidette of the Hessians, posted at a little spring, some rods above Warner's, and killing the sentinel, dashed down upon the outpost detachment, and after a quick but hard fight taking the survivors prisoners, dashed up the avenue of Van Courtlandt mansion, the reputed headquarters of the detachment. The alarm having extended to Kingsbridge, and Armand being pursued by De Lancey with his Loyalist Cavalry, he was only able to signify his presence in the valley, to the surprised officers of the Hessian detachment, by the shouts of his squadron as it hurried by in retreat, pursued by De Lancey. For miles up the valley the fight between De Lancey and Armand continued, the latter frequently turning upon the foe and inflicting severe loss. With the greater number of his prisoners, Armand regained his quarters at Croton, on this, as on other marked occasions, receiving the special thanks of Washington.... I have no record of the full military service of Colonel Armand, but it is safe to say, that in a region, with the exception of that in and about the cities and vicinity of Charleston and Savannah, more marked, during the Revolution, than any other by the ravages of distinctively partisan strife, and stirring passages of what is technically termed "combat," rather than "battle," no name stands more prominent in the records and traditions of the day than that of Col. Armand. The gallant Frenchman made his mark with his sword in many a heavy fight, as he before and afterwards made it by his grace and courtliness in the social circles of his French home.... I have frequent occasion to pass along the scenes of his exploits, by night on some parochial duty, and never, without thinking of the gallant trooper, and fancying that I hear the clatter of squadron hoofs, as I pass through the secluded glen in which is situated the fountain still bearing the name of Risley's Spring [qtd. in Ward, 11].

Armand's corps also led expeditions against the Six Nations, destroying villages, fields, and crops, keeping the valleys clear and secure for the transport of wagons which carried supplies to the Continental Army, broke the military power of the Natives, and secured the interior of Pennsylvania. The corps' services also apprehended strangers to the valley, patrolled the roads, and arrested fugitives and vagrants.

For his brave efforts, Washington assigned Armand to the command of General Kazimierz Pulaski, head of the Continental Calvary. At Brandywine and White Marsh, Charles fought with valor, joining Lafayette during a raid against Gloucester on November 24, 1777, capturing 60 Hessians, losing only one Continental soldier. Upon General Pulaski's demise in battle, a transfer to the Southern campaign combined Armand's northern unit and Pulaski's troops, forming the legendary "Armand's Legion." He fought valiantly at the Battle of Camden, South Carolina, under General Gates, his cavalry unit on the left flank, yet was unable to circumvent the ruin and defeat which followed this poorly planned battle. Apparently, according to Colonel Otho Williams, Armand strongly criticized General Gates for having put cavalry at the front of a line of battle in the dark (since silence had been encouraged in the orders), accusing Gates of doing so as a sort of revenge for Armand's challenge of Gates' decision to take horses away from officers to move artillery through the wilderness. Cavalry put at the head of the line were wounded and retreated, according to Williams, causing the whole army corps to scatter in disarray. Due to the initial onslaught, the next day's action saw Armand's corps firing ragged volleys, scattering under the pursuit of Bloody Tarleton's troops. On the afternoon following the battle, Armand effected, "I will not say that we have been betrayed, but if it had been the purpose of the general to sacrifice his army, what could he have done more effectually to have answered that purpose?" (qtd. in Southern, 116).

One of the first to recognize what he perceived as Gates' incompetence, Armand wrote to Washington, "I did not sooner begin my journey than I regreted the happiness and advantage which I lieved behind. I served under grl. Gates and by no means nature had put me when I was born under the necessity of being traited like a slave. However, it was my fate, and I subdued myself entirely to it, hopping that fortune reserved me a better one — after the defeat at Campden I went to Congress to know what were their will on respect to my legion, if it was to be remounted and reunited or not" (qtd. in Whitridge, *Marquis*, 54). To Gates himself, Charles wrote, "As this is the first time I have the honor to be under your command, I think it of my duty to revoir (report) this to your Excellency, in purpose that should I be obliged to quite the army you could know before Hand what would have been my reasons for it, since in the army my commission render me of any other immediate command except of that of the commander-in-chief of the army where I am. I am told that an officer was to come Here and take the Command of the light troops in general, perhaps not knowing the footing I have been always on in the army, and what reasons persuaded me to remain in it. You could make an arrangement by which I should be Commanded by officers which I respect, indeed, but which, by the nature of my services, are not entitled to command me, except when ordered to act in Conjunction with them in army expedition" (Colonial and State, 509). Also, frustrated when Gates assigned men he thought to be in his unit to Colonel Porterfield, he noted, "I beg leave to tell that whatsoever good are our Militia on Horse they cannot answer the most necessary purpose of mounting guards and securing a post" (Colonial and State, 537). And, finally at the end of his tether, in September 1780, he informed Gates: "The present state of the legion, of my officers and Myself Call me to Philadelphia, the only place where our affairs may be done" (Colonial and State, 590).

Washington, despite Camden, continued to laud Armand, writing to Congress: "'Tho in general I dislike independent Corps, I think a Partizan Corps with an Army useful in many respects. Its name and destination stimulate to enterprize, and the 2 officers I have mentioned [Armand and Lee] have the best claims to public attention. Colonel Armand is an officer of great merit which added to his being a foreigner, to his rank in life, and to the sacrifices of property he has made renders it a point of delicacy as well as justice to continue him the means of serving honorably" (qtd. in Whitridge, *Marquis*, 54).

Thus approved, Armand applied to Congress for a six-month leave to return to France for the purpose of raising additional money, supplies, and support for a renewed legion. As France had by this time entered into a formal alliance with America, Louis XVI forgave Armand for his impetuous youthful behavior, summoning him to Versailles and inducting him into the Order of St. Louis for his courageous efforts in America. Upon his return, Armand's unit had dwindled due to illness and combat, having served with Lafayette in Virginia during his absence, leading an attack on Tarleton near the James River. Armand found them near Yorktown, what he described as a "sickly place," and thus tendered his services to General Washington. Placed under the command of Alexander Hamilton, Armand and several of his officers served as light infantry on the assault against Redoubt #10. Colonel Hamilton praised Armand for "entering the redoubt among the first, by their gallant example contributed to the success of the enterprise" (qtd. in Haarmann, 99), securing a capture in only ten minutes of hand-to-hand fighting. Washington again sang the praises of Armand's courageous efforts to Congress, recognizing both his seniority and his achievement: "Justice to that gentleman obliges me to express the Esteem I have of him, as an intelligent, active, and very deserving officer. His promotion, I think, may take place without inconvenience" (qtd. in Whitridge, *Marquis*, 58). Congress did again promote Colonel Armand, this time to the rank of brigadier general, his new rank effectively placing him as chief of the entire Continental cavalry. He spent the final months of the war under General Nathanael Greene, dismantling isolated British outposts in South Carolina and Georgia.

Armand remained with the Continental Army until 1783, one of the first foreign volunteer officers to sail to America and one of the last to leave. During this period, he touted his idea of forming a school of cavalry as well as a peacetime cavalry unit, "pointing out deficiencies in the raising, equipping, training, tactical employment, and support of mounted units, and suggested corrective measures.... His proposals were far reaching and certainly would have gone a long way to correct the defects of the cavalry, the neglected arm of the Continental Army" (Haarmann, 100). Writing Washington, his reference to the general as father appears again: "At this period in the affairs of America, it could have been expected that my warmest wishes would be to return to France and enjoy there the fruits of my conduct here and a family happiness — but motive of attachment to your excellency, to the form of republican government and to the great quality of this people as soldiers create in me wishes stranger than those which I may gratify at home" (qtd. in Whitridge, *Marquis*, 58). Washington knew the new country could not afford a cavalry school or unit, and therefore replied: "You, my Dear Sir, cannot pass unnoticed. The great zeal, intelligence, and bravery you have shewn, and the various distinguished services you have performed, deserve my warmest thanks" (qtd. in Haarmann, 102). Armand also received the approbation of Congress in a resolution of February 27, 1784, praising him for "his bravery, activity, and zeal so often evidenced in the cause of America" (qtd. in Haarmann, 102).

Armand returned home in 1784, celebrated as a war hero, finding France on the brink of revolution. He was rather at a loss for some time regarding his future, marrying, yet losing his wife to tuberculosis within six months. He tore down his ancestral home, replacing it with a vast castle around which he planted trees from America. At first attracting the admiration of the Republican troops, he prophesied the perfect storm which became the French Revolution, recognizing the evils lurking in his land, anarchy on the one hand, despotism on the other. He also realized that though France contained men of learning, "virtuosos in art and sciences, what France lacks is men of judgment, men with any understanding of public welfare. 'These men we have not, at least none has showed himself'" (qtd. in Whitridge, *Marquis*, 60). When Armand and the Breton princes realized the distress of the royal family, instead of fleeing, they remained in France and laid plans to lead an uprising in western France to coincide with that on the opposite side of the Rhine, effectively assaulting Robespierrists simultaneously from both the east and west. Armand was placed in charge of organizing, equipping, and drilling the peasantry of the region, "making each parish the centre of a group sworn to avenge the injury done their pride as royalists or their piety as good and fervent Catholics" (Rosengarten, 238). He was well acclaimed and "used the utmost efforts to rouse the noblesse of Brittany against the plebian yoke which had been imposed upon them by the National Assembly" (Ward, 33); however, the princes, in battle, proved ineffective, and Armand and the members of the Breton revolt against the Republic ended up on the run. The Terrorists never reached Armand, for he died of a heart attack on January 29, 1793, upon hearing of the execution of Louis XVI. His friends buried him secretly by moonlight, but, alas, the Terrorists found his body and mutilated it out of revenge, placing his head on a pike, exhibiting it to the treacherous crowd.

Armand, while a true hero of two countries, remains an obscure historical figure in both France and America, unforgivable in light of his service to both nations, fighting for independence in America and sound judgment in France. As Whitridge elaborates, "It may seem strange that the man who fought so gallantly for American independence should have devoted himself no less gallantly to the destruction of the new-born republic at home. The Marquis de la Rouërie would have found nothing inconsistent in championing a republic abroad and a monarchy at home. If pressed, he would probably have argued that he was fighting against what seemed to him injustice in both cases. It is far more strange, and for this there is no easy explanation, that the man who made such a profound impression on his contemporaries, on men as different as George Washington and the Comete d' Artois, should be so nearly forgotten both in American and in his own country" (*Marquis*, 63).

Memorials

Armand's chateau remains as it stood, preserved as it appeared in Armand's day, his tomb in the woods near the house being a pile of rough stones with an iron cross, the arms bearing the insignia of Brittany and the fleur-de-lis. The inscription of the tomb reads: "Armand, Marquis de la Rouërie, died January 30, 1793: he died of his fidelity to the King."

12

HUNGARIAN HUSSAR MICHAEL KOVÁTS

Golden freedom cannot be purchased with yellow gold. — Michael Kováts to Benjamin Franklin

Having already retired from a military career in Europe, a distinguished Hussar major in the Austro-Hungarian, French, and Prussian armies from 1762 to 1776, Michael Kováts de Fabricy served the cause of American independence "most faithfully," "to the detriment of Joseph and as well for the freedom of your great Congress" (qtd. in Bako, 2, Joseph being the "emperor" of Hungary at the time, described by Jefferson as a "despot"). The only land of his time which could nourish independent, democratic governments across the globe, in Kováts' view, was America. Sailing across the Atlantic with no letter of recommendation and only the experience gained in his illustrious military career, he was appointed by a former pupil, Pulaski, as Colonel Commandant of Cavalry, training American soldiers in "Free Corps" tactics (the precursor of modern guerrilla warfare), eventually recognized by the United States Army and by Congress as "Father of Modern American Cavalry." Prophesying his own demise in (battle at the Siege of Charleston) in a letter to Benjamin Franklin before he crossed the ocean to America, Kováts, "most faithful unto death," was, at the dedication of his memorial in Washington, D.C., described by Hungarian Defense Minister Ferenc Juhász as "our freedom fighter for liberty, whose life carries a message. And the message is that irregardless of geographical location, irregardless of nationality, there is one sanctity which we all hope for, and that is liberty" (qtd. in "Opening Remarks: News Archives," n.p.).

Kováts, born August 1724, in Karcag-Uj-Szallas, Hungary, was born into a line of prominent military officers, most having fought against the invasive force of Turkish oppression; the first known, Joannes Besenew, was the King's smith and a deputy master of Royal Cavalry. Stephanus Kowach, from the 15th century, attained a general's rank and a coat-of-arms. A grand uncle from 1605, Petrus Kováts, helped to secure constitutional rights in Hungary and Transylvania, as well as the freedom of the Protestant churches in those countries, and another relative from the early 1700s was in fact elected prince of both Hungary and Transylvania. Michael's grandfather, Joannes, was commandant of the Csabrag fortress. Michael's father, Emericus, whose full last name was Kováts de Keszi et Kaal, moved to Karcag-Uj-Szallas after the Turks were expelled from Hungary. Emericus helped to rebuild this city, devastated in the Turkish wars, a market town on Hungary's Great Plains, known for prize horses and horsemanship. Thus, as Bako notes, "This Kovats family served a long succession of Hungary's monarchs, the legitimate kings of the various ruling houses including the Habsburgs, as long as they solemnly promised to uphold the constitution of the country and to defend the nation's freedom and independence. And, when they failed to do so, members of this Kovats family joined the many thousands of Hungarian patriots, and supported the efforts of the elected princes of Transylvania (up to and including Francis Rakoczi II in the early 18th century) when the rulers of that small but independent-minded remnant of the powerful medieval Kingdom of Hungary felt compelled to fight the Habsburg kings of Hungary in order to force them again and again to sign 'peace treaties' with Transylvania and to promise anew to honor their solemn oaths taken as constitutional kings of the Hungarians" (qtd. in Bako, 5). In fact, in the early 18th century, Francis Rakoczi II, ruling prince of Hungary, led a Hungarian war of independence against the House of Habsburg (1704–1711). The *Boston News-Letter*, which began publication in 1704, reported on the personalities and personal, ethical, and constitutional principles of this movement, and no doubt the founding fathers, especially Franklin, read many of these issues.

Thus born to an independent-minded and military family, his mother named Sara Tompa De Kaal, Michael most likely studied until the age of 15 at the Karcag Protestant Grammar School, versed in Latin and German, thereafter entering a Hussar training unit and distinguishing himself in "the most highly-honored branch of the military in Europe. The Hungarian Hussars were famous for their military expertise and courage, as well as their skill in training and handling a horse. The French light cavalry, as well as the Prussian, were initially organized and trained by Hungarian hussar officers" (Papp, 66). Kováts' first regiment may have deployed to Italy in 1742. He may have been captured, detained, and sent to Buda, seeking amnesty. Eventually, Kováts defected to the French regime, managing to clear himself in 1745. He entered the Royal Austrian-Hungarian army of Archduchess of Austria and Queen of Hungary and Bohemia, Maria Theresa; peace with the Prussian ruler Frederick the Great ensued only a year later, and Kováts was essentially unemployed, for a Viennese court disbanded the Hungarian Hussar units for fear of the growing strength of the Hungarian military. From 1746 to 1752, Kováts may have fought and trained with the Polish and French Hussar units.

Records become more complete thereafter, for on September 23, 1752, Kováts entered the Hungarian unit of Prussian Army Hussars, under the command of Colonel Mihály Székely, a Transylvanian who cared deeply for his Hungarian troops. A sergeant in this regiment, Kováts was promoted on merit rather than birth, as were all Prussian Hussars (not the same for the Austrian units). In 1757, Kováts was assigned to challenge the Czech Republic throughout Austria, in his own words responsible for site reconnaissance, route security, and miscellaneous security tasks, his exemplary performance earning him a promotion to lieutenant. (A battle on February 6 of this year, the Choline Way Battle, drove Frederick II from Prussia and is considered the birthday of the Habsburg Republic of Hungary.) Kováts' regiment also fought in the battles of Pirna, Gotha, Lobosits, Prague, Torgau, and Leitmeritz. When he was severely wounded in a raid against the French on October 17, 1757, his left arm unusable for a period, the Prussian Army forced Kováts to become a tax collector of sorts. Kováts balked at the task, the manner in which the poor were taken hostage if their taxes were not paid, and the overambitious tax imposed upon citizens, all in the name of improving German municipalities. Kováts at times would recover only a portion of the tax claim, witnessing the destitution of the citizens. Kováts and his troops were even subjected to an embezzlement claim, which proved moot.

Repeatedly asking for leave to receive medical care for his arm, he was rejected on several occasions, but, finally, leave was allowed in December 1760. The doctor at the spa attended by Kováts provided a certificate stating he should not return to active duty, and Michael requested retirement from the King. His request was denied; the King angrily insisted that Kováts return to the army as a major. Disobeying the King's mandate, Kováts escaped to Poland in 1761, effectively deserting the Prussian Army. In Poland, he helped the patriot movement and even trained the father of his future commander, Kasimir Pulaski (and possibly a young thirteen-year-old Casimir). Thinking all was safe, he returned to Hungary and became a spy for the Habsburg Republic against Maria Theresa. He was caught in Vienna while a double agent and subjected to questioning for high treason. Revesz notes, "The minutes of the Court Martial proceedings indicate the importance of our hero. The Minutes comprise several volumes and include among other documents, seven personal letters of Frederick the Great addressed to Kováts. After Kováts spent more than a year in military prisons, the highest military court of Austria forwarded all the papers to the Empress Maria Theresa, who ordered Kováts freed and all his personal and real property returned to him" (4). He was freed on June 13, 1762; the Empress reappointed Kováts as a major in a Hussar regiment, granting him a yearly pension of five hundred florins. Nevertheless, his every move, even his correspondence was watched carefully, and Austrian military reports indicate he lived in Eperjes, Eger, and Buda-Ujlak.

Kováts married in 1763 to Szinyei Merse Frances, her senior by nineteen years. The couple lived together for three months, but, due to his preferred lifestyle, contributing his expertise at the military headquarters, gone night after night, his wife moved back in with her parents. Kováts tried on several occasions to reconcile his marriage, to no avail. A son born to the marriage died of an unknown disease at age three. Petitioning the Court for permission to enter Poland, the request denied, the denial unheeded, Kováts entered first Poland and then Slovakia, and "achieved considerable success and recognition as a training officer of the voluntary troops of Polish patriots then organizing themselves for the liberation of their nation in a movement called the Confederation of Bar.... This was the time when Kováts met and trained his future superior in the American army, young Casimir Pulaski" (Bako, 3).

Continuing to run from Hungarian authorities due to his continuing debt (his wife had filed for alimony by this time and apparently a daughter was also supported by Kováts), he landed in France and of course heard all the chatter and news regarding America's fight for independence. Reports indicate "Major Kováts left Buda in August 1776, and according to information, he went to Bordeaux which is a port in France, from there he left for America and joined the Military Forces of the United Colonies" (qtd. in Revesz, 5). Having learned of the American agent to France, Benjamin Franklin, Kováts wrote the sage, in Latin, on January 13, 1777, a letter which is now considered immortal:

Most Illustrious Sir,
   Golden freedom cannot be purchased with yellow gold. I, who have the honor to present this letter to your Excellency, am also following the call of the Fathers of the Land, as the pioneers of freedom always did. I am a free man and a Hungarian. As to my military status, I was trained in the Royal Prussian Army and raised from the lowest rank to the dignity of a Captain of the Hussars, not so much by luck and the mercy of chance than by most diligent self-discipline and the virtue of my arms. The dangers and the bloodshed of a great many campaigns taught me how to mold a soldier, and, when made, how to arm him and let him defend the dearest of the lands with his best ability under any conditions and developments of the war. I now am here of my own free will, having taken all the horrible hardships and bothers of this journey, and I am willing to sacrifice myself wholly and faithfully as it is expected of an honest soldier facing the hazards and great dangers of the war, to the detriment

of Joseph and as well for the freedom of your great Congress. Through the cooperation and loyal assistance of Mr. Faedevill, a merchant of this city and a kind sympathizer of the Colonies and their just cause, I have obtained passage on a ship called "Catharina From Darmouth," whose master is a Captain Whippy. I beg your Excellency, to grant me a passport and a letter of recommendation to the most benevolent Congress. I am expecting companions who have not yet reached here. Your Excellency would be promoting the common cause by giving Mr. Faedevill authorization to expedite their passage to the Colonies once they have arrived here. At last, awaiting your gracious answer, I have no wish greater than to leave forthwith to be where I am needed most, to serve and die in everlasting obedience to Your Excellency and the Congress. Most Faithful unto death, Bordeaux, January 13, 1777, Michael Kovats de Fabricy [qtd. in Bako, 1].

Revesz speaks to Kováts' venture: "Kováts was fifty-three years old when he wrote that letter and had been in military service for thirty-three years. This letter is truly an historical document. At present it is in Philadelphia at the Library of the American Philosophical Society, among the papers of Benjamin Franklin" (5). Failing to await Franklin's reply, Kováts sailed to America, past commandant of a Hungarian "Free Corps," recipient of the highest military decoration in the Prussian army, the "Pour le Mérite," a staunch supporter of Polish independence, and a vehement opponent to Joseph's despotism and failure to uphold Hungary's constitution (Joseph was even contemplating recalling retired military officers for a campaign against both Turkey and Prussia at the moment of Kováts' departure.) Kováts sought service in a country true to his own ideals and values: "Human freedom and national independence. The only land where he could nurse any hopes for such promises was an independent, democratic United States of America" (Bako, 4). Kováts knew his worth and the manner in which he could serve America, for "of Frederick's twenty-two battles, fifteen were won by his cavalry and Kováts was one of his cavalrymen. Training was the secret of Frederick's success and Kováts organized for him. Kováts learned in fifteen victorious battles the dominating influence of his hussars. It was for this — and no other purpose, that he came to America, i.e. to organize hussars for Washington" (Revesz, 6).

As Franklin believed America might also have to request aid from countries such as Hungary, he did not forward Kováts' letter to Congress, for fear of offending a potential ally. (The Queen of France was a daughter of Maria Theresa and a sister to Joseph.) Finding a letter of recommendation from Major General Joseph Spencer of Providence, Rhode Island, Kováts visited Washington at his headquarters in Philadelphia in May. Washington did not immediately offer Kováts a commission, for he found the explanation of his past "conflicting" and also did not want to further offend his commanding officers by offering yet another commission to a foreign officer. Thus, during the summer months, Kováts volunteered as a recruiting officer for a Pennsylvania German unit (speaking the language fluently). He also visited and befriended the members of a Moravian Order of Lutheran Germans, both groups recommending Kováts when Major Casimir Pulaski asked General Washington to provide Kováts a commission in his legion as commandant of the cavalry.

Initially, Washington replied, "As so much has been said of the character and abilities of Mr. Kováts, I have no objection to his employment in the capacity of Master of Exercise for a few months" (qtd. in Revesz, 9). Again, on March 19, Pulaski scripted: "I would propose, for my subaltern, an experienced officer by name Kowacz, formerly a Colonel and partisan in the Prussian service" (qtd. in Papp, 66). And, on March 20, per Pulaski's and Kováts' discussions as to their frustrations regarding the implementation of a cavalry unit ("They seemed to realize that their potential authority was too great not to meet with all possible objections from the Army Headquarters at Valley Forge. The Cavalry was, at least on paper, just as important as the Infantry, and in theory, they had control over one half of Washington's potential army. Also they were of too active a nature not to feel that at the cavalry headquarters, they were more bureaucrats than soldiers; they planned on paper, organized ideas and principles only, and there was still no Cavalry with which to work. They preferred action to the writing desk. Theories can be great but they wanted a living Cavalry. They wanted to train, above all, officers, without whom they could not make a Cavalry" [Revesz, 10]), Pulaski resigned his commission. Pulaski had written Washington in February: "It is absolutely necessary that the Cavalry have a Master of Exercise, who should instruct the commissioned and non-commissioned officers in the rules of service, as, having the command, I am obliged to act with precaution; but this officer, actuated by different motives, would remove the bad habits and correct the defects of the superior officers. There is an officer now in this country, whose name is Kowacz. I know him to have served with reputation in the Prussian service, and assure your Excellency that his is every way equal to this undertaking" (qtd. in Szymanski, 120).

By March 28, the formation of a legion was sanctioned by Congress. To Kováts' delight, Congress also named him colonel commandant of Pulaski's Legion on April 18, 1778, providing the opportunity for which he had volunteered, "to organize and train hussar regiments for the American army. The recruiting of men began almost immediately.... Kováts trained these men in the tradition of Hungarian hussars; in basic form, training and organization, they were similar to their European counterparts" (Papp, 67).

Initially headquartered in Baltimore, Kováts also recruited in Easton,

Cavalry Commander Michael Kováts de Fabriczy, Hungarian Hussar and officer in the Continental Army (Pulaski's Legion).

Pennsylvania, altogether raising 320 men, remarkable in light of the fact that Washington only carried 4,000 men on the roles of the Continental Army. The newly formed cavalry (the precursor to what became the U.S. Cavalry) won numerous battles along the East Coast in late 1778 (Osborne Island on October 10 and Egg Harbor on the 14th. The Egg Harbor battle served to preserve the American haven for arms and goods on the coast of New Jersey from the force of Captain Patrick Ferguson). During the winter months, the legion trained at Cole's Fort and guarded against raids by the Iroquois Indians and Loyalists, for "Kováts had a free hand to put his ideas into practice. He took care of all the details of organization, and the Cavalry he created was, consequently, typically Hussar; Hungarian in form and in spirit" (Revesz, 11).

In February of the following year (1779), Kováts' (Pulaski's) unit was sanctioned to the defense of Charleston, South Carolina, arriving on May 8 to join the command of General Benjamin Lincoln, Kováts' horsemen reduced to 150 due to smallpox, the disease taking its toll along the path from Salem, North Carolina, to Charleston. The Southern Army, "a continuously changing amalgam of mostly militia units contributed by a number of the American states" under Lincoln's weak leadership (he was a New England patriot serving in the South and was also suffering from an incurable wound in his leg), was under siege. The British army was in the peninsula leading to the city of Charleston and expected to negotiate the terms of surrender with the city and state governor forthwith. The population of Charleston itself was overcome with terror and urged for surrender. Pulaski's charge on May 11, nevertheless, worked wonders, recharging "the will and courage of the city population, changing the opinion of the city fathers, and ... convincing the British commander of the eventually very dangerous outcome of any further aggression against Charleston, he turned around his troops of more than two thousand men, and, pursued by Pulaski's decimated Legion and some local units, led them back to the fortified city of Savannah, Georgia" (Bako, 5).

Unfortunately, during the "audacious attack," Kováts, mortally wounded by a rifle shot, fell from his horse and was buried by the British at the site where he fell, the corner of Huger Street on the lot of John Margart (his horse was also killed and buried with him). The British officers at the battle (specifically, English Brigade Major Skelly) described Kováts' unit as "the best cavalry the rebels ever had." Washington and the Congress initially hailed the saving of Charleston as "the greatest glory of the War." (Despite their differences, Kováts' wife preserved her husband's name in his home country by building Szinyei chapel [1780] in his memory.)

President Franklin D. Roosevelt, referencing Kováts, said, "Men of Hungarian blood, many of them exiles from their Fatherland, rendered valiant service to the cause of the Union, their deeds of self-sacrifice and bravery deserve to be held in everlasting remembrance" (qtd. in Revesz, 12). The *Hungarian Military Review*, in 1934, noted,

> Michael de Kováts was one of the outstanding men of his century; he embodied great initiatives, undertaking abilities and quick decisions — the very qualities we attribute to modern Americans. He had a quick wit; he was courageous; he had no handicap. He was an excellent commander, able leader and a stern disciplinarian. He was above all a gentleman, even to his enemies, and the savior of those needing protection. His excellent qualities were always appreciated. Both the English when he made the supreme sacrifice and the Austrian War Council when he was a prisoner of war, gave him full recognition for his deeds. On his personal documents we find the signature of Maria Theresa, Frederick the Great, Benjamin Franklin, George Washington. His life was dynamic. He was born in the East; He takes part

U.S. Deputy Defense Secretary Paul D. Wolfowitz shakes hands with Istvan Nyirjesy, president of the Michael Kováts Memorial Committee (right), at the bronze statue of Hungarian patriot Colonel Michael Kováts de Fabricy during an unveiling and dedication ceremony at the Hungarian Embassy in Washington, October 11, 2003 (Photograph by Gerry J. Gilmore; U.S. Department of Defense).

in every great movement of his period, always rising and moving to the West. He becomes one of the great leaders of the Revolutionary War — then disappears without any trace. After one hundred and fifty years, his name reappears so that his deeds may shine in eternal glory [qtd. in Revesz, 13].

Living and dying on his horse, an animal known for its strength and free spirit, Kováts exemplified the characteristics of the chargers who carried him into battle throughout his career: stamina, steadfastness, heart, and courage, an independent mind following the bugle call for "golden freedom." He exemplified the characteristics associated with the Medal of Freedom awarded in his name each year to an exceptional American: outstanding life achievements, dedication to freedom and democracy, promotion of transatlantic relations, and meritorious contributions to society. These qualities were certainly found in Hungarian Michael Kováts de Fabricy, a man who served, "faithful unto death," for the country which harbored his hopes.

Memorials

In Karcag, Hungary, the middle school is named in Kováts' honor, and the American and Hungarian flags fly side by side in the courtyard. Children learn of the role Kováts played in the American Revolution in history classes.

A symbolic house gate lies outside the house in which Kováts was born in Karcag, dedicated after the fall of communism in 1990.

Commemoration ceremonies are held each May 11, the date of Kováts' death, in America and Hungary.

On October 11, 2003, a statue entitled "Faithful Unto Death" was dedicated on the grounds of the Hungarian Embassy in Washington, D.C. The statue depicts the moment Kováts and his horse gave their lives for the cause of American independence (a smaller replica stands in Karcag). The military academy in Charleston, South Carolina, The Citadel, honors Kováts with a plaque and a field named in his honor.

A "Colonel Michael de Kováts Society" was formed in New York on the 200th anniversary of George Washington's birthday in 1932. On May 11 of that year, a memorial celebration commemorating Kováts' heroic death was held in Central Park, two trees planted in his memory. Attending were the Prince of Wales, King Albert of Belgium, and General Pershing.

A plaque was presented to the New York Historical Society in 1939 depicting Kováts on a horse with saber drawn, the walls of Charleston in the background.

13

SACRIFICIAL WARRIOR
BARON JOHANN DE KALB

They cannot possibly triumph in the end.—Baron de Kalb, speaking of the British Army in a letter to his wife, 1778

Ten years before the Revolutionary War began, French spies were determining the true intent and valor of the American colonists, and none other than Baron Johann de Kalb was the secret military agent dispatched by the French government. Returning to America ten years later, on April 20, 1777, companion to the illustrious Lafayette, "Baron" de Kalb was actually born a German peasant, receiving his "title" by merit. In his youth, he learned the "art" of war under Marshal Hermann Saxe; "the professor," in the words of Frederick the Great, "of all the European generals of his age," served the French during the Seven Years' War (French-Indian), and fostered France's aid to the American rebels from the very beginning. A striking figure at fifty-nine years of age when he volunteered with Lafayette for the American cause, "more than six feet tall, with greying hair, flamingly healthy cheeks, and expressive dark blue eyes" (Flood, 264), the Baron left his life's love to render his military expertise to the American cause, his army realizing immediately that "no general on the American side had more military experience, and he was using it well" (Flood, 267). Initially overlooked by Congress (as was Lafayette), Kalb proved the "Teutonic Warrior" of the American Revolution, carrying his regiments into battle, attempting to improve their plight despite incompetency, lack of supplies and rations, and inattention to his advice. At Camden, like a roaring lion, he would not leave the battlefield, though wounded and wounded again, receiving eleven injuries, eight from blades and three from bullets. Death at the hand of the British did not deter his cause, for he knew, as he wrote his beloved Emile in France, "They cannot possibly triumph in the end. Their cruelty and inhumanity must sooner or later draw down their heads the vengeance of Heaven, and blast a Government which authorizes these outrages" (qtd. in Flood, 265).

Johann was born in Huettendorf in the Bavarian District of Erlangen, on June 29, 1721. His father, John Leonard Kalb, was a yeoman, mentioned in church records as "sojourner and peasant of Huettendorf." His mother, Margaret Seitz, of Eschenbach, bore three sons, Johann being the second. He received his early education at Kriegenbronn; additional records regarding his childhood are lost, "but we know his pathway was a rugged one; that he was compelled to wring from the reluctant hand of fortune all that he gained; and that he owed everything to his exertions, character, and talents.... In the truest sense, he was self-made. The accident of birth was against him, but steadfastly relying on his own heart, and hand, and head, he carved his way from poverty and obscurity to power and fame" (Savage, 6). Becoming a waiter at the Alsatian Inn during his early teens and most likely studying the mannerisms of officers, he traveled abroad by the age of sixteen, most likely to France, where he must have cast his lot with the military, for, by 1743, he enters the historical record again as lieutenant in the regiment Loewendal of the French infantry. No doubt using his wit to advance his lot in life, Kalb somewhere was required to feign the title of "Baron," for it "is very clear that his advancement was facilitated by his assumption of nobility, and in the highest degree probable that it was achieved by some act of gallantry in the face of the enemy. But where and how he acquired the manners and the knowledge necessary to maintain his ground, is a question difficult to answer" (Kapp, *Kalb*, 3).

Johann's adoption of a noble title is not surprising based upon the fact that, in European society of that day, commoners could not be promoted and commissions could only be obtained by those whose noble "line" reached back across four generations. Thankfully, as a "partial compensation for this injustice the favored class of that day good-naturedly acquiesced in the nobility of any one who managed to assume the title and the external badges of the order, without inquiring closely into pedigree. This was particularly the case in France, where men were just awakening to a sense of the absurdity of these prejudices" (Kapp, *Kalb*, 4). History must truly appreciate and forgive this slight indiscretion on Kalb's part, for, without the title, America would not have been blessed with this hero of the Revolution.

France was at war with Austria when Kalb first entered military duty, entering a French corps commandeered by German officers, fighting in France's brilliant victory over the combined English, Austrian, and Dutch armies, under the leadership of the aforementioned Marshall Saxe. In his first year, he valiantly served in three sieges and one hotly contested battle, continuing his training under Saxe and in his "leisure" studying the modern languages, higher mathematics in association with fortification, and the organization of bodies of troops. In no time, he was promoted to captain of detail, a sort of general manager combined with judiciary duties, who "conducted the correspondence with the commanding general and the minister of war, reported the condition of the men, made requisitions to meet their wants, scrutinized and expounded the articles of war — of which each regiment then had its own — vindicated their rights as against their superiors, suggested rewards and punishments, and acted, in short, as the virtual head of the regiment" (Kapp, *Kalb*, 6). Kalb served in this capacity from the close of the Austrian war, through a time of peace, and into the Seven Years' War. As each regiment had an inclusive "code" of law so to speak, many abuses within military units were overlooked; punishments were sometimes inordinately abusive. Kalb, during his service as detail officer, attempted to correct many of these injustices, instilling humanitarian regulations within his regiment's code and recommending other regiments follow course. Kapp notes, "Kalb did what he could to redress these grievances, and corresponded with the officers of detail of all the other German regiments in the service, with the view of approximating harmony in the distribution of punishments" (*Kalb*, 8). In fact, in one instance a deserter who sold his uniform in a foreign country was sentenced to the gauntlet. Kalb petitioned for a lighter sentence, such approved due to the more humane ordinances of Kalb's regiment.

As the Seven Years' War began, Kalb proposed to M. Machault, French Minister of Marines, a means of reaching and invading English shores, writing:

> A regiment of foreign marines would be of undoubted advantage to the king. It should number from eight to twelve hundred men, and would have to serve on land, on the coast, in the colonies, and on board the navy, and be composed of Germans, Danes, Swedes, Englishmen,

inhabitants of our own seaboard provinces, but above all things of Irishmen. The latter are universally known to be the best sailors and marines of the English navy; besides, they are Roman Catholics. Their concourse to our flag might make it possible for us to people a considerable part of our colonies with them. By making this disposition of them we might secure the adherence of numbers of Irishmen in any undertaking against the naval power, the colonies, or the provinces of England, and might keep ourselves well informed of all the hostile movements of the British. All the world is aware of the hatred cherished by the Irish against the English. The former never served the latter for any other reason than the want of better employment. It is remarkable that this project has not been broached heretofore. How invaluable would such a corps have been to the State at the time when the king had sixteen thousand Irishmen in his service! For six and forty years France has had no more trusty soldiers, none who served her, on all occasions, with greater zeal and efficiency. But they would have been much more useful at sea than on land, for the former must be regarded as their native element [qtd. in Kapp, *Kalb*, 15].

Taking furlough to Paris to convince the minister of his plan, initially received by the minister, but, in line with the traditional culture of the court, expected to provide favors in association with his regimental position, Kalb returned to his duties, as "this courtly game was repulsive to Kalb's frank and open nature. He answered his friend by saying that he was advocating a public measure, in which he coveted nothing for himself except an opportunity of achieving military distinction, and that he would not stoop to the level of a flatterer or a suppliant. Preferring to renounce his plan, and preserve his military honor, he left Paris in May 1755, and returned to his garrison at Cambray, where, in the following year, he was promoted to a majority in his regiment" (Kapp, *Kalb*, 18). One of the first battles in which he was involved in the Seven Years' War found Kalb's regiment protecting the rear flank of the French at the disastrous Rossbach Battle, saving the army from total annihilation and allowing the army to find winter quarters.

Assigned to the Army of the Upper Rhine, Kalb received a promotion to Lieutenant Colonel, appointed assistant quartermaster general. His conduct at the Battle of Wilhelmsthal afforded Kalb an honor of merit. Toward the end of the year, his regiment was sent to Frankfurt to assist in the payment of debt to German families of noble descent and to lessen the chaos brought on by the war. One princess wrote Johann begging for prompt assistance: "The news of the approaching peace which I read in your favor of the 9th instant," she says, "is most welcome in this part of Germany. We would have been still more fortunate if this joyful event could have occurred eight or nine weeks earlier. Now we are all ruined. Provisions are not to be had, and lords and lieges are staggering under such a load of debt, that fifty years will be required only to clear off the worst of the rubbish. God grant that peace may be concluded in Silesia as speedily as here, so that all Germany may at last breathe freely. Is it not our beloved country whose weal and woe are in question? It gives me great pleasure to see that you, sir, take the same interest in its welfare" (qtd. in Kapp, *Kalb*, 33).

Following the war, accolades followed Kalb, including the following recommendations:

Lieutenant-colonel de Kalb," says Broglie," is one of the best and most efficient officers of my acquaintance, and as expert in the details of the service as versed in the science of war. In the late war I have found him extremely useful and reliable, and can recommend him unqualifiedly as an excellent general." "M. de Kalb," wrote the duke's brother, the Count de Broglie, at the same time, "went through the whole of the late war with me as assistant quartermaster-general, and is deserving of your projection in the highest degree. To what my brother has written in reference to him I can only add that de Kalb is an officer no less intelligent and well-informed than brave and indefatigable. I doubt whether you could find a more fitting man for the organization and instruction of your troops" [qtd. in Kapp, *Kalb*, 34].

Peace forced Kalb to purchase a commission in another regiment, Anhalt. Hoping to attain the position of assistant quartermaster for the entire army, Kalb took furlough in Paris to obtain recommendations. When the appointment did not materialize, and before his return to duty, Kalb met the love of his life, Anna Elizabeth Emilie van Robais. He soon won the heart of Emilie, "sprightly and beautiful." A blessed union ensued; the couple married on April 10, 1764, proving similar to the union of John and Abigail Adams, for in marked contrast to the dissolute manners of the time, Kalb lived exclusively for his family, while his wife, in her turn, was no less devotedly attached to her husband than solicitous of the welfare of her children. "The warmth of this attachment remained unaltered to the hour of Kalb's death, and his last letters to his wife breathe the same fervor which had inspired the first and all the others" (Kapp, *Kalb*, 34).

Following a year of marital bliss, Kalb attempted a return to active duty, yet influential French government officials required his duties elsewhere. Learning of the flattering recommendations afforded to Kalb following the war, French minister and statesman Duke de Choiseul chose Kalb for an intelligence-gathering mission to America. Determined to "eat away" at the British foe which had recently desecrated his nation, and learning of America's growing tide of disgust associated with British taxation, the minister wished to discern if an American insurrection was at hand. Special instructions for a secret mission to America were prepared for Kalb, who traveled to Versailles to receive them. They read:

1. M. de Kalb will repair to Amsterdam, and there direct his particular attention to the rumors in circulation about the English colonies. Should they appear to be well founded, he will immediately make preparations for a journey to America.
2. On his arrival, he will inquire into the intentions of the inhabitants, and endeavor to ascertain whether they are in need of good engineers and artillery officers, or other individuals, and whether they should be supplied with them.
3. He will inform himself of their facilities for procuring supplies, and will find out what quantities of munitions of war and provisions they are able to procure.
4. He will acquaint himself with the greater or lesser strength of their purpose to withdraw from the English Government.
5. He will examine their resources in troops, fortified places, and forts, and will seek to discover their plan of revolt, and the leaders who are expected to direct and control it.
6. Great reliance is placed in the intelligence and address of M. de Kalb in the pursuit of a mission requiring an uncommon degree of tact and shrewdness, and he is expected to report progress as often as possible [qtd. in Kapp, *Kalb*, 44].

After learning of British concessions to America with regard to the Stamp Act, and while Kalb was in Holland, Minister Choiseul still insisted the mission continue, writing Kalb in Amsterdam: "As it is possible, and even probable that this quiet will not be of long duration, it is the will of His Majesty that you should make immediate preparations for a speedy tour to America, in order to satisfy yourself by personal inspection as to the condition of the country, its harbors, ships, land forces, resources, weapons, munitions of war, and provisions—in short, as to the means at our command if disposed, in case of a war with England, to make a diversion in that direction. You will adopt the greatest precautions in sending me your report, and will, immediately upon your arrival, inform me where to direct such letters as I shall have occasion to write you" (qtd. in Kapp, *Kalb*, 49). The ever faithful husband replied to Choiseul, indicating his point of departure, his wish that correspondence be directed through his wife, Emilie, so as to not cause any undue suspect of his intentions while abroad, and reminding the monseigneur of his promise to care for his wife and children in the event of an unfortunate demise.

After a three and one-half–month journey over stormy winter seas, Kalb's first report to the minister as to the state of American politics, written three days after his arrival in Philadelphia, revealed:

> I am beginning to study the matters relating to my commission, such is and am in a fair way to procure reliable information as to the discontent produced in the colonies by the passage of the stamp act. This affair is very far from being adjusted. It is not the case, as was alleged in Holland, that the repeal of the act was voluntary on the part of the Government; on the contrary, although each province has its own separate and distinct assembly, they all refused to acquiesce in the measure with the same decision and unanimity as if they had jointly deliberated upon their line of action. Some, it is true, were more violent than others, but the substance of each refusal was the same. The most violent of these provincial assemblies were those of Boston and Philadelphia, where the commissioners of the new impost were even threatened in their persons. Boston has promptly renounced all commercial intercourse with London, refuses to import any more wares, and expresses a determination to content itself with the productions and domestic fabrics of the country. The women even discard tea and foreign sugar, and we are constantly told of the activity of the spinning-wheels, which have been at work, ever since the promulgation of the act, to supersede the use of English linens. With the same object the women have resolved to dispense with silks and articles of luxury, until their own country shall be in a condition to furnish them. The question is how long they will adhere to this resolution. I do not believe that Philadelphia will adopt the same policy. Although the youngest of the chief towns of the north, it is the wealthiest and most luxurious. Besides, the provincial assembly of Pennsylvania has evinced greater moderation in this respect. For the moment it is difficult to tell what the end will be. All depends upon the policy of the court, which promises to be a conciliatory one, as the advantage derived by the British people from their connection with the colonies is too great to permit the Government to stop short of any efforts to preserve this invaluable magazine of raw productions, and this most profitable market for its manufactures.
>
> During the last outbreaks the troops have treated the inhabitants with much greater circumspection than before, while the commanders have been most careful to avoid any cause of irritation. The commanding general, who has power to convene the estates of each province, to preside over them, and to suppress all attempts to impair the authority of the laws, pretends to ignore all the libels and pasquils which have appeared in public, and the names of the authors of which are in everybody's mouth. This circumstance induces me to suppose that the court have given orders to this effect, and have intended nothing but a simple experiment.
>
> The present condition of the colonies is not such as to enable them to repel force by force; but their value to the mother country is their best safeguard against any violation of their real or imaginary privileges. I have not yet found time to inform myself as to their troops and other warlike resources, but am on the point of making a tour through all the provinces, and to open correspondence at all important points, in order to enable myself to acquaint you more fully with all matters of interest.
>
> If you have any commands for me, be pleased, Monseigneur, to have them written in the same cypher, and sent to my wife, who has the necessary directions for forwarding them.
>
> The remoteness of this population from their centre of government makes them free and enterprising; but at bottom they are but little inclined to shake off the English supremacy with the aid of foreign powers. Such an alliance would appear to them to be fraught with danger to their liberties. Their taxes are very light; indeed, with the exception of the duties

on imported goods, they amount to almost nothing. The crown has even relieved the colonies of the support of a regiment of four thousand men, so that now all the troops stationed in the colonies are in the pay of England. This policy is evidently necessary under the circumstances. The troops are frequently changed, every regiment being recalled after the lapse of three years, and replaced by another.

In case of an insurrection the colonists would have nothing but their militia to depend upon, which, though very numerous, is not in the least disciplined. On the other hand, the immense extent of the country, the want of ready money, the discord among the governors of the various provinces, all independent of each other, present great obstacles to the formation of an army, and the speedy opening of hostilities in the respective neighborhoods. The odium in which the House of Commons is held, is only entrenched by the popularity of Pitt. He is called the defender of liberty, because he was the only one who opposed the stamp act in Parliament [qtd. in Kapp, *Kalb*, 53–54].

Realizing the tax on tea was the next point of conflict, Kalb wrote the Minister again the following week, indicating sedition would be the order of the day if Parliament did not act with all justice toward the American colonists, pointing out that deputies from each state were meeting in union, despite the prohibition to do so. On his attempt to reach New York, Kalb encountered a life-threatening storm as he crossed the Kill on the ferry to Staten Island. A sharp wind pushed the boat to a desolate island, the passengers and horses swimming or walking in the marsh to safety, the wind preventing anyone from hearing their cries. Huddled together throughout the bone-chilling, icy night, Kalb and his fellow survivors braved the elements, desperately attempting to keep moving to prevent sleep and death by exposure. Two of the fellow passengers died in the night, but the rest were saved around 9 A.M. the following morning. Upon reaching an inn, Kalb bathed his feet and legs in ice-cold water for fifteen minutes and was saved the frostbite injury incurred by passengers who immediately sought the comfort of a fire. While escaping with his life, Kalb lost his luggage, money, the badge of his order, and the key to his cypher. The accident report in the *New York Gazette* on February 8, 1768, stated the Baron was unable to reach New York. Thus, he could not investigate the political mood nor report to the minister before February 25. His observations in New York, however, included: "The colonies seem to entrench themselves more and more in their system of opposition and of economy" (qtd. in Kapp, *Kalb*, 60). He informed the minister the colonies were most adverse to taxation by Parliament, rather than representatives of their own particular locality.

Kalb also prophesied and observed: "All classes of people here are imbued with such a spirit of independence and freedom from control, that if all the provinces can be united under a common representation, an independent State will soon be formed. *At all events it will certainly come forth in time.* Whatever may be done in London, this country is growing too powerful to be much longer governed at so great a distance. The population is now estimated at three million, and is expected to double itself in less than thirty years. It is not to be denied that children swarm everywhere like ants. The people are strong and robust, and even the English officers admit that the militia are equal to the line in every particular" (qtd. in Kapp, *Kalb*, 63). From Boston in March, he noted the citizens carried the same spirit, "only expressed with greater violence and acrimony," noting that Massachusetts, Rhode Island, New Hampshire, and Connecticut seemed more firmly united. At that particular point in time, nonetheless, Kalb did not believe the colonies would endorse aid from the French government, for, he believed, despite differences in opinion, the colonists continued to carry a "heartfelt love" for their mother country. He referenced the conflict as a sort of family dispute which should not be tampered with, only carefully observed. He translated to French, for the benefit of the minister of state, over one hundred articles from American newspapers, placards, and pamphlets, including sermons delivered by ministers, unfavorable to English interests. Many of these publications, from such small New England towns as Newport, Salem, or Newburn, are, today, archived only in the French language, found in the libraries, museums, and historical foundations of Paris thanks to Kalb's indefatigable translations.

Remaining faithful to the French court after returning to France in April 1768, Kalb, while in blissful retirement, followed the new minister's (Comte de Vergennes) interest in America as a sore spot for the English. Eventually, due to his belief in the cause of the Colonies and his devotion to France, Kalb, encouraged by the prominent powers within the government, visited with American agent Silas Deane on November 5, 1776. Deane wrote the following day: "Count Broglie, who commanded the army of France during the last war, did me the honor to call on me twice yesterday with an officer who served as his quartermaster-general in the last war, and has now a regiment in this service, but being a German,—the Baron de Kalb,—and having travelled through America a few years since, he is desirous of engaging in the service of the United States of North America. I can by no means let slip an opportunity of engaging a person of so much experience, and who is by every one recommended as one of the bravest and most industrious officers in the kingdom; yet I am distressed on every such occasion for want of your particular instructions. This gentleman has an independent fortune, and a certain prospect of advancement here; but being a zealous friend to liberty, civil and religious, he is actuated by the most independent and generous principles in the offer he makes of his service to the States of America" (qtd. in Kapp, *Kalb*, 85). The contract with Kalb, commissioned as a Major-General in the Continental Army, was signed on December 1. Fortunately, on December 7, Deane also met nineteen-year-old Marquis Lafayette, an additional acquaintance of Broglie, Kalb's friend and patron. The contract Deane entered with Lafayette also contains Kalb's signature.

As spies for the English prime minister swarmed throughout Paris, Kalb and Lafayette's journey necessitated clandestine efforts, the planning of the voyage requiring months, requiring a hush-hush nature. Additionally, Lafayette's father-in-law was opposed to the trip and asked King Louis XVI to forbid Lafayette's journey. Kalb and Lafayette first sailed to a port in Spain for an eventual departure, but the King obliged the father-in-law's request, and, by secret order, directed Lafayette to return to his family for a trip to Italy. Lafayette sought Kalb's advice, and in a letter to Emilie, Kalb believed "it my duty to dissuade him from disregarding the wishes of his father-in-law and the commands of the king" (qtd. in Kapp, *Kalb*, 105). When Lafayette returned to Marseilles, France, by order, in an attempt to change the minds of his relatives and King, he asked Kalb "not to sail before receiving another letter from him from Toulon or some other point. If I am to wait until he gets to Marseilles, I shall have to remain here until the 26th. Lafayette's letter shows that the ship is still held in his name. He requests me to have an eye to his interests, and to see that his investment is realized as soon as possible" (qtd. in Kapp, *Kalb*, 107).

Kalb believing Lafayette received the good-will of his family and King (though he had not), the two finally set sail for America, arriving on June 13, 1777, in the port of Georgetown (near Charleston). Afraid to enter the bay for fear of British vessels, they boarded boats leading them to shore and to several slaves who directed them to the home of plantation owner Major Hueger, whose dogs notified the owner of intruders. Bullets whistled past Kalb's and Lafayette's heads as the entourage approached the plantation, Kalb saving Lafayette's life when he shouted out, in English, who approached. Hueger nourished the lost visitors and sent the two volunteers on their way to Philadelphia. Obviously, Kalb served to "ground" and protect the nineteen-year-old throughout their travels and trials, for, upon setting foot on land, Lafayette said, "I swear that I will conquer or perish in the name of independence!" Kalb pointed out the first step was discovering where they had landed.

To Kalb's astonishment, Congress did not immediately recognize the commissions endorsed by Silas Deane, informing him and Lafayette that Deane had overstepped his bounds and was not authorized to extend such high-ranking commissions, the same being above those held by American-born officers, who had grown jealous of foreign-born officers achieving higher rank within the Continental Army. Lafayette advanced his cause, nonetheless, with an offer to serve without pay. Congress, knowing the great wealth and prestige of this noble Frenchman, acquiesced. Though Lafayette demanded that Kalb's commission also be honored, his commission was not immediately accepted by Congress, and thus, Kalb wrote:

> If you will not ratify Mr. Deane's engagement and appoint me as major-general in your army, I am ready to return to Europe, but think myself entitled to ask you a sufficient sum for my going home. I received from Mr. Deane 1,200 livres French money, and certainly by going to and fro in France, by his direction, and all other expenses until my arrival at Philadelphia, I spent twice as much. And though I ardently desired to serve America, I did not mean to do so in spending part of my own and my children's fortune — for what is deemed generosity in the Marquis de Lafayette would be downright madness in me, who does not possess one of the first-rate fortunes. If I were in his circumstances I should perhaps have acted like he did. I am very glad that you granted his wishes; he is a worthy young man, and no one will outdo him in enthusiasm in your cause of liberty and independence. My wishes will always be that his successes as general-major will equal his zeal and your expectation. But I must confess, sir, that this distinction between him and myself is painful and very displeasing to me. We came on the same errand, with the same promises, and as military men and for military purposes, I flatter myself that if there was to be any preference it would be due to me. 34 years of constant attendance on military service, & my station & rank in that way, may well be laid in the scale with his disinterestedness, and be at least of the same weight and value; this distinction is very unaccountable in an infant state of a commonwealth, but this is none of my business. I only want to know whether Congress will appoint me as general-major, and with the seniority I have a right to expect this (for I cannot stay here in a lesser capacity). It would seem very odd and ridiculous to the French ministry and all experienced military men to see me placed under the command of the Marquis de la Fayette. If, on the contrary, it will not be agreeable to the U. S., I ask your excellency to give me full satisfaction for the purpose of going back, so that I may leave this country as soon as possible. I hope there will be no difficulty in fulfilling my last request, for I should be sorry to be compelled to carry my case against Mr. Deane or his successors for damages. And such an action would injure his credit and negotiations, and those of the state at court.
>
> I do not think that either my name, my services, or my person are proper objects to be trifled with or laughed at. I cannot tell you, sir, how deeply I feel the injury done to me, and how ridiculous it seems to me to make people leave their homes, families, and affairs to cross the sea under a 1000 different dangers, to be received and to be looked at with contempt by those from whom you were to expect but warm thanks [qtd. in Kapp, *Kalb*, 115].

Congress initially agreed to reimburse Kalb for his services, but, his having made acquaintance with several members of Congress, and upon consideration of the fact that this prominent officer knew the English language, Congress decided to honor Kalb's commission the day before he sailed back to France, dating his commission back to that of Lafayette's, July 31, promising him command of a vacated position. The Baron stuck to his laurels — his self-integrity, his commitment to the American cause, his foresight as to the course of history, and, as throughout his life and career, his devotion to service and duty. He resolved to leave if his appearance in the Army caused excessive discord or if the decision was disapproved in France following Kalb's ordeal with Congress.

First assigned to Valley Forge, after determining an attack at Red Bank unwise and throwing reinforcements into Jersey at Washington's command, Kalb was aghast at the condition of the American army. He wrote Emilie and Broglie as to the manner of war, the battles, and leaders of the time, many of these letters subsequently serving to preserve the history of the Revolutionary War (as had his translations). He told his wife and friend, "Everything here conspires to disgust. My blacksmith is a captain! ... The generals never think of sparing their men" (qtd. in Flood, 265). At first hard on Washington, thinking him "too slow," and "far too weak," after he discerned the character of the man who brought his army through the Philadelphia winter of 1777, he wrote Emilie: "He did and does more every day than could be expected from any general in the world.... His integrity, humanity and love for the just cause of his country, receive and merit the veneration of all men" (qtd. in Flood, 265). As Flood notes, "The professional soldier was becoming a patriot" (265). In the same letter, his fervent love for Emilie and his family ever present, Kalb hoped for the best: "I place my trust in Providence that I shall be spared to behold again the object of my most ardent love, and all that can tend to make me happy and contented for the rest of my days" (qtd. in Flood, 265).

Though dispatched on a proposed expedition to Canada by Congress, Kalb returned to Valley Forge in the spring, Lafayette, Washington, and Kalb determining the thwarted expedition to have been instigated by a jealous General Gates and even more jealous Irish officer Thomas Conway. Congress, however, soon realized the folly of such a venture, and Lafayette cheerfully wrote Washington: "I am very sensible of that goodness which tries to dissipate my fears about that ridiculous Canadian expedition. At the present time we know which was the aim of the honorable Board, and for which project three or four men have rushed the country into a great expense, and risked the reputation of our army, and the loss of many hundred men, had the general, your deceived friend, been as rash and foolish as they seem to have expected. O American freedom! What shall become of you if you are in such hands?" (qtd. in Kapp, *Kalb*, 156).

On the same day as Lafayette and Kalb returned to Valley Forge, February 6, 1778, America and France entered an alliance against Great Britain. Waiting until spring, Washington ordered May 6, 1778, a day of celebration. Writing of this event to Emilie, Kalb noted: "The alliance is, on the part of the King of France, so rational, and so generous beyond all expectation, that it has won him the hearts even of those who loved him but little before.... His (King Louis XVI) name will be inscribed upon the annals of this new empire as the interpreter of the high-hearted sentiments of that noble monarch, to whom this immense continent owes its liberty and happiness" (qtd. in Kapp, *Kalb*, 158).

Overcome with a violent fever in mid–May, one which almost took his life, Kalb was unable to serve again until mid–July. Sent to Fishkill, New York, Kalb whiled away the rest of the year in a sort of monotonous army camp life, awaiting Washington's orders and the movement of British troops, informing his wife: "You know, better than anyone else, what a sacrifice I make in this long absence from you and the children, as I might live at home more happily and peaceably than any other man. The privations to which I am subjected, the extraordinary exertions incident to the mode of warfare and to the variable climate of this country, the frequent movements from camp to camp, which makes rest and comfort unattainable even in winter, all these hardships are onerous to a man at my time of life,

Battle of Camden National Historic Landmark, South Carolina.

and make me extremely anxious to return" (qtd. in Kapp, *Kalb*, 167). Throughout another eighteen months, Kalb's troops "performed with a corps the very difficult task of guarding and defending Washington's headquarters at Morristown, protecting the country bordering on the British line, ascertaining and reporting the strength and movements of the enemy along the coasts of New Jersey and Staten Island, and securing, in the advance with an inadequate force, the safety of the American army" (qtd. in Savage, 17).

Kalb described the additional sacrifices of camp life as the summer months ensued: "What I am doing here is extremely disagreeable. Without my excellent constitution it would be impossible to bear up long under this service. Yesterday I made the most wearisome trip of my life, visiting the posts and pickets of the army in the solitudes, woods, and mountains, clambering over the rocks, and picking my way in the most abominable roads. My horse having fallen lame, I had to make the whole distance on foot. I never suffered more from heat. On my return I had not a dry rag on me, and was so tired that I could not sleep. My temperate and simple habits greatly contribute to keep me in good health. My general health is very good, and I hardly notice the annoyances of camp life. Dry bread and water make my breakfast and supper; at dinner I take some meat. I drink nothing but water, never coffee, and rarely chocolate or tea" (qtd. in Kapp, *Kalb*, 173). Commanding and moving his Maryland and Delaware divisions as necessity required over the next year and one-half, Kalb with his units ensured the northern areas occupied by the Americans remained fortified, all the while conditions in the camps worsening, Kalb finding himself "in rags," "so cold that the ink freezes in my pen," his money dwindling due to inflation, "an ordinary horse worth $20,000, I say twenty thousand dollars!" Kalb's men came to love their commander, Colonel Nicholas Rogers noting, "Besides his extreme temperance, sobriety and prudence, with his great simplicity of manners which highly fitted him for his undertaking, he had also many of the other qualifications for a soldier such as patience, long-suffering, strength of constitution, endurance of hunger and thirst, and a cheerful submission to every inconvenience in lodging, for I have known him repeatedly to arrange his portmanteau as a pillow, and, wrapping his great horseman's cloak around him, stretch himself before the fire and take as comfortable a nap as if upon a bed of eider-down" (qtd. in Savage, 16).

As the South came under siege and Charleston on the verge of occupation, Washington ordered Kalb's Maryland division to the South. The march south was just as arduous as the Northern winters, where the Army suffered "from the intolerable heat, the worst of quarters, and the most voracious insects of every hue and form" (qtd. in Flood, 266). Also, the states of North Carolina and Virginia were ignoring his plea for food and supplies. To feed his men, Kalb scrounged the countryside, finally obtaining help from the Moravian settlements, German-speaking Protestants who of course responded to Kalb's requests spoken in the German language. Flood notes, "Thus it was that American soldiers could eat again because their commander was a Bavarian" (267). Very protective of his troops, Kalb understood his division could possibly prove the only effective military force entering the Southern campaign. When they finally arrived at this command with General Gates near Camden, South Carolina, Gates convened a war council, Kalb the only officer disagreeing with his plan to attack Cornwallis on a Camden battlefield. Kalb believed: (1) the position of the Army needed additional fortification; (2) the exact number of American troops needed to be determined (Gates indicated 7,000, when the truth was more like 3,000); (3) more information about the enemy needed to be determined, most notably whether reinforcements had arrived in Cornwallis' camp; (4) the Continentals at that point needed to remain on the defensive, rather than the offensive; (5) the troops had just convened and had never mustered or maneuvered together, were unused to forming columns and certainly unable to execute difficult movements at night. (Remember, also, Colonel Armand was extremely upset about Gates placing cavalry at the front of battle at night, when silence was part of the plan.) The advice of the officer trained by one of the most highly regarded generals in European history was totally disregarded by General Gates, the impetuous and glory-seeking young commander, to the detriment of the Continental Army, as hundreds of American lives were unnecessarily taken in this particular Revolutionary War battle, as well as the life of our instant hero, Baron Johann de Kalb. (Of note: Kalb's men referred to him as "The Baron," while Gates' nickname was "Granny.") In hindsight, Gates' decisions seem almost unforgivable, for "he brought his worn-out, sick and hungry army to Rugely's Mills despite of advice and prudence, and intended at once to attack a strong post and veteran troops.... He had about fourteen hundred good troops well officered. The remainder were raw militia just collected, many of whom had never been in action, and had only just received bayonets, without instruction in their use. They had no idea of tactical formations and movements, and no provision was made for a rallying point in case of disaster.... He did not know that Cornwallis had reached Camden when he advanced, nor the weakness of his own force until he ordered the battle ... and lacked the wisdom to consult with other officers when uncertain as to the proper line of duty" (Carrington, 513–14). The loss of American life was unthinkable, and the equipment lost included the entire artillery, eight field pieces, two hundred wagons, and all luggage.

As it happened, both armies marched against each other the night of the battle, unaware of each other's design (August 16, 1780), Cornwallis wanting to overtake the Southern army and proceed to North Carolina, Gates wishing to annihilate the British army and retake Charleston. The night was hot and stifling; the sky clear and full of stars. At 2 o'clock in the morning, the armies met each other at a sandy glade in the pine forest, near the marshes halfway between Clermont and Camden (one-half mile from Saunders' Creek). A skirmish of fire from the British broke the night air. Several of Armand's cavalry were wounded, retreating to the rear, causing a general panic among the troops. The light infantry, however, returned the volley, and, both sides surprised at meeting each other, as if by consent discontinued the battle until daybreak. Adjunct General Williams learned for the first time that Cornwallis was in command of the troops, which numbered over three thousand, only five or six hundred yards from the American front. The British were equipped with two six-pounders and two three-pounders, and Bloody Tarleton's cavalry stood ready, whereas Armand's had fled in the night, having erroneously been placed at the front of the American line. Finally, though the British army was well fed, the American soldiers had eaten only molasses the night before the battle, becoming ill throughout the night due to their lack of food, weakened considerably. When Williams informed Kalb of the dire circumstances into which the American Army had marched, Kalb asked, in disbelief, if Gates had not ordered a retreat. As Flood notes, "Otho Williams had no doubt that de Kalb meant, 'let's march out of here right now'" (323).

Gates, at an apparent loss, seemed to just await the turn of events, therefore, at daybreak, the fighting ensued. A fog covered the battleground, yet Kalb formed his columns of Maryland and Delaware units, set at the right wing. He was proud of his men, having struggled alongside them for nearly two years, noting to Luzerne, French minister to the United States: "You may judge the virtues of our army from the following fact. We have, for several days, lived upon nothing but peaches, and I have heard no complaint. There has been no desertion" (qtd. in Flood, 311). Though the left wing again panicked, nineteen hundred of Gates' thirty-five hundred troops running away before firing a shot, Kalb's men on the

General Horatio Gates, who shamefully fled the battlefield at Camden, South Carolina. Mezzotint, published by John Morris, London, 1778 (National Archives and Records Administration).

right fought hard and with a degree of success, initially taking a British cannon and "a good many" prisoners, Cornwallis later speaking to the Maryland regiment's "obstinate resistance," and Bloody Tarleton paying tribute to their "great firmness and bravery." Three times Kalb rallied; three times he retreated. He may have even achieved a victory if not for the betrayal and desertion of the left flank, Gates' regiments. What gains were made by the Baron's men were overcome with the sheer numbers of British soldiers versus the now much reduced number of Continentals.

The man in the center of this hot battle was Baron Johann de Kalb, his horse unfortunately shot out from under him, leaving him vulnerable and exposed. Wearing his metal helmet and gold epaulettes, he fought without fail, brandishing his large sword, shouting orders, encouraging his men to fight to the death. His fellow commanders ran from the field, Gates, Caswell, and Smallwood (who refused to provide Kalb with extra rations of chocolate and coffee when everyone else in camp was treated), not to be found. (Gates would gallop off the battlefield and ride for miles and miles without looking back, a shameful and cowardly act which he never lived down, either in his lifetime or in perpetuity.) In this his last battle, the Baron revealed the Warrior within, not the tender husband, the intelligent agent, or the historical translator, but, instead, the sacrificial Warrior "trying with his sword and voice to offset all the neglect and wrong decisions that had brought his beloved Maryland Division to this terrible hour.... The foreigner who had threatened to sue Congress to get his commission was about to show the United States what kind of soldier it had hired" (Flood 331).

In hand-to-hand fighting, the Baron was first wounded by a saber strike to the head, despite his helmet. Bandaging his head, the adjutant general of the Delaware unit urged Kalb to retreat to the rear. The Baron put his helmet back on and redoubled his efforts, wounded again and again and again, twelve hundred British encircling five hundred fifty of Kalb's troops, these men having "forgotten there ever was a man named Gates; all they saw was their fifty-nine-year-old Baron, fighting and bleeding and roaring like a lion, and they were not going to quit before he did" (Flood, 331). Even when Tarleton's cavalry moved in, by Tarleton's own statement, the Baron "made a vigorous charge with a regiment of continental infantry through the left division of the British" (qtd. in Flood, 331). Alas, after receiving *eleven* wounds, eight from blades and three from bullets, blood streaming from every part of his body, the Baron could no longer stand. Cruelly, some of the British and Loyalist troops yanked the Baron to his feet and stripped him of his lace-lined coat, propping him against a wagon as they twisted off his clothing. Kalb clung to the side of the wagon as they left, crying in agony, blood pouring from his wounds, soaking his shirt and breeches. Cornwallis rode onto this scene, and Kalb's wounded aide, Dubuysson, crying "The rebel General! The rebel General!" informed the British commander of Kalb's status. Cornwallis looked down at the Baron and said, "I am sorry, sir, to see you, not sorry that you are vanquished, but sorry to see that you are so badly wounded" (qtd. in Flood, 332). Ordering an officer to see to the Baron's wounds, Cornwallis moved to survey his casualties, numbering sixty-four to the Americans' eight-hundred plus. An American surgeon captured by the British tried to mend Kalb's wounds, but eleven proved too much for even the Herculean Baron de Kalb. The British officer charged to care for Kalb reported the Baron stated: "I thank you for your generous sympathy, but I die the death I always prayed for: the death of a soldier fighting for the rights of man" (qtd. in Griswold, Simms, and Ingraham, 271). Visiting the house to which Kalb was taken after the battle, Cornwallis and British officer Rawdon paid tribute to the warrior, commending both his bravery (especially in light of

The death of Baron de Kalb, Camden Battlefield, August 1780. Engraving from painting by Alonzo Chappel (National Archives and Records Administration).

his commanding officer's flight) and the bravery of the Continentals in the Maryland and Delaware regiments the Baron had commanded. Unable to write, calling his aide Chevalier Dubuysson to his bedside, Kalb dictated these last words, revealing honor, forgiveness, integrity, fortitude, and service to the men of his regiment:

> Dear Generals: It is with particular pleasure I obey the Baron's last commands, in presenting his most affectionate compliments to all the officers and men of his division. He expressed the greatest satisfaction in the testimony given by the British army of the bravery of his troops; and he was charmed with the firm opposition they made to superior force, when abandoned by the rest of the army. The gallant behavior of the Delaware regiment and the companies of artillery attached to the brigades afforded him infinite pleasure. And the exemplary conduct of the whole division gave him an endearing sense of the merits of the troops he had the honor to command [qtd. in Flood, 342].

Kalb was buried by his enemies with Masonic and military honors, a solitary tree being the only mark of his resting place until 1825. Gates himself ironically reported Kalb's death to Congress: "Too much honor cannot be paid by Congress to the memory of the Baron de Kalb; he was everything an excellent officer should be, and in the cause of the United States has sacrificed his life. Here I must be permitted to say how much I think is due to the Baron de Kalb, and I am convinced Congress will declare to the world the high estimation they have for his memory and services" (qtd. in Kapp, *Kalb*, 238). Congress subsequently resolved in October 1780, to erect a monument at Annapolis (as the Baron commanded a Maryland regiment) in memory of the Baron. Ungratefully, the resolution stood unexecuted, forgotten, defunded, and forgotten after peace was ensured. Washington, when he visited Camden in

Site where Baron de Kalb was mortally wounded, August 16, 1780, Camden, South Carolina (author's photograph).

the spring of 1791, standing in front of the tree marking Kalb's grave, said, "So here lies the brave de Kalb, the generous stranger who came from a distant land to fight our battles, and to water with his blood the tree of our liberty. Would to God he had lived to share with us its fruits!" (qtd. in Kapp, *Kalb*, 253). Though South Carolina eventually raised a monument at Camden in 1825, the cornerstone lain by Lafayette himself, "the great republic for whose independence he sacrificed his life, has almost forgotten his name and services" (Kapp, *Kalb*, 263).

The contrast between the two generals on the battlefield at Camden reveals both ends of the spectrum with regard to human personality and character: the general on the left (Gates) proving incompetent, weak, cowardly, self-centered, and vain; the general on the right (de Kalb) exhibiting intelligent strategy, lion-heartedness, bravery, and self-sacrificial valor and/or duty. How has America failed to more fully honor and remember this German-born hero (in contrast to the hired mercenaries employed by the British) who endured danger in both crossing the sea and coming ashore in South Carolina, a "wishy-washy" Congress undetermined in its call for help from abroad, months and months of "ragged" existence protecting and supporting the Continental Army's fortifications, incompetency and jealousy from his fellow officers, and agonizing wounds which led to a lingering death? Ironically, it took Gates three days to flee from the battlefield, abandoning his troops to death, reaching Hillsborough, one hundred eighty miles away; on the other hand, it took Kalb three days to die from his *eleven* wounds. When will America properly resurrect his legacy?

Memorials

A monument, as mentioned above, was erected by the citizenry of Camden in 1825, underneath which lie the Baron's remains. It reads: "Here lie the remains of Baron de Kalb, a German by birth, but in principle citizen of the world. His love of liberty induced him to leave the old world to aid the citizens of the new in their struggle for independence, his distinguished talents and many virtues weighed with Congress to appoint him Major General in their Revolutionary Army. He was second in command at the battle fought near Camden on the 16th August 1780, between the British Americans and there nobly fell covered with wounds while gallantly performing deeds of valor in rallying the friends and opposing the enemies of his adopted country. In Gratitude for his zeal and service, the citizens of Camden have erected this monument."

The Federal Republic of Germany erected a monument in 1985 in front of the county courthouse in de Kalb, Georgia, which features a bust of the Baron de Kalb.

Finally, in 1886, the U.S. Congress placed a sculpture of Baron Johann de Kalb, raising his sword and leading his troops into battle, at the Maryland State Courthouse in Annapolis, Maryland.

14

THUNDERBOLT OF WAR
Count Casimir Pulaski

He was a thunderbolt of war, and always sought the post of danger as the post of honor.—Dr. David Ramsay, field surgeon in the American Revolution, congressman, and historian

Ready for action is an apt descriptor for the life of Polish hero to the American Revolution, Kazimierz (Casimir — Anglicized) Pulaski, a hero of two nations in the same vein as his compatriot, Thaddeus Kościuszko. For, like Kościuszko, Pulaski devoted his life to the advent of humanitarian governments, both in his native land, Poland, and in America. (Fortunately, his sacrifice for the ideals of the American Revolution reached fruition at a much earlier point in history.) Witnessing laws passed in Poland by a Russian/Austrian/Prussian compact which negated ancient customs, national rights, and political substance, Pulaski fought alongside his father and brother before forced by threat of death to embrace the cause of an alternative nation struggling against tyranny and despotism. Presented to General Washington by Benjamin Franklin as a gentleman who "like us is engaged in defending the liberty and independence of his country," Pulaski sailed to America, the desire and duty of his youth transferred to another locale. Remaining devoted to the cause of freedom for the whole of mankind, resolving to lend his aid in whatever fashion necessary, proving, as Franklin insisted "highly useful," Pulaski's service to the

Sketch of the dashing Polish Count Casimir Pulaski. Engraving of H. B. Hall, 1871 (National Archives and Record Administration).

Revolution intimated the historical insight of Ruhlière: "Never was there a warrior who possessed greater dexterity in every kind of service; Pulaski, by a natural ascendancy, was the chief amongst equals" (qtd. in Griswold, Simms, and Ingraham, 234). Indeed, "he was accounted the finest swordsman and one of the best horsemen in the Army.... When his horse was at gallop, he would discharge his pistol, throw it in the air, catch it on the descent, again hurl it with all his power in front of him but with one foot in stirrup pick it from the ground and time his position in the saddle" (Szymanski, 32).

Born on March 4, 1747, at a time when Poland was "a country of ancient renown, one fifth larger than France, and containing twenty millions of people ... ravaged, plundered, divided, subdued, and its political existence annihilated, by the treachery and cupidity of its three formidable neighbors, Russia, Austria, and Prussia" (Gammell, 365), Pulaski was born into a "conspiracy against the rights of men, this league of infamy between the strong to crush the weak and devour their substance ... a dark picture of selfishness, rapacity, and violence not relieved by a single spot of redeeming light" (Gammell, 365). Poland had gained, over the centuries, constitutional rights in collaboration with a highly monitored monarchy; when the Polish King died without an heir in the early 1700s, Russia, Prussia, and Austria seized the moment of weakness to march troops into the land-locked country and destroy its system of government, replacing it with the authoritarian rule of the Empress of Russia, who appointed her lover, Stanisław Augustus, as the new puppet ruler of Poland. Of course, the nobles, accustomed to a formidable constitution which embraced human rights, took up arms to resist the might of these oppressive forces. One such noble, and an able jurist in his own right, serving as chief magistrate of Warech, was Pulaski's father, who, upon his country's invasion, "suddenly exhibited traits of character, a force of purpose and energy of will, which had before been unsuspected by his countrymen, and perhaps even by himself" (qtd. in Gammell, 365). Forming an armed opposition to the enemies of freedom, he befriended Krasinski, of military reknown, convening in Bar in 1768. Pulaski's father asked his sons, whom he had placed on horseback at the tender age of five and taught to shoot a bulls-eye while riding, to join the cause, fully informing them of the danger associated with service for the opposition. All his sons, including Casimir, followed their father's lead, Casimir at the tender age of nineteen assembling Cossacks from the family's estates to join the rendezvous. Soliciting the aid of a monastery known for its miracles, the monastery of Berdichef, the conveyed troops soon numbered eight thousand. As they became bold and distributed pamphlets throughout the country to garner additional aid, the secrecy of the opposition was interrupted, and the puppet King alarmed. Note: When the Russians eventually seized the town of Bar, Father Mark mounted a rampart in front of the enemy, making the sign of a cross. At that instant, one of the Russian's cannons burst. Regarding this event as a miracle, Father Mark and a company of priests marched into the path of the assailants, carrying Christian images. The troops surrounding them drove the Russians back "with great slaughter," taking the town back along with two hundred prisoners.

As Russian troops entered the country to quell the rebellion, Pulaski's father addressed his troops:

> An execrable people, who can neither be disarmed by justice, mollified by submission, touched by favors, nor surfeited by pillage, has resolved to impose upon us the yoke of slavery. Virtues the most sacred have passed for crimes in the eyes of our oppressors; and virtuous citizens, our fathers and our exemplars, now drag out a wretched existence in the dungeons of that barbarous nation. If ever men had a duty to perform, it is that which has compelled us to take up arms. Our republic is invaded, religion outraged, the justice which was promised

to us has been converted into a snare, the rights of nations have been trodden under foot, our senators are in chains. Nations the most servile, who should be the objects of such insults and outrages, even from a legitimate sovereign, would not be so tame as to submit. The whole universe would applaud their rebellion; and the oppressions of which we complain would justify a revolt under the most despotic government. Brave confederates! Poland does not want courageous citizens prepared to sacrifice their lives for her deliverance. It is not blind despair which impels us onward, but a firm resolution, a well-founded hope, a noble sentiment, the love of country and freedom, of humanity and justice [qtd. in Gammell, 380].

This movement became known as "the Confederation of Bar," (founding date February 29, 1768), and "this staunchly Catholic and patriotic movement had as its purpose the freeing of Poland from Russian influence and from the pressure of internal religious dissenters, both Protestant and Orthodox, who were appealing to their co-religionists in Prussia and Russia and thereby were viewed widely as a threat to Poland's security" (Pienkos, 6). Pulaski's father elicited the financial aid of the Ottoman Empire (Turkey), as the Empire itself feared Russia's attempt to strengthen her already entrenched, colossal power.

Casimir found his particular calling at Father Mark's monastery, commander of three hundred men by the age of twenty-one. His post was secure for many weeks, but, finally, his supplies commandeered by the enemy, Casimir was detained, only released on the condition that he bear proposals of reconciliation to the remaining Confederates. Arriving in Moldavia to join his father, he wrote to the Russian ambassador, informing him that "he should pay no respect to a parole, which had been extorted from him by fraud and violence; that he should not advise his father, or any of the confederates, to lay down their arms, and should feel bound to fight the Russians wherever he could find them" (Spark, 385). Casimir's next two battles proved extremely successful, for he collected forage, solicited financial contributions, and secured prisoners, provisions and military equipment. He and his father also secured a "large space of country," preparing magazines for the army. Alas, the father was betrayed by a jealous compatriot, taken prisoner, guarded, and confined. He sent word for his sons to continue their efforts for the welfare of their country.

At the ancient fortress of Okopé, Pulaski built redoubts and relied upon ancient fortresses. Unfortunately, the Russians arrived with a terrifying force, setting fire to villages to continue the assault by night. Pulaski in turn set fire to his own houses and barracks within the redoubts. Overpowered by sheer numbers, Pulaski and two hundred of his men entered a frightening path along a rocky precipice, dismounting their horses and walking the treacherous trail. (Some of the horses fell into the river below.) At the bottom of the hill, Pulaski and his men rushed the body of Russians at the bottom in a column, raising a Turkish battle cry. In the ensuing confusion, they escaped, only to learn that Casimir's brother had been rushed and murdered. The entirety of Poland was overrun with Russian troops (and Poles loyal to the puppet King), who left a trail of blood and sorrow, essentially exterminating Polish patriots, yet creating a resentment among people who "claimed nothing but the quiet enjoyment of their homes, their ancient freedom, their inborn rights" (Sparks, 391) that did not abate for centuries, for "many poured out their blood like water in so righteous a cause, and left examples of a glorious martyrdom to their sons, and to men in all ages, who are thus goaded to despair by the barbed rod of an inhuman and bloodthirsty despotism" (Sparks 391).

In this atmosphere, Pulaski became a sort of Polish folk hero, an invincible warlord and guerrilla fighter. Ruhliére says,

> The name which soon eclipsed all others, and which became one of the surest hopes of the nation, when the multiplied faults of the Turks no longer permitted them to lend succors to

the Poles, was that of young Casimir Pulaski, always full of resources in misfortune, and of activity in success. After his daring flight from the summit of Okopé, he collected the scattered fragments of the confederate troops, and, by an extraordinary combination of address and courage, he escaped from the enemies who were in pursuit of him on every side. In one of these pursuits, when his rear guard was suddenly attacked and driven forward, he ran to the rescue, and heard a Russian officer demand from the prisoners, "Where is Pulaski?" Turning around, he cried out, "Here I am," and rushing upon the officer, laid him dead at his feet. By an evil inseparable from a state of anarchy, many of the confederations had been poisoned by suspicions, spread abroad by design, against the elder Pulaski, and they regarded the son with the same suspicions. Some of them, indeed, were for attacking him and taking away his troops; but the soldiers were devoted to him. His vigilance never left an opportunity for surprise; and this man, so intrepid and terrible in combat, against whom there was no reproach but that of being too fond of danger, was at all other times amiable, gentle, conciliating, and always above personal resentment. After holding interviews with those, by whose designs he might have been justly incensed, he would lead them to engage in mutual operations, and afterwards seize every occasion to afford them his assistance [qtd. in Sparks, 392].

Knowing the Russians saw him as a terror and increased the volume of their attacks in his direction, he sometimes feigned his name. On one such instance in Sambor, as he began fighting, he learned the village was under the leadership of one Francis Pulaski, his brother. The brothers rejoiced as they learned of each other's well-being, for they both thought the other dead, all the while mourning the "sad intelligence" of their father's death in prison, "to which he had been consigned by the treachery and insatiate ambition of his pretended associates" (Sparks, 393). Instead of seeking revenge, the brothers honored their father's memory by their efforts to "achieve his enterprise ... the virtue of sacrificing personal resentments to the public cause ... the time might come when they could render justice to their father, but now they had one duty to perform, a single object to attain, the deliverance of their country" (Sparks, 394). The brothers began forming new confederations, also traveling to Lithuania for recruitment purposes, Casimir the commander, Francis displaying implicit obedience. When the Russians marched upon the brothers with one thousand troops, they were routed and two hundred were left dead on the battlefield. Casimir pursued retreating soldiers into the edge of a wood, placing heads of columns at different locales in the wood to appear of a greater number, tricking the retreating enemies to lay down their arms. During another battle in the North, Casimir cunningly stationed his troops (by that time numbering four thousand) behind a marsh and sent a party out to engage the Russians, enticing them into the swamp, where they became entangled and defeated. Believing Hungary would now join their engagement, the brothers marched thereto, leaving Lithuania in the hands of one Prince Sapiéha.

This decision proved erroneous, as, in open country the brothers were assailed, Francis losing his life (his bloody clothes offered for sale in a nearby village). Reaching Hungary unharmed, Casimir reflected upon the year 1768: "He alone remained of the family, who had been the first to take up arms against the enemies of their country. His father had died in a dungeon, his youngest brother was a prisoner in Russia, his cousin had fallen in battle, and the life of Francis had been sacrificed to save his own. In Lithuania he had fought five severe battles, and, within six weeks, had traversed with his cavalry a distance of nearly five hundred leagues" (Sparks, 399). Additionally, his mother was forced to flee the family home, in disguise, to avoid Russian recrimination, the estates fairly confiscated.

In Hungary, Pulaski instigated a wintry fortress in the mountains, collecting all the rakes from nearby villages, laying the teeth upward in the path leading to his camp, the horses of the Russians disabled if they dared to approach. Like a stealth warrior, he secretly raided and carried away Russian supplies and prisoners, exchanging them for his own men. Among Pulaski's confederates "there was no one among them who had not signalized himself by some remarkable exploit. Their extreme quickness and accuracy of observation, guiding them to judge of distances, and, by crossing plains and entering woods, to cut off small Russian detachments, enabled them constantly to take many prisoners.... Pulaski had scarcely an officer whom he had not rescued from the hands of the enemy, or from some danger, and who might not say that he owed his life and liberty to his commander" (Sparks, 401).

In August of 1770, Pulaski descended from the mountains determined to march upon Warsaw. Forced to circumvent Russian pursuance, he made camp under the fortress of Czenstokow (modern spelling "Czestochowa"), a monastery located in a gorge of mountains and ancient forests surrounded by a moat and high walls. The Pope's nuncio, residing at the monastery, performed a benediction and ceremony for Pulaski's troops. When four thousand Russian troops advanced on the monastery on January 3, 1771, "the eyes of the whole nation were turned upon this siege. The monastery of Czenstokow, renowned for its sanctity, had long been regarded by the people as under the immediate protection of Heaven. The Russian general had orders to level it to the ground if any resistance should be made" (Sparks, 404). Pulaski and his men hurled fireballs, rocks, and stones down on their attackers. The assailants never made a breach in the wall, though attempting three escalades! Finally abandoning the siege, the Russians left with "two hundred men dead in the snow." Sparks notes, "The deliverance of the monastery was looked upon as a miracle by the multitude; the sleet, rain, and snow, which had fallen continually during the siege, were deemed to be prodigies; and pilgrims flocked more eagerly than ever to the sanctuary, which was thus proved to be under the protecting care of a more than human power" (Sparks, 405). Over the next year, from his fortress, Pulaski went in and out of the fortress, even to distant points, striking the enemy. At one point, he had to effect a hazardous retreat from a force of three thousand, doing so in such an expert manner, a Russian general, though reluctantly, could not help but praise his enemy (apparently wounded in the arm by a lance thrust, he fell in quicksand).

The next event in the life of the Confederacy proved to be its demise for, as Pienkos notes, "The Confederation of Bar has been called, without too much exaggeration, 'an occurrence with the highest influence on the whole of Polish society.' In raising Polish awareness of the threat to the country's very national existence, its actions asserted the need for a new sense of national patriotism linked to a revitalized, but tolerant, religious commitment. These ideals were eventually to become the bases of the modern Polish national identity, despite the country's later loss of statehood after the partitions of 1772, 1793, and 1795. They were perhaps best personified by Pulaski himself. For example, following Pulaski's example, the first uprising of students against the Russians occurred in Cracow" (Pienkos, 6). The Grand Council of the Confederates decided to abduct the Polish puppet King, Stanisław. Pulaski agreed, in the event the King was not harmed, engaging troops near Warsaw to draw troops away from the city. The party abducting the King, however, fumbled the effort, losing the King when his horse stumbled in the darkness, advancing forward and leaving the King with only one guard. This guard, hearing the advancing troops of the King behind him, surrendered. When news of the attempted abduction reached the ears of Europe, foreign financial assistance diminished. The Russians sent their finest officer, General Suvorov, "to crush the Confederates once and for all" (Pienkos, 6). All the pontiffs, including Frederick the Great and Empress Maria Theresa, wrote letters indicating the Polish troops had attempted an "assassination," labeling it an "atrocious plot." All involved in the abduction were ordered condemned to death, including Pulaski, who understood the public relations scheme of the monarchs. In defense of his honor, he wrote:

> I am not astonished that the enemies of my country, resolved on her ruin, should direct their shafts against those, who resist the most firmly their impetuosity, and that they should regard as such the brave Poles, whom they have sacrificed, and who are still repelling their most cruel attacks. Nor ought I to complain, that, having the honor to command a party of my illustrious compatriots, these enemies have chosen me for the first object of their assaults. This I might naturally expect, considering the melancholy situation of my country, and my devotion to her defence. My destiny was clear, when, at the age of twenty-one, far from yielding to the amusements common to youth, I regarded every moment as lost, which was not employed in repelling the enemies of my country. My best witness was my late father, marshal of the confederate army, who has finished his career in the public service. He would have testified to the manner in which I dared to emulate his zeal. I have endeavored to mark my course by an invincible fortitude. Neither the blood of one of my brothers, which was shed by the enemy before my eyes, nor the cruel servitude of another, nor the sad fate of so many of my relations and compatriots, has shaken my patriotism. Always faithful to my country, I flatter myself that even my enemies will regard this strong bent of my nature as a patriotic impulse. I believe I have proved, by four years' service, that I have not been influenced by interest or a false point of honor. The first calumny against me has been published in the gazettes of the enemy, in which I am named as the author of a conspiracy executed at Warsaw. To this reproach I have hitherto submitted in silence, convinced that our enemies are eager to blacken with the pen those against whom they contend with arms. But I now follow the example of the published declaration of the confederate states; and, although I have determined to defend my country only with the sword, I am induced, on this occasion, to use the pen. I declare before God, before the republic of Poland, and before all the powers of Europe, that my heart is an utter stranger to crime. My thoughts and actions have had no other end than the good of my country. It has never entered my imagination to attempt the life of any person to whom has been assigned, in any manner whatsoever, the government of the nation, or to avenge the wrongs of my country in any other way than that of open war [qtd. in Sparks, 412].

With a price on his head, and the advance of not only Russian, but also Prussian and Austrian troops, Pulaski was forced to flee from his homeland, the land of his ancestors, family, and friends, his comrades in arms, an outlaw who had sacrificed his youth to the struggle for basic human rights, "forced to leave the land of his birth, where he had buried the treasures of his heart — to sever the ties of affection which still bound him to his long-loved home" (Griswold, Simms, and Ingraham, 234). Most of the next five years of Pulaski's life are lost to history, but it is known that he escaped, miraculously, to Turkey, thereafter venturing into France, arriving shortly after the signing of America's Declaration of Independence. Of course overcome with the news of another country fighting for the same rights near and dear to his native land, freedom, independence, and justice, Pulaski surrounded himself with the American revolutionaries in France (most likely joining the Masons), namely Benjamin Franklin. Upon volunteering for the revolutionary cause, Pulaski received a letter of recommendation from Franklin.

> Count Pulaski of Poland, an officer famous throughout Europe for his bravery and conduct in defense of the liberties of his country against the three great invading powers of Russia, Austria, and Prussia, will have the honor of delivering this into your Excellency's hands. The Court here have encouraged and promoted his voyage, from an opinion that he may be highly useful to our service. Mr. Deane has written so fully concerning him that I need not enlarge, and I add my wishes that he may find in our armies under your Excellency occasions of distinguishing himself [qtd. in Szymanski, 33].

Apparently, he also became acquainted with the wife of the Marquis de Lafayette, for she sent a letter to her husband in America by way of the Count, a title adopted by Pulaski while in France, for in America a title was useful. (In Poland, such titles were "foreign to the principle of equality among nobles ... forbidden in 1638.") Plus, Pulaski "realized the benefits of a title, feeling probably morally right, especially as in France he could observe numerous titled persons, inferior socially to him, but boasting of their titles. Pulaski appropriated the title of 'comte' which was below 'marquis' but above 'baron,' 'seigneur' and 'chevalier.' ... Pulaski was using his title with discretion (at least on paper) in the manner in which some people with scientific titles use theirs when they want to impress somebody with their standing" (Szymanski, 29).

Once arriving in America, as the British occupied New York and Boston was under rumor of attack, Pulaski took a circuitous route to Philadelphia, landing outside the city at Washington's headquarters in Buck County. With Franklin's letter in tow, he wrote to either Washington or Hancock (the addressee is not clear):

> SIR: I have the honor to inclose to your excellency the letters which show the hardships that I have undergone on account of having taken up arms in defense of my country. That country no longer exists for me, and here, by fighting for freedom, I wish to deserve it. Life or death for the welfare of the state is my motto; and thereby I hope to earn the esteem of the citizens of this country. I ask your assistance, sir; it will facilitate my first efforts to obtain the honor of serving you. I inclose a statement to your excellency; if it is worthy of your attention. I shall be glad to have it laid before Congress. I hope to be excused for my lack of skill in writing as handling the pen is not my forte. I leave for the Army where I shall await orders. Your excellency's most humble and obedient servant, C. Pulaski [qtd. in Szymanski, 31].

Perhaps at headquarters, Lafayette, after receiving the letter from his wife delivered by Pulaski (speaking to her expectations of having a baby), escorted his new friend into Washington's presence and translated the ensuing conversation. Pulaski most likely looked up to Washington as they spoke, for Dr. A. Waldo described him as "a man of hardly middling stature — sharp countenance (behavior) and lively air — and he has now joined the American Army where he is greatly respected. He is also acclaimed for his martial skill and courage" (qtd. in Szymanski, 32). Washington respected Casimir's abilities immediately, for he wrote Congress on August 21, 1777:

> To the President of Congress. Sir, I do myself the honour to inclose you a Copy of Doctor Franklin's letter in favor of Count Pulaski of Poland by whom this will be handed to you. I sometime ago had a letter from Mr. Deane, couched in terms equally favourable to the character and military abilities of this gentleman. How he can with propriety be provided for you will be best able to determine. He takes this from me, an introductory letter at his own request [qtd. in Szymanski, 34].

In a letter of August 24 to Congress, Pulaski asked to be subjected only to the Commander-in-Chief "to be near the enemy, that I may more readily seize occasions of acquiring the name of a good officer" (qtd. in Szymanski, 41). He also requested command of a single company of cavalrymen, though he could conduct a division (he commanded up to four thousand men at a time in Poland). He also began serving before receiving a commission, for Howe was on the shores of Philadelphia, and Washington needed his assistance. Apparently he assisted Washington to some great length; the general reciprocated by again writing to Congress: "This gentleman, we are told, has been, like us, engaged in defending the liberty and independence of his country, and has sacrificed his fortune to his zeal for those objects. He deserves from hence a title to our respect, that ought to operate in his favour, as far as the good of the service will permit; but it can never be expected we should lose sight of this" (qtd. in Szymanski, 44). Washington also recommended Pulaski be appointed Commander of Horse.

Pulaski rode with Washington to Brandywine without a commission, serving nonetheless, more than likely the "rebel officer" described by British Major Patrick Ferguson (of King's Mountain fame) as following Washington on the field for maneuvers before the battle. Ferguson had a clear shot of both men, and could have shot each, but refused by reason of the gentlemanly rules of war. Ferguson wrote:

> We had not lain long when a rebel officer, remarkable by a hussar dress passed towards our army, within a hundred yards of my right flank, not perceiving us. He was followed by another dressed in dark green or blue, mounted on a bay horse, with a remarkably large cocked hat. I ordered three good shots to steal near to them and fire at them, but the idea disgusted me. I recalled the order. The hussar in returning made a circuit, but the other passed again within a hundred yards of us, upon which I advanced from woods toward him, on my calling, he stopped: but after looking at me proceeded. I again drew his attention, and made signs to stop him, but he slowly continued his way. As I was within that distance at which, in the quickest firing, I could have lodged half a dozen of balls in or about him before he was out of my reach — I had only to determine, but it was not pleasant to fire at the back of unoffending individual, who was acquitting himself coolly of his duty; so I let him alone. The day after I had been telling this story to some wounded officers who lay in the same room with me, when one of our surgeons, who had been dressing the wounded rebel officers, came in and told us they had been informing him that General Washington was all the morning with the light troops, and only attended by a French officer in a hussar dress, he himself dressed and mounted in every point as above described. I am not sorry that I did not know at the time who it was [qtd. in Szymanski, 51].

At Brandywine, in sight of Washington and Lafayette, still without a commission, Pulaski commanded Washington's bodyguard of about thirty horsemen. In his charge, he retarded the advancement of the enemy, allowing the defeated American soldiers time to retreat. He also noted the enemy was attempting to overtake the road to Chester, Pennsylvania, in order to recover American baggage. Communicating this observance to Washington, Pulaski was authorized to collect scattered troops to assist in maintaining supply. Advancing upon the British front and right flank with these recovered soldiers, Pulaski was instrumental in protecting the retreat, preventing the British from absconding with much needed clothing and supply. Though some historians have disputed the validity of thirty horsemen delaying the British army's advance, they may not have considered the psychological impact of Pulaski's personal combat style as described by William W. Gordon: "In the words of one of his comrades, 'the Count in battle — how he seemed to fight as if enjoying a banquet; how, again and again, he would dash into the midst of the enemy, cutting his way on the right hand and on the left, as if the strength of ten men lay in his single arm; and then wheeling, cutting his way back again, and often without loss'" (qtd. in Szymanski, 55). Plus, an unexpected charge by horses previously undetected by the British no doubt dazed their efforts and intent, and Pulaski was no stranger to battles in which the few challenged the many. As Gordon again writes, "In all the military engagements of which we have record, he was distinguished for his extraordinary personal bravery and for his handling of cavalry employing surprise and shock tactics by virtue of which he almost invariably met with success despite the use of small numbers against greater forces" (qtd. in Szymanski, 59). Perhaps the most prudent proof of Pulaski's valor at Brandywine is the fact that within days after the battle, Congress approved Pulaski's long-pending application for command of the cavalry

The Battle of Germantown, at Chew's House, an engagement in which Pulaski's Legion participated. Engraving by Rawdon, Wright, and Harch from drawing by Koeltner (National Archives and Records Administration).

with an associated rank as brigadier general. As he was the first American general of cavalry, Pulaski's legacy is today "Father of the American Cavalry." James Lovell also wrote, "The foreign officers showed themselves to great advantage in the battle.... Count Pulaski, who headed the Polanders, is now Commander of our Cavalry having first signalized himself greatly in the Battle of Brandywine" (qtd. in Szymanski, 60).

As Washington retreated to Warren Tavern, unaware the British followed, the Continental Army would have been overtaken if the ever observant Pulaski had not detected an approach. When Pulaski insisted on addressing an engaged Washington, Colonel Alexander Hamilton questioned Pulaski as to whether, in reality, he had mistaken the British troops for American. Waniczek writes, "Pulaski, with great heat, insisted that his report was accurate, and this afterwards proved to be true and it was through his intelligence and activity that further disaster was prevented" (151).

At the time Pulaski was provided a commission, the entire Continental Army Cavalry only numbered 539. Szymanski notes that if the soon-to-be cavalry had "been organized and trained as Pulaski wanted, based on his European experience, the War of American Independence would, perhaps, have ended much sooner" (68). Washington had no cavalry experience whatsoever, nor a vision as to how it could be used as a tactical force. The few officers who had attempted horsemanship in battle were either businessmen or politicians, such as Colonel Stephen Moylan, disappointed by Pulaski's appointment, and M. de la Balme, a former captain of cavalry in the French army. Baron de Kalb wrote, "As Congress has just made Pulaski Brigadier commanding the said cavalry, M. de la Balme, being discontented at this preference, intends to leave" (qtd. in Szymanski, 81). Of course, these jealousies, inconsistencies, and lack of knowledge affected Pulaski's ability to form a cavalry meeting his expectations.

The next battle for Pulaski's unit was Germantown, a strategically planned battle in which Washington hoped to push the British into the Schuylkill River. Washington placed the cavalry in position as a sort of "outlier" to guard the Army's flanks. Due to errors in timing, a fog, and the Americans' uncertainty as to the location of the enemy, the battle failed, Pulaski and Moylan assigned to "watch the enemy," instead of engagement. Pulaski and his legion were able to cover General Greene and were the last to retreat. Griswold writes: "Had our cavalry been a body acting in concert, and occupying a distinct position in the line, it would be an easy task to point out the services which it rendered. As it was, that portion of our force was limited, divided into small parties, and employed under various duties. In their performance, great assistance was given to our army; yet they were such as a cursory review must necessarily exclude; and we content ourselves with stating, that at meeting the enemy on the Lancaster road, near Philadelphia, and in the battle of Germantown, Pulaski did all his small force enabled him to accomplish, and succeeded in gaining the confidence of Washington, which was not easily won" (Grisworld, Simms, and Ingraham, 237). Definitely, Pulaski was "sorely disappointed and mortified," according to Bentalou, for the regiments of horse were not completed, guards were taken out of the regiments for Washington, his generals, or other services, "so that Pulaski was left with so few men as not to have it in his power to undertake anything of importance. This was to him a matter of regret and bitter chagrin" (qtd. in Szymanski, 95).

When Washington camped his army at Valley Forge, Pulaski and his cavalry were sent to Trenton to procure forage, before departure addressing a letter to Washington in which he remarked, "The weak state of the corps I command, renders it impossible to perform every service required. Nay, my reputation is exposed, as, being an entire stranger in the country, the least accident would suffice to injure me; yet I cannot avoid hazarding everything that is valuable in life" (qtd. in Griswold, Simms, and Ingraham, 237). (Pulaski nevertheless won a small skirmishing victory at Chestnut Hill in November 1777, killing five soldiers and taking two prisoners. He was the "lone voice" among officers with regard to the decision to camp at Valley Forge. He believed the campaign should continue and the men remain active, possibly a sound call as, at Valley Forge, starvation, smallpox, and typhus raged.) At Trenton, Pulaski made the best of the situation, dividing his men into small parties, distributing them throughout the region to obtain the necessary supply, while also using the winter months to train, discipline, and rally his troops, assisted by Officer Michael Kováts (see Chapter 12). He was also called upon in the winter months to join General Wayne in dispersing the foraging parties of the enemy. In a skirmish at Haddonsfield, in which the British attempted to surround the two detachments, Pulaski earned the respect of Wayne, capturing seven prisoners, ever on the alert, discerning the weak points of the British, and charging when an appropriate opportunity arose. Wayne later wrote that Pulaski "behaved with his usual bravery having his own with four other horses wounded — the little handful of Infantry who had an opportunity of engaging behaved with a spirit that would have done honour to the oldest veteran" (qtd. in Pienkos, 8). It seems the community of Trenton, but not the army in general, also appreciated Pulaski's efforts, for, as Bill writes in *New Jersey and the Revolutionary War*, "The town was soon further overcrowded by the arrival of the light cavalry that, owing to dearth of forage near at hand, Washington sent over from Valley Forge. Under the command of Casimir Pulaski, their scouting had been invaluable in the marches that followed battle at Chadds Ford, and they were now useful in keeping the country around Trenton clear of the gangs of Tories and outlaws that infested the Jersey side of the Delaware to the southward" (qtd. in Szymanski, 133).

Yet, frustrations continued to mount to the point Moylan disobeyed his commanding officer, Pulaski, and actually struck an aide, John Zielinski. On another occasion Zielinski unseated Moylan with a lance; on yet another a Polish officer tried to arrest two of Moylan's men, who he claimed had proved disrespectful to him. Pulaski's letters to Washington continued throughout the winter, informing him of the cavalry's needs as well as admonishing the importance of a cavalry used to the best advantage, sending his and Kováts' Regulations of Cavalry within letters such as this one from February 3, 1778:

> His Excellency General Washington: I make no doubt but your Excellency is acquainted with the present ineffective state of the Cavalry. In this situation it cannot be appropriated to any other service than that of orderlys or reconnoitering the enemy's lines, which your Excellency must be persuaded is not the only service expected from a corps when a proper footing is so very formidable. Although it is the opinion of many that from the construction of the country the Cavalry cannot aid to advantage, Your Excellency must be too well acquainted with the many instances wherein the Cavalry have been decisively serviceable to be of this opinion and not acknowledge that this corps has more than once completed victorys. To this end, I would wish to discipline the Cavalry and flatter myself by next campaign to render it essentially serviceable. What has greatly contributed to the present weak state of the Cavalry was the frequent detachments ordered to the suite of general and other officers, while a Colonel commanded, which were appropriate to everyone and the horses drove at the discretion of the dragoons. The confidence with which the Congress and your Excellence have honored me are sure guaranties to the zeal I shall ever act with in the service of the United States, but notwithstanding my great desire of rendering the Cavalry so useful as its first constitutions intended, I find it impracticable seeing that it is deficient in its principal requisitions, my reflections on which I have judged necessary to communicate to your Excellency as proof of my attachement to the good of the service and desire of executing your Excellency's designs hoping for opportunity of deserving the favor conferred upon me by your Excellency [qtd. in Szymanski, 124].

Washington obviously disagreed with Pulaski as to the manner in which cavalry might serve a higher purpose than foot, and did not understand why officers of cavalry might be provided superior rank, as was the European tradition. Colonel John Laurens aptly described Pulaski's dilemma: "The dislike of some of his officers to him as a stranger, the advantages they have taken of him, and their constant contrivance to thwart him on every occasion, made it impossible for him to command" (qtd. in Szymanski, 153). Sparks indicated: "The nature of the service was such, that these troops must be constantly separated into small parties, remote from each other, subject to the command of the general officers of the different divisions of the army, and of course not capable of acting upon any general system, or with important effect upon any one point" (424). Pulaski was at his wit's end, writing his sister: "It will be enough for you, Dear Sister, to know that I am in good health. My fortune varies as it is usual in the time of war. Here, I am commanding the whole cavalry, and I took part in different attacks successfully enough. I do not intend to stay here long. The native customs cannot agree with my temper, and additionally, my service here is a waste of time. I cannot do anything good. People are very jealous, and everything is antagonistic. But the next campaign I shall be here. In future, if it would be possible, I shall become a merchant which is here the most useful" (qtd. in Szymanski, 144).

By February 28, Pulaski had resigned his commission in the Continental Army. Washington replied: "Your intention to resign is founded on reasons which I presume make you think the measure necessary. I can only say therefore that it will always give me pleasure to bear testimony of the zeal and Bravery which you have displayed on every occasion" (Szymanski, 153). Pulaski, within a month, proposed command of an independent, partisan corps to Washington, who concurred. Congress, when presented with the idea by Washington ("The Count, far from being disgusted with the service, is led by his thirst for glory, and zeal for the cause of Liberty"), also approved the proposal, and authorized Pulaski to raise and equip a corps of sixty-eight light horse and two hundred foot, to be called *Pulaski's Legion*. Sparks believes "the scheme of independent legions seems to have been first suggested by Pulaski; and it proved of the greatest importance in the subsequent operations of the war, and above all in the southern campaigns. Lee's and Armand's legions were formed upon a similar plan" (426).

Recruiting for the legion was no easy task, and Michael Kováts helped Pulaski in these efforts. Washington determined that the legion should consist of "native-born Americans with ties of property and family connections," and allowed the nucleus to consist of two mounted, armed and equipped troopers of his choosing from each of the four Continental Light Dragoon regiments. Finally, the corps was selected, with Paul Bentalou, Pulaski's most trusted officer, appointed captain; John Zielinski, the aide who unhorsed Moylan, lieutenant; and Michael Kováts, commander of lancers. Forming an association with the Moravians of German-speaking Maryland and Pennsylvania communities afforded additional recruits, as did Hessian deserters. While in this area of the country, the Moravian Sisters of Bethlehem, Pennsylvania, presented him with a crimson banner, from which he never parted and which is preserved in the collection of the Historical Society of Baltimore. The banner itself was made famous in one of Longfellow's poems (1825), entitled "Hymn of the Moravian Nuns of Bethlehem — at the Consecration of Pulaski's Banner."

Pulaski was first sent to Little Egg Harbor, New Jersey, to prevent the British from further devastating the harbor where Americans had received privateers prior to the British moving from New York by land to the harbor, destroying the ships, burning the homes, and committing other unspeakable acts against the inhabitants. The legion was to protect the village; nonetheless, one of the Hessian deserters who had joined the legion turned face once more and informed the British of Pulaski's position. Pulaski's Lieutenant Colonel De Bosen was particularly targeted by the deserter, whose name was Charles Juliet, for when a surprise unit landed and attacked the colonel's unit, no quarter was given, forty men were murdered, and De Bosen was stabbed over and over again with a bayonet. (Apparently, Juliet and De Bosen had argued before the desertion, as De Bosen despised men who deserted their colors.) Pulaski rushed to the scene of this attack with his additional troops, preventing further disaster. Pursuing the fleeing British, Pulaski's horsemen took several prisoners, yet the removal of planks from a bridge and a swamp prevented a full capture. Bentalou reported the incident:

> Pulaski formed his camp in front of the enemy, placing the infantry of the legion, under the command of Lieutenant Col. Baron De Bosen, at some distance on his right: the first troops of light dragoons of the legion, with the militia, formed his left, under the command of the captain of the troop. During the preceding winter, three Hessian officers had deserted to us from the enemy, and the youngest of these men (who certainly deserved neither reception nor

countenance) was sent to Pulaski by the Board of war, without a commission indeed, but with orders to let him do the duty of a sub-lieutenant in the legion. This man was treated with such severity by De Bosen, whose high sense of honour led him to despise one who, though a commissioned officer, could be guilty of deserting his colours, that he determined to revenge himself in a manner that could not have been foreseen or imagined. Under pretence of fishing, he one day left the camp, with two other men, and as they did not return, and it could not be supposed he would have the hardihood to return to the enemy, they were thought to be drowned. It seems, however, that he ventured to go back, and the enemy, under his guidance, and the cover of the night, landed and penetrated, before break of day, to De Bosen's quarters. On the first alarm, the Lieutenant Colonel rushed out, armed with his sword and pistols; but though he was a remarkably stout man, and fought like a lion, he was overpowered by numbers and killed. The instant the news reached headquarters, the cavalry went full speed to the spot; but we had the mortification to see the enemy already in their boats, on the return to the ships, with the exception of a few stragglers, whom we made prisoners in numbers greater than our own loss. The principal object seemed, indeed, to have been De Bosen. The voice of the deserter was distinctly heard exclaiming, "this is the Colonel — kill him"; and De Bosen's whole body was found pierced with bayonets. That the Colonel did not sufficiently consult his own safety is very probable; but what mighty disgrace attaches to Pulaski or his legion from this surprise, is not so obvious. The fault belongs, if anywhere, to the Board of War, who sent the traitorous Hessian to Pulaski [qtd. in Szymanski, 209–100].

Next stationed at Minisink near the Delaware River for the winter months, at a locale where the Cherry Point Massacre and other acts of hostility by the Indians and Tories proved dangerous to the frontier and its inhabitants, Pulaski safeguarded the area, though he facetiously wrote to Washington: "I demand to be employed near the enemy's line, and it is thought proper to place me in an exile which even the savages shun, and nothing remains but the bears to fight with" (qtd. in Szymanski, 221). Once again, Pulaski wished to leave America, for "first of all, he was sick of intrigues, persecutions, petty harassment and lack of scope for his ambitions. Unable to convince the Americans of the European tactical use of cavalry as a strike force, he had opted for a small Legion to imitate his famous hit and run tactics so successful against the Russians, only to be frustrated again. Neither he nor his Legion were trained for Indian fighting, which was best left to the frontiersmen. The area was 'unsuitable' ... and lacked forage for the horses. Militarily, it was the wrong mission for the wrong unit. He considered the Indians not worth fighting and even a victory over them would bring no honor. He was too restless a fighter to do garrison duty or protectionist defense. He had come to fight the British, to hit, to strike, and strike again in the manner of cavalry warriors. He was a dashing cavalry leader with no place to dash in the Minisink forests. We could liken him to a George Patton, caged in England, while the allies landed and expanded their Normandy beaches without him. In any event, in such a mood of despair and frustration, Pulaski saw no future in continuing" (Szymanski, 228). On December 4, 1778, he wrote to Congress, "I have given my reason to the General of the army for which I had a mind to depart for Europe, but this is not at this time when I am in some activity. I love my profession, and I cannot employ this better as in the cause of freedom.... After a tree mounts trouble must begin upon new. This is not the way, Gentleman, to reward the pain we take to serve you well, pleading is not my study I only beg you without Delay to finish the matter upon any manner. I claim, Gentlemen, for your generosity, this is the appearance of noble minds that becomes a people who expounds their lives in throwing off the Yoke of Tyranny. Let me ungo oppression and you will oblige me" (qtd. in Szymanski, 233).

Congress, unlike Washington, decided to employ Pulaski's strategies, sending him to the Southern campaign under General Lincoln on February 2, 1779. During those winter months, as he readied his troops for the march, recruiting as late as April 10 in Annapolis, Maryland, the British captured Savannah, threatening Augusta, Georgia, and Charleston, South Carolina. Taking twenty-nine days to reach Charleston, reinforcing Lincoln's troops with supply, Pulaski's timing could not have proved more advantageous, one division arriving by land on May 8, another by shore May 11, along with a group of local volunteers known as the "Raccoons." (General Prevost of the British command crossed the Savannah River on the 11th with the intention of capturing Charleston; Count Pulaski crossed the Cooper River.)

The battle began that same day, Prevost at first distinguishing himself in battle against Generals Lincoln and Moultrie, who defended with a combined force of around fifteen hundred, to include Pulaski's Legion. Moultrie and Pulaski determined "to fight it out," and Pulaski determined to raise the spirit of the inhabitants of Charleston. Many young men of the area even procured a horse and placed themselves under his command. Pulaski met the British in the only road at that time leading to the city, around Noisette's Garden. The resulting charge helped the Americans "feel the enemy," making an impression on the minds of the British, who did not dare charge the cavalry. Pulaski's horses, nevertheless, exhausted from the journey, could not advance further, and when striking again, lost several members of the corps, to include Colonel Kováts, second in command. The *Boston Gazette* reported: "The Count attacked a detachment of the enemy, took several prisoners and obliged the remainder to save themselves by flight.... Early in the morning of the 13th Count Pulaski went out with a small party of horse to reconnoiter, and the surprise can scarcely be conceived, which was occasioned by his sending an intelligence of the enemy having decamped and recrossed Ashley Ferry" (qtd. in Szymanski, 256). Despite the costly loss of life, Casimir was praised for his attack, for it had delayed the British as a result of its fierceness, and consequently the city was saved when reinforcements arrived. As Pienkos notes, "Pulaski's activities at Charleston were pivotal; credited with the rescue of the town and the restoration of American honor by his daring attack upon a larger force, he became the man of the hour and was from that time onward included in the deliberations of inner military circles" (Pienkos, 8). Pulaski might have even pursued the British and attacked them on James Island, but the want of boats deterred such a plan, together with the inception of a "low country" fever incurred in the marsh.

During the summer months, Pulaski was incessantly asked for accountings associated with funds disbursed for the cavalry, no matter that he had never received any compensation for his services and was owed 10,000 livres. He replied to Congress on August 19, noting, "Disregard for death made me enlist in your ranks, and I flattered myself that I should work to your satisfaction and earn your approval. It must be my fate, that nothing but honor, to which I have ever been faithful, makes me continue in this service; but I am disheartened by ungenerous treatment.... Be just, gentleman, and think that I could not bow before the powers of Europe I came here to sacrifice everything for the independence of America. I wish to live in a free country, and before I settle down here I wish to fight for that country's freedom. The campaign will start soon; maybe I shall still have opportunity to prove that I am a friend to your cause, though I have not been lucky enough to commend myself to some persons" (qtd. in Waniczek, 154).

This letter proved prophetic, for Pulaski would die for the American cause by October 11. In September, the French admiral Count d'Estaing, Lincoln, and Pulaski planned a movement for the recapture of Savannah, Pulaski's Legion to initially attack outposts, which proved successful and allowed American soldiers to join French troops on the coast. Thirty men were assigned to this duty, requiring a crossing of Fubly's Ferry. When a solitary canoe was found, rather than boats ordered from Augusta, Pulaski accompanied each of his men over, one at a time, leading a horse swimming by his side. Captain Bentalou, who wrote numerous accountings which preserved Pulaski's legacy while in America, led the undertaking, and "while pushing forward towards the town, in the night, he was surprised by the voice of Pulaski, who had hastened on with the remainder of the legion to aid his friend in any possible emergency" (Griswold, 240). When d'Estaing was able to land, he dispatched Pulaski, stating "he was sure he would be the first to join him." Upon meeting, they happily embraced, marching for Savannah the following morning. D'Estaing planned to attack on October 9, British intelligence immediately learning of the plan. Savannah was surrounded by the river on the south and north, to the west a thick swamp and woody morass. A line of five redoubts and batteries lined the last side, thus the infantry had to open a line for cavalry. The plan was for the French to form in three columns, two for assault, one for reserve, with the main attack against the Spring Hill redoubt. As at Valley Forge, Pulaski objected, proposing three points of attack, one on the British right flank, one on the left wing, and the main attack near the right center.

Strategy unwound however; the French were late, the Continentals marched in one straight column, their spirits dimmed by the sound of bagpipes. D'Estaing began the attack before the left flank could form, the column confused and breaking away, under heavy fire. In a mass of confusion, d'Estaing attempted to rally the soldiers. Pulaski was to attack to the left of the Spring Hill redoubt and at the rear of the columns, but the column to open way for the cavalry was forced to retreat, and d'Estaing wounded. Attempting to rally d'Estaing's scattered troops, Pulaski was mortally wounded, "leading not an absurd cavalry charge 'but a desperate push at the British lines'" (qtd. in Szymanski, 273). Bentalou again described the incident:

> D'Estaing led in person the French corps of attack. Wishing to avoid a circuitous advance round a swamp, and supposing the ground at the bottom to be sufficiently firm, he marched directly through it. The enemy had been informed of his plan by spies. They knew the intended point of attack, and the direction in which the approach of the assailants was to be made. Accordingly, they collected all their force where it would be required, and at the first alarm opened a tremendous and deadly fire. Pulaski, impatient to know when he was to act, determined, after securing his cavalry undercover as well as the ground would admit, to go forward himself, and called to accompany him one of the captains of his legion, who is yet living but far advanced in years. They had proceeded only to a small distance, when they heard of the havoc produced in the swamp by the hostile batteries. D'Estaing himself was greviously wounded. Aware of the fatal effect which such a disaster was likely to produce on the spirits of French soldiers — and hoping that his presence would reanimate them, Pulaski rushed on to the scene of disorder and bloodshed. In his attempt to penetrate to the murderous spot he received a swivel shot in the upper part of his right thigh; and the officer who had accompanied him was, while on his way back, wounded by a musket ball — The enterprise upon Savannah was abandoned by the allied armies [qtd. in Szymanski, 274].

Harry Lee wrote of Pulaski's charge: "Count Pulaski, at the head of two hundred horse, threw himself upon the works to force his way into the enemy's rear. Receiving a mortal wound, this brave officer fell, and his fate arrested an effort which might have changed the issue of the day" (qtd. in Szymanski, 275). Major Maciej Rogowski wrote: "After calling upon God's help, Pulaski shouted 'forward,' and we, two hundred strong, rode after him at a gallop so that earth shook under us. The first two minutes went well. We hurried like knights into the danger, but as we passed the gap between the two batteries, a crossfire like a shower confused our ranks. I looked. O painful moment which is ever to be remembered: Pulaski was on the ground. I jumped from my horse, thinking that perhaps his wound was not serious, but, great misfortune, a shot had hit his leg and blood was also flowing from his chest, probably from another wound. As I got to my knees and tried to lift him, he said in a faint voice, 'Jesus, Mary, Joseph.' Further I do not know because in the same moment a carabine shot wounded me" (qtd. in Pienkos, 9).

Pulaski and Bentalou were conveyed on board the United States brig, the *Wasp*, to return to Charleston. Several skillful French surgeons attempted to stop Pulaski's arterial bleeding and prevent suppuration, to no avail. Gangrene set in, and Pulaski died three days later. By most accounts, including that of Bentalou, Pulaski was assigned to a watery grave. However, Joseph Johnson wrote in *Traditions of the American Revolution*, "Another report of his interment has lately been received from my friend I. K. Tefft of Savannah. Charles Litomisky, a Polander, said that he was at the siege of Savannah, as aide de camp to General Count Pulaski, and had the consoling satisfaction of supporting this hero in the struggles of death and that he assisted in consigning his mortal remains to its kindred earth under a large tree, about the bank of the creek leading from Savannah to Charleston. I believe this statement to be true" (Szymanski, 277). And Henry Williams, making a speech during the laying of the cornerstone for the Pulaski Monument in Savannah, on October 11, 1853, said: "On this day seventy-four years ago, Pulaski died, yet remarkable to relate surrounded as he was by friends and companions in arms, prominent as was his station, and gallant as were his deeds, no evidence exists which designate with certainty the place where his remains were deposited. Whether the sea received him, or whether he lies under some spreading oak upon St. Helena's Island in our sister State or sleeps beneath the sod of Greenwhich by the banks of our own beautiful streams, an hour's pilgrimage from the spot where he fell, remains to this day a mystery" (qtd. in Szymanski, 277).

Entering Charleston Harbor, the flag of the *Wasp* was set half-mast, the signal repeated by all the ships in harbor, and at all the forts and batteries. The governor and council of South Carolina and the city of Charleston held a hero's funeral to honor Count Casimir Pulaski, and according to Bentalou, "the procession was grand, magnificent, suited to the occasion. The pall was carried by three American and three French officers of the highest grade — followed by the beautiful horse which Pulaski rode when he received his mortal wound, with all the accoutrements, armour, and dress which he then wore. So immensely large was the mournful procession that it was found necessary to make a circuit round the whole city to the church, where an eloquent and impressive discourse was delivered by the chaplain of the army" (qtd. in Szymanksi, 275).

General "Light Horse Harry" Lee continued the tribute, describing Pulaski: "He was sober, diligent, and intrepid, gentlemanly in his manners, and amiable in heart. He was very reserved, and when alone, betrayed strong evidence of deep melancholy. Those who knew him intimately, spoke highly of the sublimity of his virtue, and the constancy of his friendship. Commanding his heterogeneous corps, badly equipped and worse mounted, this brave Pole encountered difficulty and sought danger. Nor have I the smallest doubt if he had been conversant in our language and better acquainted with our customs and country, but that he would have become one of our most conspicuous and useful officers" (Szymanski, 287). The Marquis de Lafayette noted, "He was one of the first members of the Confederation of Poland, the most distinguished officer and the most dangerous enemy of the tyrants

Statute to Casimir Pulaski, Monterey Square, Savannah, Georgia, cornerstone laid 1825 by Lafayette (author's photograph).

of his country" (Szymanski 290). Historian Sparks said, "From early youth, Pulaski's energies were devoted to the cause of freedom.... Poland was beyond his aid; and when he saw her expire beneath the powerful grasp of a usurper, and felt that she was dead, he forsook the scenes where he had buried the virgin aspirations of his soul — never to look upon them again. He heard of another nation, struggling to attain the end he had hoped to secure for his own, and immediately resolved to lend his aid.... Pulaski was true to the principles he advocated in his youth, and he never ceased to cherish a sincere wish for their ultimate success" (qtd. in Sparks, 242).

Indeed, Pulaski left a legacy in both the Old World and the New. For, in Poland, "by his undaunted courage, shown in twenty battles, attacks, defenses, and raids, as well as by the unceasing zeal with which he incited thousands of others, he contributed to the preservation of the Polish spirit. He was the man who, with Kościuszko, inculcated in the younger generation a strong faith in the restoration of Polish independence" (Waniczek, 156). In the Old World, perhaps his strongest accolade was spoken by his arch-enemy and puppet King Stanisław Poniatowski: "Pulaski has died as he lived — a hero — but an enemy of kings" (qtd. in Szymanski, 290).

In the New World, Pulaski not only sacrificed his life in dedication to political freedom and human rights (John Adams called attention to Pulaski's "universal service for mankind") and saved lives both in battle and on the frontier, averting the full wrath of the British army on multiple occasions, but also "began the initial organization of the American cavalry, an important element in the national military organization up to World War I. For this effort, he has rightly been honored as its 'father.' Pulaski's concrete role in properly defining the role of the cavalry was real enough too; he was the first to stress the importance of cavalry in a military engagement, to insist upon special training for the cavalry, and to organize a unified cavalry command. He also issued many directives which were later incorporated into cavalry training and maneuvers and followed by succeeding officers in this service" (Pienkos 10).

Rash, bold, and active, both in life and death, Pulaski's spirit faileth not, remaining sprightly even in the 21st century, as monuments, shrines and foundations erected and organized in his name remind nations to defend freedom, indeed serve it. In Illinois, on the first Monday of each March, schoolchildren stay out of school to reflect upon the sacrifices of this hero from another world, far across the sea. Should not every American take five seconds each and every day to pull in the reins and reflect upon our handsome land and the lofty values and principles toward which Pulaski, without fail, galloped at breakneck speed, crying "Forward!"

Memorials

One of the first tributes to Pulaski was paid when George Washington on November 17, 1779, issued a challenge and password set for identifying friend and foe when crossing military lines: "Query: *Pulaski*, response: *Poland*."

A memorial to Pulaski, reaching to the heavens, from the state of Georgia, erected in 1825, stands in Monterey Square in Savannah.

A statue to Pulaski depicting his stature in battle was erected in Freedom Plaza in Washington, D.C., in 1910, encouraged by Polish-American societies, especially the one found in Chicago.

Memorials and statues are found in Little Rock, Arkansas; Philadelphia, Pennsylvania; Pennsauken, New Jersey; Utica, New York; Baltimore, Maryland; Stevens Point and Milwaukee, Wisconsin; Buffalo, New York; and Detroit, Michigan.

In 1929, Congress specified October 11 as an annual Pulaski commemoration day, issuing a two-cent stamp in his memory.

Waniczek says, "There is hardly a state in the Union that does not have a county or town, street or square, monument or tablet, school or highway named in grateful memory of General Pulaski," to include at least six counties, twenty towns and villages, two parks, six streets and squares, two schools, stores, banks, savings and loans, and clubs. Such is the case in Pulaski County, Virginia, a name given at the suggestion of the family of Colonel George Hancock of Montgomery County, Virginia. According to his descendants, Hancock served as aide-de-camp to the count, receiving his body in his arms when he fell from his horse in the siege of Savannah. Also, bridges, streets, roads, skyways, and schools throughout America are named in his honor.

Kentucky, since 1942, has recognized a General Pulaski Day. The state of Illinois celebrates Casimir Pulaski Day on the first Monday of March. Wisconsin and Indiana extend a similar recognition, and Milwaukee and New York City hold an annual parade.

Foundations in America which preserve Pulaski's memory include the Polish Roman Catholic Union, the Polish National Alliance, the Polish-American Historical Association, and the Casimir Pulaski Foundation of Philadelphia.

Poland has always included Pulaski as one of its national heroes, with the exception of the period of communism, formed in the country following World War I. During this regime, Pulaski's birthplace, Winiary, was completely neglected (having been a popular tourist attraction), except for the Statue of the Virgin under which Pulaski was said to have prayed. Nonetheless, today, the Kazimierz Pulaski Museum stands in Warka, Poland, the estate preserved, a monument from the United States government commemorating the hero. Visitors are once again enthusiastically welcomed.

The U.S. Congress passed a resolution in 2009, subsequently signed by President Barack Obama, honoring Count Casimir Pulaski with an honorary citizenship, only the seventh person in U.S. history to receive such an honor.

15

WASHINGTON'S ONE-MAN ARMY
Peter Francisco

As for me, give me liberty or give me death.—Patrick Henry, 1775

Anyone kidnapped at the tender age of five, carried across the sea away from home and family, set on shore in another country, alone, left to the "vultures," either consciously or subconsciously, might have a "bone to pick" with any human who would oppress or tyrannize another. Such was the psychological makeup of Portuguese-born Peter Francisco, the "Hercules of the American Revolution," a giant man who single-handedly lifted a 1,100-pound cannon, carrying it from the battlefield and away from British capture; cut down eleven men in succession at Guilford Courthouse; and fought off nine of Tarleton's Bloody Dragoons at Ben Ward's Tavern. His brave and superhuman feats throughout the Revolution earned him a distinguished status throughout the army, his stories of military success reiterated across the Colonies. Presented a dress sword by Colonel Mayo after Francisco saved his life, and a six-foot broadsword by Washington, forged specifically for Francisco as the effective weapon of a giant, rather than the standard sword of the time, this 6'6", 260-pound soldier, as an adult, could protect himself from harm and abduction in any instance, contributing his strength, might, fortitude, and fearless heart to the cause of freedom. How ironic, yet fitting, that a man who was an illiterate indentured servant before joining the revolutionary cause received the highest accolade of the commanding officer of the Continental Army, General Washington remarking: "Without him, we would have lost two crucial battles, perhaps the war, and with it our freedom. He was truly a one-man army!" (qtd. in Hull, 31).

Five-year-old "Pedro" Francisco arrived on the shores of America, at City Point (Hopewell), Virginia, on June 23, 1765, a child abductee from the Portuguese Azores Islands. The ship in which he had been carried across the Atlantic anchored, lowered its longboats, and two crew members rowed the frightened child to shore, leaving him to an uncertain fate. Hull notes, "Large for his age, later research seems to indicate he was a few weeks short of five. Olive-skinned, with black hair and dark eyes, he had a brave bearing and an engaging manner despite his predicament. He spoke a foreign gibberish—what might have been Portuguese mixed with French, or Spanish—and kept repeating the name 'Pedro Francisco'" (Hull, 25). Most likely, Pedro, renamed Peter by the Colonists, was born into nobility on July 9, 1760, nine hundred miles off the coast of Portugal in the Azores. The studies of John E. Manahan in 1960, two hundred years later, revealed a birth record, family history and

"Give me liberty, or give me death!" Patrick Henry delivering his great speech on the rights of the colonies, before the Virginia Assembly, convened at Richmond, March 23, 1775, concluding with the above sentiment, which became the war cry of the revolution. Currier & Ives, 1876 (Library of Congress).

parental home of one Pedro Francisco in the seaside town of Porto Jedeu on the island of Terceira. Another researcher, Robert McKee, studying Spanish court records, found evidence of "the head of the House of Francisco, was in severe disfavor with the King ... and a secret order had been given that one of the Francisco children be killed to atone for the father's guilt" (qtd. in Hull, 26). Another theory postulates that Pedro's own parents arranged his kidnapping and transport to the American colonies for his own safety. Thus, so seated, the boy, kidnapped and left to the shore of Virginia, was wearing a soiled suit, of the very highest quality with a lace collar and cuffs, and silver-buckled shoes with the initials "P.F." engraved thereupon.

From day one, Peter was "all the news," for as the story spread, his guardian-to-be, Judge Anthony Winston (uncle to Patrick Henry), arranged to meet the child, who had been given a bed in a dock warehouse and food by the men and women of City Point, as well as the protective eye of the wharf's night watchman. As Peter proved amiable despite his circumstance, Judge Winston took him under his care, transporting him to his 3,600-acre plantation, known as Hunting Tower, situated on the road from Lynchburg to Richmond, in Buckingham County, Virginia. In time, he became an indentured servant and Winston's personal bodyguard. After learning English, Peter recalled living in a mansion overlooking the sea. He fondly spoke of a younger sister and a beautiful mother, whom he loved deeply. One day, as he was playing in the garden of his parents' home, two men lured

Pedro and his sister to the garden gate with cakes and seized the children. A blanket was thrown over Peter's head; he was bound and gagged, carried aboard a waiting ship. Somehow, Peter's sister escaped (perhaps bearing credence to the theory about the appearance of kidnapping for safety purposes), but Peter was transported across the ocean. Or, perhaps the work of Algerian corsairs, Peter was unharmed for the purpose of a sale into slavery, for as Azorean historian Pedro de Merelim noted, "We all know how they infested these islands and ravaged their peoples" (qtd. in Hull, 26). Yet, if the pirates went to this much trouble in kidnapping and transporting the child, why did they thereafter simply set him ashore and leave?

Trained in the trade of blacksmithing and denied any formal schooling due to his status as a servant, Peter was still always noticed, not just for his height, but for his superhuman strength. Dixon notes, "He was a born athlete. He could throw down, outrun, or whip any boy in Buckingham County, and the wonderful feats performed by him won for him the respect and confidence of the whole community" (4). When he traveled with Winston to a meeting of the Virginia Convention in Richmond (March 1775), just shy of fifteen years of age, he demonstrated this strength by breaking up a tavern dispute, "lifting the combatants into the air and banging them together until they ceased their argument" ("Gustaitus," 2). As the Convention heated up and tempers flared in association with the debates over the colonies' status with the mother country, Peter, no doubt guarding Winston from any threatening altercation, stood outside the door and windows of St. John's Church and heard Patrick Henry's immortal speech:

> MR. PRESIDENT: No man thinks more highly than I do of the patriotism, as well as abilities, of the very worthy gentlemen who have just addressed the House. But different men often see the same subject in different lights; and, therefore, I hope it will not be thought disrespectful to those gentlemen if, entertaining as I do, opinions of a character very opposite to theirs, I shall speak forth my sentiments freely, and without reserve. This is no time for ceremony. The question before the House is one of awful moment to this country. For my own part, I consider it as nothing less than a question of freedom or slavery; and in proportion to the magnitude of the subject ought to be the freedom of the debate. It is only in this way that we can hope to arrive at truth, and fulfill the great responsibility which we hold to God and our country. Should I keep back my opinions at such a time, through fear of giving offence, I should consider myself as guilty of treason towards my country, and of an act of disloyalty toward the majesty of heaven, which I revere above all earthly kings.
>
> Mr. President, it is natural to man to indulge in the illusions of hope. We are apt to shut our eyes against a painful truth, and listen to the song of that siren till she transforms us into beasts. Is this the part of wise men, engaged in a great and arduous struggle for liberty? Are we disposed to be of the number of those who, having eyes, see not, and, having ears, hear not, the things which so nearly concern their temporal salvation? For my part, whatever anguish of spirit it may cost, I am willing to know the whole truth; to know the worst, and to provide for it.
>
> I have but one lamp by which my feet are guided; and that is the lamp of experience. I know of no way of judging of the future but by the past. And judging by the past, I wish to know what there has been in the conduct of the British ministry for the last ten years, to justify those hopes with which gentlemen have been pleased to solace themselves, and the House? Is it that insidious smile with which our petition has been lately received? Trust it not, sir; it will prove a snare to your feet. Suffer not yourselves to be betrayed with a kiss. Ask yourselves how this gracious reception of our petition comports with these war-like preparations which cover our waters and darken our land. Are fleets and armies necessary to a work of love and reconciliation? Have we shown ourselves so unwilling to be reconciled, that force must be called in to win back our love? Let us not deceive ourselves, sir. These are the

implements of war and subjugation; the last arguments to which kings resort. I ask, gentlemen, sir, what means this martial array, if its purpose be not to force us to submission? Can gentlemen assign any other possible motive for it? Has Great Britain any enemy, in this quarter of the world, to call for all this accumulation of navies and armies? No, sir, she has none. They are meant for us; they can be meant for no other. They are sent over to bind and rivet upon us those chains which the British ministry have been so long forging. And what have we to oppose to them? Shall we try argument? Sir, we have been trying that for the last ten years. Have we anything new to offer upon the subject? Nothing. We have held the subject up in every light of which it is capable; but it has been all in vain. Shall we resort to entreaty and humble supplication? What terms shall we find which have not been already exhausted? Let us not, I beseech you, sir, deceive ourselves. Sir, we have done everything that could be done, to avert the storm which is now coming on. We have petitioned; we have remonstrated; we have supplicated; we have prostrated ourselves before the throne, and have implored its interposition to arrest the tyrannical hands of the ministry and Parliament. Our petitions have been slighted; our remonstrances have produced additional violence and insult; our supplications have been disregarded; and we have been spurned, with contempt, from the foot of the throne. In vain, after these things, may we indulge the fond hope of peace and reconciliation. There is no longer any room for hope. If we wish to be free, if we mean to preserve inviolate those inestimable privileges for which we have been so long contending, if we mean not basely to abandon the noble struggle in which we have been so long engaged, and which we have pledged ourselves never to abandon until the glorious object of our contest shall be obtained, we must fight! I repeat it, sir, we must fight! An appeal to arms and to the God of Hosts is all that is left us!

They tell us, sir, that we are weak; unable to cope with so formidable an adversary. But when shall we be stronger? Will it be the next week, or the next year? Will it be when we are totally disarmed, and when a British guard shall be stationed in every house? Shall we gather strength by irresolution and inaction? Shall we acquire the means of effectual resistance, by lying supinely on our backs, and hugging the delusive phantom of hope, until our enemies shall have bound us hand and foot? Sir, we are not weak if we make a proper use of those means which the God of nature hath placed in our power. Three millions of people, armed in the holy cause of liberty, and in such a country as that which we possess, are invincible by any force which our enemy can send against us. Besides, sir, we shall not fight our battles alone. There is a just God who presides over the destinies of nations; and who will raise up friends to fight our battles for us. The battle, sir, is not to the strong alone; it is to the vigilant, the active, the brave. Besides, sir, we have no election. If we were base enough to desire it, it is now too late to retire from the contest. There is no retreat but in submission and slavery! Our chains are forged! Their clanking may be heard on the plains of Boston! The war is inevitable and let it come! I repeat it, sir, let it come.

It is in vain, sir, to extenuate the matter. Gentlemen may cry, Peace, Peace but there is no peace. The war is actually begun! The next gale that sweeps from the north will bring to our ears the clash of resounding arms! Our brethren are already in the field! Why stand we here idle? What is it that gentlemen wish? What would they have? Is life so dear, or peace so sweet, as to be purchased at the price of chains and slavery? Forbid it, Almighty God! I know not what course others may take; but as for me, give me liberty or give me death!

Henry's entire speech is reiterated herein to analyze the tremendous psychological impact these words must have wrought upon Peter's psyche, a young adult not yet fifteen whose very life story imitated the images contained in the speech: Peter had listened to the song of the sirens by being attracted to the pirates' treats, effectively betrayed by a kiss; he had been blindfolded and gagged, having eyes seeing not, having ears, unable to hear; he had been the victim of the worst truths associated with his family history, spurned from his family's social standing, at "the foot of the throne"; by the lamp of experience, he carried firsthand knowledge of the horrors of confinement and suppression, of the binding of hand

and foot; he had been exposed to a fleet whose purpose was subjugation (the ship which carried him away from home and family), sent solely to "bind and rivet"; he had been fighting against his own personal oppression for ten years, this particular number mentioned twice within Henry's speech, deceived with regard to his societal potential by the hand of his guardians; he had heard the clanking of chains on the plantation, witnessing the price of peace at the hand of the mighty. Small wonder Peter, while still in the churchyard, offered to enlist. Of course, despite the unjustified social standings of the era, "Winston loved like a son the young giant who could do the work of three men" (Hull, 26), and made Peter promise to wait one more year, until he gained the age of sixteen, at which time he would give him permission to join the Continentals, and, as a result, earn his freedom.

In December 1776, both Winston and Francisco fulfilled their promises to each other, and Francisco voluntarily enlisted as a private in the 10th Virginia Regiment under Colonel Hugh Woodson, sent to Middlebrook, New Jersey, for basic training, "devoted passionately to the cause which he had made his own ... no such picturesque figure in the whole Continental line" ("Peter Francisco: American Soldier," 214), "without an ounce of superfluous flesh, an extremely handsome face, with black hair and piercing black eyes ... a veritable giant with an eye like a hawk, the spirit of a king eagle, a breast like a lion, strong as a buffalo, and with the breath of a hound" (Dixon, 5). He served the Northern campaign for three years, his first experience on the line occurring on September 11, 1777, at the Battle of Brandywine. Along this little creek south of Philadelphia, Washington attempted to circumvent the advance of the British army under Generals Howe and Cornwallis. Washington, expecting a frontal assault, yet confronted by Cornwallis' decision to complete a circular flanking, fought desperately to no avail. In an attempt to save his army, Washington sent several field units onto the field to halt the advance and bide time for a retreat, including the 10th Virginia, which took position at Sandy Hollow Gap. These units held the field for a full forty-five minutes, providing Washington the time to save his army. Receiving his first of six injuries incurred during the war, Francisco took a musket ball in the leg and recovered at a temporary hospital organized at a Moravian community north of Philadelphia, Bethlehem, whereby he met fellow patient Marquis de Lafayette, also injured during the battle. The two men developed a friendship while convalescing, which lasted a lifetime.

Recovering quickly, Francisco next fought at the battle of Germantown on October 4, the Continentals attempting to hold their forts on the Delaware River five miles north of Philadelphia. General Nathanael Greene held the line for a significant amount of time, proving the British army could be defeated, yet a counterattack proved excessive. Again, Francisco was in the "thick" of holding the forces at bay long enough for Greene to organize a retreat. During the remainder of the fall months, Francisco served at Fort Mifflin on Mud Island (Delaware River). British ships incessantly shelled the Fort, Dixon stating, "Day after day, the besieged withstood the bombardment of the enemy with persistent energy and bravery, until the block houses were beaten down, the palisades demolished, and the guns dismounted. Many of the brave defenders were killed or wounded, and when the few still left were unable to longer defend the fort, they set fire to whatever was combustible, and crossed the river at night by the light of the flames. Young Francisco, during this terrible siege, stood side-by-side with the bravest of the defenders and was the peer of the best" (7). Transitioning to the winter months, "he and the rest of Washington's oft-defeated army wintered at Valley Forge, enduring the nightmare of hunger, bitter cold and exposure that was the lot of the Colonial soldier there. Like many, he became ill and spent two bitter winter months in the hospital" (Hull, 28). The spring months proved healing, and Francisco

The Battle of Stony Point, Joseph Brightly, engraver (c. February 14, 1857). Print shows General "Mad" Anthony Wayne and his men, including Peter Francisco, attacking a British fortification (Library of Congress).

reenlisted. On June 28, 1778, Francisco was wounded for the second time during the war at the Battle of Monmouth, near present-day Freehold, New Jersey. The wound was to the right thigh, a musket ball entering therein, the tissue and bone damage causing Francisco pain for the remainder of his life.

Francisco's next feat for the Army is memorable in that he was chosen as one of twenty to take part in a surprise attack on Stony Point on the Hudson River, a British stronghold north of New York City. Moving out at 11:30 P.M. on July 15, 1779, under the command of Major General "Mad" Anthony Wayne, the group known as "forlorn hope," cleared the way for light infantry by cutting a path through the undergrowth with axes, scrambling quickly up a cliff when sighted by the Redcoats. Of the twenty members, only three survived the spearheading efforts, one such survivor being Francisco, though he did sustain a 9-inch bayonet slash across his abdomen (the third injury of the war) while killing three grenadiers. In spite of this wound, he charged to the flagstaff, eliminated the color bearer, seized the flag and collapsed, watching the Continentals confiscating British ammunition and supply. The next morning, Francisco delivered the flag to Lieutenant Colonel François-Louis Teissèdre de Fleury, a French army engineer. Captain William Evans, also in the battle, wrote: "Francisco was the second man who entered the fort and distinguished himself in numerous acts of bravery and intrepidly.... In a charge which was ordered to be made around the flagstaff, he killed three British grenadiers and was the first man who laid hold of the flagstaff and being badly wounded laid on it that night and in the morning delivered it to Colonel Fleury. These circumstances brought Mr. Francisco into great notice and his name was reiterated throughout the whole army."

After recuperating from wound number three, Francisco enlisted for a third time and joined a militia regiment under Colonel William Mayo. The war moved South due to a change in British strategy (they hoped to rally Loyalists in the area). Led by General Horatio Gates, the regiment first fought at Camden, South Carolina (August 15, 1780), a battle doomed to fail as a result of poor planning, haste, and an inexperienced militia, most of whom had never seen battle or even drilled in military technique. In this battle, labeled by historian John Fiske as "the most disastrous defeat ever inflicted on an American Army," Francisco did not join the panic of the moment, and in vain attempted to "rally the running, screaming men around him, but he too was forced to retreat through the pine woods" (Hull, 29). As he ran, he came upon a British grenadier attempting to bayonet his regiment's commander, Colonel Mayo. He shot the offender, an act thus noticed by one of Bloody Tarleton's dragoons, who charged the pair. Standing his ground to the green-coated cavalryman, who raised his sword and ordered Francisco to throw down, Francisco simply sidestepped and bayoneted the cavalryman, tossing him from his saddle and mounting the horse. As he rode through the pines and sand, Francisco impersonated a Tory, yelling, "Huzzah, my brave boys! Yonder goes the damned rebels!" As he rode, he noticed, among the Tories, Mayo had been taken prisoner. Charging the Loyalists, he freed his commanding officer, and noticing Mayo's fatigue, offered his charger for a ride to safety. (In appreciation for saving his life, Mayo later promised to bequeath Francisco 1,000 acres in Kentucky, which never occurred due to a dispute in title, and also presented him with his personal dress sword, now preserved by the Richmond-based Virginia Historical Society.)

Francisco was far from finished in attempting to recover losses incurred during the Battle of Camden, described as a defeat which caused the "Laurels of Saratoga to change to Southern willows," a reference to the unforgivable personal retreat by General Gates, in which he galloped off the battlefield and to a location near Charlotte, North Carolina, in record time! As Gates sped away, labeled as a coward in perpetuity, Francisco became a legend for all time. Noticing a cannon abandoned by the Continentals during their retreat, as well as the horse pulling the fieldpiece lying on the battlefield, obviously dead, Francisco, determined the British would not capture the artillery, risked his life by running for it, unhitching the carriage, and lifting the 1,100-pound cannon onto his back, staggering under its weight, yet carrying it off the battlefield and toward a group of Continentals. Of note: "Some historians have questioned whether such a feat is possible, but during the American bicentennial celebrations of 1975–76, the U.S. Postal Service saw no reason to doubt it and issued a commemorative stamp showing the hulking Peter Francisco performing this stupendous deed" (Gustaitus, 3). Tarleton's dragoons not yet finished with Francisco, another trooper, finding him exhausted under a tree, reared his horse above Francisco and admonished: "Surrender or die!" Francisco replied his musket was unloaded and offered the dragoon the butt end. As the dragoon reached for the gun, Francisco twirled it around and pushed the bayonet into the green-coated chest. Pushing the dead dragoon from his horse, he mounted and galloped, again, past the Tories, chased by Tarleton's Legion as he rose in the stirrups, once more crying "Huzzah, my brave boys! We've conquered the rebels!" the trick leading him to safety a second time.

Following Camden, Francisco began complaining about the swords he had been using in battle, referring to them as "more like a toothpick than an effective weapon. General Washington heard of his predicament and gave special orders for a suitable broadsword to be forged for him. Six feet long and with a 5-foot blade, the new sword was delivered to Francisco on March 13, 1781—two days before the most sensational day of his fighting career and one of the bloodiest battles of the Revolution" (Hull, 30). This battle was "long, obstinate, and bloody," and came to be known as the Battle of Guildford Courthouse.

Note: According to Peter's petition to the Virginia House of Delegates years later, on his way to join the Battle of Guilford Courthouse, he displayed another example of his unlimited bravery (Francisco using the third person):

> We then fell in with the British army of about five or six hundred at a place called Scotch Lake. About a hundred yards from the lake, they fortified themselves in upon the top of a hill resembling a sugar loaf; as soon as he got in sight of the lake, he tied his horse and ran under the bank thereof to discover the situation that the enemy were in, and, after getting opposite to the fort, he discovered thre was no danger under the foot of the mount where all of their tents and marquees as they stood pitched, and where there were several hogsheads; and after walking about for some time, when about to return went into one of their marquees, threw down one of the hogsheads, down on the bulge, and rolling some distance, placed himself upon his belly, with his head under cover of the hogshead, and, by drawing it down gently by each chime, got it to the lake, the British firing at the same time, and firing several balls through the hogshead. The British, being surrounded by our cavalry and infantry, they could not come out of the fort. When he arrived at his journey's end, General Johnson and his piquet being placed there, the General opened the hogshead, and the contents were shirts and overall, and othr clothing, which he divided amongst Washington and Lee's men, who were bare for such necessaries'; General Johnson himself wore some of the pantaloons. He then mounted his horse and rode around the north side of the mount, where he discovered eight horses belonging to British officers, about one hundred yards from the fort. He borrowed a whip and rode between the fort and the horses under fire, and brought them safe into the camp and gave them to Colonel Washington [qtd. in "Letter to," 218].

The Southern Continental Army, now under the leadership of General Nathanael Greene, in the words of Lord Cornwallis, "fought like demons," on paper won by the British, but, effectively, helping America to win the war, as the British suffered a grave loss of lives. Wielding his new sword, Francisco seemed invincible as he led Washington's cavalrymen down the slope. Benson Lossing reported in his 1850 *Pictorial Field Book of the Revolution* that Francisco felled eleven soldiers before a British guardsman pinned him to his horse with a bayonet, Peter's fourth injury of the war. Lossing wrote, "Forbearing to strike, he assisted the assailant to draw his bayonet forth, when, with terrible force, he brought down his broadsword and cleft the poor fellow's head to his shoulder" (qtd. in "Gustaitus," 4). Peter's own son, Dr. B. M. Francisco, wrote later that continuing his soldiering duties, Peter charged on, killing two more Redcoats before incurring a fifth injury in which an upward-thrust bayonet "impaled his right thigh the whole length of the bayonet, entering above the knee and coming out at the socket of his hip" (qtd. in Hull, 30). Overcome with pain, Peter wheeled and rode off a short distance before passing out and falling from his horse. Fortunately, a Quaker by the last name of Robinson who was scouting the field for survivors found Francisco among a group of four dead men, took him home, and tended to his wounds, nurturing him back to health, this intense wound taking six to eight weeks to heal. Washington, so impressed with Francisco's deeds, offered him an officer's commission, which Francisco declined due to his unfortunate lack of education. General Greene presented Francisco a handmade razor case as "a tribute to his moral worth and value" (qtd. in Hull, 30). (The case is preserved in the Guildford Courthouse Museum in Greensboro, North Carolina.)

Despite Francisco's perceived inability to accept the commission, upon *walking* home to Virginia, he did accept an offer to become a scout, quite the honor for a private solider, his duty to monitor the comings and goings of Bloody Tarleton's Dragoons, the cavalrymen who had pursued him at Camden, for "Tarleton's hated dragoons were raiding army posts and settlements" in Francisco's home state. On one such search, Francisco stopped for refreshment at Ben Ward's Tavern in Amelia (Nottoway County). While sitting in the inn yard drinking ale, he was surrounded by nine of Tarleton's Dragoons, eight entering the inn and one demanding Francisco's acquiescence. With saber drawn, the Dragoon quipped, "Give up instantly all that you possess of value, or prepare to die!" (qtd. in Hull, 30), specifically targeting the silver buckles on Francisco's shoes. Francisco replied, "They were a present to me from a valued friend. Give them into your hands, I never will. You have the power; take them if you think fit" (qtd. in Hull, 30). The trooper placed his sword under his arm to retrieve the buckles, yet Francisco took a step backward from the dragoon's grasp, grabbed his saber and slashed the man's head and neck. Before expiring, the horseman drew a pistol and fired at Francisco, the bullet grazing Francisco's side and constituting his sixth injury of the war, Francisco reacting by nearly excising the dragoon's hand as well. The

Engraving depicting Continental Army Soldier Peter Francisco in a fight with Bloody Banastre Tarleton's Dragoons, Amelia County, Virginia, July, 1781. Engraving by D. Edwin, 1814.
  Print shows Peter Francisco in a clearing near a tavern, with sword raised, assaulting a British soldier on horseback, another soldier at his feet, dead or wounded, and seven other dragoons fleeing on foot toward Lieutenant-General Tarleton's cavalry in the background. Includes a remarque of George Washington at bottom center (Library of Congress).

noise drew the other eight dragoons from the inn, and several versions of what happened next exist, however, it appears that when one of the eight aimed a musket at Francisco, which misfired, he grabbed it from the assailer, knocked him from the saddle, and galloped off. Some works indicate, that "Francisco, quick-witted and cool-headed, called aloud as if shouting out his own command of men. The British standing near him were deceived by this pretense and fleeing precipitately left their horses behind them. Thereupon Francisco dashed into the saddle of one of the deserted horses, and driving the others before him escaped down an obscure road, though Tarleton's troopers were dispatched in all directions in search of him. With characteristic independence, Francisco sold his British horses at Prince Edward Courthouse, retaining one for himself, which he rode for many years, calling him Tarleton" ("Peter Francisco: American Soldier," 215).

Francisco wrote in his pension petition: "He had then neither sword nor pistol of his own, but fought with his adversary's own weapon, which he took from him. He wounded and drove off the others, and took eight horses, with their trappings, out of nine; the ninth man escaped with a large cut upon his back. They all joined Tarleton, who was about a mile off, except the slain man. This is the last favor I ever did the British" (qtd. in "Gustaitus: American Soldier," 219).

Triumphantly, Francisco was next heard of on the line with his friend, Lafayette, to watch the surrender of Yorktown on October 19, 1781, the two returning to Richmond afterwards, where, supposedly, as they strolled and talked one day in front of St. John's Church, "a young lady who was leaving the building tripped and was caught by the strapping young veteran. And that was how Francisco first encountered Susannah Anderson, the woman he would marry" ("Gustaitus," 4). Following the war, Francisco's legend grew to one mimicking the characteristics of the Paul Bunyan tall tales: supposedly, he rescued a cow and calf from the mud, carrying one under each arm, and threw a shoddy carpenter onto the roof of a barn. Supposedly, he tossed a challenger from Kentucky named Pamphlett over a four-foot fence, along with his quadruped. What is real is that after the war, Francisco received another chance at life, one based in freedom and justice. He entered the private school of John McGraw next to young children ages five and up, excelling to the point he was reading the classics within three years, becoming an avid reader who assembled his own library. He "became prosperous, acquired property, raised children, and served on juries. The fame of Francisco's combat prowess slowly gave way to the legacy of a quiet-spoken, kind-hearted giant who shelled corn for the poor and habitually left the table to take food to old servants.... He was appointed sergeant-at-arms in the Virginia Legislature in 1825. His acquaintances there included such distinguished contemporaries as Chief Justice John Marshall and Henry Clay, the senator and Whig Party leader" (Hull, 31). Francisco, now a member of the gentry, pursued the happiness associated with independence by enjoying matrimonial bliss (Susannah until her death in 1790, this marriage resulting in one son and one daughter; Catherine Brooke in 1794 and until her death in 1821, the progeny from this marriage being three sons and one daughter; and Mary Grymes West in 1823), dressing well (he loved waistcoats, high hats, and silk stockings), enjoying fishing and hunting outings, as well as house parties, during which he would sing with a fine voice, described by one visitor as powerful and deep yet carrying a sweetness of tone and remarkable potency. He was granted a monthly pension by the Virginia Assembly in his elder years (Congress ungratefully and astonishingly did not approve his petition for a pension) and enjoyed a return visit from his friend, Lafayette, in 1825.

Succumbing to appendicitis on January 16, 1831, at the age of 70, Francisco died in

Richmond, the Virginia Assembly adjourning in respect for the patriot who was "no common man," and "whose striking example of bravery ... and exploits have scarcely ever been excelled" (qtd. in Hull, 31). The proceedings from the Virginia House of Delegates, January 17, 1831, read: "By nature he had been endowed with extraordinary strength, the most determined intrepidity, and the warmest patriotism. It was not his lot to be advanced in rank during our Revolutionary struggle. But, as a private soldier, he gave a striking example of bravery, and performed exploits that have scarcely ever been excelled. Not only in the North, but the South, he displayed his heroism. And the achievements which he performed in Virginia, overcoming three or four of the enemy, and causing them to fly, leaving their property in his possession, has seldom been equaled" (qtd. in Dixon, 11).

Francisco's funeral with full military honors was held in the House of Delegates Hall on January 18, the Reverend Channing Moore, Episcopal Bishop of Virginia, presiding. Present were the "governor, legislators, citizens and units of the light infantry, artillery, dragoons, and the Public Guard" (Hull, 31).

In his petition to the Virginia House of Delegates for receipt of a pension, Francisco noted "he never felt satisfied, nor thought he did a good day's work, but by drawing British blood, and if that was not the case, could not have a good night's repose" (qtd. in "Peter Francisco: American Soldier," 217). Francisco, of all the volunteers mentioned in this book, was the most terrorized victim of tyranny and injustice, indeed enduring the loss of personal freedom in association with his right-of-birth and skin color. He pushed that victimization aside, however, using his other God-given gifts to not only go out of the box, but burst it, changing the composition of an old adage: Might is in the Right, but only when freedom is at stake! (Otherwise, gentle, artful living is the order of the day, per Francisco's example.) Certainly, Francisco was in the right when he fought for his own personal freedom as well as the freedom of millions and millions of Americans yet to be born! Graciás, Pedro!

Memorials

A granite column marking the spot where Francisco felled 11 British soldiers was unveiled at the Guilford Courthouse National Military Park in 1904. At the commemoration ceremony, Dixon noted, "How very fitting that a tablet to the memory of Peter Francisco should be unveiled today upon this battlefield, where he did some of his most heroic deeds, and where he poured out his blood so freely for American Independence. How seldom do we find tablets unveiled or monuments erected to the man behind the guns, but officers of an army could make no renown if they had no brave men to do the fighting. I take my hat off to the private soldier, to the man who never wavered in battle or on the march, whose brawny arm and trusty broadsword thinned the ranks of the enemy wherever he went, the man whose memory we honor today by yonder tablet, the typical American soldier, Peter Francisco" (12).

Peter is buried in Richmond's Shockoe Cemetery, his tombstone simply stating, "A Soldier of Revolutionary Fame."

A Liberty Tree representing Virginia was planted around 1899 at the Golden Gate State Park in San Francisco, California, nourished by soil taken from the grave of Peter Francisco.

Since 1953 three states have designated March 15, the anniversary of the Battle of Guilford Courthouse, as Peter Francisco Day: Virginia, Massachusetts, and Rhode Island.

In 1957 the Portuguese Continental Union of the United States established a silver, gold, and enamel Peter Francisco Award. Candidates are "persons or organizations that contribute to the promotion of Luso-American relations and the preservation of Portuguese heritage and culture. The medal bears the motto of Prince Henry the Navigator, the famed Portuguese explorer: 'Talent De Bein Faire' (the desire to do well). The first recipient of the award was President John F. Kennedy" (Hull, 31).

In Hopewell, Virginia, at City Point, a marker depicts the spot where a young five-year-old Pedro Francisco was deposited on the shores of America on June 23, 1765, supposedly left to oblivion, instead, at the hand of truth and justice, remembered by the ages.

16

THE REVOLUTIONARY PEDAGOGY OF DRILLMASTER BARON FRIEDRICH WILHELM VON STEUBEN

If I am Possessor of some talents in the Art of War, they should be much dearer to me, if I could employ them in the service of a Republick such as I hope soon to see America. — Baron von Steuben to the Continental Congress, December 6, 1777

It is a rare individual who understands how to motivate and gain the respect of an adult learner. Yet, in the winter of 1778 at Valley Forge, Pennsylvania, volunteer drillmaster Baron Friedrich Wilhelm von Steuben, a Prussian-born officer who had personally served Frederick the Great, focused on three essentials associated with reaching the disenchanted, diseased, and starving soldiers (for the last thing they needed was an arrogant European to remind them of their failings): 1) appreciate strengths apparent; 2) provide an example; 3) encourage, enable, and get out of the way. Appreciating the Continentals' strengths, Steuben wrote a friend, explaining he did not think a European army could bear up under such privations. And, as John Laurens noticed, "He is not so much a systematist as to be averse from adapting established forms of stubborn circumstances. He will not give us the perfect instructions absolutely speaking, but the best which we are in a condition to receive" (qtd. in Danckert, 3). Serving as an example, Steuben was the first on the parade field each morning, drilling a model company, allowing this company to train another, who trained others, thus contributing to exponential growth. He also set the standard by writing the first "blue book" of military technique for the American army. And, finally, Steuben instilled in his men "a relish for their trade, to make them feel a confidence in their own skill," by encouraging self-directed learning in which the soldiers came to understand their own deficiencies by means of questioning, in turn receiving respectful answers which fostered a commitment to the task at hand and to a spirit of pride. As William Wordsworth would write a generation later, due to Steuben's professional teaching methods, which proved ahead of their time, the men camped at Valley Forge "found comfort in themselves and in their cause." Nonetheless, despite this enlightened pedagogy, Steuben, though "genial, benevolent, and generous to excess ... would not allow the slightest deviation from military usages, the slightest waste of military stores, or the slightest infringement of military dignity ... for upon these points he had all the spirit and chivalry of the best days of knighthood" (Griswold, Simms, and Ingraham, 248).

Baron von Steuben on horseback (Library of Congress).

Steuben's family in fact harked back to the days of chivalry; the surname can be traced back six hundred years, written variously Steube, Stoebe, Stoyben, and finally Steuben, and first heard of in Franconia, a village lying along the River Main, South of Saxony, Germany. The family broke tradition by placing themselves on the side of the Reformation, losing their estates as a result. Steuben's paternal line included a miller, tenant-farmer, and an ambitious self-made man and minister, Augustin, according to Palmer. Yet, Lockhart believes, "One aspect of his origin, however, is very clear, though historians have needlessly made it a point of controversy: his social status. Friedrich von Steuben was nobly born" (2). Bloodline aside, his father was born Wilhelm Von Steuben, who "entered the Prussian military service in 1715, and held one military post after another, part of the time in Russia" (Doyle, 8). From Wilhelm's union with Mary Dorothea Von Iagow was born the Revolutionary hero, Friedrich Wilhelm (named after his honorary godfather, Friedrich I, an indication that this King "who loved his Army more than his children, more than anything other than his serious and vengeful God—would not have agreed to stand in as godfather to just anyone. His doing so for this baby that day showed that the Steuben family was high in his favor, that Friedrich's father was on his way up in the world, and that baby Friedrich would not have an ordinary life. Should he survive into manhood, he would grow up to be a soldier, too, and great things would be expected of him. What no one present that day could have anticipated was the Friedrich von Steuben would win his fame not in the battlefields of central Europe, but in distant America" (Lockhart, 2).

Friedrich's mother appears to have provided a traceable "blue blood" line in her son's veins, as genealogists "trace the blood of his grandmother, Charlotte Dorothea von Effern, step by step back to 'Karl the Great' and St. Elizabeth ... On the one side the blood imperial of Charlemagne; on the other side that of a successful self-made man, a rare phenomenon in eighteenth-century Prussia" (Palmer, 15). Baptismal records place his birth at Madgeburg, a fortress on the Elbe, on September 17, 1730 (though Kapp provides a date of November 15, 1730), born a subject of Friedrich William I. The first of ten children, Friedrich, in a letter to a friend on his 56th birthday, placed his birth as "the seventeenth of September 1730, at six o'clock in the evening." Friedrich grew up "among guns, drums, trumpets, fortifications, drills and parades. His uncle had written one of the standard books on fortifications, and his father was a major of military engineers" (Bobrick, 332).

Little is known of Friedrich's childhood, but it is clear he was reared in poverty, as captains of the period earned a meager pay. As Palmer notes, it was the "peculiarly painful poverty of the shabby genteel" (23), and since his grandfather, Augustin, had purloined the use of "von," as a family name to help the family "rise" in the world, each family member, now considered nobility when the surname was heard, had to prove him or herself a gentleman or a lady. Thus, Friedrich's father moved to Russia when he was one year old, with the permission of the King, in an attempt to "win wealth and honors at the cannon's mouth" (Palmer, 23). For eight years, Friedrich witnessed "pictures of crowded garrison life at Cronstadt and other fortresses; glimpses of his mother's frugal housekeeping in her crowded billet; of his father marching off to fight the Turks in Crimea; of merry games with the children of other officers and the rough horseplay of hirsute soldiers in their barracks. There were other pictures of the palaces, the churches and the crowded streets of St. Petersburg, the pageantry of the Imperial Guards marching in review before some exalted personage on horseback, perhaps the great soldier of fortune, Marshal Münnich himself. There may even have been a picture of the Empress Anne surrounded by her brilliant staff" (Palmer, 24). Five of Friedrich's brothers and sisters were buried in Russia, never surviving the cold

Russian winters. When nine, he traveled back to Germany with his parents and sister, Dorothea, never having known the grandparents in Brandenburg who died during his absence.

Friedrich spent the remainder of his childhood, up through and until the age of seventeen, in the new Prussian province of Silesia, as Frederick the II (Frederick the Great) ascended to the throne, began his military campaign, and kept his soldiers on the home front. (Friedrich also witnessed two more young infant brothers pass away during this period.) Friedrich's father was promoted to major and earned decorations for his services under Friedrich the Great, earning the Order *Pour le mérite* (a reward for loyal subjects with outstanding service — the use of a French term considered stylish during this period). As Palmer notes, "We may be sure that his father was his principal military tutor. Major von Steuben was an educated man and an accomplished military engineer. Nor was he a purely theoretical instructor. When he went to the Second Silesian War in 1744, he took his son with him. There Frederick William, as a boy of fourteen, was present at the siege of Prague and began his practical training for the siege of Yorktown" (27). Lockhart says, "Young Friedrich was hooked — by the smoke and the noise and the excitement, by the respect that his father's office carried and by the great responsibility that his father bore for the King" (3). Pursuing his education at the Jesuit Colleges in Silesia, Steuben was proficient in math, history, German, and French (all of which helped him perform his duties at Valley Forge). With regard to his education, Steuben wrote: "The troubles of a military life, the narrow circumstances of my parents and their frequent changes of residence, did not permit them to give me any better education than that which a poor young nobleman in Prussia always receives. But while other young officers led a dissolute and extravagant life, I applied myself closely to study, and exerted myself not only to learn my profession, but to enlarge my knowledge of belles-letters and the practical science. Nevertheless, from want of time and the necessary means, I made only slow progress" (qtd. in Doyle, 9). Palmer indicates Steuben's thoughts regarding his education were "unduly modest," for "Steuben was much better educated than the average Prussian officer of the day. He wrote better German than most of his contemporaries. He also spoke and wrote French fluently.... His letters are full of allusions to the important literature of the day. The Jesuit fathers in Breslau gave him more than mathematics. They led him into the world of books" (28). Works Steuben particularly loved included Voltaire's *Candide* and *Don Quixote.*

Steeped in the military life, Steuben joined the Prussian army at the age of seventeen, quartered in Breslau where his father was stationed and where he still had access to the university and library. Proving successful in his early military career, Steuben was first promoted to ensign on May 3, 1749, and thereafter to second lieutenant on November 26, 1752. The importance of drill and discipline was preeminent to his training, for "he was one of the cogs in the most perfect military machine in the world. There were few idle hours in the military day. Every day throughout the year there were rigid drills and the drill year culminated in prolonged field maneuvers under the eye of Frederick the Great himself. Steuben's regiment was a strict school in which he learned every detail of the military business and above all the secret of discipline. To say that he was a lieutenant in King Frederick's Lestwitz Regiment is to say that he was a member of the most highly trained corps of infantry officers in the world" (Palmer, 29), for Prussian soldiers were trained in "linear tactics" in which infantry could change formations, from column of march to line of battle, even while under fire. Young cadets, in their blue coats bordered by rose-colored cuffs, white waistcoats, and white breeches, were also taught humility (seasoned officers, despite their rank, would conduct drills in the field themselves, to include the King) and empathy, encouraged to appreciate the burdensome life of a private. No doubt, Steuben also sharpened his social graces during this initial military experience, for, while at Valley Forge, the wives of Washington, Greene, Duane, and Peters "enjoyed his witty conversation and his courtly old-world manners," and William North spoke to his "graceful entry and carriage in a ball room" (Palmer, 31). Alternatively, it seems throughout life, Steuben, in the words of North, always "wanted to eat his calf while it was still in the cow's belly," a reference to his undisciplined spending practices, which contrasted with the highly disciplined manner in which he performed his duties as a soldier.

While enjoying a youthful life, Steuben also spent his time "in the trenches," literally, as his career was budding. He wrote in a letter to friend Count von Donnersmark in 1754:

> While you, my dear Count, are figuring in the temple of Themis, I am condemned to a most revolting occupation. A work that M. De Balby (engineer) has traced across a cemetery, requires the cutting of a deep ditch, in the course of which half-decomposed dead bodies are continually disinterred. I fear for my poor soldiers. The noisome exhalations will become more insupportable as the season advances. I order vinegar, brandy, tobacco, in short, everything that I can think of for their protection.... As yet I have no sick, but I fear the month of July. In order not to alarm them, I am continually at work, notwithstanding my disgust for this abominable occupation, and my subordinates are obliged to follow my example—*ora pro nobis!* (Latin for pray for us) [qtd. in Doyle, 10–11].

In the same letter, Steuben went on to predict the war between Frederick the Great and Maria Theresa (Austria) and Czarina Elizabeth (Russia), exclaiming to his friend, "Yes, my dear Henry, if there is a war, I promise you, at the end of a second campaign, that your friend will be either in Hades, or at the head of a regiment" (qtd. in Doyle, 11). As a lieutenant, Steuben's additional duties included "leading his company in hours of drill, keeping a watchful eye on the discipline and cleanliness of his men, maintaining the company's accounts and other paperwork, supervising the distribution and cooking of rations, and all of the other elements of the stultifying but necessary routine" (Lockhart, 17).

Steuben's prophesy proved correct, for by 1756, the Seven Years' War was on, and, ironically, during his second campaign, he earned his baptism of fire. During the battle of Prague, which Carlyle described thusly: "Battle of Prague, one of the furious battles of the World; loud as Doomsday: the very Emblem of which, done on the Piano by females of energy, scatters mankind to flight who love their ears" (qtd. in Palmer, 35), Steuben served in the "free battalion," organized of volunteer adventurers (notoriously difficult to command) who wished to perform swift raids and other special missions (scouting, reconnaissance, and raiding) away from the main army. He was wounded twice, but not severely, having ridden into battle under the eyes of King Frederick himself. Due to his service, he was elected staff officer of the battalion, a tribute to his professionalism and a certain indication of the King having noticed his abilities. Palmer notes that "more important still, his experience with irregular troops broadened him for his future role in America" (36), and Doyle believes, "Here it was that Steuben learned thoroughly those tactics and infantry management generally which were to prove so valuable in later years" (13). During this period, in which he was promoted to first lieutenant and quartermaster, "an officer qualified to assist a general in his strategic capacity and not merely in his administrative capacity" (Palmer, 38), performing intelligence and strategic planning, he also became friends with the King's brother, Prince Henry, a friendship that would last for a lifetime, even when Steuben eventually fell from the King's favor.

Steuben was wounded for the second time at Kunersdorf, as was the King. The King's army was failing due to the coalition formed against him (Russia, France, Austria, Sweden), yet Steuben continued to maintain a bold front to his foes, assisted by a strong British contingent, ally to Prussia. While on the Russian line at Treptow, Steuben was taken prisoner and escorted to St. Petersburg, though probably for a short period of time due to prisoner exchanges. Using his knowledge of the Russian language to his advantage, Steuben became friends with Duke Karl Peter Ulrich, who had an affinity for all things Prussian. It appears Steuben may have sent the news of the Czarina's death to the King from St. Petersburg, as the King personally wrote Steuben on January 24, 1762: "Be assured of my most gracious recognition for the news which you sent me on the occasion of the death of the later Empress of Russia," and again on February 8, 1762, asked Steuben to serve as a sort of temporary ambassador (as the war ended due to the Czarina's death, Duke Peter, heir apparent, took the throne) within the Prussian embassy in Russia, "such a letter from a monarch to a junior officer is most unusual and indicates the King's confidence in his intelligence, fidelity, and discretion" (qtd. in Palmer, 44). Steuben stayed in St. Petersburg in the spring of 1762 and, apparently, while serving as attaché, also entered into some sort of youthful adventure which a magazine article described as a tragic-comic role which almost became dangerous.

Upon his return to Prussia, Friedrich the Great invited von Steuben to enter his newly created "Special Class on the Art of War," an intensive course the King would teach himself. One of thirteen initially selected to be schooled in strategic planning and army leadership, Steuben "was being groomed for a general's rank, with the greatest soldier of the age as his personal tutor" (Lockhart, 25). Yet, as quickly as his fate had improved, it changed, for, after completing the school in February 1763, he was demoted to a command in the far western edge of the kingdom (Wesel), a remote location "clearly not a mark of royal favor. Only a couple of months later, he was dismissed from the service entirely" (Lockhart, 27). Historians have pondered the reasoning behind Steuben's dismissal. Some believe the gossip from St. Petersburg reached the King and Prussian kingdom (though we know not what the gossip entailed). Some believe Steuben earned the "rancor" of an "implacable enemy," to use Steuben's words, General Wilhelmi von Anhalt, a jealous and misanthropic man who stood, unfortunately, in the King's favor and who earned a reputation for "wrecking the careers of officers for whom he had taken a dislike — and there were many of them. Whatever or whoever authored Steuben's fall from grace, it happened in the blink of an eye" (Lockhart, 27). Steuben himself later claimed the fall came as a result of "an inconsiderate step and an implacable personal enemy" (qtd. in Doyle, 19). Based upon this statement, conjecture might say that Anhalt used the news of Steuben's youthful tragic-comic escapade to destroy the reputation of Steuben before his King.

Steuben, nonetheless, had amassed an unheralded store of military knowledge during this career in the Prussian army, to include training in the King's specialized military school and training from Prince Henry and a dozen other general officers. Lockhart relates that during his service as an "NCO, a company commander, an adjutant, a general in training, and a junior diplomat," he gained crucial military experience, having "led an infantry company into battle, and served on staffs at the battalion, regimental, brigade, and army levels. He had watched his men die, and in turn he had been wounded in battle twice, so he knew what it was like to fall in combat.... He had learned from the best soldiers in the world how to gather and assess intelligence, how to read and exploit terrain, how to plan marches, camps, battles, and entire campaigns.... In the Seven Years' War alone, he built up a record of professional education that none of his comrades in the Continental Army — Horatio

Gates, Charles Lee, the Baron Johann de Kalb, and Lafayette included — could match" (30). Yet, in the end, the Prussian army, whose allies included the British, "spat him out ungratefully." Having given his life to military service, Steuben had no home, no money, and no other career. Eventually, he must have been ordered out of the country, for he writes in a letter to his benefactor, that "my adverse fate forced me to leave my country, my friends and my support and perhaps renounce them for life" (qtd. in Palmer, 57).

Unemployed, somehow Steuben traveled throughout Europe during the remaining months of 1763 in an effort to find a job, first becoming acquainted, ironically, with Count de St. Germain at Hamburg, a distinguished French general then in the service of Denmark who would, fourteen years on, in his capacity as French minister of war, recommend Steuben to Benjamin Franklin "as the man of the hour so vitally needed in America" (Palmer, 54). First, however, he was to serve Princess Margravine Frederica Dorothea of Württemberg, as chief minister to the court at Hohenzollern-Hechingen in the Black Forest region of the kingdom. (The princess herself was the favorite niece of ol 'Fritz, Friedrich the Great, an attractive woman five years younger than Steuben. Apparently, the friendship between Steuben and the princess flourished, for just as he was destitute from his life experiences, the Princess was suffering as well, from an abusive husband. Years later, according to Kapp, when Steuben was moving from New York to his country estate in the upper Mohawk Valley, a miniature portrait fell from his cabinet. A friend asked the subject of the portrait, at which time Steuben, overcome with emotion, replied, "She was a matchless woman.")

Baron von Steuben, ¾ length. Reproduction of painting by Ralph Earl (1751–1801). Note the military medals and Order of Fidelity Star of which Steuben was so proud (National Archives and Records Administration).

This position was in reality a sort of social secretary in which Steuben served as household manager for the prince and "supervised the daily administration of the court and its personnel, advising his master on matters of economy and personal finance, responsible for the education and rearing of the prince's children" (Lockhart, 49). Steuben served in this position from September 17, 1764 (his thirty-fourth birthday) until the spring of 1777, a few months before his departure for America. During his stay in Hechingen, the princess also bestowed upon her friend an honorable order of knighthood, the Order of Fidelity, which provided Steuben the use of the title "Baron," meaning "free lord." (The German prince of Baden-Durlach, at the princess' insistence, actually was the benefactor.) The princess herself pinned upon Steuben's chest the distinctive insignia of the order, founded to reward chivalry five decades prior thereto, and, in Steuben's time to "reward subjects for faithful service, outstanding achievements, or high moral character" (Lockhart, 50). The insignia itself was a Maltese cross mounted on an eight-pointed silver star carrying the motto *Fidelitas*. Note: Steuben submitted a family tree revealing his noble descent back six generations, the great-grandfather, Ludwig von Steube, Knight of St. John, questioned by historians. At the same time, he also changed his baptismal name from *Friedrich Wilhelm Ludolf Gerhard Augustin* to *Friedrich Wilhelm Augustus Henry Ferdinand*. (Steuben's reasoning for changing his name is not known.)

A portrait of Steuben from the time, commissioned by Prince Josef, does not resemble a military officer, but rather an artist. His hair hangs in curls, his face is lush, his clothing of silk and lace, the eight-pointed star of the Order of Fidelity embroidered on his frock. Yet, having enough of a more peaceful life, the finances of his courtly family diminishing, by 1771, Steuben began seeking other employment, to no avail. As his employer, Prince Josef, moved to Lyons in 1772 to avoid the expense of the royal court, the small province almost bankrupt, Steuben joined his courtly family, the stay in France broadening his outlook, his "last vestiges of German provincialism" disappearing, his acquaintance with Count St. Germain renewed. Traveling to Baden in the spring of 1777 to, yet again, seek employment, Steuben met Peter Burdett, an English cartographer sympathetic to the American cause and friend to Benjamin Franklin. Burdett revealed to Steuben that Franklin and Silas Deane were in fact seeking military leaders, or at least those with high levels of military leadership. Expressing interest, Burdett sent Steuben to Paris to meet with Franklin, sending along the following letter of recommendation:

> Sir! The bearer is Baron Steuben of whom I had the honor to write to you by the hands of a Friend about a month since. He is a gentleman of Family, merit and great experience, well known to some of the First personages in Europe, and hereby gives you Sir a strong proof of his ambition to make the acquaintance of Doctor Franklin in actually performing a Journey from Germany to Paris for that purpose [qtd. in Palmer, 83].

Before meeting with Franklin, however, Steuben visited his old friend, St. Germain, who took the initiative into his own hands, thrilled with the baron's idea. Not only might he receive Franklin's recommendation, but also the powerful support of the French government. St. Germain was aware of Steuben's accomplishments and knew "the real secret of Friedrich's victory at Rossbach" and of the inferiority of French military training to that of the Prussians, aware "the France of his day could send no gospel of military efficiency to Washington" (Palmer, 88). Secretly, St. Germain arranged for letters of recommendation from Franklin, Deane, and Beaumarchais, arranging for the merchant company of Hortalez and Company to not only provide a ship carrying munitions and arms to America, but also a certain Lieutenant General Baron von Steuben (his rank elevated for the purpose of proving to Congress his qualifications). Hoping for a commission, which Franklin and Deane could not guarantee, for "so many foreign officers had gone to America that they had become a source of embarrassment to Washington and to the Continental Congress," Steuben was not discouraged as "the American adventure so appealed to his imagination that he decided to go as a volunteer and take a gambler's chance on finding employment" (Whitridge, "Steuben," 430). All concerned were convinced "that once he got to America Steuben's credentials and his engaging personality would easily win him a place in the Continental service" (Whitridge, "Steuben," 431). Thus, giving up lifetime associations, a civilized military, and his language to embrace an uncertain future, guaranteed only a passage 3,000 miles across the ocean and a bit of spending money from Beaumarchais, Baron Friedrich von Steuben left Paris for America in September 1777, accompanied by his secretary, a body-servant, a French cook, and his Italian greyhound, arriving in Portsmouth, New Hampshire, on December 1 after an eventful trip involving a terrific storm and a mutiny at sea. (Steuben, despite the hellish trip, put his mind to mathematical calculations, target practice, and the works of Abbé Raynal, a French philosopher concerned with democratic principles, also educated by Jesuits.)

Steuben stepped ashore "on a sunny afternoon, wearing the gold star of the Order of Fidelity on his lieutenant-general's uniform. It was a happy occasion, all the more so as he brought with him 52 brass cannon, 22 tons of sulphur, and 17 hundred weight of powder, all of which the patriot army badly needed.... From Portsmouth Steuben wrote a letter to the Continental Congress, offering his services to the cause of freedom. It reached Henry Laurens, the President of Congress, on January 12, 1778; and two days later, notwithstanding the hostile attitude of Congress to all foreign officers, Congress passed an enthusiastic resolution accepting the services of Lt. General Baron von Steuben.... Washington was delighted. He had already recommended that an inspectorship be formed; and by God's good grace a very master of the art of war, a loyal and trusted servant of Frederick the Great, had offered his services, waiving at the same time all embarrassing claims to rank or pay" (Whitridge, "Steuben," 432).

The party stayed in Portsmouth for ten days, Steuben receiving a hero's welcome in diametrical contrast to the unemployment and neglect left behind in Europe. Steuben wrote, "All of the inhabitants of the place crowded together as if to look at a rhinoceros" (qtd. in Lockhart, 52). Steuben's aide Duponceau said, "Only fancy to yourself, an old German Baron with a large brilliant star on his breast, three French aides-de-camp and a large, spoiled Italian dog, and none of that company could speak a word of English" (qtd. in Lockhart, 53). En route to Philadelphia and the Continental Congress, however, the reception made a 360-degree turn. While passing through Spencer, Massachusetts, on a miserable snowy night, the entourage stopped at a tavern owned by one Whitt-more, a Tory sympathizer who informed the party he had neither food nor lodging. Pleading for shelter, the Baron's party was refused. Enraged, Steuben called to his body servant, Vogel: "Pistolen!" Vogel returned with one of the Baron's horse pistols; Steuben cocked the hammer and shoved it into the proprietor's face. Duponceau recalled "Steuben and his staff then stayed up well into the night eating, drinking, and talking around the hearth, with the innkeeper waiting patiently on the group as if nothing unpleasant had happened" (Lockhart, 61).

Before Congress, Steuben asserted his goal of serving a republic and the principles thereof, making no demands: "I have made no condition with your Deputies in France, nor shall I make any with you." To Washington he said, "If the distinguished ranks in which I have served in Europe should be an obstacle, I had rather serve under your Excellency as a Volunteer, than to be a subject of Discontent to such deserving Officers as have already distinguished themselves amongst you" (qtd. in Lockhart, 63). Steuben's only condition was that if Congress determined he contributed something of real value to an American victory, that he be reimbursed for his travel to America and be given an annual salary of six hundred guineas, retroactive to the summer of 1777, with interest, from the end of hostilities until his death, a sort of pension based upon merit. Congress was ecstatic; here was an exemplary officer from Europe who would work for free up until the point he proved worthy and who would require no contract of commission. Hosting an "entertainment" in his honor, in the words of Richard Peters, Board of War member, Steuben was entreated "with every mark of distinction ... with more particular attention ... than I had known given to any foreigner" (qtd. in Lockhart, 67). To John Hancock and Samuel Adams, who had befriended and assisted Steuben while in Boston, the Baron wrote: "My journey has been extremely painful, but the kind reception I have met with from Congress and G. Gates at my arrival here have made me Soon forget those past incommodities. Now Sir I am an American and an American for life; your Nation has become as dear to me as your Cause already was" (qtd. in Lockhart, 68).

Steuben's work was ahead of him, and he rode into the throes of the "skeleton of an army," half-clothed and underfed, on February 24, 1778, Washington greeting "this illustrious Stranger" on the outskirts of camp, though rather coolly. Steuben's first supporters included the twenty-three-year-old John Laurens, son of Henry Laurens, president of the Continental Congress when Steuben arrived in America, as well as Alexander Hamilton (who fought after the war to secure the Baron's compensation). Dining with Washington "no fewer than ten times in his first fourteen evenings in camp," the seasoned military veteran went straight to work, allowed complete access to the camp. He was open with Washington as to the army's deficiencies, made friends at the drop of a hat, won the affection of the officer's wives, and made himself a legend by inviting junior officers to his home for a meal and several rounds of high-proof "Salamanders," admission thereto requiring "that none should be admitted that had on a whole pair of breeches" (qtd. in Palmer, 149). During his first three weeks, Steuben poked his head into the leaking log huts the soldiers had constructed for shelter, inquiring as to the privates' health, rations, officers, and camp life, for, as mentioned previously, officers trained in the Prussian service took notice of and concerned themselves with the welfare of their men. Thus earning the respect of citizens, not subjects, Steuben's appearance drew the American soldiers out of their stupor. Ashbel Green, a sixteen-year-old private who later became the president of the College of New Jersey and chaplain to Congress, wrote, "Never before, or since, have I had such an impression of the ancient fabled God of War as when I looked on the baron. He seemed to me a perfect personification of Mars. The trappings of his horse, the enormous holsters of his pistols, his large size, and his strikingly martial aspect, all seemed to favor the idea" (qtd. in Bobrick, 332). Steuben was no less impressed with the "ordinary" Continental soldier, admiring their resilience in the face of adversity, some even boiling their shoes and leather accessories for food, as well as their mindset, such admiration fueling his now famous quote: "The genius of the nation is not to be compared with that of the Prussians, Austrians, or French. You say to that soldier, 'Do this,' and he doeth it; but here I am obliged to say, 'This is the reason why you ought to do that: and then he does it'" (qtd. in Bobrick, 334). Bobrick comparatively notes Steuben's great talent: "Steuben's genius was his ability to unite Prussian virtues to those of the American mind" (334).

Dealing with an organizational mess, "the words company, regiment, brigade and division were so vague that they did not convey any idea upon which to form a calculation, either of the particular corps or of the army in general.... I have seen a regiment consisting of thirty men, and a company of one corporal.... No captain kept a book" (qtd. in Bobrick, 334) leaves of absence and dismissals unrecorded, army property (muskets, bayonets, clothing) scattered here and yon, Steuben instituted a requirement of accountability. Record-keeping was initiated, as were monthly inspections, guard duty, and equipment accountings. Cleanliness and order in personal and camp hygiene was also stressed; carcasses were carried far away from camp, clothing was boiled to rid the camp of lice.

Yet, what of drill? Steuben would have three months to train an entire army in a

Baron von Steuben drilling the Continental soldiers at Valley Forge, March 1778 (National Archives and Records Administration).

universally accepted tactical military technique (difficult since each state regiment brought to camp its own techniques), while also instilling a sense of discipline among the troops, "a collection of farmers, landless laborers, tradesman, and Irish and German immigrants" (Lockhart, 97). Steuben accomplished this massive undertaking by creating a bond between himself and the Continentals. In addition to visiting them personally in their log huts, he insisted that officers drill their own soldiers instead of condescendingly assigning the task to someone of a lesser rank and created a model company (train-the-trainer technique) which he personally drilled himself. One American colonel wrote: "To see a gentleman dignified with a lieutenants general's commission from the great Prussian monarch take under his direction a squad of ten or twelve men in the capacity of a drill sergeant, commanded the admiration of both officers and men" (qtd. in Bobrick, 335). Additionally, Steuben exhibited his humanity to his men, not only his authority, by (1) pantomiming positions; (2) correcting the bearings of soldiers with his own hands; (3) singing out cadence in his strong voice (think of today's drill sergeant); (4) taking up muskets to demonstrate and illustrate usage; (5) using comedy in moments of stress; (6) and exhibiting empathy for suffering comrades (remember the Salamander dinner).

The moment that helped Steuben become "one of the most popular figures in the affections of the plain soldiers of the Continental Army" occurred during an early drill when after a drill command, some men went one way and some another when he provided hastily learned English commands. Steuben then tried the command in French, then German, to no avail. Red-faced, the Baron began swearing in German and French. He even attempted sign language, cursing with the only English curse word he knew, "Goddam!" The men chuckled in the ranks. As Steuben later wrote, just then an angel from heaven appeared, for a young officer by the name of Captain Benjamin Walker of the New York regiment stepped forward, addressing the Baron in French and offering his services as an interpreter. Palmer notes, "The Baron gave the instructions again through his new interpreter and the maneuver was executed without a fault. Here was a touch of comedy to make the whole play a success" (148). Steuben had learned a lesson; from that moment forward, he delighted the soldiers at Valley Forge by swearing in French and German, calling upon certain soldiers to also curse in English, using laughter to curtail any resistance to methods of discipline. He later wrote: "My good republicans wanted everything in the English style; our great and good allies everything according to the French mode. When I presented a plate of sauerkraut dressed in the Prussian style, they all wanted to throw it out of the window. Nevertheless, by the force of proving by *Goddams* that my cookery was the best, I overcame their prejudices" (qtd. in Bobrick, 334).

His first drill for the model company having begun on March 19, by March 24, the whole army was at drill: "Each regiment was divided into squads of twenty men. Each brigade inspector was supervising the exercises with his brigade. The Baron galloped from parade ground to parade ground, taking a hand here and there, impressing his personality everywhere. Thanks to the example already given by the Guard Company, all of the drillmasters and most of the soldiers knew exactly what to do because they had seen it done" (Palmer, 150). John Laurens wrote to his father that same day: "The Baron Steuben has commenced the functions of inspector general.... The Baron discovers the greatest zeal, and an activity which is hardly to be expected of his years. The officers in general seem to entertain a high opinion of him, and he sets them an excellent example in descending to the functions of a drill-sergeant" (qtd. in Palmer, 150). Writing his own drill regulations as he went, Steuben adapted the Prussian practice to American use, tossing aside European pride to also incorporate useful American techniques, such as loose body formations, the use of sharpshooters, shock troops and advance guards, and aiming accuracies. The complete compilation of these regulations, in essence a new military manual, referred to by Continental officers as the "Blue Book," was officially accepted by Congress on March 29, 1779, and published as *Regulations for the Order and Discipline of the Troops of the United States*, remaining the official manual until the War of 1812, and an exemplary manual for generations thereafter.

The drills instituted by Steuben, "continual" until May of 1778, included Attention; Dress Rank; a "fast-time" marching step performed without fifes and drums and in absolute silence, without stirring of the hands, blowing the nose, or talking: "the key ingredient to well-ordered infantry tactics, which in the Baron's estimation was the most obvious shortcoming of the Continentals;" 90 degrees to the right; and 90 degrees to the left (which required wheeling). Modeling each move, Steuben walked down each line to check efficiency, "not hesitating to point out deficiencies, his big hands roughly pushing men into the correct posture as if he were arranging scenery on a stage. His ministrations were gruff and never tender, but even when playing the role of drill sergeant he could not hide his essential affability. He complimented those who got it right; he joked and swore, effortlessly, at those who did not" (Lockhart, 100). Steuben's routine continued day after day.

> No one beyond the Baron's little circle knew that he was making it up as he went along. Each evening when he retired to his quarters, he took a quick dinner before returning to his desk and working out the lesson for the next day in his hastily scribbled, inelegant French, which he then gave to Duponceau for translation and revision. After several hours working by candlelight, he turned in, only to rise again at three o'clock in the morning to do it all over again — to dress, drink his coffee, and smoke his pipe, to study the day's lesson and practice the words in English. Then, promptly at nine o'clock, just as on the first day of training, he and his staff galloped through the snow to the Grand Parade. "There was no waiting for a tardy aide-de-camp, and those who followed wished they had not slept," one of his assistants recalled. "Nor was there need of chiding. When duty was neglected or military etiquette infringed, the Baron's look was quite sufficient." The instruction of the model company

followed the same pattern each day: the review of the old lessons, the separation into squads, the explanation of the new lesson for the day. Steuben's assistants would give personalized instruction to each of the squads. The Baron, in the meantime, flitted about from one squad to the next, fussing, fuming, correcting, praising. When he was satisfied that the men had been coached enough, the company reassembled and performed the new lessons again, together. And thus the instruction proceeded each morning and each afternoon [qtd. in Lockhart, 102].

Washington honored Steuben by appointing him as inspector general of the entire army, to the dismay of Irish-born Officer Thomas Conway, by March 28, providing the rank of Major-General:

Baron Steuben, a Lieutenant General in Foreign Service and a Gentleman of great military experience having obligingly undertaken to exercise the office of Inspector General in this Army, The Commander in Chief 'til the pleasure of Congress shall be known desires he may be respected and obeyed as such.... The Importance of establishing a Uniform System of useful Manuevers and regularity of discipline must be obvious, the Deficiency of our Army in these Respects must be equally so; the time we shall probably have to introduce the necessary Reformation is short [qtd. in Lockhart, 107].

Steuben also served as a talent scout, picking up two more additions to the core of his staff: Colonel François-Louise Teissèdre de Fleury, a French engineer, and British-born Benjamin Walker, the aforesaid interpreter and line officer. His bureaucracy also included sub-inspectors Colonel William Davies of Virginia, Colonel Francis Barber of New Jersey, Colonel John Brooks of Massachusetts, and a French Colonel Ternant. As soon as he received Washington's directive to train the entire army, Steuben began sketching detailed instructional plans — a syllabus — for the coming weeks, in which each lesson would be taught to sub-inspectors and brigade inspectors, who in turn, would teach a selected twenty-man squad from each brigade. Captains of infantry companies would also follow this regimen, until the whole Army was trained and drills in large formations could commence. Lockhart relates, "No officer was exempt from participating in the drills. They would have to work as hard as the men, if not harder, and they would have to learn exactly as the men did: every afternoon, the brigade inspectors would assemble all majors, captains, and most lieutenants, drilling them on the day's lesson as if they were privates themselves" (107).

The resulting transformation in the American Continentals' morale and effectiveness was, by all reports, miraculous, Steuben having instilled a sense of service as a soldier who could defeat a Redcoat within the men. Alexander Scammell wrote to Timothy Pickering, member of the Congressional Board of War, "Discipline flourishes and daily improves under the indefatigable efforts of Baron Steuben — who is much esteem'd by us" (qtd. in Lockhart, 113). On May 1, word reached Valley Forge that the French had signed an alliance with the United States. Washington decided to celebrate the treaty while also honoring his new inspector general, Baron von Steuben. He asked Steuben to choreograph a Grand Review, which he "pounced upon as if he were starved for work. In just a couple of days, he worked out all the intricate details, writing instructions for each brigade and regiment, even drawing diagrams" to effect an elaborate display called a *feu de joie*, the coordinated, rolling fire of muskets. John Laurens described the event: "The order with which the whole was conducted, the beautiful effect of the running fire which was executed to perfection, the martial appearance of the Troops, gave sensible pleasure to every one present.... The plan as formed by Baron von Steuben succeeded in every particular, which is in a great measure to be attributed to his unwearied attention and to the visible progress which the troops have already made

Statue of Baron von Steuben, Valley Forge, Pennsylvania (author's photograph).

under his discipline.... Triumph beamed in every countenance" (qtd. in Lockhart, 115). Washington took the moment to spring the surprise on the Baron that he was a volunteer no more, but an American general, inspector general on top of that. Lockhart relates, "On the whole it was the most satisfying moment of his life. The forcibly retired infantry captain who so feared dying as an unknown, a mediocrity, was now a major general and the object of sincere accolades. After just about a month of hard work, the army bore his personal imprint more than that of any other man. The army was, of course, a creation of the American people, of the individual states, and of Washington himself, but its metamorphosis was his, its current shape and form were his" (116).

As Washington was ready to move his men into battle, Steuben began drilling the men in more advanced practices, including forming columns of platoons and firing drills (including moving fire and firing by platoons in retreat). These drills made a difference between "an army that could attack, retreat, and change formation quickly, and an army that found it an almost insurmountable challenge just to form up for battle. It was this marriage of fluidity, rapid motion, and constant firepower that had set the Prussian army apart from its foes and allies" (Lockhart, 127). A Philadelphia militia officer wrote that the Continentals were "as well disciplined as any of the British troops can be, they performed several maneuvers with great exactness and dispatch, under the direction of Baron Stueben, and ... I am informed that our whole army are in as good order as them 15 regiments." Members of Congress were delighted, William Henry Drayton congratulating the Baron: "Because of the rapid advance of our young Soldiers in the art military under your auspices, you are my Dear Baron, entitled to the thanks of every American." And, Richard Peters told Timothy Pickering he "continued to be pleased with the appearance of everything at Valley Forge. Discipline seems to be growing apace and America will be under lasting obligations to the Baron Steuben as the Father of it. He is much respected by the officers and beloved by the Soldiers who themselves seem to be convinced of the propriety and necessity of his regulations. I am astonished at the Progress he has made with the Troops" (qtd. in Lockhart, 128).

When the army left Valley Forge due to the British move from Philadelphia on June 17, Steuben served to gather intelligence, observing British movements from the rear as a type of scout, completing a task for which he had been trained over twenty years ago: "to collect and analyze intelligence so that his commander could employ his army as the situation warranted" (Lockhart, 148). Riding for three days with hardly any rest, in the elements, he finally came upon the British line, riding so close to British positions he was recognized and chased by dragoons. Steuben paused only long enough to "draw both of his enormous horse pistols from the holsters lashed to his saddle and fire each of them at his pursuers, then he turned his horse about and galloped to safety, so fast that his cocked hat flew off his head during the retreat" (Lockhart, 154).

Leaving the battle field on November 13, 1778, heading to Philadelphia to sequester himself for the purpose of creating America's first military code, Steuben wrote without letup from the time he entered the city until the following April (1779). He chose elements from the Prussian and French military systems, adapting them to American conditions, utilizing five translators and scribes. Steuben described, "I have rejected everything which tended only to Parade and confined myself to what alone appeared to me absolutely necessary" (qtd. in Lockhart, 191). When he finally submitted the manuscript, Congress ordered that the regulations be printed immediately, for "after four long years of fighting the British, the Continental Army finally had a standardized military code" (Lockhart, 190). The Blue Book, as it came to be known, included three parts: a drill manual for the infantry, a set of official regulations for the use of the entire army (to include court-martial procedure, inspection of troops, and safety and well-being), and a treatise on the conduct of officers and enlisted men (comparing an officer-ship to the love of an ideal father, stern, yet patient and caring). He stated, "The preservation of the soldiers' health should be the first and greatest care. His first object should be to gain the love of his men, by treating them with every possible kindness and humanity" (Lockhart, 195). The Board of War and Washington praised the manual, Washington writing to Steuben: "You will, I flatter myself, shortly have the satisfaction, so rarely enjoyed by Authors, of seeing your precepts reduced to practice — and I hope your Success will be equal to the merit of your work" (qtd. in Lockhart, 196).

As inspector general, Steuben spent the summer of 1779 inspecting camps in New Jersey, the Hudson Highlands, and Rhode Island. Nothing escaped his eye: muster rolls were required, soldier's books were checked against supply, surgeons were interviewed regarding cleanliness and health, reports and statistics were compiled. As a result, loss of property and equipment dropped, a healthy spirit of competition spread throughout the barracks, appropriate appearances were encouraged. All of Steuben's work paid off, for on July 15, 1779, two American columns scaled the rocky heights at Stony Point, surprising the enemy and taking those not killed in battle prisoner. A month later, at Paulus Hook, nearly 160 British and Hessians were taken prisoner. The Baron wrote to Benjamin Franklin, "Tho' we are so young that we scarce begin to walk, we can already take Stoney Points & Powles Hook with the point of the Bayonet, without firing a single shot" (qtd. in Lockhart, 211).

Steuben continued his inspections, reports, and pleas to Congress to support the buildup of the army's numbers, traveling to Philadelphia on one occasion in snow "man-high" to argue his case, chastising congressional negligence with regard to the recruitment and care of American soldiers. His affable nature toward the troops continued; he served on the board which court-martialed Major John André, Benedict Arnold's accomplice, for he regarded with "abhorrence and contempt" the traitor. While inspecting West Point in October 1780, the Baron noticed a man by the name of Jonathan Arnold on the roles. Calling him forward, the Baron "asked him how he could stand having such a name.... The terrified young soldier stammered out that he hated the name but didn't think he could do anything about it. Delighted at the response, Steuben put Arnold at his ease. Assuredly the name could be changed, he said, and offered 'Steuben' as a substitute" (Lockhart, 230). The soldier listened to his commander's wishes and, in 1783, petitioned the Connecticut General Assembly to change his name, Steuben supporting the petition and further asking the state to pay the soldier a lifetime pension.

Steuben grew to love the idea of America more each year, remarking to Chancellor Frank, "What a beautiful, happy land is this without kings, without high princes ... and without idle barons.... Here we are in a republic and a baron does not count for more than any James or Peter. Our general of artillery (Knox) was a book printer in Boston — a worthy man who understands his craft from the bottom up, and who carries out his present position with much honor" (qtd. in Lockhart, 231). Thus, after attempting to chase down Benedict Arnold in Virginia with just the state militia (traveling through the state to deliver plans for a fort at Hood's Landing to Jefferson), and asked by Greene to remain in Virginia in an attempt to prevent further invasion by the traitor until the French fleet arrived, the Baron acquiesced and commanded four militia battalions, holding the British advancement toward Petersburg and securing the Pocahontas Bridge which would allow the militia to retreat, if necessary, across the Appomattox. Under the Baron, the militia disputed every inch of ground, fighting with muskets, bayonets, and even their fists as each battalion retreated across the

Bridge, the rear guard ripping up the planks per Steuben's orders. The battle held up the British just long enough for Lafayette, with his light infantry one thousand strong, to enter Manchester, Anthony Wayne's Pennsylvania line not far behind. Jefferson wrote Steuben, "I cannot but congratulate you on the initiation of our militia into the business of war" (qtd. in Lockhart, 255).

At Yorktown, Washington entrusted the Pennsylvania brigade of Anthony Wayne and the Maryland brigade of Mordecai Gist to the Baron, who led his troops into the trenches by day, digging closer parallels by night, all while under fire. His division was on duty when Cornwallis surrendered on the 17th and also during the surrender ceremony, on the 19th, for, as he told Lafayette, "tradition dictated that those on duty in the trenches when peace overtures were first made should remain at their posts until the surrender was signed. The Baron planted the American flag on one of the captured British redoubts with his own hand.... After he had done so much to make this day possible — both by training the victorious army and by holding Virginia until Lafayette could take his place — Steuben no doubt felt that he deserved the honor" (Lockhart, 270).

Perhaps the highest honor Steuben was given as the war ended was when Rochambeau's French generals, stopping by the Continental encampment before sailing home, witnessed a review of the American Army, commenting, "Both its direction and the ease and precision of its movements really astonished us.... I admire the celerity and exactitude with which your men perform." The highest accolade, nevertheless, came from Rochambeau himself: "You must have formed an alliance with the King of Prussia. These troops are Prussians!"

Victory at Yorktown, October 1781 (National Archives and Records Administration).

(qtd. in Lockhart, 276). In 1783–4, Steuben devoted his time to advocating for a permanent, standing army to defend the United States, writing a pamphlet presented to Congress entitled *A Letter on the Subject of an Established Militia, and Military Arrangements, Addressed to the Inhabitants of the United States*. He also wrote a document for Secretary of War Lincoln detailing the characteristics of an American military academy, gaining high order in the Society of the Cincinnati and joining George Washington on the balcony of Federal Hall as the new president took his oath of office in 1789.

True to his comment to John Hancock in early 1778 on becoming an American for life, naturalized on the Fourth of July 1786, Steuben lived out the remainder of his days in America, specifically in the state of New York, which afforded him a grant of land in the upper Mohawk valley upon which he built a log cabin, never lacking for friends or social occasions, as no foreign officer, even Lafayette, was more beloved in the day. Congress did not treat Steuben appropriately, failing to afford him the pension promised for meritorious duty. Succumbing to a stroke on November 28, 1794, according to his instructions, the Baron was wrapped in his cloak, ornamented with the star of the Order of Fidelity, and laid to rest in the forest which adjoined his cabin, provided "a simple and impressive close to a long life of virtue and usefulness, began in courts, amid pomp and despotism, and closed in a log-house in the shade of primeval woods, blest in the fruition of human freedom" (Sparks, 252).

Trained in every aspect of war, infantry, intelligence, and administration, Steuben's highest calling, his very fate, led him to a disheveled army camp in Valley Forge, Pennsylvania, a ravaged, cold, and snowy outdoor classroom, which transformed this eminent Prussian officer into the Great Teacher of the American Revolution. The Baron equipped a destitute, hodge-podge group of American soldiers with the knowledge, discipline, and pride needed to compete on the battlefield against one of the world's most advanced armies, preparing their lesson plans, writing their textbooks, modeling their duties, training their trainers, caring for every physical and emotional need. This turnaround and progression was instituted in "fast-time," comparative to the cadence of the march taught by Steuben. At a time when America is not destitute, yet just the opposite, drowning in a pool of excess and overspending, in a sinkhole of disregard, citizens ignoring the well-being of the whole for the sake of individual comfort, shall we not pickup the pace, open our manuals, and muster the troops, drilling the principles for which Steuben and the additional volunteers in this book risked their lives, back into the heads, the daily walk, of the American people, filling our hearts, once more, with a sense of collective pride, as we strive to protect our rights, our values, the cause of freedom.

Memorials

Von Steuben is one of four European military leaders who assisted the American cause during the Revolution honored with a statue in Lafayette Square, just north of the White House. Other statues of Steuben can be found in Utica, New York, and the garden of the German Embassy in Washington, D.C., as well as within the grounds of Valley Forge Historical Park in Pennsylvania.

In Germany, statues of the Baron may be found in Potsdam and in Steuben's hometown of Madgeburg. In Berlin, Germany, one stands near the Allied Museum on Clayallee in the former American sector of the divided city.

Benjamin Franklin and John Jay signing the Preliminary Treaty of Peace at Paris, November 30, 1782. Print by John D. Morris & Co. after painting by German artist Carl Wilhelm Anton Seiler (1846–1921) (Library of Congress).

The home presented to Steuben as a gift for his services in the Continental Army is located at New Bridge Landing in Rivers Edge, New Jersey, maintained by a historical society and opened for special occasions.

Other tributes include Steuben Field, the stadium of the Hamilton College football team, Von Steuben having laid the cornerstone of the school. Upon graduating, all Hamilton seniors receive as a gift from the college a cane with a tricorn hat at its top in reference to von Steuben.

At Steuben's gravesite, on a granite boulder near his tomb, a bronze tablet reminds the world that his services were "Indispensable to the Achievement of American Independence."

BIBLIOGRAPHY

Allen, Gardner. *A Naval History of the American Revolution.* New York: Russell & Russell, Inc., 1913.

Amler, Jane Frances. *Haym Salomon: Patriot Banker of the Revolution.* New York: Rosen Publishing Group, 2004.

Babits, Lawrence and Joshua Howard. *Long, Obstinate and Bloody: The Battle of Guilford Courthouse.* Chapel Hill: University of North Carolina Press, 2009.

Bako, Elemer. "The Solution of an Age-Old Mystery: The Family Background as the Key to the Character and the European Heritage Values of Colonel Michael Kováts de Fabricy." *Hungarian Heritage Review* 16.8 (1987): 1–11.

Balderston, Marion. "The Flag John Paul Jones Really Fought Under." *Huntington Library Quarterly* 33.1 (1969): 77–83.

Barnes, James. *With the Flag in the Channel: Or the Adventures of Captain Gustavus Conyngham.* New York: D. Appleton and Co., 1902.

Bell, Malcom, Jr. *Major Butler's Legacy: Five Generations of a Slaveholding Family.* Athens: University of Georgia Press, 1987.

Billias, George Athan. *American Constitutionalism Heard Round the World, 1776–1989: A Global Perspective.* New York: New York University Press, 2009.

Bobrick, Benson. *Angel in the Whirlwind: The Triumph of the American Revolution.* New York: Simon and Schuster, 1997.

Bowen-Hassell, E. Gordon, Dennis M. Conrad, and Mark L. Hayes. *Sea Raiders of the American Revolution: The Continental Navy in European Waters.* Washington, DC: Naval Historical Center, Department of the Navy, 2003.

Bowman, Travis. *Hercules of the Revolution.* Davidson, NC: Bequest Publishing, 2009.

_____. *The Peter Francisco Story: George Washington's "One Man Army."* DVD. Bequest Publishing, 2010.

Brady, Cyrus Thomas. *Commodore Paul Jones.* New York: D. Appleton and Associates, 1906.

Branchi, E. C. "Memoirs of Philip Mazzei." *The William and Mary Quarterly, Second Series* 9.4 (1929): 247–264.

Carrington, Henry Beebee. *Battles of the American Revolution: 1775–1781.* New York: A.S. Barnes, 1888.

Chamberlain, John. "A Reviewer's Notebook: World Citizen." *The Freeman* 32.4 (1982): 1–3. Web. http://www.fee.org/the_freeman/detail/a-reviewers-notebook-world-citizen#axzz2Z8yISAAv.

Clark, William Bell. *Gallant John Barry, 1745–1803: The Story of a Naval Hero of Two Wars.* New York: MacMillian, 1938.

Coghlan, Francis. "Pierce Butler, 1744–1822, First Senator From South Carolina." *The South Carolina Historical Magazine* 78.2 (1977): 104–119.

Colonial and State Records of North Carolina. State of North Carolina Department of Cultural Resources. "Letter from Charles Armand Tuffin, Marquis de La Rouerie to Horatio Gates, July 26, 1780." *Documenting the American South.* University of North Carolina at Chapel Hill. March 28, 2010. Web. November 24, 2012.

_____. "Letter from Charles Armand Tuffin, Marquis de La Rouerie to Horatio Gates, August 8, 1780."

_____. "Letter from Charles Armand Tuffin, Marquis de La Rouerie to Horatio Gates, September 4, 1780."

Conway, Moncure Daniel. *The Life of Thomas Paine.* New York: Putnam, 1892.

Conyngham, David Hayfield. *Reminiscences of David Hayfield Conyngham, 1745–1834.* Wilkes-

Barre, PA: Wyoming Historical and Geological Society, 1904.

Conyngham, Gustavus. "Narrative of Captain Gustavus Conyngham, U.S.N., While in Command of the 'Surprise' and 'Revenge,' 1777–1779." *Pennsylvania Magazine of History and Biography* 22.4 (1898): 479–488.

Danckert, Stephen. "Baron von Steuben and the Training of Armies." *Military Review* 74.5 (1994): 29–35.

Dixon, B.F. *Peter Francisco: An Address*. Greensboro, NC: Guilford Battle Ground Co., 1910.

Doyle, Joseph Beatty. *Frederick William von Steuben and the American Revolution: Aide to Washington and Inspector General of the Army*. HC Cook Company, 1913.

Downing, Margaret Brent. "Foreign Heroes in Washington Parks." *Records of the Columbia Historical Society* 24 (1922): 8–22.

Elzas, Barnett Abraham. *The Jews of South Carolina: From the Earliest Times to the Present Day*. Philadelphia: J.P. Lippincott, 1905.

Fast, Howard. *Haym Salomon: Sons of Liberty*. New York: Julian Messner, Inc., 1941.

Feingold, Henry L. *Zion in America: The Jewish Experience from Colonial Times to the Present*. New York: Hippocrene Books, Inc., 1974.

Feldberg, Michael. *Blessings of Freedom: Chapters in American Jewish History*. Hoboken, NJ: KTAV Publishing House, 2002.

Fowler, William M. *Rebels Under Sail: The American Navy During the Revolution*. New York: Charles Scribner's Sons, 1976.

Flood, Charles Bracelen. *Rise and Fight Again: Perilous Times along the Road to Independence*. New York: Dodd, Mead, & Co., 1976.

Fruchtman, Jack, Jr. *Thomas Paine: Apostle of Freedom*. New York: Four Walls Eight Windows, 1994.

Furman, Bess. "Signed, Sealed—and Forgotten!" *Daughters of the American Revolution Magazine* 71 (1937): 1,004–1,009.

Gammell, William, William B. Sprague and Jared Sparks. *Lives of Roger Williams, Timothy Dwight, and Count Pulaski*. Boston: Little & Brown, 1845.

Gilmore, Jodie. "True Father of the American Navy." *The New American* 26.8 (2010): 35.

Greene, Jack P. *Understanding the American Revolution: Issues and Actors*. Charlottesville: University Press of Virginia, 1995.

Griffin, Martin. *The Story of Commodore John Barry*. Philadelphia: Published by the author, 1897.

Griswold, Rufus, William Simms, and Edward Ingraham. *Washington and the Generals of the American Revolution*. Philadelphia: Lippincott, 1856.

Gummere, Richard M. *Seven Wise Men of Colonial America*. Cambridge: Harvard University Press, 1967.

Gustaitus, Joseph. "One Man Army." *American History*. (October 1998): 1–4. Web. January 5, 2013.

Guthorn, Peter J. "Kościuszko as Military Cartographer and Engineer in America" *Image Munei* 29 (1977): 49–53.

Haarmann, Albert W. "General Armand and his Partisan Corps, 1777–1783." *Military Collector and Historian* 12 (1960): 97–102.

Haiman, Miecislaus. *Kościuszko in the American Revolution*. Boston: Gregg Press, 1972.

Haywood, Marshall Delaney. "Major George Farragut." *Gulf States Historical Magazine* (September 1903).

Headley, Phineas Camp. *Old Salamander: The Life and Naval Career of Admiral David Glascoe Farragut*. Boston: Lee and Shepherd, 1883.

Hirschfeld, Fritz. *George Washington and the Jews*. Cranbury, NJ: Associated University Presses, 2005.

Hirschman, Elizabeth, and Donald Yates. *Jews and Muslims in British Colonial America*. Jefferson, NC: McFarland, 2012.

Hull, Michael. "George Washington's One Man Army." *Military History* (July/August 2006): 25–31.

Jones, Charles Henry. *Captain Gustavus Conyngham: A Sketch of the Services He Rendered to the Cause of American Independence*. Philadelphia: Pennsylvania Society of the Sons of the Revolution, 1903.

Kapp, Frederick. *The Life of Frederick William Von Steuben*. New York: Mason Brothers, 1859.

_____. *The Life of John Kalb: Major-General in the Revolutionary Army*. New York: Henry Holt, 1884.

Kaye, Harvey J. *Thomas Paine and the Promise of America*. New York: Hill and Wang, 2005.

Kessler, John. *A Biographical Sketch of Commodore John Barry*. Philadelphia: Insheep and Bradford, 1813.

Kite, Elizabeth. "Charles Armand Tuffin." *Légion d'honneur Magazine* 10 (1940): 451–462.

Knight, Vick, Jr. *Send for Haym Salomon!* Alhambra, CA: Borden Publishing Co., 1976.

"Letter of Peter Francisco to the General Assembly." *William and Mary Quarterly* 13.4 (1905): 217–219.

Lewis, Joseph. *Thomas Paine, Author of the Declaration of Independence.* New York: Freethought Press Assn., 1947.

Lipscomb, Terry W. *The Letters of Pierce Butler: 1790–1794.* Columbia: University of South Carolina Press, 2007.

Lockhart, Paul Douglas. *The Drillmaster of Valley Forge: The Baron de Steuben and the Making of the American Army.* Washington, DC: Smithsonian, 2008.

Lorenz, Lincoln. *John Paul Jones: Fighter for Freedom and Glory.* Annapolis, MD: United States Naval Institute, 1943.

Lumpkin, Rosa. *From Savannah to Yorktown: The American Revolution in the South.* Lincoln, NE: toExcel Press, 1987.

Mahan, Alfred Thayer. *Admiral Farragut.* New York: Appleton and Co., 1893.

Marchione, Margherita. *The Adventurous Life of Philip Mazzei.* Lanham, MD: United Press of America, Inc., 1995.

_____. *Philip Mazzei: Jefferson's Zealous Whig.* New York: American Institute of Italian Studies, 1975.

_____. *Philip Mazzei: The Constitutional Society of 1784.* Morristown: New Jersey Historical Commission, 1984.

Marcus, Jacob Rader. "Jews and the American Revolution: A Bicentennial Documentary." *American Jewish Archives* 27.2 (1975): 103–269.

Marraro, Howard R. "Mazzei's Correspondence with the Grand Duke of Tuscany during His American Mission." *William and Mary Quarterly, Second Series* 22.3 (1942): 275–301.

_____. "Philip Mazzei on American Political, Social, and Economic Problems." *Journal of Southern History* 15.3 (1949): 354–378.

_____. *Philip Mazzei, Virginia's Agent in Europe: The Story of His Mission as Related in His Own Dispatches and Other Documents.* New York: New York Public Library, 1935.

Masini, Giancarlo. *How Florence Invented America.* New York: Marsilio Publishers, 1998.

Mazzei, Philip. *Philip Mazzei: My Life and Wanderings.* Morristown, NJ: American Institute of Italian Studies, 1980.

McGrath, Tim. *John Barry: An American Hero in the Age of Sail.* Yardley, PA: Westholme Publishing, 2011.

Meany, William Barry. *Commodore John Barry: Father of the American Navy.* New York: Harper Brothers, 1911.

Mizwa, Stephen P. *Great Men and Women of Poland.* New York: The MacMillan Company, 1942. Print.

Morison, Samuel Eliot. *John Paul Jones.* New York: Little Brown and Company, 1959.

_____. "The Willie Jones-John Paul Jones Tradition." *William and Mary Quarterly* 16.2 (1959): 198–206.

Munro, Richard K. "Seaman, Guerrilla, Artilleryman, and Calvary Officer George Farragut Was a Versatile Hero." *Military History.* 21.4 (2004): 12–15.

Nagy, Tibor. "Fabricy Michael Smith: Founding Father of the U.S. Light Cavalry." Lovasok. n.d. Hungarian Web. 15 December 2012. http://www.lovasok.hu/index.php?i=42974.

Neeser, Robert Wilden. *Letters and Papers Relating to the Cruises of Gustavus Conyngham.* New York: DeVinne Press, 1915.

Nelson, Craig. *Thomas Paine: Enlightenment, Revolution, and the Birth of Modern Nations.* New York: Viking, 2006.

"Opening Remarks: News Archives." *Embassy of Hungary.* n.d. Web. 15 December 2012. http://www.huembwas.org/NEws%20Archive/StatueSpeeches.htm.

Palmer, John. *General von Steuben.* New Haven, CT: Yale University Press, 1937.

Papp, Susan M. *Hungarians and Their Communities in Cleveland.* Cleveland, OH: Cleveland State University, 1981.

Paullin, Charles Oscar. *The Navy of the American Revolution.* New York: Haskell House Publishers, Ltd., 1971.

Pencak, William. *Jews and Gentiles in Early America: 1654–1800.* Ann Arbor: University of Michigan Press, 2005.

"Peter Francisco: Remarkable American Revolutionary War Soldier." *American History* (October 1998): 5–12.

"Peter Francisco: The American Soldier." *The William and Mary Quarterly* 13.4 (1905): 213–216.

Peters, Madison C. *Haym Salomon: The Financier of the Revolution.* New York: The Trow Press, 1911.

Pienkos, Angela. "A Bicentennial Look at Casimir Pulaski: Polish, American, and Ethnic Folk Hero." *Polish American Studies* 33.1 (1976): 5–17.

Powell, David. *Tom Paine: The Greatest Exile.* New York: St. Martin's Press, 1985.

Powell, William Stevens. *Dictionary of North Carolina Biography.* Chapel Hill: University of North Carolina Press, 1986.

Pula, James S. *Thaddeus Kościuszko: The Purest Son of Liberty.* New York: Hippocrene Books, 1999.

"Pulaski's Legion." *Military Illustrated* 116 (1998): 8–15.

Rappaport, Doreen, and Joan Verniero. *Victory or Death! Stories of the American Revolution.* New York: Harper Collins, 2003.

Reilly, Richard M. "The Father of the American Navy." *Journal of American History* (1907).

"Resolution by the New York State Convention of the Ancient Order of Hibernians endorsing the Commodore John Barry Memorial at the United States Naval Academy." July, 2009. New York State Convention of the Ancient Order of Hibernians. Web. July 27, 2012.

Revesz, Coloman. *Colonel-Commandant Michael de Kovats: Drillmaster of Washington's Cavalry.* Pittsburgh: Verhovay Fraternal Insurance Association, 1912.

Rezneck, Samuel. *Unrecognized Patriots: The Jews in the American Revolution.* Westport, CT: Greenwood Press, 1975.

Rosengarten, J. G. "Colonel Armand of the Revolutionary War." *Pennsylvania Magazine of History and Biography* 22.2 (1898): 234–242.

Russell, Charles E. *Haym Salomon and the Revolution.* New York: Cosmopolitan Book Corporation, 1930.

Savage, George. *In Memoriam: The Baron de Kalb.* Baltimore: James Young Press, 1886.

Sayen, John J., Jr. "Oared Fighting Ships of the South Carolina Navy, 1776–1780." *South Carolina Historical Magazine* 87.4 (1986.): 213–237.

Schwartz, Laurens R. *Jews and the American Revolution: Haym Salomon and Others.* Jefferson, NC: McFarland, 1987.

Seitz, Don C. *Paul Jones: His Exploits in English Seas During 1778–1780.* New York: E. P. Dutton & Co., 1917.

Solyom, Gwen. "Hussar Hero: Michael Kovats, Father of the U.S. Cavalry." *Magyar News Online.* Magyar Studies of America. 2009. www.magyarnews.org/news:php?viewStory=802. 22 December 2012.

Southern, Ed, ed. *Voice of the American Revolution in the Carolinas.* Winston-Salem, NC: John Blair Publishers, 2009.

Sparks, Jared. *The Library of American Biography.* Boston: Little and Brown, 1845.

Stewart, Charles W., ed. *John Paul Jones Commemoration at Annapolis April 24, 1906.* Washington, DC: United States Congress Joint Committee on Printing, 1907.

Storozynski, Alex. *The Peasant Prince: Thaddeus Kościuszko and the Age of Reason.* New York: St. Martin's, 2009.

Stutesman, John. "Colonel Armand and Washington's Calvary." *New York Historical Society Quarterly* 45.1 (1961): 5–42.

Szymanski, Leszek. *Casimir Pulaski: A Hero of the American Revolution.* New York: Hippocrene Books, 1979.

Taylor, Jeanette. *Life and Times of John Paul Jones including His Narrative of the Campaign of the Liman.* New York: Clerk, Southern District of New York, 1830.

Thomas, Evan. *John Paul Jones: Sailor, Hero, Father of the American Navy.* New York: Simon and Schuster, 2003.

"200th Birthday of Colonel Commandant Michael Kovats de Fabricy." *American Hungarian Federation.* http://www.americanhungarianfederation.org/news_michael_kovats_200thAnniversary.htm. 15 December 2012.

Ulmer, S. Sidney. "The Role of Pierce Butler in the Constitutional Convention." *The Review of Politics* 22.3 (1960): 361–374.

Van der Weyde, William. *The Life and Works of Thomas Paine.* New York: Thomas Paine National Historical Association, 1925.

Waniczek, Helena. "Casimir Pulaski, The Father of American Cavalry." In *Great Men and Women of Poland*, edited by Stephen P. Mizwa, 144–156. New York: MacMillan, 1942.

Ward, Townsend. "Charles Armand Tuffin, Marquis de La Rouërie, Brigadier-General in the Continental Army of the American Revolution." *Pennsylvania Magazine of History and Biography* 2.2 (1878): 1–34.

Whitridge, Arnold. "Baron von Steuben, Washington's Drillmaster." *History Today* 26 (1976): 429–436.

_____. "The Marquis de la Rouërie, Brigadier General in the Continental Army." *Proceedings of the Massachusetts Historical Society* 79 (1967): 47–63.

Williamson, Audrey. *Thomas Paine: His Life, Work, and Times.* London: George Allen & Unwin, Ltd., 1973.

Wood, Gordon S. *Revolutionary Characters: What Made the Founders Different.* New York: Penguin, 2006.

Woodward, W. E. *Tom Paine: America's Godfather.* New York: Dutton, 1945.

Young, Alfred F., Gary B. Nash, and Ray Raphael. *Revolutionary Founders: Rebels, Radicals, and Reformers in the Making of a Nation.* New York: Alfred A. Knopf, 2011.

INDEX

Adams, Abigail 144
Adams, John 5, 8, 15, 17–8, 25, 49–50, 67, 71, 76, 87, 126, 144, 174
Adams, John Quincy 26
Adams, Samuel 25, 197
Adirondacks 113, 124
Age of Enlightenment 5, 14
Age of Reason 31
Agrarian Justice 31
Agriculture 7, 10, 16, 20, 57, 108–9
Albermarle County, Virginia 10, 11–2
Alfred 76–7
Allen, Richard (alias) 65
Alliance 54–6, 58, 84, 86
ambush 44–6
Amelia, Virginia 184
American Crisis 18, 28
American Daily Advertiser 57
ammunition 12, 43–4, 93, 110, 114, 181
Amsterdam 86, 144
Ancient Order of the Hiberians 52, 60
Anglicanism 19
Annapolis 60, 73, 88, 154, 156, 170
Anthony, Susan B. 31
aristocracy 15, 20, 20, 105
aristocrat 8, 22, 46, 97, 105, 125
Armand, Charles 125–32, 151–2, 207–8, 210
Armand's Legion 130
Armstrong, General John 112–3, 117–8, 152
Arnold, Benedict 113, 118, 127, 203
artillery 94, 108, 113–4, 121–2, 127, 130, 144, 151, 154, 182, 186, 203
attaché 193
Austin, Sarah 52
Australia 117, 124

Austria 33, 100, 121, 134–5, 142, 158, 162, 192–3
autocracy 121
Azores Islands 176

backcountry 43–4, 105
Bank of North America 29, 38
Barbados 48, 73
Barcelona 91
barracks 113, 115–6, 159, 190
Barry, John 47–60
battalion 192–3, 203
battlefield 117, 141, 151–4, 156, 160, 176, 182, 186, 205
Bavarian 141, 151
bayonet 114, 151, 168–9, 181–3, 197, 203
Beaumarchais 110, 195
Bellini, Carlo 12
Bentalou, Captain 166, 168, 171–2
Berdichef Monastery 158
Beth Elohim 42
Bill of Rights 27, 39–40, 43
Black Prince 49
Blackden, Colonel Samuel 87
blacksmithing 6, 149, 178
bloodline 190
Bloody Tarleton 91, 94, 120, 130, 152–3, 182, 184
Bonaparte, Napoleon 18, 32
Bonhomme Richard 71, 83–4, 90
Boston 12, 48–9, 56, 75, 97, 106, 134, 145–6, 163, 179, 197, 203
Boston Gazette 170
Boston Newsletter 134
Boston Tea Party 48
Brandywine, Battle of 128, 130, 164–5, 180
bravery 33, 54, 57, 61, 86, 88, 125, 131, 138, 153–4, 156, 162, 164, 166, 168, 180–1, 183, 186
brig 49, 61–2, 66–7, 72–3, 172
British 8, 10–1, 14–5, 18, 39; anti-British 25, 42; Army 41–4, 68, 78, 81, 93, 96, 98–9, 100–3, 112–4, 116–8, 120, 125, 141–3, 149–56, 163–71, 174, 180–5, 193–4, 202–3; capture 1, 176; Crown 15, 25, 28, 43, 53, 103; culture 34, 48, 52, 76, 81, 96; Empire 8, 10–2, 41, 47–8, 62, 64, 74, 76, 80, 92, 144, 178–9; horses 185; intelligence 171; Navy 48–9, 52–3, 55–6, 61, 64, 66, 68, 71, 74, 77–8, 80, 82–6, 93, 110, 115, 126, 131, 138, 147, 180; officers 14, 48, 56, 91, 93, 97, 99, 113, 120, 127, 138, 153, 156, 164; people 18, 49, 145, 156, 200; prisoners 39, 80, 100, 117, 121; soldiers 52, 55, 153, 182, 186; taxation 1, 34, 144
broadsword 176, 182–3, 186
Broglie, Count de 143, 147, 149
buccaneer 81
Burdett, Peter 195
Burgoyne, General 78, 113–4
Bush, George H.W. 32
Bushneff, Albert 39
Butler, Pierce 96–104

cadets 108, 116, 191
Camden, Battle of 130, 141, 150–2, 154–6, 182, 184
Canada 14, 97, 149
Candide 191
cannons 53–4, 64, 91, 158
Cape Canaveral 56, 58
Caribbean 67–8, 75, 79, 92
Carnegie, Andrew 31
Carrickfergus Harbor, Northern Ireland 80, 88
Case of Officers of Excise 23
Catherine the Great 33, 109, 120–1
Catholic 33, 36, 47, 60, 107, 122, 159, 175

Index

Chappel, Alonzo 51, 119, 154
Charles XII 108
Charleston, South Carolina 42, 44–6, 91, 93, 96–7, 99–100, 105, 120, 129, 133, 138, 140, 151–2, 170, 172
Charlotte, North Carolina 118, 182
Cherokee 43–4
Chesapeake Bay 126, 128
Chevalier 36, 87, 90, 154, 163
chevaux-de-frise 115
Chicago, Illinois 37, 40, 124, 174
chivalry 188, 190, 195
Choiseul, Duke 144–5
church 6, 12, 19, 33, 48, 58, 72, 75, 98, 100, 105, 141, 172, 178, 185
The Citadel 140
City Point (Hopewell), Virginia 176–7
Coleridge, Samuel Taylor 124
Colonel Michael de Kováts Society 140
combat 49, 91, 97, 129, 131, 160, 164, 185, 193
combatants 55, 178
commerce 1, 61, 64
commission 56, 58, 61, 64–5, 68–9, 75–7, 79, 87, 96–8, 100, 112, 130, 136–7, 144, 148, 153, 163–5, 168–9, 183, 195–6, 198
Common Sense 11, 18, 25–8, 31
compatriot 115, 157, 159
Confederation of the Bar 33, 135, 159, 161
Congress 13–4, 17, 29, 30, 34, 36, 39, 49, 51, 56, 58, 64, 69–70, 76–9, 87, 98, 103, 111, 120, 126–8, 130–1, 133, 136–8, 141, 148–9, 153–4, 156, 163–4, 166–70, 175, 185, 195–7, 199, 200, 202–3, 205
Connecticut 52, 113, 146, 203
El Conquistador 91
Constitution 15, 17, 27, 31, 37, 39, 57, 100, 103
Constitutional Convention 17, 96, 100, 102
Constitutional Society 14–5, 17
Continental Congress 11, 27, 35, 43, 76, 96, 127, 188, 195–7
Continentals 79, 113, 119–20, 126, 151, 153–4, 171, 180–2, 188, 198–200, 202
Conway, Dr. Moncure 20, 25, 32, 207
Conway, Thomas 149, 200
Conyngham, Gustavus 1, 61–70, 86
Conyngham and Nesbitt 61–2
Cooper, James Fenimore 49, 53, 69

The Copelands, Battle of 80
Cornwallis, Lord 28, 30, 56, 58, 91, 93–4, 118–20, 151–3, 180, 183, 204
Coronoca 42–3
courage 3, 6, 9, 49–50, 88, 113, 125, 129, 134, 138–9, 160, 163, 174
Cowpens 91, 94, 118
credentials 13–4, 43, 195
Crown (British) 20, 25, 27, 35, 43, 98, 101, 103, 146
crypt 90
Czartoryski 107

Dan River 119–20
Deane, Silas 64, 67, 79, 126, 147–8, 162–3, 195
Declaration of Independence 11–2, 17, 26–8, 37, 46, 57, 69, 71, 98, 111, 113, 126, 162
de Fleury, Colonel François-Louis Teissèdre 181, 200
Deism 109
de Kalb, Baron Johann 2, 141–56, 166, 194
Delaware 150–4
Delaware River 18, 28, 52–4, 58, 68, 77–8, 112, 128, 167, 169, 180
delegates 11, 27, 100–1, 183, 186
delegation 41, 43, 87, 121
despotism 9, 131, 136, 157, 159, 205
d'Estaing, Count 170–1
divide et impera 10
division 151, 153–4, 163, 170, 197
Don Quixote 191
Donegal, Ireland 61
dragoons 87, 128–9, 167–8, 186, 202
Drake 80–1, 88
Drayton, John 45
drills 190–2, 197–9, 200, 202
Dunkirk Pirate 61, 63
Dunmore, Lord 10, 12, 52
Duponceau 196, 199
Dutch 22, 36, 42, 62, 68, 86, 100, 117, 142
Dylan, Bob 31

eagle 57, 180
East India Company 42
Effingham 52–3
Egg Harbor 138, 168
elections 5, 27
electoral college 101
electors 103
Elizabeth, Czarina of Russia 109, 192–3
enemy 9, 31, 39, 41, 45, 49–50, 53–4, 64–5, 68–9, 76–7, 80–1, 84–5, 87, 91, 94, 97, 99, 112–4, 117, 120, 128, 142, 150–

1, 158–9, 161–4, 166–72, 174, 179–80, 183, 186
engineer 30, 54, 106–17, 144, 181, 190–2, 200
English 13, 15–6, 18, 22, 26, 33, 36, 41–2, 47, 54–5, 61–6, 68–9, 72, 76–7, 79–81, 86, 91, 108, 120, 125, 127, 138, 142–8, 177, 195–6, 198–9
English Channel 61, 64–5, 69, 86
Euclid 72
Europe 5, 10, 12, 14–6, 30, 33–4, 36, 41–2, 47–8, 52, 62, 64–5, 68, 107–8, 111, 122, 133–4, 138, 141–2, 148, 151, 161–2, 165, 167, 169, 170, 188, 190, 194–6, 199, 205
Evans, Captain William 181
exciseman 22–3

"faithful unto death" 133, 136, 140
Farragut, George 91–4
Father Mark 158–9
Federalist 27, 31
Ferguson, Captain Patrick 22, 138, 164
feu de joie 200
flag 52, 56–7, 64, 71, 76–7, 79–80, 84–5, 90, 94, 143, 172, 181, 204
flagstaff 17, 181
fleur-de-lis 132
Florence 6–9, 11
Florida 14, 56, 58
Fly 77
foes 56, 84, 129, 144, 174, 193, 202
fog 62, 152
"forlorn hope" 181
Fort Ticonderoga 34, 112–3
fortification 108, 112, 142, 151, 181
fortress 112, 117–8, 121, 133, 159–61, 190
Four Letters on Interesting Subjects 27
France 13–5, 30–1, 36, 54–7, 62, 64, 68–9, 79, 81, 86, 88, 90, 94, 108, 110, 114, 125–6, 131–2, 135–6, 141–3, 147–9, 158, 162–3, 193, 195–6
Francis, Rakoczi II 134
Francisco, Dr. B.M. 183
Francisco, Peter 176–187
Franklin, Benjamin 1, 2, 3, 5, 8, 13–5, 22–5, 54–5, 61, 64, 67, 69, 71, 73, 79, 81, 83, 86, 111–2, 133–6, 139, 157, 162–3, 194–5, 203, 206
Frederick the Great 29, 134–5, 139, 141, 161, 188, 191–2, 196
Fredricksburg 73, 76, 90
freedom 2, 9, 12, 14–7, 23, 25,

27–8, 33, 38–9, 41, 46–7, 71, 76, 88, 93, 96, 98, 105–7, 111, 121, 124, 133–6, 139, 146, 149, 157–9, 162–3, 169–70, 174, 176, 178, 180, 185–6, 196, 205
Freeman's Farm 113
French 14–6, 22, 32–4, 36, 38, 54, 65–9, 73–4, 79–80, 85, 87, 91–2, 96–7, 103, 107, 109–10, 112–14, 118, 122, 125–7, 129, 131, 133–4, 141–4, 146–8, 152, 164, 166, 170–2, 176, 181, 191, 194–200, 202–4
Frost, Robert 48, 54

garrison 143, 169, 190
Gates, General Horatio 100, 112, 115, 121, 130, 149, 151–4, 156, 182, 194, 197
genius 16, 40, 61, 71, 88, 91, 197
George III 10–1, 41
Germantown, Battle of 128, 165–6, 180
Germany 2, 64, 143, 156, 190–1, 195, 205
Gist, Mordecai 204
Golden Gate State Park 186
Grafton, Duke of 20
Great Britain 8, 9, 15, 18, 25–6, 29, 38, 49, 62, 64, 75, 77, 86, 92, 101, 114, 149, 179
Greene, Nathanael 28–9, 94, 99, 117–21, 129, 131, 166, 180, 183, 192, 203
grenadiers 181
guerrilla 81, 91, 118, 128, 133, 159
Guilford Courthouse 176, 183, 186

Habsburg Kings 134
Haiti 93, 110
Hamilton, Alexander 1, 34, 54, 131, 165, 197
Hamilton, William 85
Hancock, John 12, 49, 52, 64, 77, 112, 163, 197, 205
Harvard 39, 56
Henry, Patrick 5, 12, 14, 76, 176–9
Henry the Navigator 187
Hercules of the American Revolution 1, 176
Hessians 28, 34, 52–3, 78, 127, 129–30, 203
History of the American Revolution 26
History of the United States Navy 49
Holland 36, 41, 62, 64, 79, 86, 108, 144–5
Hopewell, Virginia 176, 187
horses 23, 43, 45, 76, 113, 122, 129–30, 134, 138–40, 150–1, 153, 158, 161, 164, 166, 168, 170–2, 175, 182–3, 196–7, 202

Hudson River 38, 113–8, 124, 128, 181
Hudson Valley 129, 203
Hull, Agrippa (Grippy) 117
human rights 3, 30, 88, 162, 174
Hungary 2, 8, 133–6, 140, 160
Hunting Tower plantation 178
hurricane 48, 111
Hussars 133–5, 137–8, 164
Hutchinson, Amy 20

Illinois 37, 40, 74–5
independence 1, 5, 9, 11, 16, 43, 46, 70–1, 77, 87, 111, 118, 120, 127, 132–36, 140, 146, 148, 156–7, 162–3, 165, 170, 174, 185–6, 206
Independence Hall 58–9, 102, 104
Independence National Historical Park 16–8, 25–7, 31–2, 39
Indiana 124, 175
industry 8, 48, 120
informant 17
Inquisition 41–2
inspector general 199, 200, 202–3
Instructions to the Freeholders of Albemarle County to Their Delegates in Convention 11
instructor 72, 108, 191
Iredell, James 99
Ireland 13, 16, 25, 47–8, 55, 58, 61, 75, 80, 96–8, 101
Irish 47–8, 50, 52, 58, 60–2, 80, 94, 96–8, 100, 143, 149, 198, 200
Italy 5–12, 14, 17, 33, 134, 147, 196

Jackson, Andrew 32
Jamaica 74
Jefferson, Thomas 1, 5, 9–17, 28, 37, 40, 57, 87, 106, 117, 119, 121–2, 133, 203–4
Jews 33, 39, 41; Sephardic 41–3, 45–6, 106
Jones, John Paul 1, 3, 37, 52, 68–9, 71–90
Juhász, Ferenc (Hungarian Defense Minister) 139
justice 1, 8, 10, 12, 14, 16, 19, 25, 31, 41, 57, 67, 75, 91, 109, 121, 125, 131, 146, 158–60, 162, 185, 187

Karcag, Hungary 133–4, 140
Kennedy, John F. 17
Kewoee River 44–6
knighthood 87, 188, 194
Knox, Henry 56, 203
Kościuszko, Tekla 107
Kościuszko, Thaddeus 106–124
Kościuszko's Garden 116

Kováts, Michael 133–140
Kraków 106, 122

Lafayette, Marquis de 1, 2, 16, 36–7, 54, 56, 58, 90, 128, 130, 131, 141, 147–9, 156, 163–4, 172–3, 180, 185, 194, 204–5
Latin 2, 21, 23, 29, 134–5, 192
Laurens, Henry 46, 196–7
Laurens, John 30, 54, 167, 188, 197, 199, 200
Lee, Charles 111, 194
Lee, "Light Horse" Harry 172
Lee, Richard Henry 50
Lexington 49–50, 52
Lexington, Massachusetts 30, 49, 80, 93
Lincoln, Benjamin 93, 99, 138, 170
Locke, John 42, 107
London 8–10, 13, 16–7, 19, 21–4, 41–2, 46, 49, 67, 69, 77–8, 82–3, 86, 113, 128, 145–6, 152
London Evening Post 83
Long Island 13, 28, 77
Longfellow 168
Los Angeles 40
Louis XVI 1, 30–1, 36, 85, 87, 110, 125–6, 131–2, 147, 149
Loyalists 1, 44, 93, 105, 118, 138, 182
Luzerne, Chevalier de la 36, 70, 152

Madgeburg, Germany 190, 205
Madison, James 1, 10, 12, 14, 16, 33, 37, 40, 101, 103
Manahan, John E. 176
Maneuvers of Horse Artillery 122
manifesto 28
man-o-war 71, 74, 81, 84, 86
marches 167, 186, 193–4
Margravine Frederica Dorothea of Württemberg 194
Maria Theresa, Empress of Hungary 134–6, 139, 161, 192
Mason, George 10–12
Massachusetts 66, 117, 146, 186, 196, 200
Mayo, Colonel William 176, 182
McDougall, Alexander 34–5, 115–6
Melville, Herman 31, 71
memorials 3, 17, 32, 39, 46, 58, 70, 90, 105, 124, 132, 140, 156, 174–5, 186, 205
Merelim, Peter 178
Mikveh Israel 35, 39
militia 12, 39, 43–4, 94, 96, 99, 113, 116, 121, 130, 138, 146, 151, 168, 182, 202–3, 205
Minorca 91–2, 94
Mohawk Valley 194, 205
monastery 125, 127, 158–9, 161

Monmouth, Battle of 181
Monroe, James 10, 14, 31, 37
Monterey Square, Savannah 174
Monticello 9, 12
Moravian 136, 151, 168, 180
Morgan, Daniel 94, 99, 114, 118
Morris, Robert 37–8, 40, 48–9, 56, 61, 67, 77, 79, 83, 126–7
Mulholland, General St. Clair 58
muskets 44, 51, 55, 81, 91, 121, 197–8, 200, 203
muster 203, 205
mutiny 29, 55, 67, 80, 196

National Archives and Records Administration 35, 50–1, 73, 82–3, 106, 119, 128, 152, 154, 16, 194, 198, 204
National Register of Historic Places 90, 124
Natural History of Virginia 21
Naval Biography 49, 54
Naval Documents of the American Revolution 49
Navy 36, 47, 49–50, 52, 54, 56–8, 61–2, 64–5, 67–71, 73–4, 76–81, 83–4, 87–8, 90–4, 114, 141
Netherlands 42, 86
New Hampshire 103, 146, 196
New Rochelle, New York 30, 32
New World 9, 24, 26, 174
New York 17, 30, 32, 34, 54, 58, 124, 128, 140, 149, 175, 198, 205
New York City 13–4, 28, 32, 34–5, 42, 68, 77–8, 115, 117, 120, 140, 146, 163, 168, 175, 181, 194
New York Gazette 146
Niemcewicz, Julian Ursyn 109
Ninety-Six, South Carolina 42–3, 46
Non-Importation Resolves 48, 61
Norfolk, Virginia 12, 92
North Carolina 65, 76, 78, 87, 94, 99–100, 118, 138, 151–2, 182–3
North Sea 86
Nova Scotia 78, 96–7
Nyirjesy, Istvan 139

one-man-army 176
Order of Fidelity Star 194–6, 205
Order of St. Louis 131

Pacta Coventa 107
Paine, Thomas 18–32
pamphlet 18, 23, 25–7, 205
Paris 6, 13, 15–6, 32, 56, 65–7, 75, 86–8, 90, 108, 110, 122, 125–6, 143–4, 147, 195–6, 206

Parliament (British) 9–10, 23, 41, 49, 96–7, 101, 107, 146, 179
patriotism 29, 33, 36, 39, 57–8, 101, 108, 111–2, 161–2, 178, 186
pauper 20–1, 87
Pearson, Captain 83–5
pedagogy 188–205
penal laws 20, 47
Pennsylvania 8, 24–5, 28–30, 34, 36–9, 54, 56, 58–9, 68, 70, 90, 102, 104–5, 124, 127–9, 136, 138, 145, 164, 168, 175, 188, 201, 204–5
Pennsylvanian Magazine 24–5
physician 7–8, 52, 88
Pickens, Andrew 43–4
Pictorial Field Book of the Revolution 183
pirates 1, 67–8, 178–9
pistols 80, 120, 169, 196–7, 202
plantations 97, 99–100, 103, 107, 147, 177, 180
Pocahontas Bridge 203
Poggio-a-Caiano, Italy 6, 17
Poland 1–2, 16, 33, 39, 62, 107–110, 121–2, 124, 155, 157–9, 162–3, 172, 174–5
Polish American Historical Association 175
Polish American Kościuszko Foundation 124
Polish Biographical Dictionary 124
Poniatowski, Stanislaw 16, 33, 174
Poor Richard's Almanack 22, 71
Porto Jedeu 177
Portugal 1, 20, 33, 42, 66, 176
Potomac 16, 90
Potter, General Horace 88
pounders 51, 54, 56, 68, 93, 152
Pour le Mérite 136, 191
powder 50–2, 55, 62, 85, 91, 93, 110, 196
Prague 134, 191–2
primogeniture 6, 96
Princeton 29, 52–3
prisoner 13, 34, 52, 66, 69, 75, 80, 83, 86–7, 93, 96, 99, 117, 139, 159–60, 182, 193, 203
privateer 13, 21–2, 36, 55, 64–5, 68, 78, 83, 93–4, 168
privations 149, 188
Providence 77
provincial 27, 42–3, 46, 108, 145
provisions 11, 65, 67, 100, 116, 143–4, 151, 159
Provost 34–5
Prussia 22, 33, 121, 129, 134, 136, 158–9, 162, 190–1, 193, 204
psyche 110, 179
Pulasaki, Francis 160
Pulaski County, Virginia 175

Pulaski, Kazimierz (Casimir) 2, 33, 128, 130, 133–8, 157–175
Pulaski's Legion 137, 168
Putnam, Israel 112

Quaker 18–9, 20–1, 24, 28–9, 183
quartermaster 143–4, 147, 192
quisque suae fortunae faber 23

raccoons 170
Race to the Dan 119
Racławice, Poland 121, 124
Ranger 52, 79–81, 83, 90
Rappahanock River 12–3
rations 38, 117, 141, 153, 192, 197
Raynal, Abbé 15, 196
razor 183
Reagan, Ronald 31
rebel 49, 93, 96, 113, 153, 164
reconnaissance 134, 192
Redcoats 35, 114, 118–9, 181, 183
redoubt 112–7, 131, 159, 171, 204
regiment 35, 81, 96–9, 122, 134–5, 142–4, 146–7, 153–4, 180, 182, 191–2, 197–200
Regulations for the Order and Discipline of the Troops of the United States 199
religious freedom 12, 14, 17, 33, 41, 46
Remembrancer 45
Republic 16, 26, 39, 77, 79, 132, 134–5, 156, 158, 162, 196, 203
Republican 15–6, 27, 105, 121, 125, 131
retreat 94, 113, 119, 129, 152–3, 161, 164, 166, 171, 179, 180, 182, 202–3
Revenge 61, 65–70, 93
rhetoric 28, 31, 100
Rhine river 132, 143
Rhode Island 28, 30, 54, 136, 146, 186, 203
Richards, Samuel 116
Richmond, Virginia 14, 117, 177–8, 182, 185–6
The Rights of Man 30, 32
Robespierrists 132
Rochambeau 1, 38, 204
Roosevelt, Franklin 31, 40, 138
Roosevelt, Theodore 88, 90
Rouërie, Marquis de la 125, 132
royal 12, 22, 43, 52, 62, 78, 84, 90, 97, 108–10, 122, 125, 132–5, 193, 195
Ruhlière 158–9
rum 73, 78
Rush, Benjamin 25, 57–8, 114
Russia 33, 107, 109, 121, 158–60, 162, 190, 192–3

saber 7, 140, 153, 184
St. Germain, Count 194–5

St. John's Church 178, 185
St. Petersburg 121–2, 124, 190, 193
Salamanders 197–8
Salomon, Haym 33–40
Salvador, Francis 41–45
Sandy Hollow Gap 180
Saratoga, Battle of 106, 113–5, 182
Saxe, Marshall Hermann 141–2
Schuyler, General 34, 112–3
Scotland 67, 71, 73–5, 80, 84, 87, 90
scout 183–4, 200–2
Senate 40, 101, 103
Seraphis 71, 83–87
Seven Years' War 34, 64, 92, 141–3, 192–3
Shakespeare 21, 74
silver 12, 30, 80, 94, 100, 128, 177, 184, 187, 195
Six Nations 129
skirmish 97, 120, 128, 152, 166
slave trade 74, 111
slavery 11, 29, 74, 103, 107, 158, 178–9
slaves 12, 47, 99, 116–7, 120–1, 147
Smyrna 8
Society of the Cincinnati 120–1, 205
soldier 18, 28, 57, 97, 113, 116–7, 120, 130, 135, 149, 151, 153, 176, 180, 184, 186, 190, 192–3, 197, 200, 203
Sons of Liberty 33–35
Sosnowski, Ludwika 109–10
South Carolina 1, 13, 41–3, 45–6, 93, 96–100, 103, 105, 118, 130–1, 138, 140, 150–2, 155–6, 170, 172, 182
Spain 36, 42, 66–9, 86, 114, 147
Spanish 1, 7, 33, 36, 41, 64, 66–7, 91–4, 110, 176–7
speech 10, 12, 25, 103, 172, 177–80
spies 45, 141, 147, 171
squad 198, 200
Stamp Act 10, 61, 96, 144–6
Stanisław, King 33, 109, 161
Stanton, Elizabeth Cady 31
staymaker 18, 21–2
Stony Point, Battle of 181, 203
Surprize 61, 64
Switzerland 108, 122, 124
synagogue 33, 38, 41–2

Tales of the Garden of Kościuszko 116
tavern 14, 114, 165, 176, 178, 184, 196
taxes 11, 26, 33, 48, 62, 108, 134, 145–6
Tennent, William 43
Tennessee 94–5
Terceira 177
terrain 193
Terrorists 132
Thetford, England 19–22, 32
Thomas Paine, Author of the Declaration of Independence 28
Thorne 122, 179, 191, 193
Timoleon 107
tolerance 42, 48, 97, 105–6, 111
Tories 16, 26, 43, 46, 49, 167, 169, 182
Traditions of the American Revolution 172
Transylvania 133–4
Treaty of Utrecht 64
trenches 112, 192, 204
Trenton, New Jersey 28–9, 52–3, 166–7
Trenton, Battle of 28
troops 9, 12, 25, 28–9, 34–5, 38, 44, 52–4, 65, 94, 99, 108, 113–5, 118–21, 130–1, 134–5, 138, 142, 144–6, 149–54, 156, 158–62, 164–8, 170–1, 192, 198–200, 202–5
Turkey 7–8, 136, 159, 162
Tuscany 5, 8, 11–4, 16
Tuscany, Grand Duke of 5, 8–9, 12, 14
Twain, Mark 31
tyranny 5, 18, 24, 28, 36, 77, 95, 107, 157, 169, 186

Valley Forge, Pennsylvania 53–4, 128, 137, 149, 166–7, 171, 180, 188, 191–2, 198–202, 205
Van Robais, Anna Elizabeth Emilie 144–5, 147, 149
Vergennes, Comte de 64, 147
Versailles 68, 86–7, 126, 131, 144
Virginia 8–14, 16, 21, 48–50, 52, 73, 75, 90, 92, 110, 117, 120, 125, 131, 151, 175–8, 180, 182–6, 200, 203–4
Virginia Assembly 9–10, 12, 177, 185
Virginia Convention (1775) 178
Virginia Gazette 10–1

virtues 47–8, 69, 100–1, 105–6, 135, 152, 156, 160, 164, 172, 197, 205
volunteer 1, 3, 43, 46, 49, 110–1, 127, 131, 188, 192, 195–6, 202
von Steuben, Baron Friedrich Wilhelm 1, 37, 40, 115, 188–205

Wałęsa, Lech 107
Walker, Captain Benjamin 198
War of 1812 57, 69, 122, 199
Ward, Ben (Tavern) 176, 184
warrior 58, 81, 91, 95, 141, 153, 158, 161
Warsaw 16, 108–9, 121, 161–2
Washington, Booker T. 122
Washington, George 5, 10, 12, 18, 26, 28–30, 35, 37–40, 52–8, 76–7, 81, 87, 99, 101, 110, 112, 115–7, 119, 120–1, 125, 127–133, 136–38, 149–51, 154, 157, 163–70, 174, 176, 180, 182–4, 192, 195–7, 200, 202–5
Wasp 172
Wayne, Anthony "Mad" 53, 166, 181, 204
West Indies 42, 48, 57, 66, 74, 78
Wheatley, Phyllis 74
Whigs 5, 12, 16, 26, 39, 42, 185
Whitman, Walt 31–2
Wilkes, John 9–10
Williamsburg, Virginia 9, 11–2, 14, 17, 48
Williamson, Major Andrew 41–5
Wilson, Woodrow 58, 115
Winiary 175
Winston, Judge Anthony 177–8, 180
Wisconsin 175
Wolfowitz, Defense Secretary Paul 139
Woodsworth, William 188
wounds 45, 55–6, 74–6, 94, 100, 121, 124, 138, 153, 156, 171–2, 181–3
Wythe, George 5, 10

Yeats, John 124
Yiddish 33
Yom Kippur 38
Yorktown 38, 55, 114, 125, 131, 185, 191, 204

www.ingramcontent.com/pod-product-compliance
Lightning Source LLC
Chambersburg PA
CBHW081555300426
44116CB00015B/2888